Cultural Models of Emotions

Victor Karandashev

Cultural Models of Emotions

 Springer

Victor Karandashev
Department of Psychology and Counselor Education
Aquinas College
E. Grand Rapids, MI, USA

ISBN 978-3-030-58437-5   ISBN 978-3-030-58438-2   (eBook)
https://doi.org/10.1007/978-3-030-58438-2

This Springer imprint is published by the registered company Springer Nature Switzerland AG
The registered company address is: Gewerbestrasse 11, 6330 Cham, Switzerland

*Dedicated to the memory of my parents and parents-in-law –
gone, but never forgotten*

Acknowledgment

I appreciate the numerous and extensive studies that a number of scholars from various disciplines have conducted in cross-cultural research of emotions. Abundance of references and citations in the book recognizes their important contributions.

I also acknowledge the outstanding contributions in cross-cultural emotion research – pertinent to development of cultural models of emotions – of such scholars as Paul Ekman, James Russell, David Matsumoto, Shinobu Kitayama, Hazel Markus, Nico Frijda, Batja Mesquita, Klaus Scherer, Jeanne Tsai, William Gudykunst, Anna Wierzbicka, Zoltán Kövecses, and their multiple collaborators.

In addition, I express my great appreciation to the editorial team at Springer that has been very supportive to my book proposal and patient regarding my perfectionism in preparation of the manuscript. They knew that *"Everything takes longer than we think it will."*

I appreciate the grant of Faculty Development Committee of Aquinas College that helped me to successfully prepare this book for publication.

Introduction

Throughout several decades, especially from the1990s to 2010s, cross-cultural research of emotions has become a popular topic of scholarship in several disciplines, such as anthropology, sociology, psychology, and communication studies. Empirical research has been prolific and developed its robust disciplinary traditions and methods. Summaries of the findings in those fields were published in review articles and books on specific areas of emotion research demonstrating variations of emotions in many cultural contexts. Scholars of anthropology, sociology, and communication studies have been especially productive in these endeavors. Psychologists have joined this area of research later and embraced the topic with great interest, energy, and productivity.

Although some scholars in those disciplines may think that they are self-sufficient in their theoretical frameworks and methodologies, I believe that the *construction and exploration of cultural models of emotion* need *interdisciplinary approach* to describe the models comprehensively. Methodologies, which have been developed in cultural and cognitive anthropology, social and cultural psychology, sociology, and communication studies, enrich all disciplines involved in emotion research.

Throughout decades, researchers have identified many similarities across cultures, yet they have discovered the major differences between Western and Eastern patterns of experience and expression of emotions. The cultural differences in the societies within Western and Eastern cultural regions have been also recognized in multiple studies. The diversity and complexity of emotional life have taken into account their cultural aspects. Cultural differences in experience of positive and negative emotions, their intensity, and verbal and non-verbal expression of emotions have been found.

These differences were typically attributed to *individualism-collectivism* of those societies. However, later researchers found that *individualism* and *collectivism* are *complex cultural dimensions* with variations depending on the context of social life. Scholars have revealed the role of other cultural dimensions as well.

Numerous empirical reports, articles, and chapters in edited volumes have covered the topic from multiple angles in different cultural contexts, mainly contrasting the broadly understood Western and Eastern cultural values and norms. The more global and detailed picture, however, still remains piecemeal and patchy.

This book aims to integrate the findings from various disciplines in a *comprehensive interdisciplinary description* of *cultural models of emotions*. The special focus of the book is on how *cultural parameters of societies* affect *emotional life of people in different cultural contexts*.

The book concisely and extensively reviews such parameters of culture as *individualism-collectivism, uncertainty avoidance, power distance, gender roles equality (cultural femininity) and gender roles inequality (cultural masculinity), context differentiation*, and their relations with various aspects of emotional life in societies. The book, however, goes beyond these traditional parameters and presents other cultural dimensions, which have been so far in the shadow of the mainstream research: *immediacy, cultural temporal patterns, relational mobility, various cultural values*, and others. Showing their role in emotional life of people, Chap. 2 encourages researchers to include these dimensions in their studies of people's experience and expression of emotions.

Chapters 1 and 2 expand the concept of culture, providing the reasons why ethnicity, nations, and global cultures are not the only cultures that deserve cross-cultural investigation. Regions of countries, religious groups, the circles of people with certain socio-economic status, and mixed cultures should also be considered as cultural groups.

The content of the book is still structured around traditional dichotomy of West-East cultural contrast because very many studies have been conducted in this comparative perspective. Nevertheless, many parts of the book show that within both Western and Eastern cultural contexts, there is a great diversity of cultural experience and expression of emotions.

This book follows an integrative approach and intends to provide a general representation of how cultural diversity of emotional experience and expressions builds up a *typology of cultural models of emotions*. This comprehensive review should set up the background and perspectives for future cross-cultural investigation of emotions.

Key features of the book

– A comprehensive review of the classical and most recent theories and research findings on emotions pertinent to construction of cultural models
– A comprehensive review of cultural models of emotions from interdisciplinary perspective
– A comprehensive review of cultural models of emotions from international perspective

The book can be of interest to scholars working in various disciplines – anthropology, sociology, linguistics, social and cultural psychology, and communication science. The primary audience is scholars interested in emotions. The accessible language of the book makes it valuable for researchers, practitioners, as well as undergraduate and graduate students. Professors in colleges and universities in many countries can teach the courses on emotions and can use materials from different chapters.

In general, the book consists of *three groups of chapters*, which are closely intertwined and inter-referenced.

Chapters 1 and 2 are like societal guides to cultural models. They are about *concepts of cultures and their societal dimensions*. The materials of these chapters are supposed to be on the top of the models' constructions.

Then, *Chap. 3* is a main designer center of cultural models of emotions, in some respect. It is about theory and methodology of cultural models. It is about *how to construct and explore these models*.

Chapters 4, 5, and 6 are like production factories of cultural models. They review multiple studies and their findings about cultural patterns of emotional life, which can be used as the building blocks for construction of models. The chapters also propose several examples of the cultural models of emotions based on compilation of findings from studies, which have already completed. The materials of these chapters are supposed to be on the bottom of the models' construction.

Chapter 1, "Diversity of Cultures," presents a general introduction to the concept of culture. It shows the diversity of types of cultures, going beyond traditional, global, national, and ethnic understanding of culture. Regional, religious cultures and the cultures of communities with different socioeconomic status and social class also deserve their research attention. Mixed and multicultural cultures are the new cultural realities that need to be explored.

Chapter 2, "Cultural Parameters and Their Influence on Emotions," presents a brief overview of cultural dimensions, which are worthwhile to study to better understand cultural conceptualization of emotional life, experience, and expression of emotions. Among those are *collectivism and individualism* – taking into account its multifaceted nature, *power distance, gender roles equality* versus *gender roles inequality (cultural femininity-masculinity), immediacy, context differentiation, temporal dimensions* of cultures, *reaction to ambiguity and uncertainty, survival and self-expression values* of societies, *relational mobility, embeddedness* versus *autonomy, hierarchy* versus *egalitarianism*, and *mastery* versus *harmony*.

Chapter 3, "Theories, Examples of Cultural Models, and Methods To Explore Those," presents the conception of cultural models and provides examples. The chapter also describes *pan-cultural, cross-cultural, and cultural approaches* to the study of emotional constructs, along with typology and diversity of possible cultural models of emotions. In this regard, *Chap. 3* is *in the core of the book*: it is based on Chaps. 1 and 2, which introduce cultural parameters of possible models, and evolves into the following Chaps. 4, 5, and 6, which describe the cultural patterns of emotional life.

Chapter 3 also briefly presents *methodology of research on cultural models of emotions*, including such topics as *conceptual* and *measurement equivalence, adequacy*, and *bias* in cultural research of emotions. These materials provide the conceptual background, while the following parts bring the overview of *descriptive, comparative,* and *structural methodologies*, with a *summary of statistical methods* available for *construction of cultural models of emotions*.

Chapter 4, "Emotional Processes in Cultural Contexts," describes the structure of emotional life and functions of emotions in cultural contexts, including the concepts of *emotional control* and *regulation, emotional differentiation*, and *complexity*. This chapter also reviews *cultural models of emotions* in the *culture of self* and *culture of relating*.

Chapter 5, "Cultural Models of Emotional Experience," describes the physiology and body sensations, associated with subjective experience of emotions, and factors affecting cultural appraisals of situations. The chapter presents multiple studies which have explored the cross-cultural similarities and differences in the norms and actual experience of emotions across cultures. It reviews the findings about the ways how people experience the qualities, positive and negative valence, and intensity of emotions. In this chapter, I have compiled several *cultural models of emotions*. They are based on *subjective locus of emotions, salience of specific emotions* in particular cultural contexts, *valence*, and *intensity of emotional experiences*.

Chapter 6, "Cultural Models Based on Expression of Emotion," presents the studies which have explored the norms and the real behaviors of how people express their emotions across cultures. Based on the findings obtained in those multiple studies, I have compiled the description of *expressive* and *non-expressive cultural models*, the *models of direct* and *indirect expression of emotions*. The chapter also demonstrates the diversity of ways and channels in which people express their emotions in different cultures, including the most visible – facial expression.

Conclusion summarizes the cultural models that are evident from the results of multiple studies reviewed in the book. It also sets up the new methodological perspectives in exploration of cultural models of emotions in the future.

Contents

Chapter 1
Diversity of Cultures

1.1 Multifaceted Concept of Culture

1.1.1 Definitions of Culture

General Concept of Culture

Throughout recent several decades, many authors have defined the concept of culture. Despite multiplicity of definitions, they are revolving around the same general idea. Culture is the system of historically derived and socially constructed information, ideas, and meanings shared by a group of people and transmitted across generations throughout values, beliefs, practices, languages, rituals, artifacts, and so on (Kroeber & Kluckhohn, 1952; Markus & Conner, 2013; Matsumoto & Hwang, 2012). The cultural cycle includes (1) the people's generation of ideas, which (2) affect the way how individuals feel, think, and behave in certain situations and circumstances. Over time, people's psychological processes and their individual thoughts and actions generate cultural norms and practices, while these cultural norms and practices have a tremendous impact on their psychological processes, thoughts, and actions (Lehman, Chiu, & Schaller, 2004; Triandis, 2007).

A culture teaches them what is good (or bad), right (or wrong), moral (or immoral), acceptable (or unacceptable) in their daily life (Markus & Conner, 2013; Shweder, 2003). Culture includes such constituents as the methods that people use to share services, goods, and technology (*material culture*), the ideas and knowledge which a group of people share (*subjective culture*), and the institutions and rules of social behavior which they share (*social culture*; Chiu & Hong, 2006).

© The Author(s), under exclusive license to Springer Nature Switzerland AG 2021
V. Karandashev, *Cultural Models of Emotions*,
https://doi.org/10.1007/978-3-030-58438-2_1

Variety of Definitions of Culture

The definitions of culture, which have been proposed throughout recent decades (see for review Matsumoto, 2006a, p. 220), differ in various disciplines, such as anthropology, sociology, psychology, and communication studies. Which is right and most comprehensive? It is unlikely that one single and all-comprehensive definition of culture is possible. I would agree with Cohen (2009) that the way how scholars define culture depends on what form of culture and what domain within that culture they take into account.

Some tend to focus on meaning. Geertz (1973), for instance, views culture as an interpretive search for meaning. In the same vein, D'Andrade (1984) defines culture as a learned system of meaning. Shweder and Haidt (2000) maintain that culture includes meanings, conceptions, and interpretive schemes. These researchers, who are interested in morals and values, perceive culture in terms of meaning.

Others focus on information and knowledge. Boyd and Richerson (1985) define culture as information that can affect the phenotypes of individuals, which they learn via imitation and teaching from other species. Lumsden (1989, p. 15) states that culture is a system of knowledge shared among members of a society, which individuals socially learn. These researchers, who are interested in the cultural evolution and adaptation, consider culture in terms of information.

Taking into account a broad range of forms of culture can help us extend our understanding of what the culture is, promote new views on culture, and comprehend how the diverse cultures resemble each other and still differ from each other.

1.1.2 How Culture Develops

The Basic Background for Culture Development

How do cultures develop? All societies have the same basic needs, ideas, and even meanings (to some extent), yet they make some of those needs, ideas, and meanings more accessible and elaborated, but deemphasize and devaluate others. Culture evolves as an adaptation process when humans interact with their environments.

Culture is a complex set of human and societal responses to the demands of life in given ecological, environmental, and social contexts (DeKay & Buss, 1992; Georgas, van de Vijver, & Berry, 2004). Culture consists of the typical ways and methods, which people use to solve their problems and to meet their biological and social needs in a society.

Different Local Conditions for Culture Development

People in different parts of the world, in different geographical and climate conditions, have different resources available to meet their needs. These factors determine the way how they survive and thrive. According to Matsumoto (2006a), culture appears as the product of the interaction between "universal biological needs and functions, universal social problems created to address those needs, and the contexts in which people live" (pp. 219–220). To address the universal social problems and biological needs, people adapt to their environments in order to survive and thrive. Culture results from the process of individuals' attempts to adapt to their contexts. In this regard, Matsumoto also defines culture as "a shared system of socially transmitted behavior that describes, defines, and guides people's ways of life, communicated from one generation to the next" (p. 220).

Cultures in Flux

How rapidly does the culture of behavior, thought, and emotions evolve and change? This can take centuries. For example, the cultural patterns of analytical and holistic cognition—attention, perception, reasoning, and thinking—reflecting intellectual traditions of Greek philosophy in North America, and Confucianism and Daoism in East Asia (Nisbett, Peng, Choi, & Norenzayan, 2001), have been persisting for centuries. However, some cultural patterns can transform in a few decades. For example, nowadays many cultures, including traditionally collectivistic Japan, have become more individualistic than several decades ago. Even though this tendency is equivocal, and the modern collectivism in Japan has been carried forward with Japanese representation of their culture, the cultural shift is noticeable (Hamamura, 2012). Another example is the shift in traditional social engagement and civic participation in American society. Putnam (2000) documented the decline of this cultural value throughout recent several decades.

1.2 National and Regional Cultures

1.2.1 National and Transnational Cultures

Nations as Units of Cultural Research

National cultures, as the cultures typical within country territories, have developed over time. Historically, individuals and communities within national boundaries have shared the same cultural traditions and practices, social institutions, and normative social influences. Many countries are mono-cultural, yet many other are multi-cultural.

Assuming the former, researchers have frequently used nations as the units for the cultural as well as for individual level of analyses. The vast majority of cross-cultural research on emotions in the twentieth century was conducted comparing nations and countries, frequently one country (typically the United States) as a representative of Western culture while another (typically Japan or China) as a representative of Eastern culture. Such geographical regional cultures probably exist, according to some cultural dimensions. However, in many cases the broad generalization is not quite adequate. Many European countries, being considered as Western, substantially differ from North America.

Throughout decades, cross-cultural studies have commonly used countries as the cultural units for research comparison. The studies of Hofstede (e.g., 1983, 2016) on cultural dimensions of societies, of Schwartz (e.g., 2006, 2014) on cultural value orientations, and of many others cited in this book have used *national cultural samples* (of students, teachers, employees), for their data collection and analysis. Obtaining the same results on different samples within the same countries reassured the validity of national division of cultures.

Validity of National Cultures

Some scholars (see for review, Minkov & Hofstede, 2012b) contended that the cultural diversity within some nations can be significant, while the people across national borders can be similar.

However, the results of a comprehensive cross-cultural study (Minkov & Hofstede, 2012b), which analyzed the data from World Values Survey, showed the validity of the national cultural division for the global distribution of values:

> 299 in-country regions from 28 countries in East and Southeast Asia, sub-Saharan Africa, Latin America, and the Anglo world overwhelmingly cluster along national lines on basic cultural values, cross-border intermixtures being relatively rare. This is true even of countries like Malaysia and Indonesia, or Mexico and Guatemala, despite their shared official languages, religions, ethnic groups, historical experiences, and various traditions. Even the regions of neighboring African nations, such as Ghana, Burkina Faso, and Mali, do not intermix much when they are clustered on the basis of cultural values. (p. 133)

That means that the concept of national culture is viable and the countries as the units of analysis are worthwhile for cross-cultural research. It should be noted, however, that some studies of emotions (see those in further chapters) have showed that *within-country variation* of emotional variables can be higher than *intercountry variations*. That means that other within-country and typological differences may play important role.

In support that national culture is a viable unit of cross-cultural research, three studies investigated cultural differences between Brazilian states using the Hofstede cross-national dimensions. All these studies have demonstrated that the Brazilian national culture is common across Brazil's states. The similarities between states within the country are more substantial than with Latin American countries, as well as countries worldwide.

Global Transnational Cultures

National cultures share some similarities with other neighboring countries, due to geographical and historical traditions, and religious and political factors. Some global regions of the world may be substantially different in many cultural aspects. One source of these cultural differences is the ancient philosophical views, which are still transmitted to modern generations. Throughout recent centuries, many scholars have noticed and actively entertained the opposition of Western and Eastern cultural civilizations, the mental and cultural perspectives of which are drastically different in many regards.

Cultural and cross-cultural studies have actively engaged in empirical investigation of these global differences. Comparing the United States, the Netherlands, and sometimes other European countries as representative of Western culture, while Japan and China as representative of Eastern culture, researchers have found many interesting cultural differences between these two global cultures of the world. Typically, they referred to individualism and collectivism, or similar societal conceptions as an explanatory cultural framework.

The question, however, remains: whether the United States is representative to all (so-called) Western countries, or whether Japan (or China) is representative of other (so-called) Eastern countries. What does the West mean? What does the East mean? For example, there are many differences between East Asian and South Asian cultures, between American and West European cultures. There is variety of cultural differences between West European countries.

Therefore, researchers began to dig deeper in a global cultural variety of the world. For example, based on the dimensions of cultural values (see details in the followings sections of this book), Schwartz (2014) identified eight *transnational cultural regions* of the world: English-speaking, West European, East Central and Baltic European, Orthodox East European, Latin American, South Asia, Confucian influenced, and African and Middle Eastern. Each of those transnational regions is characterized by a typical pattern of cultural values. Eight cultures, however, have not fit in expected regions.

Among other findings, Schwartz (2014) highlighted cultural differences in the "West." He commented, in particular, that it is not quite adequate to characterize Western culture as individualistic. The complex analysis of cultural orientations has demonstrated considerable differences within the West. Schwartz and Ros (1995) revealed substantial differences on six of the cultural value orientations between the samples in the United States and in Western Europe. In the United States, mastery, embeddedness, and hierarchy were higher, whereas in West European countries, intellectual autonomy, egalitarianism, and harmony were higher.

According to the analysis (Schwartz, 2014), the transnational regions are based on geographical proximity. Therefore, their cultural similarity can be understood because of the cross-national border transmission of values, norms, and practices. Language, histories, religion, and other cultural factors also played their role.

1.2.2   Regional and Local Cultures

Regional Cultures of Nations

Nations are also not necessarily unitary and monocultural systems (Smith & Bond, 1999). In this sense, it is not quite valid to treat India, Russia, the United States, and other multiethnic and multicultural countries as national cultures. This kind of treatment hides the diverse natures of their subcultures, or even different cultures united under one country. The United States, as a country of immigrants, is especially multicultural in this regard. So, it seems that the concept of American culture in literature largely refers to the culture of European Americans. The cultures of African Americans, Asian Americans, Latino Americans, and Native Americans are sometimes viewed as the cultures of minorities.

The country Germany is smaller than the United States, yet there is substantial regional diversity. The distinct differences exist between southern, northern, and eastern lands of Germany. For example, Munich is culturally different from Mannheim, in such aspects as, for instance, work ethic and time system. The German industrialized areas of the north, such as Frankfurt, Stuttgart, Dusseldorf, and Hamburg, are more influenced culturally from other countries, due to international trade (Hall & Hall, 1990). Some regions, such as Bavaria, have their cultural origins and prefer pursuing their cultural heritage to some degree. Historically, Bavaria is Catholic (even though the number of Catholics is recently on the decline), while many other German territories are Protestant. Bavarian German has a strong language dialect.

The French, the people of northern France, are also different from southern French. The weather and surrounding countries have impact on the cultures of northern and southern parts of France. The northern France resembles to some degree Belgium and Germany as North European cultures, while southern France may look more like Italy and Spain as Mediterranean cultures. People in the north of France are a little more reserved and less flamboyant than southern French people. It should be noted, however, that the recent migration flow in France mixed French cultures even more.

In many countries, the regions with distinctive cultures try to preserve their historical societal or communal identities, for example, Bavaria in Germany, Texas in the United States, Quebec in Canada, Scotland in the United Kingdom, and Catalonia in Spain.

Regional Cultural Diversity in the United States

In the United States, there is great regional and ethnic diversity of the population. Therefore, it is difficult to generalize the typical cultural characteristics of Americans. Quite frequently, when researchers use the term Americans, they refer to the people descended from Northern and Western Europe. These are the people from the middle-class, well-educated, living in Chicago, New York, Washington, D.C., Los Angeles, and San Francisco. Other borders exist deep within the territory of North America. It is an imported border that is expressed through a dynamic, continuing recombination of cultures.

For example, the northern and southern parts of the United States are considered as different cultures (e.g., Vandello & Cohen, 1999; Vandello, Cohen, & Ransom, 2008). Other regions of the United States are also culturally different from each other.

The cultural values, norms, and practices of people in different geographic regions within a country may vary in some respects, such as individualism and collectivism, or the importance of honor (Cohen, 2009). According to earlier analysis, the cultures of herding societies tend to attach more importance to honor compared to cultures of agrarian societies (Cohen, Nisbett, Bowdle, & Schwarz, 1996). Based on this fact, Cohen and colleagues explain that since white population in the southern United States historically mostly originate from Scotch-Irish herding societies, the values of honor are more prevalent among Southerners, and they more violently respond to insults. On the other side, the original white settlers and inhabitants in the northern United States are mainly the descents from farmers.

The surveys revealed that white Southerner men tend to use a violent response in case of threats to a person's honor more frequently, compared to Northerners. They strongly believe that it is important for a man to fight a person who insulted his wife. In the lab experiments, the behavior of white Southern men asserted their masculinity, they were more aggressive and confrontational, and they responded with anger when they were insulted. Physiologically, they displayed spikes in their level of testosterone and salivary cortisol, the hormones associated with aggression and stress. Different from this, white Northern men tend to respond with confusion when they were insulted. It is worth noting that patterns of behavior in South areas different in their climate, history of slavery, or socioeconomic status are not associated with these factors.

The cultures of socioeconomic classes play their role in gender role specific norms of emotion expression. For example, in the middle- and upper-middle class of European Americans, society expects that women display less such a negative emotion as anger (Brody & Hall, 2008). This feminine display rule to internalize anger reflects a woman's cultural gender role oriented on nurturing, accommodating, interpersonal relations (Zahn-Waxler, Cole, & Barrett, 1991). However, in low-income or working classes of America, a woman's gender role also encourages them to look "tough." Therefore, women's socialization in these social conditions permits them to openly express anger in order to protect themselves in a potential unsafe neighborhood (Brown, 1999; Eisenberg, 1999; Miller & Sperry, 1987).

Neighboring with Mexico and proximity to other Latino countries can also explain the specific cultural features of southern parts of the United States, including the use of language. "Spanglish" as a mix of Spanish and English is commonly used in Latino communities of the United States among people who grew up with two languages and two cultures (Morales, 2003). "Spanglish" is not just a language;

for Mexican-Americans it is also a merged culture of "Chicanos" that developed under the influence of Mexico and other Latino countries, including Puerto Rico and Cuba.

Regional Cultural Diversity in Japan

Japan also has regional differences. For instance, Kitayama, Ishii, Imada, Takemura, and Ramaswamy (2006) explored Japan's northern frontier region (Hokkaido). The residents of this Japan's "Wild North," where jobless samurai settled during the Meiji government in the late 1800s, have certain common historical features with the American Wild West frontier. A desire for personal achievement and wealth motivated early settlers to arrive to a frontier and to promote their self-reliance in order to survive. Since settlers were goal oriented, this promoted their beliefs in internally motivated behavior and individualism. American authors (Oyserman, Coon, & Kemmelmeier, 2002) provided the same reasoning for individualism in the United States as partially originating from American frontier history. Research showed (Kitayama et al., 2006) that people in Hokkaido consistently display behavior, which is more individualistic than is thought as typical for Japanese. For example, residents of Hokkaido demonstrate the individualistic pattern of attribution considering dispositional (internal) factors as more important than situational (external) factors in causing behavior. These differences reflect on emotional experience and expression. While traditionally for Japanese, only socially engaging positive emotions are associated with happiness, for people in Hokkaido, disengaging positive emotions (e.g., pride) as well as social-harmony-promoting emotions (e.g., friendly feelings) are related to happiness.

Modern scholarship encourages revising the concept of culture going beyond national and regional cultures. The concept of cultural community perfectly fits to the concept of culture. Communities are the units with which members share aesthetic/expressive, cognitive, and moral meanings. Through this belonging they gain a sense of group identity and identity of the boundary between members and nonmembers. Such communities are constructed symbolically being engaged in meanings and rituals and providing the opportunity to construct and reconstruct social relationships over time (Cohen, 1985). Modern understanding of culture goes further rethinking the relations between concepts of culture, community, locality, transnationalism, and diaspora in the age of globalization. In modern age of globalization, transnational cultures—communities across borders—became yet other types of culture. Such cultural communities are not limited by particular physical locations. They are liberated from dependence upon direct interpersonal relations and locality, still sustaining community of migrants across borders (Kennedy & Roudometof, 2002).

Regional Cultural Diversity in Brazil

The Brazilian societal culture is hierarchical and structured. It is above global average on Power Distance and Uncertainty Avoidance and average on Individualism and Masculinity. The Brazilian culture manages to balance individuals versus ingroups and achievement versus caring. It is characterized by fairly Long-Term Orientation. It values persistence more than tradition (Hofstede, Garibaldi de Hilal, Malvezzi, Tanure, & Vinken, 2010).

Despite this overall commonality, there are five distinct regions of Brazil:

1. The South: European and prosperous, is more hierarchical, less formal, more individualist, and more masculine (achievement-oriented).
2. The Southeast plus Brasilia: urban, industrial, densely populated, and ethnically mixed, is less masculine and also shorter term-oriented.
3. The Central-West: a borderline region of settlers, is less formal.
4. The Northeast: tropical, colonial heritage, poor, and Afro-Brazilian, is less hierarchical, more formal, and less masculine, that is, more caring.
5. The North: the Amazon basin and the homeland of Brazil's native Indians, is very informal, collectivist, and very masculine, which in this case may mean assertive. (Hofstede et al., 2010, p. 347–348)

Large Cities and Small Towns as Cultures

Another point of regional cultural differences is between small towns and large cities. In this regard, there might be consistent patterns across countries. For instance, small towns in Japan may be similar to small towns in Australia.

Researchers (Kashima et al., 2004) probed this theory investigating regional differences in the concept of self in a large metropolitan city (Tokyo) and in a regional city (Kagoshima) in Japan, in parallel with a large metropolitan city (Melbourne) and a regional city (Wodonga) in Australia. Authors were interested in such aspects of the individualistic self as agency ("I act more on the basis of my own judgment than on other people's decision") and assertiveness ("I assert my opposition when I disagree strongly with other people"), and such aspects of the collectivistic self as the relational self ("I feel like doing something for people in trouble because I can almost feel their pains") and the collective self ("I would act as a member of my group rather than alone as an individual"). Naturally, at the national level they found that the Australians are more individualistic, with higher scores on agency and assertiveness, compared to the Japanese, which in turn are higher on the relational self and the collective self. Women are more relational than men. But it is more interesting that metropolitan residents are less collectivist in their *self* than regional residents in both countries.

The study cited above is unique in terms of cultural samples. Unfortunately, few cultural studies of emotions have been conducted in small towns and rural areas, despite a reasonable expectation that emotions of people in urban and rural communities may differ.

1.3   Multicultural Cultures

1.3.1   Ethnic and Multiethnic Cultures

Ethnic Cultures

Ethnic and racial background of participants is traditionally considered as a basis for cultural division within a society. It is a common place that such demographic information is collected in American studies. The small sample size of some minorities in those studies, however, does not always allow incorporating the cultural variable of ethnicity in analysis.

The variable of ethnicity is more evident when ethnic differences are the targets of cross-cultural research (e.g., Bray, 1970; Matsumoto, 1993; Phinney & Alipuria, 2006; Tsai, Chentsova-Dutton, Freire-Bebeau, & Przymus, 2002; Tsai & Levenson, 1997; Van de Vijver, Blommaert, Gkoumasi, & Stogianni, 2015). In many other studies, an ethnic culture as a type of culture frequently becomes the topic of sociological, psychological, and anthropological research.

Ethnic and Cultural Coexistence

Cultural borders are frequently associated with national, state, or tribal boundaries with clearly identifiable markers. A culture is commonly equated with a territory (Delgado-Gaitan & Trueba, 1991; Ewing, 1998; Lugo, 1997). It is assumed that once the distinct societies are separated from each other by borders, a researcher should expect cultural distinctiveness. In the modern age of mass migration, it is often not adequate to reality.

Modern world exposes people to various cultures that might be more or less compatible to each other. Nevertheless, neighboring cultures tend to mix with each other. The culture mixing has become the reality nowadays (Hao, Li, Peng, Peng, & Torelli, 2016; Harush, Lisak, & Erez, 2016; Martin & Shao, 2016).

Culture mixing refers to "the coexistence of representative symbols of different cultures in the same space at the same time" as a new paradigm of polyculturalism in the culture and psychology research (Hao et al., 2016). Besides American, Chinese, and German cultures, there might be European and Californian cultures, which are not necessarily associated with ethnicity. Besides American and Mexican, there might be a Mexican-American culture.

Cultures on the national borders sometimes mix with each other, sometimes not. The concept of *cultural borderland* was proposed to define a space where two or more cultures inhabit the same territory (Foley, 1995). Generally, it refers to a psychological space at the conjuncture of two cultures in multicultural societies. Individuals in these lands crossing borders frequently experience bicultural or multicultural identities deciding which culture—their cultures of origin or of adoption—they would prefer to identify with. The Mexican-American borders are the examples of such lands where some students may experience the dilemma in preferences to read "gringo" (White) poetry and Chicano poetry (Saenz, 1997).

1.3.2 Mixed Cultures

Multicultural Mixing

The diversity of forms of culture, their mixture and overlapping within a cultural group, and increasing multicultural identity of individuals put additional challenge for definitions of culture. Different forms of cultures can be defined and measured along similar as well as different cultural dimensions. Cultural groups can have a mixed culture belonging to different forms of culture: national, socioeconomic, religious, regional, and possibly others. The same way, modern individuals are less likely to be monocultural and more likely to be multicultural, especially in the era of mass migration. And this multiculturalism might be not only in terms of national or ethnic mixture of cultural identities, but also in terms of mixture of socioeconomic status, social class, of being religious (or nonreligious, or atheistic), and of living in a particular region within a country.

Some large or small dynamic communities have great variation in ethnic and national origins of people living together (e.g., Van de Vijver et al., 2015). Individuals in those communities experience multiple influences developing polycultural identity. Polyculturalism implies that "individuals take influences from multiple cultures" (Morris, Chiu, & Liu, 2015, p. 631).

Multicultural Identity

For some individuals, it may be challenging to identify themselves according to one cultural identity since they rather have a mixture of two cultures. Researchers now pay more attention to multicultural individuals (Martin & Shao, 2016) and the concept of bicultural identity integration attracts attention of researchers (Benet-Martínez & Haritatos, 2005; Harush et al., 2016). Immigrants can experience a bicultural identity and keep the elements of ethnic identity from the culture of their origins, yet they already acquired some aspects of the culture where they live now. Studies demonstrated strong evidence of the positive behavioral and relationship consequences of being bicultural and having bicultural integration (e.g., Cheng, Lee, Benet-Martínez, & Huynh, 2014).

In daily life, individuals may develop multiple cultural identity and act according to different cultural roles. According to the role theory in social psychology, an individual in any given episode of his/her everyday activity acts out of a socially defined social category (e.g., daughter, father, factory worker, grandmother), with each role fulfilling certain values, norms of behavior, and expectations. The same way in cultural psychology, an individual can act out of his/her cultural category being influenced by one or another cultural identity in any given episode of his/her life.

When an individual cultural identity from diverse cultures is incorporated, instead of remaining separate from each other, then cultural boundaries within an individual become blurred. Chang (1999) provides the illustrative examples of multicultural individuals with close connections with Korea, who currently live in the pluralistic US society.

Jean Kohl, a 9-year-old daughter of a German father and a Korean mother, was born and raised in the United States. Her parents, fluent speakers of German and Korean respectively, adopted English as the primary language at home. "I am an American," proclaimed she, but she often ended her proclamation with an addendum that she was also German and Korean. For several summers she traveled to visit her maternal or paternal grandparents in Korea or Germany, during which she was exposed to her parents' native cultures and languages. The German, Korean and U.S. heritage blended in her cultural repertoire. For Jean, where does the "American" cultural border end and other cultural borders begin?

Carrie Baumstein, a 20-year-old woman, was born in Korea and adopted by a Messianic Jewish-American couple when she was 2 years old. She has lived in the States ever since. She was not exposed to much Korean culture and language when she was growing up, but was instead surrounded by her parents' Jewish tradition. Despite her primary identity with the Jewish culture, she was often reminded by her relatives and neighbors of her Korean-or Asian-linkage. She was in an identity search for Asianness when she was attending a small Christian college on the East Coast. For Carrie, where do the cultural borders lie between the Korean and the American and between the Messianic Jew and the Christian?

Peter Lee, a 15-year-old, was born in the States to immigrant parents from Korea. His parents own and operate a dry cleaning shop in a suburb of Philadelphia. Their English is functional for the business but they prefer speaking Korean on all other occasions. Peter's family attends a Korean church regularly, which usually serves as a cultural community as much as a religious one. Peter's Korean is so limited that he usually speaks English, although his parents speak Korean to him. He is definitely an American in his mind and heart, perhaps a Korean-American occasionally. But his preference of Korean-American peers to others is a curious phenomenon. Where lies the cultural border that divides the Korean and the "American" for Peter?

Elaine Sook-Ja Cho, 50 years old, immigrated to the States 30 years ago to marry a Korean bachelor 10 years her senior. Her husband came to the States as a student and found employment upon completion of his study. Elaine was a housewife for 20 years before undertaking a small grocery business. She speaks "Konglish" (a mixture of Korean sentence structure and English words) but she seems to be at ease speaking English. She is Korean in her heart but "Americanized" in her own words and by her life style. For Sook-Ja how far does the Korean cultural border stretch to meet the "American" culture? (Chang, 1999, p. 4)

What is the cultural typology of these individuals? How would they cross the cultural borders daily? Would it be possible to be culturally Korean in the morning, German during lunch, "American" in the afternoon, and Korean once again in the evening?

These within-group and within-individual cultural variations put an additional challenge for cross-cultural studies. Some cultural traits can be imperfectly represented and available in people's minds at any given moment (Adams & Markus, 2004). The definition of culture nowadays, when a mixture of cultures and their blending take a rapid growth and expansion, encounters another research challenge.

1.4   The Cultures of Socioeconomic Status and Social Class

1.4.1   Social and Economic Cultures Within Countries

Variety of Cultural Groups Within National Cultures

There is a variety of forms of culture, which can be classified according to such criteria as demographic background, socioeconomic status, and social class. The people who share certain cultural parameters belonging to such groups can be considered as cultures, or subcultures. They have various kinds of group affiliation and dynamics, which can be considered culturally different and demonstrate cultural diversity. Other kinds of cultures are possible. Here are some examples.

Based on gender affiliation, these can be manhood culture (Basso, McCall, & Garceau, 2013; Gilmore, 1990; Vandello, Bosson, Cohen, Burnaford, & Weaver, 2008) and womanhood culture (e.g., Hancock, 2019; Rapoport & El-Or, 1997; Roberts, 2002; Underwood, 1985), with androgynous and LGBT—lesbian, gay, bisexual, and transgender—cultures (e.g., Driver, 2008; Herdt, 1997; Ramet, 2002) in between, or beyond.

There are cultures according to the age and generation differences (e.g., Baker, Buttigieg, & Robards, 2015; Brake, 1985; Bucholtz, 2002; Hodkinson, 2016; Hodkinson & Deicke, 2007; Nilan & Feixa, 2006), as well as various cultures attached to the art, music, and other types of activities and interests. They are often called subcultures (Gelder, 2007; Hodkinson & Deicke, 2007).

In light of this diverse use and relatively ambiguous interpretation of the construct of *culture*, some authors began to doubt that culture is an adequate concept for cross-cultural research (see for review, Fischer & Poortinga, 2018; Poortinga, 2015). Indeed, the modern definition and operationalization of *culture* deviate from the original one (also diverse). It may be the time to reevaluate and revise it. Meanwhile, a good other solution could be if authors would conceptually and operationally define the concept of *culture* in their writing, according to the meaning they have in mind.

Socioeconomic and Social Classes as Cultural Groups

Social class and socioeconomic status as the forms of cultures deserve special consideration because they represent a large variation in the values, beliefs, norms, and practices shared by large groups of people and transmitted from generation to generation (Cohen, 2009). They are comparable to nationality and ethnicity in this regard.

Socioeconomic and social classes can be considered as cultural groups since they differ in their values, norms, and practices. Individuals in those cultural groups have similar views on many aspects of life. For example, people of high socioeconomic status generally prefer rock music and people of low socioeconomic status prefer country music. What does it tell us about these cultures? According to content analysis, the rock music highlights self-actualization and making the world to accommodate and conform. The country music, on the other side, tends to highlight adapting to challenges and maintaining resiliency and integrity (Snibbe & Markus, 2005).

1.4.2 Research of Social and Economic Cultures

Adaptation Versus Control Beliefs Associated with Socioeconomic Status

In terms of general views on life, the culture of high socioeconomic status respects the values of control and agency, while the culture of low socioeconomic status favors the values of flexibility, integrity, and resilience. People of high socioeconomic status believe that they are able to influence others and control their environments. People of low socioeconomic status believe that they cannot control their environments and, therefore, have to adapt to their surroundings and maintain their integrity (Snibbe & Markus, 2005). Therefore, they highly value resilience in time of adversity, compared to people of high socioeconomic status, who focus on altering their environments. For example, people from lower social class may be less motivated to solve their health problems and think that it is an appropriate way to deal with them. They may rather adapt to their health problems with integrity. In addition, low socioeconomic status correlates with high religiosity. Therefore, people from low socioeconomic status may believe that their health problems are God's will and have some greater meaning (Cohen, 2009). Thus, different cultural membership can bring different interpretation of data and cultural variables.

Cultural Differences Between Socioeconomic Statuses Are Larger Than Between Countries

Let us consider one more example of cross-cultural research taking into account socioeconomic status. Researchers (Haidt, Koller, & Dias, 1993) compared adults and children of higher and lower socioeconomic statuses in three cities in the United

States and in Brazil. They asked participants to judge the actions that were highly disrespectful or disgusting, even though not harmful to others. Authors found that Brazilians judged these actions more immoral than Americans. People of low socioeconomic status in both countries judged these actions as immoral, rather than a violation of a social convention or a personal choice. What is especially important, the differences based on socioeconomic status were larger than the country differences.

The cultural dimension of *individualism* may also depend on social class, and social and economic conditions of living. Thus, generalization of individualism as a cultural characteristic of the United States might be not quite adequate, and other societal and cultural factors play their role. For example, Snibbe and Markus (2005) found that the pursuit of uniqueness and self-expression is valued as more important for Americans with a *high socioeconomic status* than for those with a *low socioeconomic status*. Other studies also indicate that individualism is a more descriptive value for Americans with *high socioeconomic status*, rather than with low *socioeconomic status* (Kraus, Piff, & Keltner, 2009; Stephens, Markus, & Townsend, 2007).

On the other cultural side, in Philippines, China, and Japan—traditionally considered as collectivistic cultures—*individualism* is higher among people with *high socioeconomic status*, compared to those with low *socioeconomic status* (Guthrie, 1977; Hamamura, Xu, & Du, 2013; Kameda, Takezawa, & Hastie, 2005). Thus, this effect of *socioeconomic status* on the cultural dimension of individualism is identified and found across cultures.

Socioeconomic Development and Emotions

Some studies (e.g., Arrindell et al., 1997; Basabe et al., 2000; Diener, Diener, & Diener, 1995; Wallbott & Scherer, 1988) found that subjective well-being and experience of positive emotions are strongly associated with socioeconomic development and high income in countries. In less developed countries, people perceive social life as more socially stressful and uncontrollable. As a result, they experience less pleasant emotions.

1.5 Religious Cultures

1.5.1 Religion as a Culture

Cultural Nature of Religion

Religion is the search for significance related to the sacred things, those that believers perceive as "holy, 'set apart' from the ordinary, and worthy of veneration and respect" (Pargament, Magyar-Kussell, & Murray-Swank, 2005, p. 668). Beliefs about the mighty and merciful nature of God and prayers affect emotional well-being and bring a powerful emotional experience of closeness to the sacred

(Silberman, 2005), which transfer to corresponding emotional attitudes toward other people. Such emotional dispositions as love, hope, gratitude, humility, forgiveness, and self-control are highly prized in Muslim, Hindu, Buddhist, Christian, and Jewish traditions and have been extensively investigated (Emmons & Paloutzian, 2003).

All religions consist of (1) cognitions and beliefs related to the people's perception of transcendence, (2) moral rules and practices, (3) individual and collective rituals, along with emotions that create close affiliation of people with each other and with transcendence, and (4) the feelings of personal identification with greatly valuable and timeless groups (Saroglou, 2011). These constituents of all religions across history (even nontheistic religions) include (1) believing, (2) behaving, (3) bonding, and (4) belonging. They are present in all religions with variability across cultural and religious groups.

Religion in Cultural Context of Nation

Religion is frequently viewed as a category dissociated from broader culture. Some scholars think that this tendency reflects the Western bias influenced by Christianity. They believe that religion substantially influences cultural dimensions of societies, yet it is an overlooked dimension in cross-cultural psychology (Cohen, 2009; McCutcheon, 1995; Tarakeshwar, Stanton, & Pargament, 2003; Tsai, Koopmann-Holm, Miyazaki, & Ochs, 2013).

Religious cultures resemble *national cultures*, yet they also differ from national cultures in important ways. Religion, like national and ethnic cultures, can also be considered as a form of culture and cultural system (Cohen, 2009; Saroglou & Cohen, 2013). Religions can also become subcultures in the same country. For instance, Hinduism is a subculture of the broader Indian culture. A religious parameter of culture correlates with other cultural dimensions. These correlations make it difficult to distinguish a special role of religion from other cultural dimensions.

Religious Groups as Cultures

Religion is difficult to define as a unitary cultural construct or dimension since it embraces a diverse set of cultural groups, such as monotheistic Islam, Judaism, Christianity; polytheistic Hinduism, Taoism, Shinto; or atheistic Buddhism. They present a set of values, beliefs, practices, and symbols which establish pervasive, powerful, and long-lasting moods and motivations that are similar among a large group of people. They formulate conceptions of universal existence with an aura of facts which make the moods and motivations uniquely realistic (Geertz, 1973, p. 90).

Religion can be viewed as a set of cultural religious groups, rather than a single and unitary dimension, and each group might be analyzed in various cultural dimensions. For example, Tarakeshwar et al. (2003) proposed a five-dimensional framework of religion, which includes ideological, ritualistic, experiential, intellectual, and social dimensions. Authors suggest this framework for cross-cultural research of religion.

1.5.2 A Cross-Cultural Perspective on Religion

Cultural Dimensions of Religions

Researchers were able to identify several major dimensions of religiousness (see for detailed review, Saroglou & Cohen, 2013), which are present across many religions and denominations with some cultural differences. *Fundamentalist (orthodox)* expressions versus *questing* expressions of religious beliefs and practices are distinguished among Muslims, Christians, Jews, and Hindus. *Intrinsic* versus *extrinsic* religious orientations are identified among Catholics, Protestants, Orthodox, Muslims, and Jews. The dimension of organized traditional *religiousness* versus modern individual *spirituality* exists in many cultural contexts. The *mystical dimension* of religion, focusing on the spirituality of the mystics, is common in many religions. The mystic experiences appear similar between American Christians and Iranian Muslims as well as Israeli Jews, Indian Hindus, and Tibetan Buddhists' religiousness (see for detailed review, Saroglou & Cohen, 2013).

Interaction of Religious and Cultural Parameters in Society

Religions interact with other cultural parameters influencing cultural and emotional life of people. National and ethnic cultures can be closely connected with religious cultures. For instance, European Americans is an individualistic culture, and they are largely affiliated with Christianity (Protestants are also individualists). Japanese, on the other side, is a collectivistic culture and they are commonly affiliated with Eastern religions (Buddhists are also collectivists). The cultural differences between the West and the East are pervasive and stable across centuries, partially due to religious aspects of their cultural heritage.

Religious people are also generally more interdependent than those who are not (Cohen & Rozin, 2001; Cukur, de Guzman, & Carlo, 2004, Triandis, 1995), yet religions differ in their degree of interdependence, contingent on being monotheistic (more independent) or nontheistic (more interdependent). The Protestant societies tend to be mostly individualist and egalitarian, the Confucianist societies are usually collectivist, and Islamic societies are typically hierarchical (Basabe & Ros, 2005).

Historically, religion frequently shaped cultural patterns of nations (Norris & Inglehart, 2004), even though the reversed influence also took place. A culture of country caused a religious development in a certain way. For instance, anthropological studies showed (Wikan, 1988) that Islam can endorse different values in different cultures. Religion comes through culture being modified and transformed. Even though Muslim communities in the countries of Bali and Egypt have a common religion and follow the same Islamic beliefs, nevertheless, they are consistent with their cultural customs.

1.5.3 Religious Teachings About Emotions

Religious Cultural Norms of Emotions

Religious cultural traditions substantially influence emotional values of people (Emmons, 2005; Silberman, 2005; Snibbe & Markus, 2002) and teach them which feelings and acts are virtuous, moral, good, and desirable to feel, and what an *ideal affect* is. Religious cultures also teach which feelings and behavior are immoral, sinful, and undesirable and, therefore, should be avoided, and what an *avoided affect* is (Koopmann-Holm, 2013; Tsai, 2007; Tsai, Knutson, & Fung, 2006; Tsai et al., 2013).

Religions prescribe not only which emotions are appropriate, but also which are preferable, how intense they should be (Silberman, 2005), and how a person can cultivate intense positive emotions and regulate negative emotions. Generally, people prefer an experience of positive emotional states. However, they want to avoid an experience of negative emotional states more than positive ones. There are cultural variations and religious differences in how people want to avoid certain feelings (Koopmann-Holm, 2013). The studies on how cultural aspects of different religions impact emotional life of people elucidate the diversity of love experience since love is a central tenet of many religious beliefs.

The Value of Positive and Negative Emotions in Religious Cultures

Many religions value traditions and are quite conservative suggesting moderation in the search of pleasure, novelty, and excitement. Catholics, Protestants, Greek Orthodox, Jews, and Muslims—to a greater or lesser extent—discourage such emotional values as novelty, change, and pursuing pleasure in life (Schwartz & Huismans, 1995; Saroglou, Delpierre, & Dernelle, 2004). A study among Dutch Roman Catholics, Dutch Protestants, Dutch nonaffiliated, and Israeli Jews showed that religion favors traditional motivation and discourages hedonic motivation (Huismans & Schwartz, 1992).

Some cultural variability is still evident. According to lexical content analyses, Christian texts more frequently than Buddhist classical texts encourage *high-arousal positive* states. The findings from empirical studies are in accordance with cross-cultural differences in the importance of *high-* versus *low-arousal positive* emotions in North American (predominantly Christian) versus East Asian (predominantly Buddhist) cultures (Tsai et al., 2006).

According to the old fundamental texts—Gospels in Christianity and Lotus Sutra in Buddhism—as well as with typical practices in the two religions, high-arousal positive emotions, such as excitement, are valued more, whereas low-arousal positive emotions, such as calm, are valued less in Christianity than in Buddhism. These differences correspond to the data obtained in empirical studies. Comparing the *ideal affect* of Christian and Buddhist practitioners, researchers (Tsai, Miao, & Seppala, 2007) found that Christian and Buddhist texts and practices really influence their ideal affect. Results showed that Christian practitioners value *high-arousal positive affective* states more and *low-arousal positive affective* states less than did Buddhist practitioners (Tsai et al., 2007).

The Value of Specific Emotions

Exploring the desirability of love, happiness, pride, gratitude, sadness, guilt, shame, anger, and jealousy, researchers found that *Christians* prefer to experience ideally and really experience love more frequently than Muslims and Buddhists. *Muslims*, however, prefer ideally and really experience shame and sadness more than Christians, Jews, Buddhists, and Hindus. *Buddhists* feel fewer dips or peaks in any emotional experience compared to Christians, Jews, Hindus, and Muslims (Kim-Prieto & Diener, 2009). According to Buddhism, life is full of sorrow, grief, and suffering. The best way to end this suffering is to achieve "enlightenment" (Smith, 1991).

The cultural norms of emotions in the same religion can vary across countries. For example, Muslim people in Bali and Egypt have different attitudes toward expression of emotions (Wikan, 1988). The Balinese consider emotional expressions as a threat to others and oneself interfering with judgment. Egyptians regard emotional expressions as the cultural norm, which are vital for positive health. Emotional reactions to death are also different in two cultures. People in Bali react to the death of a child with calm emotions, whereas in Egypt with precipitated intense emotional reactions.

1.5.4   Impact of Religions on the Experience and Expression of Emotions

Religions and Experience of Specific Emotions

Religious cultures have always profoundly affected believers' emotions influencing their emotional experience, expression, and emotional health (Saroglou, 2010, 2011; Tsai et al., 2013).

Emotional experience of gratitude is perhaps the most closely associated with religiosity. A cross-cultural study (McCullough, Emmons, & Tsang, 2002) found that, according to self- and peer ratings, religious people tend to have a grateful disposition in their life. In Christianity, gratitude, thankful joy, and love toward God have been always the signs of genuine emotional experience. People with high levels of spirituality experience more gratitude in their daily moods (McCullough et al., 2002). A small study of Catholic priests and nuns (Samuels & Lester, 1985) showed that out of 50 emotions, gratitude and love are the most frequently experienced toward God. Other religions, such as Buddhism, Hinduism, Islam, and Judaism, greatly value gratitude, which is a desirable and important emotional attitude for living a good life (Emmons & Crumpler, 2000; Kim-Prieto & Diener, 2009). Religion can shape the desirability of other prosocial emotions as well; for example, across different religions, religious people rate the value of being forgiving higher than nonreligious people (Rokeach, 1973). However, we should keep in mind a possible variation in the meaning of forgiveness in religious cultures (Cohen, Malka, Rozin, & Cherfas, 2006).

It seems that the feelings of guilt and anxiety drive believers in Catholicism more than Protestantism (Patock-Peckham et al. 1998). In the United States, Protestants are more emotionally positive in their personality traits, such as high extraversion and low neuroticism, and feel less discomfort with openness to experience, compared to Catholics in Europe (Saroglou, 2010). Protestant couples have less negative emotional effects of divorce on their well-being than Catholic couples (Clark & Lelkes, 2005).

In Germany, Protestants are also higher than Catholics in their trust, and both Protestants and Catholics are higher than nonreligious people (Traunmiiller, 2011). Protestants agree more with dispositional (internal and personal) attributions of situation and emotion than do Catholics (Li et al., 2012).

The differences are even larger when comparing more distinctive religions. People who identify themselves with Christian or Buddhist religion value low-arousal positive states more than those who do not. Besides, Christians are in favor of high-arousal positive states more and low-arousal positive states less than Buddhists (Tsai et al., 2007).

Religions and Well-Being

Individuals following religious beliefs and engaging in religious practices tend to be *more* satisfied and happier. They experience more positive feelings on a daily basis (Koenig, 2001; Koenig, George, & Titus, 2004). They are more hopeful and have a meaningful purpose in life. They have less anxiety, feel fewer depressive symptoms, and are *less* vulnerable to depressive episodes (Koenig, 2001; Koenig et al., 2004; Masters & Hooker, 2013; Park & Slattery, 2013). The studies using physiological measures also showed that religious practice promotes well-being (Davidson et al., 2003; Inzlichrt & Tullett, 2010).

It should be noted, however, that some religions do not have the same ideal affect as others and interpret well-being differently across religious cultures (Tsai et al., 2013). Other national and religious cultures may have different desired or ideal emotional states. For instance, high-arousal positive states, such as enthusiasm and excitement, are suitable measures of emotional well-being for Christians, but can be inadequate for Buddhists (Tsai et al., 2007). These cultural differences place a challenge in interpretation of empirical data since emotional satisfaction can result from achieving high levels of ideal affect, or alternatively, from the lowering of the ideal affect.

Religious Teaching About Expression of Emotions

Do religions suppress emotions, as psychoanalysis assumed? Freud considered sublimation, as the defense mechanism of rechanneling of unacceptable urges into creative pursuits (Freud, 1905/2000). In a series of studies, Kim, Zeppenfeld, and Cohen (2013) explored the suppression of anger and its consequences for sublimation. Researchers asked Catholic, Protestant, and Jewish participants either to recall an anger-provoking incident and suppress thinking about it, or recall an anger-provoking incident and suppress thinking about another harmless topic (e.g., a horse), or to recall a neutral event and suppress thinking about a harmless topic.

Then, researchers asked participants to engage in creative tasks (e.g., making a collage, making a sculpture, creating captions for cartoons). The results showed that while suppression of anger did not affect creativity among Catholic and Jewish participants, the suppression of thinking about an anger-provoking incident stimulated much more creative and angry products of art among Protestants (by opinion of expert judges; Tsai & Clobert, 2019, p. 308). These findings demonstrate that emotional suppression is useful, yet consequences and the product of suppressed emotions vary across religions.

Several other studies have demonstrated the role of religious values in experience and expression of emotions. Even though there is a common opinion that Protestantism and Muslim beliefs, as well as the overall higher level of religiosity and orthodoxy, encourage the suppression of emotions, empirical studies do not support this notion (Van Hemert, Poortinga, & van de Vijver, 2007; Veenhoven, 1994).

Contrary to the hypothesis that "countries with more Protestants show lower levels of positive emotions" (van Hemert et al., 2007, p. 918), meta-analysis revealed that the higher percentage of Protestants positively correlates with self-reports of positive emotions. Also, contrary to the hypothesis that "countries with a higher percentage of Muslims show lower levels of general emotional expression" (van Hemert et al., 2007, p. 918), meta-analysis discovered that the percentage of Muslims in a country does not significantly correlate with cultural differences in emotional expression.

Overall, the expectation that "countries with higher levels of religiosity may be more restrictive in their expression of emotions" (van Hemert et al., 2007, p. 918) was not supported. The findings of meta-analysis demonstrated that "expression of emotions and particularly positive emotions was higher in more religious countries" (van Hemert et al., 2007, p. 933).

Religious Teachings About Emotion Regulation

Various religious traditions have developed emotional regulation techniques that can modulate people's everyday emotional experience (Schimmel, 1997; Watts, 1996). In particular, many spiritual traditions foster the cultivation of transpersonal states (McCraty, Barrios-Choplin, Rozman, Atkinson, & Watkins, 1998). Zen meditation brings positive emotional benefits (Gillani & Smith, 2001). The contemplative tradition encourages to regulate emotions via calming the passions and developing emotional tranquility. In some religions, the ascetic view (Allen, 1997) suggests the greater awareness of emotion and the creative ways to express emotions.

Religions provide spiritual rationales and methods to handle the disruptive nature of such emotions as guilt, depression, and anger. For example, Christian and Jewish teachings have traditionally suggested the ways to master anger, pride, envy, and other destructive emotions (Schimmel, 1997).

References

Adams, G., & Markus, H. R. (2004). Toward a conception of culture suitable for a social psychology of culture. In M. Schaller & C. S. Crandall (Eds.), *Psychological foundations of culture* (pp. 335–360). Mahwah, NJ: Erlbaum.

Allen, D. (1997). Ascetic theology and psychology. In R. C. Roberts & M. R. Talbot (Eds.), *Limning the psyche: Explorations in Christian psychology* (pp. 297–316). Grand Rapids, MI: Eerdmans.

Arrindell, W. A., Hatzichristou, C., Wensink, J., Rosenberg, E., van Twillert, B., Stedema, J., & Meijer, D. (1997). Dimensions of national culture as predictors of cross-national differences in subjective well-being. *Personality and Individual Differences, 23,* 37–53.

Baker, S., Buttigieg, M. B., & Robards, B. (Eds.). (2015). *Youth cultures and subcultures: Australian perspectives.* Surrey, UK: Ashgate Publishing.

Basabe, N., Paez, D., Valencia, J., Rimé, B., Pennebaker, J., Diener, E., & González, J. L. (2000). Sociocultural factors predicting subjective experience of emotion: A collective level analysis. *Psicothema, 12*(Suppl 1), 55–69.

Basabe, N., & Ros, M. (2005). Cultural dimensions and social behavior correlates: Individualism-collectivism and Power distance. *International Review of Social Psychology, 18*(1), 189–225.

Basso, M., McCall, L., & Garceau, D. (2013). *Across the great divide: Cultures of manhood in the American west.* New York, NY: Routledge.

Benet-Martínez, V., & Haritatos, J. (2005). Bicultural identity integration (BII): Components and psychosocial antecedents. *Journal of Personality, 73*(4), 1015–1050. https://doi.org/10.1111/j.1467-6494.2005.00337.x

Boyd, R., & Richerson, P. J. (1985). *Culture and the evolutionary process.* Chicago, IL: University of Chicago Press.

Brake, M. (1985). *Comparative youth culture: The sociology of youth cultures and youth subcultures in America, Britain and Canada.* London, UK: Routledge.

Bray, D. H. (1970). Extent of future time orientation: A cross-ethnic study among New Zealand adolescents. *British Journal of Educational Psychology, 40,* 200–208.

Brody, L. R., & Hall, J. A. (2008). Gender and emotion in context. In M. Lewis, J. M. Haviland-Jones, & L. F. Barrett (Eds.), *Handbook of emotions* (pp. 395–408). New York, NY: Guilford Press.

Brown, L. M. (1999). *Raising their voices: The politics of girls' anger*. Cambridge, MA: Harvard University Press.

Bucholtz, M. (2002). Youth and cultural practice. *Annual Review of Anthropology, 31*(1), 525–552.

Chang, H. (1999). Re-examining the rhetoric of the "cultural border". *Electronic Magazine of Multicultural Education, 1*(1), 1–7. Retrieved from http://www.edchange.org/multicultural/papers/heewon.html

Cheng, C. Y., Lee, F., Benet-Martínez, V., & Huynh, Q. L. (2014). 13 variations in multicultural experience: Influence of bicultural identity integration on socio-cognitive processes and outcomes. In V. Benet-Martínez & Y. Hong (Eds.), *The Oxford handbook of multicultural identity* (p. 276). New York, NY: Oxford University Press.

Chiu, C.-Y., & Hong, Y.-Y. (2006). *Social psychology of culture*. New York, NY: Psychology Press.

Clark, A., & Lelkes, O. (2005). *Deliver us from evil: Religion as insurance*. ffhalshs-00590570f. Retrieved from https://halshs.archives-ouvertes.fr/halshs-00590570/document

Cohen, A. B. (2009). Many forms of culture. *American Psychologist, 64*, 194–204.

Cohen, A. B., Malka, A., Rozin, P., & Cherfas, L. (2006). Religion and unforgivable offenses. *Journal of Personality, 74*, 85–118.

Cohen, A. B., & Rozin, P. (2001). Religion and the morality of mentality. *Journal of Personality and Social Psychology, 81*, 697–710.

Cohen, A. P. (1985). *The symbolic construction of community*. Chichester, UK/London, UK: Ellis Horwood and Tavistock Publications.

Cohen, D., Nisbett, R. E., Bowdle, B. F., & Schwarz, N. (1996). Insult, aggression, and the southern culture of honor: An experimental ethnography. *Journal of Personality and Social Psychology, 70*, 945–960. https://doi.org/10.1037/0022-3514.70.5.945

Cukur, C. S., de Guzman, M. R. T., & Carlo, G. (2004). Religiosity, values, and horizontal and vertical individualism-collectivism: A study of Turkey, the United States, and the Philippines. *Journal of Social Psychology, 144*, 613–634.

D'Andrade, R. G. (1984). Cultural meaning systems. In R. A. Shweder & R. A. LeVine (Eds.), *Culture theory: Essays on mind, self, and emotion* (pp. 88–119). Cambridge, UK: Cambridge University Press.

Davidson, R. J., Kabat-Zinn, J., Schumacher, J., Rosenkranz, M., Muller, D., Santorclli, S., et al. (2003). Alterations in brain and immune function produced by mindfulness meditation. *Psychosomatic Medicine, 6S*, 564–570.

DeKay, W. T., & Buss, D. M. (1992). Human nature, individual differences, and the importance of context: Perspectives from evolutionary psychology. *Current Directions in Psychological Science, 1*(6), 184–189.

Delgado-Gaitan, C., & Trueba, H. (1991). *Crossing cultural borders*. New York, NY: The Falmer Press.

Diener, E., Diener, M., & Diener, C. (1995). Factors predicting the subjective well-being of nations. *Journal of Personality and Social Psychology, 69*, 851–864.

Driver, S. (2008). *Queer youth cultures*. Albany, NY: SUNY Press.

Eisenberg, A. R. (1999). Emotion talk among Mexican American and Anglo American mothers and children from two social classes. *Merrill-Palmer Quarterly, 45*(2), 267–284.

Emmons, R. A. (2005). Emotion and religion. In R. F. Paloutzian & C. L. Park (Eds.), *Handbook of the psychology of religion and spirituality* (pp. 235–252). New York, NY: Guilford Press.

Emmons, R. A., & Crumpler, C. A. (2000). Gratitude as a human strength: Appraising the evidence. *Journal of Social and Clinical Psychology, 19*, 56–69.

Emmons, R. A., & Paloutzian, R. F. (2003). The psychology of religion. *Annual Review of Psychology, 54*(1), 377–402.

Ewing, K. P. (1998). Crossing borders and transgressing boundaries: Metaphor for negotiating multiple identities. *Ethos, 26*(2), 262–267.

Fischer, R., & Poortinga, Y. H. (2018). Addressing methodological challenges in culture-comparative research. *Journal of Cross-Cultural Psychology, 49*(5), 691–712.

Foley, D. E. (1995). *The heartland chronicles*. Philadelphia, PA: University of Pennsylvania.

Freud, S. (2000). *Three essays on the theory of sexuality*. New York, NY: Basic Books. (Original work published 1905).

Geertz, C. (1973). *Interpretation of cultures: Selected essays by Clifford Geertz*. New York, NY: Basic Books.

Gelder, K. (2007). *Subcultures: Cultural histories and social practice*. London, UK: Routledge.

Georgas, J., Van De Vijver, F. J., & Berry, J. W. (2004). The ecocultural framework, ecosocial indices, and psychological variables in cross-cultural research. *Journal of Cross-Cultural Psychology, 35*(1), 74–96.

Gillani, N. B., & Smith, J. C. (2001). Zen meditation and ABC relaxation theory: An exploration of relaxation states, beliefs, dispositions, and motivations. *Journal of Clinical Psychology, 57*(6), 839–846.

Gilmore, D. D. (1990). *Manhood in the making: Cultural concepts of masculinity*. New Haven, CT: Yale University Press.

Guthrie, G. (1977). A social-psychological analysis of modernization in the Philippines. *Journal of Cross-Cultural Psychology, 8*, 177–206.

Haidt, J., Koller, S. H., & Dias, M. G. (1993). Affect, culture, and morality, or is it wrong to eat your dog? *Journal of Personality and Social Psychology, 65*, 613–628.

Hall, E. T., & Hall, M. R. (1990). *Understanding cultural differences*. Yarmouth, ME: Intercultural Press.

Hamamura, T. (2012). Are cultures becoming individualistic? A cross-temporal comparison of individualism–collectivism in the United States and Japan. *Personality and Social Psychology Review, 16*(1), 3–24.

Hamamura, T., Xu, Q., & Du, Y. (2013). Social class and independence and interdependence among Chinese adolescents. *International Journal of Psychology, 48*(3), 344–351. https://doi.org/10.1080/00207594.2011.647030

Hancock, M. (2019). *Womanhood in the making: Domestic ritual and public culture in urban South India*. New York, UK: Routledge.

Hao, J., Li, D., Peng, L., Peng, S., & Torelli, C. J. (2016). Advancing our understanding of culture mixing. *Journal of Cross-Cultural Psychology, 47*(10), 1257–1267. https://doi.org/10.1177/0022022116670514

Harush, R., Lisak, A., & Erez, M. (2016). Extending the global acculturation model to untangle the culture mixing puzzle. *Journal of Cross-Cultural Psychology, 47*(10), 1395–1408. https://doi.org/10.1177/0022022116670261

Herdt, G. H. (1997). *Same sex, different cultures: Exploring gay and lesbian lives*. Boulder, CO: Westview Press.

Hodkinson, P. (2016). Youth cultures and the rest of life: Subcultures, post-subcultures and beyond. *Journal of Youth Studies, 19*(5), 629–645.

Hodkinson, P., & Deicke, W. (Eds.). (2007). *Youth cultures: Scenes, subcultures and tribes*. New York, NY: Routledge.

Hofstede, G. (1983). Dimensions of national cultures in fifty countries and three regions. In J. B. Deregowski, S. Dziurawiec, & R. C. Annis (Eds.), *Expiscations in cross-cultural psychology* (pp. 335–355). Lisse, NL: Swets & Zeitlinger.

Hofstede, G. (2016). *Country comparison tools*. Retrieved August 15, 2016, from http://geert-hofstede.com/tools.html

Hofstede, G., Garibaldi de Hilal, A. V., Malvezzi, S., Tanure, B., & Vinken, H. (2010). Comparing regional cultures within a country: Lessons from Brazil. *Journal of Cross-Cultural Psychology, 41*(3), 336–352.

Huismans, S., & Schwartz, S. H. (1992). Religiosity and value priorities: A study of Protestants, Catholics, and Jews. In S. Iwawaki, Y. Kashima, & K. Leung (Eds.), *Innovations in cross-cultural psychology: Selected papers from the tenth international conference of the International Association for Cross-cultural Psychology held at Nara, Japan* (pp. 237–249). Amsterdam, The Netherlands: Swets & Zeitlinger.

Inzlicht, M., & Tullett, A. M. (2010). Reflecting on God: Religious primes can reduce neurophysiological response to errors. *Psychological Science, 21*(8), 1184–1190.

Kameda, T., Takezawa, M., & Hastie, R. (2005). Where do social norms come from? The example of communal sharing. *Current Directions in Psychological Science, 14*, 331–334.

Kashima, Y., Kokubo, T., Kashima, E. S., Boxall, D., Yamaguchi, S., & Macrae, K. (2004). Culture and self: Are there within-culture differences in self between metropolitan areas and regional cities? *Personality and Social Psychology Bulletin, 30*, 816–823.

Kennedy, P. T., & Roudometof, V. (2002). *Communities across borders under globalising conditions: New immigrants and transnational cultures.* Abingdon, UK: Routledge.

Kim, E., Zeppenfeld, V., & Cohen, D. (2013). Sublimation, culture, and creativity. *Journal of Personality and Social Psychology, 105*, 639–666.

Kim-Prieto, C., & Diener, E. (2009). Religion as a source of variation in the experience of positive and negative emotions. *The Journal of Positive Psychology, 4*, 447–460.

Kitayama, S., Ishii, K., Imada, T., Takemura, K., & Ramaswamy, J. (2006). Voluntary settlement and the spirit of independence: Evidence from Japan's "Northern Frontier". *Journal of Personality and Social Psychology, 91*, 369–384.

Kitayama, S., Mesquita, B., & Karasawa, M. (2006). Cultural affordances and emotional experience: Socially engaging and disengaging emotions in Japan and the United States. *Journal of Personality and Social Psychology, 91*(5), 890–903.

Koenig, H. G. (2001). Religion and medicine II: Religion, mental health, and related behaviors. *The International Journal of Psychiatry in Medicine, 31*(1), 97–109.

Koenig, H. G., George, L. K., & Titus, P. (2004). Religion, spirituality, and health in medically ill hospitalized older patients. *Journal of the American Geriatrics Society, 52*, 554–562.

Koopmann-Holm, B. (2013). *The negative feelings that people want to avoid: Cultural differences and consequences for compassion.* Dissertation, Stanford University. http://purl.stanford.edu/qn512fn5267

Kraus, M., Piff, P., & Keltner, D. (2009). Social class, the sense of control, and social explanation. *Journal of Personality and Social Psychology, 97*, 992–1004.

Kroeber, A. L., & Kluckhohn, C. K. (1952). *Culture: A critical review of concepts and definitions.* Cambridge, MA: Harvard University Press.

Lehman, D. R., Chiu, C.-Y., & Schaller, M. (2004). Psychology and culture. *Annual Review of Psychology, 55*, 689–714.

Li, Y. J., Johnson, K. A., Cohen, A. B., Williams, M. J., Knowles, E. D., & Chen, Z. (2012). Fundamental(ist) attribution error: Protestants are dispositionally focused. *Journal of Personality and Social Psychology, 102*, 281–290.

Lugo, A. (1997). Reflections on border theory, culture, and the nation. In D. E. Johnson & S. Michaelson (Eds.), *Border theory* (pp. 43–67). Minneapolis, MN: University of Minnesota.

Lumsden, C. J. (1989). Does culture need genes? *Ethology and Sociobiology, 10*, 11–28.

Markus, H. R., & Conner, A. (2013). *Clash! Eight cultural conflicts that make us who we are.* New York, NY: Penguin.

Martin, L., & Shao, B. (2016). Early immersive culture mixing: The key to understanding cognitive and identity differences among multiculturals. *Journal of Cross-Cultural Psychology, 47*(10), 1409–1429.

Masters, K. S., & Hooker, S. A. (2013). Religion, spirituality, and health. In R. F. Paloutzian & C. L. Park (Eds.), *Handbook of the psychology of religion and spirituality* (pp. 519–539). New York, NY: Guilford Press.

Matsumoto, D. (1993). Ethnic differences in affect intensity, emotion judgments, display rule attitudes, and self-reported emotional expression in an American sample. *Motivation and Emotion, 17*(2), 107–123.

Matsumoto, D. (2006a). Culture and nonverbal behavior. In V. Manusov & M. L. Patterson (Eds.), *The SAGE handbook of nonverbal communication* (pp. 219–235). Newbury Park, CA: Sage.

Matsumoto, D., & Hwang, H. S. (2012). Culture and emotion: The integration of biological and cultural contributions. *Journal of Cross-Cultural Psychology, 43*(1), 91–118.

McCraty, R., Barrios-Choplin, B., Rozman, D., Atkinson, M., & Watkins, A. D. (1998). The impact of a new emotional self-management program on stress, emotions, heart rate variability, DHEA and cortisol. *Integrative Physiological and Behavioral Science, 33*(2), 151–170.

McCullough, M. E., Emmons, R. A., & Tsang, J. A. (2002). The grateful disposition: A conceptual and empirical topography. *Journal of Personality and Social Psychology, 82*(1), 112–127.

McCutcheon, R. T. (1995). The category "religion" in recent publications: A critical survey. *Numen, 42*, 284–309.

Miller, P., & Sperry, L. L. (1987). The socialization of anger and aggression. *Merrill-Palmer Quarterly, 33*(1), 1–31.

Minkov, M., & Hofstede, G. (2012b). Is national culture a meaningful concept? Cultural values delineate homogeneous national clusters of in-country regions. *Cross-Cultural Research, 46*(2), 133–159.

Morales, E. (2003). *Living in Spanglish: The search for Latino identity in America.* New York, NY: Macmillan.

Morris, M. W., Chiu, C.-Y., & Liu, Z. (2015). Polycultural psychology. *Annual Review of Psychology, 66*, 631–659. https://doi.org/10.1146/annurev-psych-010814-015001

Nilan, P., & Feixa, C. (Eds.). (2006). *Global youth?: Hybrid identities, plural worlds.* London, UK: Routledge.

Nisbett, R. E., Peng, K., Choi, I., & Norenzayan, A. (2001). Culture and systems of thought: Holistic versus analytic cognition. *Psychological Review, 108*, 291–310.

Norris, P., & Inglehart, R. (2004). *Sacred and secular: Religion and politics worldwide.* New York, NY: Cambridge University Press.

Oyserman, D., Coon, H. M., & Kemmelmeier, M. (2002). Rethinking individualism and collectivism: Evaluation of theoretical assumptions and meta-analyses. *Psychological Bulletin, 128*(1), 3–72.

Pargament, K. I., Magyar-Russell, G. M., & Be Murray-Swank, N. A. (2005). The sacred and the search for significance: Religion as a unique process. *Journal of Social Issues, 61*, 665–687.

Park, C. L., & Slattery, J. (2013). Religiousness/spirituality and mental health. In R. F. Paloutzian & C. L. Park (Eds.), *Handbook of the psychology of religion and spirituality* (2nd ed., pp. 540–559). New York, NY: Guilford Press.

Patock-Peckham, J. A., Hutchinson, G. T., Cheong, J., & Nagoshi, C. T. (1998). Effect of religion and religiosity on alcohol use in a college student sample. *Drug and alcohol dependence, 49*(2), 81–88.

Phinney, J., & Alipuria, L. (2006). Multiple social categorisation and identity among multiracial, multi-ethnic and multicultural individuals: Processes and implications. In R. Crisp & M. Hewstone (Eds.), *Multiple Social categorisation: Processes, models and applications* (pp. 211–238). New York, NY: Psychology Press.

Poortinga, Y. (2015). Is "culture" a workable concept for (cross-)cultural psychology? *Online Readings in Psychology and Culture, 2*(1), 1–21. https://doi.org/10.9707/2307-0919.1139

Putnam, R. (2000). *Bowling alone: The collapse and revival of American community.* New York, NY: Simon & Schuster.

Ramet, S. P. (Ed.). (2002). *Gender reversals and gender cultures: Anthropological and historical perspectives.* Routledge.

Rapoport, T., & El-Or, T. (1997). Cultures of womanhood in Israel: Social agencies and gender production. *Women's Studies International Forum, 20*, 573–80.

Roberts, M. L. (2002). True womanhood revisited. *Journal of Women's History, 14*(1), 150–155.

Rokeach, M. (1973). *The nature of human values.* New York, NY: Free Press.

Saenz, B. A. (1997). In the borderland of chicano identity, there are only fragments. In D. E. Johnson & S. Michaelson (Eds.), *Border theory* (pp. 68–96). Minneapolis, MN: University of Minnesota.

Samuels, P. A., & Lester, D. (1985). A preliminary investigation of emotions experienced toward God by Catholic nuns and priests. *Psychological Reports, 56*, 706.

Saroglou, V. (2010). Religiousness as a cultural adaptation of basic traits: A five factor model perspective. *Personality and Social Psychology Review, 14*, 108–125.

Saroglou, V. (2011). Believing, bonding, behaving, and belonging: The big four religious dimensions and cultural variation. *Journal of Cross-Cultural Psychology, 42*, 1320–1340.

Saroglou, V., & Cohen, A. B. (2013). Cultural and cross-cultural psychology of religion. In R. F. Paloutzian & C. L. Park (Eds.), *Handbook of the psychology of religion and spirituality* (2nd ed., pp. 330–354). New York, NY: Guilford Press.

Saroglou, V., Delpierre, V., & Dernelle, R. (2004). Values and religiosity: A meta-analysis of studies using Schwartz's model. *Personality and Individual Differences, 37*(4), 721–734.

Schimmel, S. (1997). *The seven deadly sins: Jewish, Christian, and classical reflections on human psychology*. New York, NY: Oxford University Press.

Schwartz, S. (2006). A theory of cultural value orientations: Explication and applications. *Comparative Sociology, 5*(2–3), 137–182.

Schwartz, S., & H., & Huismans, S. (1995). Value priorities and religiosity in four Western religions. *Social Psychology Quaterly, 58*, 88–107.

Schwartz, S. H. (2014). National culture as value orientations: Consequences of value differences and cultural distance. In *Handbook of the economics of art and culture* (Vol. 2, pp. 547–586). Amsterdam, The Netherlands: Elsevier.

Schwartz, S. H., & Ros, M. (1995). Values in the west: A theoretical and empirical challenge to the individualism-collectivism cultural dimension. *World Psychology, 1*, 99–122.

Shweder, R. A. (2003). *Why do men barbecue?: Recipes for cultural psychology*. Cambridge, MA: Harvard University Press.

Shweder, R. A., & Haidt, J. (2000). The cultural psychology of the emotions: Ancient and new. In M. Lewis & J. M. Haviland-Jones (Eds.), *Handbook of emotions* (2nd ed., pp. 397–414). New York, NY: Guilford Press.

Silberman, I. (2005). Religion as a meaning system: Implications for the new millennium. *Journal of Social Issues, 61*(4), 641–663.

Smith, H. (1991). *The world's religions: Our great wisdom traditions*. New York, NY: HarperCollins.

Smith, P., & Bond, M. H. (1999). *Social psychology across cultures* (2nd ed.). Needham Heights, MA: Allyn & Bacon.

Snibbe, A. C., & Markus, H. R. (2002). The psychology of religion and the religion of psychology. *Psychological Inquiry, 13*, 229–234.

Snibbe, A. C., & Markus, H. R. (2005). You can't always get what you want: Educational attainment, agency, and choice. *Journal of Personality and Social Psychology, 88*, 703–720.

Stephens, N., Markus, H., & Townsend, S. (2007). Choice as an act of meaning: The case of social class. *Journal of Personality and Social Psychology, 93*, 814–830.

Tarakeshwar, N., Stanton, J., & Pargament, K. I. (2003). Religion: An overlooked dimension in cross-cultural psychology. *Journal of Cross-Cultural Psychology, 34*(4), 377–394.

Traunmiiller, R. (2011). Moral communities?: Religion as a source of social trust in a multilevel analysis of 97 German regions. *European Sociological Review, 27*, 346–363.

Triandis, H. (1995). *Individualism and collectivism*. San Francisco, CA: Westview Press.

Triandis, H. C. (2007). Culture and psychology: A history of the study of their relationships. In S. Kitayama & D. Cohen (Eds.), *Handbook of cultural psychology* (pp. 59–76). New York, NY: Guilford Press.

Tsai, J. L. (2007). Ideal affect: Cultural causes and behavioral consequences. *Perspectives on Psychological Science, 2*(3), 242–259.

Tsai, J. L., Chentsova-Dutton, Y., Freire-Bebeau, L., & Przymus, D. E. (2002). Emotional expression and physiology in European Americans and Hmong Americans. *Emotion, 2*(4), 380–397.

Tsai, J. L., & Clobert, M. (2019). Cultural influences on emotion: Empirical patterns and emerging trends. In S. Kitayama & D. Cohen (Eds.), *Handbook of cultural psychology* (2nd ed., pp. 292–318). New York, NY: Guilford Press.

Tsai, J. L., Knutson, B., & Fung, H. H. (2006). Cultural variation in affect valuation. *Journal of Personality and Social Psychology, 90*(2), 288–307.

Tsai, J. L., Koopmann-Holm, B., Miyazaki, M., & Ochs, C. (2013). The religious shaping of feeling: Implications of affect valuation theory. In R. F. Paloutzian & C. L. Park (Eds.), *Handbook of the psychology of religion and spirituality* (2nd ed., pp. 274–291). New York, NY: Guilford Press.

Tsai, J. L., & Levenson, R. W. (1997). Cultural influences on emotional responding: Chinese American and European American dating couples during interpersonal conflict. *Journal of Cross-Cultural Psychology, 28*(5), 600–625.

Tsai, J. L., Miao, F., & Seppala, E. (2007). Good feelings in Christianity and Buddhism: Religious differences in ideal affect. *Personality and Social Psychology Bulletin, 33*, 409–421.

Underwood, J. O. (1985). Western women and true womanhood: Culture and symbol in history and literature. *Great Plains Quarterly, 5*, 93–106.

Van de Vijver, F. J. R., Blommaert, J. M. E., Gkoumasi, G., & Stogianni, M. (2015). On the need to broaden the concept of ethnic identity. *International Journal of Intercultural Relations, 46*, 36–46. https://doi.org/10.1016/j.ijintrel.2015.03.021

Van Hemert, D. A., Poortinga, Y. H., & van de Vijver, F. J. (2007). Emotion and culture: A meta-analysis. *Cognition and Emotion, 21*(5), 913–943.

Vandello, J. A., Bosson, J. K., Cohen, D., Burnaford, R. M., & Weaver, J. R. (2008). Precarious manhood. *Journal of Personality and Social Psychology, 95*(6), 1325–1339. https://doi.org/10.1037/a0012453

Vandello, J. A., & Cohen, D. (1999). Patterns of individualism and collectivism across the United States. *Journal of Personality and Social Psychology, 77*, 279–292.

Vandello, J. A., Cohen, D., & Ransom, S. (2008). U.S. Southern and Northern differences in perceptions of norms about aggression: Mechanisms for the perpetuation of a culture of honor. *Journal of Cross Cultural Psychology, 39*, 162–177. https://doi.org/10.1177/0022022107313862

Veenhoven, R. (1994). Is happiness a trait? Tests of the theory that a better society does not make people any happier. *Social Indicators Research, 32*, 101–160.

Wallbott, H. G., & Scherer, K. R. (1988). How universal and specific is emotional experience?: Evidence from 27 countries on five continents. In K. R. Scherer (Ed.), *Facets of emotion: Recent research* (pp. 31–56). Hillsdale, NJ: Lawrence Erlbaum Associates.

Watts, F. N. (1996). Psychological and religious perspectives on emotion. *The International Journal for the Psychology of Religion, 6*(2), 71–87.

Wikan, U. (1988). Bereavement and loss in two Muslim communities: Egypt and Bali compared. *Social Science and Medicine, 27*, 451–460.

Zahn-Waxler, C., Cole, P. M., & Barrett, K. C. (1991). Guilt and empathy: Sex differences and implications for the development of depression. In J. Garber & K. A. Dodge (Eds.), *The development of emotion regulation and dysregulation* (pp. 243–272). New York, NY: Cambridge University Press.

Chapter 2
Cultural Parameters and Their Influence on Emotions

2.1 Collectivism and Individualism as Cultural Parameters

2.1.1 The Constructs of Collectivism and Individualism

Multiple Dimensions of Culture

Throughout decades of cross-cultural research scholars in sociology, psychology, and anthropology proposed many cultural dimensions, in which countries, nations can differ. Some researchers (Lytle, Brett, Barsness, Tinsley, & Janssens, 1995) identified 75 cross-cultural dimensions. Among the most prominent are individualism-collectivism, power distance, masculinity-femininity, egalitarianism-hierarchy, motivational values, honor, activity-reactivity, contact-noncontact, uncertainty avoidance, and modernization. Let us consider some of those, which researchers extensively used in their studies throughout recent decades, especially in relations to their influence on cultural experience and expression of emotion. I have included some of these cultural dimensions as the good candidates for the construction of cultural models of emotions. The studies presented in this and following chapters provide sufficient evidence in support of this proposal.

The Cultural Characteristic of Collectivism Versus Individualism

Individualism-collectivism was the cultural construct that theorists across disciplines identified and elaborated in early cross-cultural research (e.g., Hofstede, 1980/1984; Marsella et al., 1985; Triandis, 1995). The relations between an individual and a group define the cultural variable of *collectivism* and *individualism*, which is currently prevalent across various social and psychological domains. *Collectivism* and *individualism* as the societal characteristics describe the degree to which people in a society are integrated into groups. Societies are characterized as

V. Karandashev, *Cultural Models of Emotions*,
https://doi.org/10.1007/978-3-030-58438-2_2

individualistic or *collectivistic* when these value orientations characterize the majority of individual members (Hui & Triandis, 1986), even though within a given society, individual differences in the prevailing cultural orientation exist. People in a particular culture may be more or less collectivistic and individualistic in the different areas of relationships: with their parents, kin, neighbors, co-workers, or friends.

2.1.2   Values and Emotions in Collectivistic Cultures

Values in Collectivistic Cultures

In *collectivist cultures* people are integrated into strong, cohesive in-groups, and extended families. A paramount value is the individual's loyalty to a group, which in turn protects the interests and well-being of an individual, and opposes other groups. The group encourages certain social actions in order to facilitate mutual support and shared experiences. Personal privacy is abridged, a sense of personal identity is based on one's place in one's group, and people are emotionally dependent on a group. In personal motivation, people subordinate individual goals to the goals of a collective; group goals have precedence over individual goals. Collectivistic cultures emphasize in-group beliefs rather than individual ones; value in-group views over individual ones, collective norms of the in-group, rather than individual pleasure.

People in collectivistic cultures (highly embedded in their relationship) tend to distinguish more strongly their behavior toward those individuals from their in-group versus out-group compared to people in individualist cultures (highly autonomous) (Smith & Bond, 1999).

Collectivistic values emphasize interpersonal bonds, group harmony and solidarity, consciousness and greater awareness of and responsiveness to the needs of others, obligation, emotional interdependence, and a sense of interconnectedness (Hofstede, 1980/1984; 2011; Hui & Triandis, 1986; Gelfand, et al., 2000; Kashima, et al., 1995; Triandis, 1995). A sense of obligation, duty toward the group, as well as in-group harmony and working in groups are the core facets of collectivist beliefs (Oyserman, Coon, & Kemmelmeier, 2002).

Triandis and his colleagues (Triandis, 1995; Triandis, Bontempo, Villareal, Asai, & Lucca, 1988) identified the relations with family (unity, loyalty, and integrity) as the collectivistic values. Friendships are predetermined by stable relationships formed early in life. People in collectivistic cultures apply different standards for members of their in-groups and out-groups (Hofstede, 1980/1984): they are collectivistic in relations with their in-group members (family, friends, etc.), yet they can be individualistic in relations with out-group members (strangers and people from other cultural groups).

Relational values in collectivistic cultures encourage cooperation within a group and harmony of interpersonal relationships more than the assertion of an individual

(Noon & Lewis, 1992). Therefore, cultural beliefs view emotions as interactive rather than individual experiences, reflecting the people's social context rather than their internal self. Emotions are deemed as situational cues about relationships between people.

Collectivism and Emotional Experience

People in collectivistic cultures admit that positive and negative emotions can co-occur at the same time and feel pretty comfortable with a dialectical mixture of both emotions (Aaker, Drolet, & Griffin, 2008; Hong & Lee, 2010; Kim et al., 2014; Williams & Aaker, 2002).

The beliefs of collectivistic cultures suggest people in those societies to moderate their experience and expression of emotions. Their desired norms are to experience both positive and negative emotions remaining untroubled, calm, and peaceful. They prefer low frequency, duration, and intensity of emotions (Bond, 1993; Tamir et al., 2016; Tsai, Knutson, & Fung, 2006; Tsai, Miao, Seppala, Fung, & Yeung, 2007).

As for real experience, people in *collectivistic cultures* tend to feel their emotions with relatively low intensely (Basabe et al., 2000; Markus & Kitayama, 1991; Scherer, Matsumoto, Wallbott & Kudoh, 1988; Matsumoto, 1991).

According to several studies (Kitayama et al., 2000; Kitayama et al., 2006; Uchida & Kitayama, 2009), people in *collectivistic cultures* experience in their life *socially engaging emotions* (such as respect, friendliness, and sympathy) more frequently than *socially disengaging emotions* (such as self-esteem, pride, and frustration).

Collectivism and Emotional Control

For people in collectivistic cultures, *external interactional aspects of their emotions*—thinking of how their actions and emotion affect others—are very important. Therefore, cultural norms of collectivistic cultures consider *control of emotion* as high priority. People typically display lower levels of general emotional expression (Potter, 1988; van Hemert et al., 2007). Collectivistic cultures do not accept public expression of "negative" emotions as appropriate since it can decrease the group harmony. Collectivism dimension is likely associated with cultural endorsement of such emotional regulation strategy as suppression.

The typical examples of collectivistic societies are some Asian countries, such as Singapore, Taiwan, Hong Kong, Pakistan, and Latin American countries, such as Colombia, Venezuela, Chile, and Peru. People from Arab and African countries and from Eastern Europe also endorse collectivist beliefs, yet to a lesser degree (Basabe & Ros, 2005).

2.1.3   Values and Emotions in Individualistic Cultures

Typical Values in Individualistic Cultures

Individualistic cultures emphasize the individual's goals, while collectivistic cultures stress that group goals have precedence over individual goals. In individualistic cultures, "people are supposed to look after themselves and their immediate family only," while in collectivistic cultures, "people belong to in-groups or collectivities which are supposed to look after them in exchange for loyalty" (Hofstede & Bond, 1984, p. 419).

Individualistic cultures emphasize the individual's goals, personal autonomy, personal independence, a primacy of personality uniqueness, personal goals and actions, self-realization and individual initiative, the individual's rights rather than duties, one's self-interest and that of one's immediate family, high value of one's independence, and less concern for other persons' needs and interests. Personal identity is defined by the individual's attributes. In personal motivation, people subordinate the goals of the collectivities to individual goals. The ties between individuals are loose. The typical examples of individualistic societies are Australia, New Zealand, the United States, Canada, Great Britain, the Netherlands, Italy, Belgium, and Denmark, mostly Western countries (Hofstede, 1984; 2011; Hui & Triandis, 1986; Gelfand, et al., 2000; Kashima, et al., 1995; Triandis, 1995).

Triandis and his colleagues (Triandis, 1995; Triandis, Bontempo, Villareal, Asai, & Lucca, 1988) identified personal freedom, personal autonomy, personal initiative, and self-reliance as the values related with individualism in a culture, while family unity, family loyalty, and family integrity as the values related with collectivism. People in individualistic cultures establish personal and specific friendships. They are universalistic and tend to apply the same standards to all.

People in individualistic cultures, with high value of autonomy, frequently exhibit the similar behavior directed to others from their in-groups and out-groups, while people in collectivistic cultures, with high value of embeddedness tend to differentiate more their behavior toward others from their in-group versus out-group (Smith & Bond, 1999).

Individualism and Emotional Experience

Individualism as a cultural dimension is associated with frequency of experience of certain emotions and the relative pleasantness/unpleasantness of emotions that people experience in their life. Research suggests that in the countries high in *individualism dimension,* people experience the *lower level of negative emotions* and the *high level of positive emotions* (Basabe et al., 2002).

An interesting fact concerning differences in the experience of emotions in *individualistic* and *collectivistic* cultures came from another study (Chentsova-Dutton & Tsai, 2010). Their results revealed that attention of European American participants to the *individual aspects of the self* had amplified their emotional experience, whereas attention of Asian Americans to the *relational aspects of the self* had amplified their emotional experience.

According to a series of studies (Kitayama et al., 2000; Kitayama et al., 2006; Uchida & Kitayama, 2009), people in *individualistic cultures* experience in their life more *socially disengaging emotions* (e.g., self-esteem, pride, and frustration) than *socially engaging emotions* (respect, friendliness, and sympathy).

Individualism and Happiness

How can *individualism* as a cultural dimension affect emotional life of people in different cultural contexts? A comprehensive study of 21 thousands of adult respondents (*M* age = 30.2 year) across 48 countries in three time periods of 1980–2000s (Steel, Taras, Uggerslev, & Bosco, 2018) explored the relations between subjective well-being and individualism. Authors anticipated that culture can predict satisfaction with life and relationships above wealth.

The results *at the individual* level showed that individualism was negatively correlated with all aspects of subjective well-being. Even after controlling for wealth, individualism negatively predicted life and family satisfaction. The values associated with individualism and autonomy does not seem beneficial in terms of well-being at the individual level. Authors explain this result by positive association of individualism with introversion (found in other study, Migliore, 2011), which in turn, as a personality trait, negatively correlates with subjective well-being (Steel et al., 2008).

Contrary to this finding, at the national level, happy nations are typically high in *individualism*. At the national level, high *individualism* positively correlates with high subjective well-being. Although the effect of *individualism-collectivism* on subjective well-being is related to political and economic circumstances in a country, yet it is still partially independent from those parameters.

Individualism and Expression of Emotions

Individualism dimension is likely associated with cultural endorsement of such emotional regulation strategy as expression. Highly individualistic cultures display greater levels of general emotional expression (van Hemert et al., 2007). Since individualistic cultures appreciate and promote separateness, autonomy, and uniqueness of individuals (Markus & Kitayama, 1991), then people in these cultures believe that they have a right to express their emotions as important personal experiences. Individualistic cultures (such as American) encourage external displays of emotions, as expressions of individuality, exaggerating the strength of the emotional experience (Matsumoto, Takeuchi, Andayani, Kouznetsova, & Krupp, 1998).

2.1.4   Multifaceted Nature and Diversity of Individualism-Collectivism

Dynamic Nature of Individualism and Collectivism

The picture in real cultural comparisons, however, is more multifaceted than the simple dualistic distinction *collectivistic* versus *individualistic*. Here are the examples from several societies showing that cultures are not static in this regard, but rather in constant flux across time and across individuals within cultures (Hamamura, 2012; Matsumoto, Kudoh, & Takeuchi, 1996; Putnam, 2000).

In the United States and Japan, it was demonstrated in a series of studies (Matsumoto, Kudoh, & Takeuchi, 1996) exploring the diversity of *collectivism* and *individualism* and their transformation during recent decades. The authors analyzed social changes in the United States and Japan and challenge the stereotypic notions of individualism-collectivism in those cultures. Empirical data examining within-individual and within-culture variability on *individualism-collectivism* highlighted the dynamic nature of culture in both countries.

China also undergoes rapid cultural transformations over recent decades, many of which are driven by younger generation, the China's millennial youth. The most prominent cultural change is the development of a new kind of individualism. This new cohort is known as the *ku* generation. This slang word is the Chinese version of the American term *cool* and it is pervasively used as a symbol of the youth rebellion striving to transform the older generation's cultural values (Moore, 2005). Individualism and self-indulgence are two major values associated with the term *ku*. In the past, these values were not endorsed among the people in mainstream Chinese society. The Millennial Chinese describe these new individualistic tendencies in terms of freedom, with the strong focus on freedom as a measure of the individualism that they appreciate. The self-indulgence does not have the same negative implication for the young educated urbanites, as in earlier Chinese generations.

Individualism and Collectivism in the Process of Acculturation

Chinese people moving and residing in the United States experience other cultural transitions. They are affected by double cultural influence: of the *collectivistic culture*, where they were raised, and of the *individualistic culture*, via exposure to the new values and behaviors in America (Tsai, et al., 2000). Through acculturation, they gradually adopt the dominant cultural values and behaviors (Feldman, et al., 1992). These Chinese residents are at a cultural crossroad: they may be more individualistic than Chinese native spouses, but less individualistic than North American spouses. The results of Fitzpatrick et al. (2006) revealed the multilayered patterns in distinction between individualistic and collectivistic cultures. They discovered more complex results: participants from three groups—Chinese native, Chinese residents, and North American—had some unexpected similarities and differences.

In particular, their results revealed that North American husbands were less individualistic than Chinese (resident or native) husbands. But, no group differences appeared between North American and Chinese wives. Chinese native wives were less collectivistic than North American or Chinese resident wives, and so on. These results are probably due to a confluence of cultures (Fitzpatrick, et al., 2006). The cultures mix and merge in various ways. Chinese spouses may acquire more individualistic values as they are exposed to Western lifestyles. When North Americans are exposed to Eastern values and cultures, they may become more collectivistic. Chinese traditional values and modern Western equity in the marriages of urban Chinese couples co-exist (Pimental, 2000). Many correlational findings of Fitzpatrick et al. (2006) are in agreement with this conception, for example, collectivism was found positively related to individualism in majority groups. Thus, we see that these cultural orientations are not the oppositional constructs. They appear in diverse and intertwined ways. As Tsai et al. noted (2000), Chinese immigrants living in the United States may express and follow varied cultural orientations in different contexts: Chinese values—more commonly in home and other private settings, while American values—in school, work, and other public settings.

2.1.5   Variation of Individualism and Collectivism

Diversity of Individualistic and Collectivistic Beliefs

In 1980–1990s many authors considered collectivism and individualism as the polar and opposite dimensions of cultures or societies (Chan, 1994; Hofstede, 1984, 2001; Hui & Triandis, 1986; Kitayama, Markus, Matsumoto, & Norasakkunkit, 1997) and usually contrasted Western (European and American) versus Eastern (East Asian) countries.

However, the constructs of *individualism* and *collectivism* engage more cultural complexities. The recent studies demonstrated the multilayer and amalgamate picture (e.g., see for review Oyserman, Coon, & Kemmelmeier, 2002). On the scale of *individualism,* Europeans and Latin Americans are similar to North Americans, while higher than Japanese, and substantially higher than people on the Indian subcontinent and Africa. The biggest difference on this dimension is between the United States and China, Taiwan, Hong Kong (as Confucianist countries), whereas no difference from Australia, Germany, and Canada. Killen and Wainryb (2000) have demonstrated the complexity of *individualism* and *collectivism* using examples from the empirical research conducted in Japan, the Middle East, and Colombia.

It was found that variations of individualist beliefs between nations are smaller and less distinctive than differentiation in collectivist beliefs (Basabe & Ros, 2005). The parallel presence of collectivism and individualism becomes more evident in many countries, with an entangled amalgamation of cultural values. Here are some examples.

In Thailand—a highly collectivist country —the study of dual resident marriages (Schvaneveldt et al., 2001) discovered the occurrence of "non-assertive individualism," which lacks the directness of traditional individualism, yet this reflects in-group values tied to collectivism.

In the United States—a highly individualist country—European Americans are indeed more individualistic since they value personal independence and less collectivistic because they feel less duty to *in-groups*. However, the results of studies (Oyserman, Coon, & Kemmelmeier, 2002) demonstrated that European Americans are not more individualistic than Latinos, or African Americans, and not less collectivistic than Koreans or Japanese. Asians are also not homogeneous in their cultural characteristics. Among those, only Chinese revealed distinctive differences, being both less individualistic and more collectivistic.

Oyserman, Coon, and Kemmelmeier (2002) found that in *individualistic beliefs* Latin Americans, Europeans, and North Americans had the similar high scores, while the people of Africa, India, and Japan had the lower scores on this dimension. On the other side, people in China, Taiwan, and Hong Kong—the Confucianism countries—had substantially lower scores of individualism than people in the United States. People in Australia and Germany had no different scores in individualism compared to people in Canada and the United States (Oyserman, Coon & Kemmelmeier, 2002). In *collectivistic beliefs,* Chinese were higher in these scores compared with people of English-speaking countries. People from Eastern Europe, Arab countries, and Africa, and Latin Americans were high in collectivist beliefs. The greatest differences were between North Americans and people of Asian and African countries.

Although the nations substantially differ in their degree of individualism and collectivism, these constructs and corresponding dimensions should not be conceptualized as unitary, but rather as multidimensional concepts (Basabe & Ros, 2005; Neto, 2007; Oyserman, Coon, & Kemmelmeier, 2002). Cultures can share some similarities along some facets of collectivism, yet still vary in other aspects of collectivism (Brewer & Chen, 2007; Fiske, 2002). For instance, we can say that Hindu Indians, Chinese, Japanese, Koreans, and Mexicans share collectivism as a cultural dimension. Nevertheless, these national cultures are different and specific in many regards.

Overall, the results of several studies (e.g., Stephan, Stephan, Saito, & Barnett, 1998) suggest that *individualism-collectivism* is not a single and specific dimension of nonmonolithic nature. It is rather a broad set of several cultural dimensions.

Diversity of Individualism and Collectivism Within a Country

The facets of collectivism and individualism dimensions vary also within nation across social classes, religions, regions of countries, and may across other cultural groups. For example, it might be inadequate to treat North American culture as exclusively individualistic. The regions of the US culture differs in their individualism and collectivism (Vandello & Cohen, 1999) in such state-level variables of these constructs as the percentage of people living alone (as an indicator of individualism), the percentage of households with grandparents in them, and the percentage of people with religious affiliations (as an indicators of collectivism). On these parameters, the *individualism* is highest in the Mountain West and Great Plains and *collectivism* is highest in the Deep South and Hawaii. The latter state is especially collectivist, probably due to the high proportion of people of Asian descent living there. The researchers found (Vandello & Cohen, 1999) that in terms of economic system, plantation farming correlate with collectivism, while self-run farms—with individualism. Ethnic minorities were usually more collectivistic than individualistic.

Donohue (1990) highlighted complexity of these two cultural dimensions and asserted that individualism and collectivism can co-exist: American freedom assimilates both individual rights and collectivistic community involvement, that it is NOT exclusively related to general cultural individualism.

Idiocentrism and Allocentrism as Individual Dimensions of Individualism and Collectivism

While *individualism* or *collectivism* is the dimension of culture at the country level, *idiocentrism* or *allocentrism* is the dimensions of personality at the individual level. *Idiocentrism* is an individualistic personality trait and *allocentrism* is a collectivistic personality trait. *Idiocentric* and *allocentric* individuals are present in both *individualistic* and *collectivistic* societies. Nonetheless, *individualistic cultures* typically have more *idiocentric individuals*, whereas *collectivistic cultures* have usually more *allocentric individuals* (Eid & Diener, 2001; Lay et al., 1998; Matsumoto, & Kupperbusch, 2001; Triandis et al., 1995).

Other theories and research (see for review Basabe & Ros, 2005) suggested other dimensions of cultural values. For example, Schwartz (1994) and his colleagues proposed to distinguish different types of collectivism. Cultures of *egalitarian commitment* encourage individuals to voluntary cooperate with others and care for their welfare. The cultures emphasizing *conservation* tend to promote the maintenance of the status quo. The cultures stressing *hierarchy* promote differences in power and hierarchical systems of roles.

Competitive Individualism and Egalitarian Individualism

Another variable within individualism as a cultural value, which can explain cultural model of experience of emotions, is competitive individualism versus egalitarian individualism. Competitive individualism (typical for North Americans) accentuates the importance of having high self-esteem, standing out among others, and achieving personal success. Egalitarian individualism (typical for Belgians), on the other side, highlights the integrity of individuals within their social network of equal rights (Schwartz & Ros, 1995).

A study comparing Americans and Belgians (Boiger, De Deyne, & Mesquita, 2013) hypothesized that anger is more beneficial in the culture of American individualism (more competitive), whereas shame is more beneficial to the culture of Belgian individualism (more egalitarian). Anger is a socially disengaged emotion, and emphasizing personal desires over others'; it contradicts egalitarian individualism. The communication effect of shame is different; it signals a person's attempt to repair damaged social relationships. It is more consistent with the egalitarian values emphasizing the maintenance of egalitarian relationships and conformity. The results of the study, which employed experience sampling over a period of seven days, showed that Americans experienced anger more and shame less than Belgians.

The cultures of interdependent contexts are also heterogeneous, even though the similar emotional patterns have been found across those cultural contexts. For example, the similarity of engaging versus disengaging emotions was revealed in the samples of Japanese and Mexicans compared to Americans (Savani, Alvarez, Mesquita, & Markus, 2013).

Nevertheless, the value of affective states is still different in other interdependent cultural contexts. The studies showed that Mexicans have a substantially more preference for high arousal positive versus low arousal positive states. Chinese, on the other side, have revealed a preference for low arousal positive over high arousal positive states. The Mexican pattern of ideal affect resembled that of European Canadians (Ruby, Falk, Heine, Villa, & Silberstein, 2012). These results confirmed that not all collectivistic cultures have the same ideal affect.

2.1.6   The Independent Versus Interdependent Models of Culture

Independent and Interdependent Self-Construals

People across cultures differ in the conceptions of personhood, in their *construals of the self*, *of others*, and *how self and others are related*, being independent and interdependent. Throughout recent decades, scholars have largely focused on Eastern–Western cultural comparison because these two cultural regions are probably most distinctive and contrasting in many regards. Since the samples in analysis and research are predominantly North American (specifically of European American descent), on one side, and Japanese and Chinese, on another side, it is more adequate to call these two broad regions of the world as *European–American culture* and *East Asian culture*. Despite their within-regional variations in each of these world regions and their diversity, people in the countries within each of the two regions share many cultural ideas, practices, and social institutions.

The difference in *independent model of self* (prevalent in *individualistic* cultures) and *interdependent model of self* (prevalent in *collectivistic* cultures) was proposed as an explanatory framework for exploring the cultural differences of emotions in *independent model* and *interdependent models of culture* (Markus & Kitayama,

1991; Mesquita & Leu, 2007; Tsai & Clobert, 2019). Being associated with *individualism* versus *collectivism* dimension of culture, this approach focuses on *independent* and *interdependent models of self*, respectively, in attempts to explain cultural patterns of emotions (Kitayama, & Markus, 2000; Markus & Kitayama, 1991; Tsai & Clobert, 2019). Markus & Kitayama (1991) suggested using these different models of self to describe and explain cultural patterns of emotional experience. Tsai and Clobert (2019) have provided a quite comprehensive review of the emotional experience in these two types of cultures.

East Asian interdependent cultures

The conceptions of individuality in many East Asian cultures imply that individuals in community are basically related to each other. Cultural norms emphasize the importance of connectedness among individuals and their harmonious interdependence, including interdependence of a personal self with others. This *self-in-relationship-with-others* idea embraces people's motivation, emotions, thought, and actions. The psychological boundaries between the *personal self* and the *selves of others* are invisible and fuzzy. Even though the *personal self* is important, yet this self includes the *selves of others* involved and various connections with those.

An individual with *interdependent models of self* is aware of him/herself as being related to others, as having his/her duties and affiliations with others, with priorities of others' needs (over his/her own), being encouraged to adjust to others (i.e., change personal desires, preferences, and beliefs to be consistent with environments). Personal self develops through immersion in close relationships and identification with significant others (or rebellion against them). *Standing in* and *adjusting to* relationships are more important for Japanese than standing-out and influencing others (Morling, Kitayama, & Miyamoto, 2002; Tsai & Clobert, 2019; Weisz, Rothbaum, & Blackburn, 1984).

Conceptions of the interdependent nature of humans are widespread in East Asian cultures (e.g., Markus & Kitayama, 1991; Uchida, Norasakkunkit, & Kitayama, 2004). Individuals in those cultures feel strongly motivated to fit and adjust themselves to relevant social and interpersonal relations. They are committed to their social roles, social obligations, and ready to respond to social expectations (Morling, Kitayama, & Miyamoto, 2002; Weisz, Rothbaum, & Blackburn, 1984).

European American Independent Cultures

According to European American conception of individuality, individuals in a society should keep their autonomy and independence from others by realizing and expressing their unique self. An individual with *independent models of self* is aware of him/herself as *separate from others*, as having own personal desires, preferences, and beliefs, with priorities of personal needs (over those of others), being encouraged to *influence others* (i.e., change the environments to be consistent with personal desires, preferences, and beliefs).

These cultures—with *independent models of self*—appreciate an individual's distinctiveness, autonomy, and personal achievement. Therefore, their prevalent cultural values emphasize *personal self* and *individual distinctiveness*.

The *individual self* in this conception is the center of people's motivation, emotions, thought, and actions. Although individuals value their social relations, yet the relationships and interactions assume the independence of their selves. This means that they have a choice to enter and exit the relationships. Standing out and influencing others are more important in European American culture than standing in and adjusting to relationships (Morling, Kitayama, & Miyamoto, 2002; Weisz, Rothbaum, & Blackburn, 1984).

Independent Model of Self and Emotional Experience

Individual emotional experiences in *independent cultural contexts* tend to be more self-focused. European Americans experience and express more intense emotions when they think of themselves (vs. family members) (Chentsova-Dutton & Tsai, 2010; Uchida, Townsend, Markus, & Bergsieker, 2009). People in independent cultures (i.e., United Kingdom, United States, and Germany) generally experience the socially engaging feelings of being connected with others, friendly, guilty, ashamed, less frequently and intensely, while socially disengaging emotions, such as feeling proud, superior, frustrated, and angry, more frequently and intensely, compared with people in Eastern cultures (i.e., Japan) (Kitayama, Mesquita, & Karasawa, 2006; Kitayama, Park, Sevincer, Karasawa, & Uskul, 2009). These differences emerge early in childhood (Furukawa, Tangney & Higashibara, 2012), and therefore, American people tend to encounter situations eliciting anger more frequently, while situations eliciting shame less frequently than Japanese (Boiger, Mesquita, Uchida, & Barrett, 2013).

Interdependent Model of Self and Emotional Experience

Different from this, Eastern cultures—with *interdependent models of self*—appreciate fitting in with others, interpersonal connectedness, and group achievement. Consequently, their prevailing cultural values of emotional life emphasize connection with others.

Individual emotional experiences in interdependent cultural contexts tend to be more other-focused. Asian Americans experience and express more frequent and intense emotions when they think of family members and other relationships (vs. themselves) (Chentsova-Dutton & Tsai, 2010; Uchida, Townsend, Markus, & Bergsieker, 2009). People in interdependent cultures (e.g., Japan) generally experience such socially engaging emotions as being connected with others, friendly, guilty, ashamed, more frequently and intensely, while socially disengaging emotions, such as feeling proud, superior, frustrated, and angry, less frequently and intensely, compared with people in Western cultures (i.e., United Kingdom, United States, and Germany) (Kitayama, Mesquita, & Karasawa, 2006; Kitayama, Park, Sevincer, Karasawa, & Uskul, 2009). These differences emerge early in childhood (Furukawa, Tangney & Higashibara, 2012), and thus, Japanese tend to encounter situations eliciting shame more frequently than Americans, whereas, situations eliciting anger less frequently than Americans (Boiger, Mesquita, Uchida, & Barrett, 2013).

Diversity of Independent and Interdependent Cultural Contexts

It should be noticed, however, that there is a substantial cultural diversity within each group of this dichotomy: *East Asian/interdependent* versus *Western/independent* societies (Mesquita & Leu, 2007; Tsai & Clobert, 2019). It is not quite adequate to assume that there are only two ways of experiencing and expressing emotions: according to *independent* and *interdependent* models.

Emotions in various *interdependent cultures* (including not only East Asian, but also non-East Asian interdependent societies), as well as in *independent cultures* (including not only European Americans, but also various West European societies) can be experienced in a diversity of ways. For instance, a study revealed that people in *Mexican interdependent contexts* experience emotions differently compared to people in *Japanese interdependent contexts*. Thus, other dimensions—beyond *independence* and *interdependence*—should be taken into account in development of *cultural models of self* and *relating* (Mesquita & Leu, 2007).

There might be also an overlapping of cultural norms and models among these two seemingly opposite types of cultures. For instance, in a cross-cultural study of frequency and intensity of emotions, researchers (Eid & Diener, 2001) found that Taiwanese respondents were similar to Australians and Americans in their experience of many positive emotions. *Pride* was the only positive emotion where Taiwanese were similar to Mainland Chinese. Taiwanese were also similar to Australians and Americans in the frequency of negative emotions. However, in the intensity of negative emotions, the differences between Taiwanese and respondents from those two individualistic societies were stronger. Authors explain these findings that the modern Taiwanese culture is under influence of two cultural traditions. It is a society historically associated with Chinese collectivistic values, yet in the modern time it is strongly connected to individualistic values (Eid & Diener, 2001).

Another example is about diversity of Western cultural norms between European Americans and European German. Although European Americans and Germans hold Western individualistic values, yet there are important dissimilarities between two cultural groups. These differences are in the way how their ancestors reacted to religious persecution and economic hardship in Europe of previous centuries. Early American settlers from Germany immigrated to America in search of a better life, while their European Germans remained in their homelands and adjusted to their difficult circumstances.

In light of these historical differences, a study of Koopmann-Holm and Tsai (2014) anticipated that this "frontier spirit" might be associated with their differences in views of negative emotions. The results have demonstrated that European Americans really believe in frontier values more than Germans, and because of this European Americans prefer to avoid negative affective states more than Germans. These differences in the desire to avoid negative emotions also allow predicting how people in these cultures express sympathy for another person.

> When imagining that a close acquaintance has lost a loved one, European Americans were more likely to send a sympathy card that focused on the positive (e.g.,!"Remembering . . . let time heal your soul") than one that focused on the negative ("A severe loss... take time to grieve") compared to Germans. (Tsai & Clobert, 2019, p. 307)

2.2 Power distance as a Cultural Parameter

2.2.1 High Versus Low Power Distance Cultures

Construct of Power Distance

The cultural parameter of *power distance* was proposed by Hofstede's to describe how societal cultural norms expect and accept that power, status, and "vertical" relationships in society is distributed unequally (Hofstede, 1998, 2001).

The construct of *power distance* defines how a society views the importance of hierarchy of power and social status for interpersonal interactions and relationships. As a cultural dimension, *power distance* measures the extent to which people recognize and accept the social norms that social distance and power between individuals of low and high status, low and high ranking in status are distributed unequally. In other words, it is a measure of inequality (vs. equality) of status and power between people in a society.

High-Power Distance Cultures

In *high power distance cultures*, these differences in power of "superiors" and "subordinates" seem to be natural and reflect an "existential inequality" (Hofstede, 1980/1984). In a *high power distance culture*, less powerful members accept and expect that power is distributed unequally within a society. Authorities (e.g., managers, elders, and parents) and subordinates (e.g., commoners, youngsters, and children) are emotionally distant from each other. Formal submission and respect for higher status people are especially treasured. Japan, Philippines, Singapore, Malaysia, India, Mexico, Guatemala, Venezuela, Colombia, and Brazil are the examples of high power distance societies (Hofstede, 1980/1984).

Low-Power Distance Cultures

In *low power distance cultures,* people are viewed as equal. In a low power distance culture, there are expectations of egalitarianism and equality in relationships and power, participative and consultative style of communication prevails. New Zealand, Israel, Switzerland, Denmark, Sweden, Norway, Finland, Austria, and Ireland are the examples of low power distance countries (Hofstede, 1998, 2001; Würtz, 2005). The United States is lower than the median in power distance (Andersen, Hecht, Hoobler, & Smallwood, 2003).

2.2.2 Power Distance and Emotional Life

Power Distance Is Predictive for Emotional Experience

Does *power distance* as a cultural dimension affect emotional life of people in different cultural contexts? Traditionally, emotion research (see for review Basabe et al., 2000) compared samples from societies *high in collectivism* and *high in power distance* with cultural samples *high in individualism* and *low in power distance.* These two dimensions —*individualism* and *low power distance*—often correlate with each other in many societies. Authors explained cultural differences in emotions typically as individualistic versus collectivistic differences. However, as the multivariate analysis of several studies (Basabe et al., 2000) demonstrated, actually *power distance* in societies is a more relevant predictor, which explains cultural differences in emotional experience. Thus, one can see that *power distance* as a cultural dimension substantially affects emotional experience.

Individuals in the societies *high in power distance* tend to be moody and experience higher frequency of such negative emotions as anger and sadness (Arrindell et al., 1997; Basabe et al., 2000). Several studies (see for review Basabe et al., 2000) showed that *power distance* in a society reflects on the people's experience of *anxiety, stress, fear, depression*, and *guilt*. This prevalence of negative emotions is probably due to strong social and hierarchical differentiation that is typical for this type of societies (for instance, Malaysia and Guatemala). High frequency of sadness, anger, and other negative emotions, which people feel, indicates a potential or real conflict between norms and actual emotional experience of life. Thus, frequent experience and lower intensity of negative emotions make high power distance society a suffering emotional culture (Basabe et al., 2000).

Power Distance and Well-Being

An extensive study of 21 thousands of adults (*M* age = 30.2 year) across 48 countries in three time periods of 1980–2000s (Steel, Taras, Uggerslev, & Bosco, 2018) discovered that at the individual level, power distance showed a weak negative relationship with life and relationship satisfaction. Power distance does not seem beneficial for well-being of individuals.

At the national level, the results were similar: *happy nations* have *low power distance*. *High power distance*, on the other end, strongly correlates with *low subjective well-being*. According to the data for the decade 2000–2009, happy and low power distance countries, like Norway and the Netherlands, were on the top, the less happy and high power distance countries, like the Philippines and China, were at the bottom. Although the effect of power distance on subjective well-being is related to political and economic situations in countries, yet it is still partially independent from those parameters.

Power Distance and Expression of Emotions in Relationships

It can be expected that power distance should reflect on interpersonal relationships and close relationships, in particular (i.e., old–young generation, parent–child, romantic, and marital relationships). High power distance cultures (e.g., India) may limit interpersonal interaction and forbid free interclass dating and marriage. Individuals are expected to display only positive emotions to those with high status and show negative emotions to those with low status (Matsumoto, 1991; Porter & Samovar, 1998). Subordinates experience bodily tension and smile habitually in attempt to conciliate superiors and look polite (Andersen & Bowman, 1999). This is why many Asians frequently smile creating and maintaining smooth social relations. Paralinguistic and vocalic cues of speech also adapt to this type of relationships.

For Japanese, a lower body position communicates respect and acceptance; it is a sign that a person is accepting, trustworthy, and loving (Ishii, 1973). Downcast eyes signal attentiveness and agreement (Cambra & Klopf, 1979).

People in low power distance cultures are less aware of this aspect of communication. They are not cognizant that vocal loudness, noisy, and exaggerated vocal tones can be perceived as offensive to others or appear as childlike (Andersen, 2000; Condon &Yousef, 1983). For Americans, body position below that of another and downcast eyes are commonly interpreted as subordination (Cambra & Klopf, 1979).

One can expect that power distance should determine how people express their emotions in formal and informal relationships. In high power distance cultures, the individuals and the organizations are more interdependent than in low power distance cultures, and they accept the differences in power. Therefore, in *high power distance* cultures the emotional expression should be acceptable in superior–subordinate relationships. Different from this, in *low power distance* cultures the expression of emotions should be suppressed in superior–subordinate relationships.

2.3   Gender Roles Equality and Gender Roles Inequality

2.3.1   The Construct of Cultural Masculinity-Femininity

Equality and Inequality in Gender Roles

The cultural parameters of *masculinity-femininity* (Hofstede, 1980/1984; Hofstede & Bond, 1984) was associated with the typical gender stereotype of that time, not real gender differences between men and women in a society. In my opinion, this dimension can be more adequately and precisely named as *gender roles equality* and *gender roles inequality*.

In terms of social and economic characteristics, *feminine cultures* can be classified as *welfare societies*, while *masculine cultures* as *competitive societies*. Cultural norms in *feminine cultures* encourage the value of sympathy, concern for the weak persons, and pay attention to interpersonal relationships (Hofstede, 1991)

The Cultures of Gender Roles Inequality (Masculine Cultures)

In highly masculine cultures, the gender roles are strongly differentiated. Such cultures suggest people to act within a constricted set of gender-related behaviors emphasizing importance of traditional gender role identification (Andersen, 1988). *Masculinity* of culture means the prevalence among men such typical masculine traits as strength, assertiveness, achievement, ambitiousness, and competitiveness. Success and money—attributed as the typical men's preferences—as dominant cultural values. The countries with high masculinity are Japan, Austria, Venezuela, Italy, Switzerland, Mexico, Ireland, Great Britain, Germany, and the Caribbean (Hofstede, 1984).

The Cultures of Gender Roles Equality (Feminine Cultures)

In highly *feminine cultures*, the gender roles are fluid. Such cultures do not impose gender-related behaviors and traditional gender role identification. *Femininity* of culture means the prevalence of caring for others and quality of life—attributed as the typical women's preferences—as dominant cultural values. The countries with high femininity as a cultural dimension are the Netherlands, Denmark, Sweden, Norway, Finland, Portugal, Chile, and Thailand.

Machismo and Marianismo

In Latin American societies, the traits of dominant masculinity among men is called *machismo*, whereas the feminine traits, such as emotionality, affection, compassion, nurturance, and purity are strongly attributed to women *marianismo*. From the lists of countries above, it seems that many South American cultures do not exhibit the typical Latin pattern of machismo. As Hofstede (1984) suggested that machismo is prevalent in the Caribbean region, but not evident in other South American countries.

2.3.2 Gender Roles Equality (Femininity) Versus Gender Roles Inequality (Masculinity) in Society and Emotional Life

Cultural Femininity-Masculinity and Emotional Experience

How does cultural *masculinity-femininity* affect emotional life of people in different cultural contexts? Some empirical studies (e.g., Arrindell et al., 1997; Paez & Vergara, 1995) found that *cultural femininity* substantially influences emotional experience and expression. Other studies showed that people in *feminine cultures* experience positive emotions, such as joy, more frequently and negative emotions, such as anger and sadness, less frequently than in masculine cultures (Basabe et al., 2000; Diener et al., 1995). Basabe et al. (2000) explain this prevailing *positive emotionality* in feminine societies by higher frequency of positive and lower frequency of negative events. It seems that *masculine cultures* are more normative and emotionally inhibited (Basabe et al., 2000).

Cultural Femininity Is Conducive for Well-Being

As for the effect of *cultural femininity-masculinity*, the studies (e.g., Arrindell et al., 1997; Paez & Vergara, 1995) discovered that *cultural femininity* is greatly associated with subjective well-being of individuals. People in *feminine cultures* are happier.

A study of 21 thousands of respondents (*M* age = 30.2 year) across 48 countries in three time periods of 1980–2000s (Steel, Taras, Uggerslev, & Bosco, 2018) found that at the individual level, masculinity was negatively related to life and relationship satisfaction. Feminine individuals tend to be happier.

Cultural masculinity as a trait is strongly linked to materialism, yet materialistic values are problematic for well-being. Materialistic consumption definitely increase happiness, but the effect is typically temporary, not long staying. Studies across a range of nations have demonstrated this finding (Dittmar, Bond, Hurst, & Kasser, 2014).

Although the effect of *masculinity-femininity* on subjective well-being is related to political and economic institutions, yet it is still partially independent from those parameters. At the national level, happy nations are high in *femininity*. At the national level, high *masculinity* positively correlates with low subjective well-being and high stress. Men may harm their health when they internalize emotions rather than externalize as women often do (Buck, 1984). *Androgynous* behavioral patterns, which combine both feminine and masculine, can result in higher social competence, success, and self-esteem for both males and females.

One can expect that these cultural parameters of masculinity and femininity may have an impact on gender differences in the expression of emotions across cultures. Masculine cultures should manifest gender differences, whereas feminine cultures should not. One also can expect that this cultural dimension should influence interpersonal relationships, and close relationships, in particular. However, there are no studies, which investigated these aspects of emotional life, so far.

2.4 Immediacy as a Cultural Parameter

2.4.1 The Concept and Measures of Immediacy

Individual Aspect on Immediacy

Each individual has a preferable personal space around them as an invisible bubble which expands beyond their body. This personal space can depend on the relationship with the people nearby, on the emotional state of person, the activity being performed, as well as on cultural background. In multiple studies, the personal space was investigated as a function of personal attitudes, individual, gender, and age characteristics of communicators, as well as cultural parameters of societies.

Immediacy is a territorial aspect of communication. This dimension characterizes interpersonal relationships in a society in terms of behavioral and psychological closeness. People communicate interpersonal closeness through a series of actions, which can be verbal, but mostly nonverbal expressions. The *immediacy* dimension ranges from a close proximity to a remote distance in interpersonal interaction and communication. The close proximity is frequently interpreted as approach tendency, accessibility and warmth, whereas a remote distance—as avoidance tendency, inaccessibility, and distant (Andersen, 1985). However, this interpretation may vary across cultures.

In terms of nonverbal behavior, *immediate relationship* includes open body positions, closer proximity in interaction, touching, eye contact, smiling, more vocal animation, and expressiveness. In a positive relationship, persons tend to reciprocate such immediate behaviors (Andersen & Andersen, 1984). *Distant relationship* includes close body positions, greater distance in interaction, lack of touching, lack of eye contact, lack of smiling, less vocal animation, and less expressiveness.

The proxemic theory and research of 1960s (Hall, 1966) extensively investigated the types of distance that people prefer to maintain during interaction. They were classified as

(a) *public distance* (above 210 cm; in this distance, voice shifts to higher volumes, and eye contact is minimized);

(b) *social distance*, maintained during more formal interactions (122–210 cm, this distance precludes all but visual and auditory stimuli);

(c) *personal distance*, maintained during interactions with friends (about 46–122 cm, vision is no longer blurred, vocalizations increase); and

(d) *intimate distance*, maintained in close relationships (from 0 to 46 cm, this distance is characterized by poor and blurred vision, and increased perception of heat and olfactory stimuli; Hall, 1966, cited in Sorokowska, et al., 2017, p. 579).

Cultural Aspect of Immediacy

Territoriality in human societies has developed under a strongly influence of culture (Hall & Hall, 1990). Therefore, the territorial space, which is labeled as "mine," varies across cultures and depend on several factors. An individual feel uncomfortable or aggressive when someone penetrates this personal territory. They can tolerate it only for short periods of time.

The people in some cultures are more sensitive to crowding and invasion of their personal space by others. In north America and many northern European countries, such as Germany, England, Netherlands, and Sweden, these personal bubbles are large and people tend to keep their distance all times. In Italy, Spain, Greece, and southern France, however, these bubbles are smaller. A conversational distance, which is typical for people in the southern European cultures, can be perceived as too close and intimate for people in the north. Related to this aspect of spatial communication, people in northern Europe usually feel uncomfortable when someone touches them or brushes of the overcoat sleeve.

The perception of interpersonal space is multisensory (Karandashev et al., 2019), including auditory, kinesthetic, touch, thermal, and olfactory space. There are cultural differences and preferences in this regards. Americans and Germans, as low-context people, rely on auditory screening, while the high-context people in Italy and Spain reject auditory screening and thrive on being open to interruptions and in tune with what goes on around them.

2.4.2   High-Contact Versus Low-Contact Cultures

Conception of High-Contact and Low-Contract Cultures

Immediacy can be also considered as a cultural dimension of a society. The culture, which has typical social norms of interpersonal immediacy, is categorized as *high-contact culture*. People in these societies keep an open body position, stand closer to each other, touch more, and tend to use more sensory stimulation during interpersonal interaction, compared to societies with a *lower-contact culture* (Hall, 1966). These *high-contact* versus *low-contact* patterns of behavior are present in everyday life and affective relationships (Patterson, 1983).

Hall (1966) proposed and extensively studied so-called *contact* versus *noncontact* cultures. According to this conception, cultural norms define the social distance, which people prefer. People from *high-contact* cultures favor immediate nonverbal behaviors, compared to those from *low-contact* cultures, and they may interpret the same distance differently, depending on the typical cultural norms of spatial behavior. An intimate distance in one culture may be considered as personal or social in another.

In *high-contact* cultures, people use a shorter interpersonal distance and more touch during communication, while people in *noncontact* cultures prefer to keep on distance and from touch. Persons from *high-contact cultures* (e.g., Arabs, Latin Americans, and southern and eastern Europeans) construct immediacy in relations increasing sensory input, interacting at closer distances, maintaining more direct body orientations, and touching more frequently than those from *low-contact cultures* (e.g., Asians, North Americans, and northern Europeans). Theory was that such differences can be attributed to variations in climate and/or conditioning. Because of the persons from high-contact cultures prefer tactile and olfactory modes of communication more than those in low-contact cultures do (Andersen, 1988; Sussman & Rosenfeld, 1982).

Research on High-Contact and Low-Contact Societies

Subsequent research brought some support to this theory, even though results were not perfectly convincing. It was found that distance, gaze, and touch as nonverbal indicators of liking, friendliness, and intimacy are culturally specific. Studies brought somewhat mixed results and interpretation (see for review, La France & Mayo, 1978; Andersen, Hecht, Hoobler, & Smallwood, 2003). As interpretation, many authors suggested a climate factor.

Many *high-contact cultures*, such as Latin Americans, Arabs, and the Mediterranean, are closer to the equator in warmer countries, whereas *low-contact cultures*, such Scandinavian and other North European countries, are usually located at high latitudes in cooler countries. For example, Surinamese people display liveliness in their body movements, smile, and laugh more frequently than the Dutch. That supports the theory of the warmer nature of people residing closer to the equator (Vrij & Winkel, 1991).

North Americans and Australians are *moderately high-contact cultures* and located in moderate climate conditions (Andersen, Hecht, Hoobler, & Smallwood, 2003, p.75; Patterson, 1983). Even within the United States, the southern regions with warmer latitudes tend to display *higher-contact cultures*. The recent tendency of Americans to migrate to the Southeast and Southwest may be among the reasons for the American increased immediacy found in recent studies (Andersen et al. 1987).

Asian societies as *low-contact cultures* (Barnlund, 1975; Klopf & Thompson, 1991; McDaniel & Andersen, 1998), however, do not fit to this the latitudinal pattern for climate interpretation. The historic origin of Asian cultures, such as influence of Confucianism, which emphasizes self-control, proscribes public displays of emotion, and encourage nonexpressive in interpersonal contact can be among causes of their low-immediacy.

Later research demonstrated that North America and Northern Europe might be considered as relatively *high-contact* cultures. It seems that the Western countries, including the United States, became more *high-contact* cultures than previously viewed.

Latin American and Arab societies are high-contact cultures compared to North America. North Americans may feel uncomfortable and anxious being in spatial closeness, which is typical for Latin Americans and Arabs. North Americans prefer a more distant style of interaction with the lack of olfactory contact and tactile behavior that can be viewed by Latin Americans and Arabs as alienated (Almaney & Alwan, 1982; Shuter, 1976). Asian societies are definitely *low-contact* cultures (McDaniel & Andersen, 1998; Remland, Jones, & Brinkman, 1991) with low immediacy in interaction preferring even more distant communication with the lack of sensory contacts, and the lack of tactile and expressive behavior.

Proliferating research of 1960–1980s on cultural aspects of nonverbal communication discovered both similarities and differences, supporting relations between cultural parameters and proxemic behavior. For instance, people in Mediterranean cultures such as southern Italians and Greeks preferred closer distances than northern Europeans such as Swedes and Scots (Little, 1968). Other studies (see for review, La France & Mayo, 1978; Remland, Jones, & Brinkman, 1991) compared Americans with Arabs, Latin Americans, Mediterraneans, Pakistanis, Germans, Italians, Japanese, and Venezuelans. Studies also found differences between Australians and Indonesians, among Arabs, southern Europeans, and Latin Americans, when compared with Asians, Near Eastern people, and northern Europeans. Certain patterns of differences regarding high-contact versus low-contact distinction were found in the studies of touch.

A seating position during interaction is another example of proxemic behavior, which varies across cultures illustrating the dimension of immediacy. For instance, according to the two different cultural habits, Taiwanese usually prefer to seat side-by-side while interacting with same-sex partners, while Americans mostly prefer corner seating (Cline & Puhl, 1984).

2.4.3   Factors Affecting Interpersonal Distance Across Cultures

Interpersonal Distance During Interaction

In European samples (Remland, Jones, & Brinkman, 1991), researchers recorded naturally occurring interactions in dyads. They found that the Dutch preferred more interpersonal distance than the French and English, while the French preferred more distance than the English. Authors also revealed that the French tend to sit farther apart during conversation, yet keep more direct body orientation than Dutch and English partners. The same-sex dyads touched less often than the mixed-sex dyads.

The later study of 1990s (Remland, Jones, & Brinkman, 1995) brought controversial results, despite expectations that the Greeks and Italians (as the dyads from the contact countries) should keep less distance than the dyads from England, Ireland, Scotland, and the Netherlands (as the noncontact countries). Interpersonal distance among the standing Irish and Scottish dyads was closer than among the Italian, Greek, French, and English dyads. The results of other study of that time (Regan, Jerry, Narvaez, & Johnson, 1999) were in agreement with conception of high-contact versus low-contact cultures. In naturalistic observation of Asians versus Latin Americans, while they were walking through the campus of a large western university, researchers investigated public touching behavior as a function of the race and ethnicity. In such public circumstances, Latin American male–female dyads (as more contact-prone) were more likely to embrace than Asian male–female dyads (*low-contact* cultures).

Other studies, however, were inconclusive (see for references and detailed review, Sorokowska, et al., 2017; Remland, Jones, & Brinkman, 1995). Overall, despite evidence of cross-cultural variability in interpersonal distances, those results could not explain the division of cultures: whether they were based on geographical location, *environmental factors* (e.g., temperature of a region and population growth rate), or *socio-psychological factors* (e.g., collectivism/individualism and wealth of the society). Many early studies did not specify whether they studied distances among strangers, acquaintances, and close persons. However, this latter parameter might be important to take into account.

As the early research demonstrated, the perceived closeness toward in- and out-group members varies across cultures (Triandis, 1994). For instance, Chinese students feel closer to their mother, father, and spouse (their ingroup members) than did Americans; however, they feel more distant from their roommates and friends (their outgroup members) than did the Americans (Triandis, McCusker, & Hui, 1990).

A recent study (Safdar et al., 2009) compared the feeling of closeness in relationships among Japanese, US Americans, and Canadians. Authors found that the degree of subjective closeness of the relationship between a person and a target figure varies across cultures, yet depends on a range of closeness with that individual. Three groups were *close* (family members and two close friends), *medium* (acquaintances and classmates), and *distal* (professors in three countries).

> Japanese reported being significantly closer to the distal group than Americans, they also reported being closer to the medium group than Canadians and Americans, and less close to the close group than the Canadians and the Americans. (Safdar et al., 2009, p.5)

These results seem different and opposite from the earlier study with Chinese students (Triandis, McCusker, & Hui, 1990) and need an additional cultural interpretation and replication.

Recent Studies of Interpersonal Distance

The interest to the topic of interpersonal distance as a culturally dependent variable revived recently. A study of Sorokowska, et al. (2017) was unique in this regard. It investigated preferences in interpersonal distance with a total sample of 8943 people in 42 countries (53 study sites) of the globe.

Results indicated that climate demands play their role, even though wealth resources should be taken into account in understanding cultural tendencies. Distance preferences depend on mean temperature. The unipolar, mean temperature is associated with psychological variables, and the latter can be used instead, or in addition to the climatic demand variable. It is interesting that the effect of temperature was different for social and intimate distance (Sorokowska, et al., 2017).

In warmer countries, people prefer to keep closer distances toward strangers. These results are in agreement with previous studies (e.g., IJzerman & Semin, 2010), which revealed that warmer conditions (compared with colder ones) predispose to closer social proximity. Even within one country (e.g., the United States), people living in warm latitudes display a closer contact behavior and more touch than in colder climates (Andersen, 1988).

As for the intimate distance, in warmer countries, people preferred to keep farther distance toward their intimate partners. Both cold and heat are challenging environmental conditions. However, the negative effects of colder climate can be lessened in closer intimate distances.

That study (Sorokowska, et al., 2017) also discovered gender differences in preferred *personal* and *social distance*: women tend to prefer more distance in interaction. For social distance, this effect of gender was especially evident among participants in Switzerland, Malaysia, Saudi Arabia, Hong Kong, Brazil, Austria, and India. For personal distance, it was particularly apparent among participants in Switzerland, Malaysia, China, Saudi Arabia, Brazil, Poland, and Nigeria. Explanation for these differences was challenging, yet, some aspects of questionnaire could play its role—authors did not specify the gender of an approaching individual.

These results—that women prefer more distance in interaction than men—are different from previous studies, which found that women preferred closer interpersonal distances than men (Aiello, 1987; Horenstein & Downey, 2003; Ozdemir, 2008; Patterson & Edinger, 1987). Further research to verify and replicate these findings is needed.

Similar to earlier studies (Aiello, 1987; Gerin-Lajoie et al., 2006; Rapp & Gutzmann, 2000; Webb & Weber, 2003), researchers also found that age allows predicting preferences in personal and intimate distance: younger people tend to engage in physical contact with others (Sorokowska, et al., 2017).

2.5   Context Differentiation as a Cultural Parameter

2.5.1   Context and Functional Relativity

Attention to Context

Context includes all information associated with a particular message, and it is bound up with the meaning of that message. Individuals as well as cultures differ in the extent how much value they place on messages and contexts in coding and decoding a meaning, which they convey.

Cultures and people differ in their attention to the details of the context, in which they act, ascribing different importance to the particulars of situations, verbal, and nonverbal behaviors. This cultural dimension was named as *context differentiation* (Hall, 1976, 2000; Hall & Hall, 1990; Matsumoto, Yoo, & Fontaine, 2009).

The theoretical framework that considered *context* as a cultural dimension was proposed in the early 1970s (Hall, 1976, 2000; Hall & Hall, 1990) to explain communication patterns and expressive behavior prevalent in a culture. It distinguished *high-context* and *low-context* cultures, with major differences in the way how people in those cultures take into account the *context* (vs. *content*) of messages in their interactions: the *high-context* cultures are context-oriented, implicit, indirect, and nonverbal, while *low-context* cultures are content-oriented, explicit, direct, and verbal.

High-Context Cultures

Generally, Eastern societies tend to be high-context cultures, whereas Western societies are more frequently low-context cultures. Some scholars (Gudykunst & Matsumoto, 1996) contended that people in collectivistic cultures prefer high-context messages, while those in individualistic cultures prefer low-context messages.

Among the *high-context cultures* are Japan, China, Korea, Taiwan, Arabs, African Americans, Native Americans, Mexican Americans, Spain, and Latinos (Andersen, Hecht, Hoobler, & Smallwood, 2003; Hall, 1976, Hall & Hall, 1984; Lustig & Koester, 1999). American Indians with their roots in East Asia are *high-context cultures* and they resemble in this regard contemporary Oriental culture (Hall, 1984). Most Latin American cultures are also *high-context cultures*, being influenced by Iberian (Spanish and Portuguese) and indigenous traditions. People in southern and eastern Mediterranean, such as Greeks, Turks, and Arabs also belong to *high-context cultures*.

Low-Context Cultures

Among the *low-context cultures* are Germany, Switzerland, Sweden, Norway, Finland, Denmark, Canada, and the United States (Andersen, Hecht, Hoobler, & Smallwood, 2003; Hall, 1976, 1984; Lustig & Koester, 1999). Some cultures, such as England, France, and Italy, combine the characteristics of both *high-context and low-context cultures*. People in those societies are less explicit in their communication that other Western European and North American cultures.

A Fallacy of Overgeneralization

It is also worthwhile to say a word of caution against overgeneralization of the cultural similarities in the traits related to high-context and low-context communication (Andersen, 1999). Although many people in a culture have such traits as relatively common, due to cultural norms in a society, they still may behave individually or typologically different. It is wrong to attribute all of the features of a culturally specific behavior to any individual; they are typical rather than essential.

Another fallacy of overgeneralization is implicit ethnocentrism. Unfortunately, people belonging to those two opposite cultures—high-context and low-context—are not fully aware and understand these basic differences in their communication, behavior, and context (Andersen, Hecht, Hoobler, & Smallwood, 2003). They tend to quickly misattribute the causes for behavior of each other. Such misattribution and wrong interpretation are the widespread causes of misunderstanding.

Functional Relativity

Principle of functional relativity explains the ways how social and cultural groups develop and use functional features of their language depending on the social and cultural contexts and depending on the goals, which they want to achieve in a situation (Bernstein, 1971; Hall, 1976, see for detailed review Lim, 2003).

Communicators apply different linguistic codes and switch those in different culturally suitable situations (Palmer, 1996; Philipsen, 1992). In specific social and cultural contexts, they are able to use not only grammatically correct, but also pragmatically adequate sentences (Hymes, 1971).

Over years, researchers have explored such diverse cultures and languages as those of the African countries, of the Papua New Guinean, the Native South American, Indonesia, and people of Pohnpe, Micronesia (see for review Lim, 2003, p. 57), and demonstrated that syntactic structures and lexical items of languages reflect the specific experiences of local communities and their cultural values. This research suggests the importance of understanding how individuals in cultural groups communicate in a specific local, not global anglo-centric, perspective (Lim, 2003, p. 57).

Messages in Context

Recent research on language usage across cultures has mostly employed functional relativism rather than linguistic relativism. Functional relativism admits that the forms, which the grammatical systems of language take, fulfill the social and personal needs that the language serves (Halliday, 1973, 1978). A message of speech reflects the circumstances and social position of a person. It also expresses the social and cultural view. Since cultures are situated in different environments, have different beliefs, attitudes, and values, their languages also differ.

Hall (1976) applied the earlier theoretical perspective (Bernstein, 1971) on the relations between language use and context to the theory of cultural context. He argued that understanding of the context in speech is vital for adequate comprehension of the message since the meaning, the linguistic code, and the context of communication are closely intertwined. However, the proportion of the context in the message can be different.

Hall (1976) applied the *theory of context* to explain how the *context dependency* reflects on the cultural differences in people's use of language. In the low-context messages, the major portion of information is explicitly stated in the code, with little left in the context. In the high-context messages, the substantial portion of information is located in the context of a situation, or implicitly known by a person, with little left in the in the explicit coded and transmitted part of the message (Hall, 1976, p. 79).

2.5.2   *Interpersonal Communication in High-Context Cultures*

Values of Verbal Communication

Mediterranean people, Arabs, and Japanese peoples maintain the extensive close relationships with their family and friends (Hall & Hall, 1990). Therefore, their normal interactions in daily life already imply such in-depth known information that means a lot for them in understanding of each other. They do not need the detailed elaboration of a message. High-context people can be irritated and impatient when people from low-context cultures request from them or give the information they do not need. When there is too much information, people may feel that they are being talked down to.

Traditionally, the holistic worldview, the beliefs in unity and harmony have been the vital tenets of all major East Asian religions (Buddhism, Taoism, and Confucianism, Yum, 1988). From those origins, it is expected that Eastern cultures are *high-context cultures*. They believe that language imposes biases on the capability of thinking, imagination, and they have a holistic attitude toward communication. The words are only the part of the total communication context, which includes the personal characters and the nature of interpersonal relationships between them (Gudykunst & Kim, 1984). The Easters cultures place little emphasis and faith in

words and prefer to communicate and meditate beyond the words. They believe that
the meanings are the context specific and, therefore, a total understanding involves
mental unification with the other person.

Pauses in conversation and silence are not feared, but rather valued (Hasegawa &
Gudykunst, 1998; Morsbach, 1976; Oliver, 1971). The silence, however, is not
always good. People prefer silence to words only when words can threat the face of
self or the other. These might be the cases of challenge, disagreement, breaking
peace by initiation of conversation, or interrupting the other. However, when the
other person expects active and responsive participation, then keeping silent is considered impolite. Japanese, for example, may view silence as negative in some situations (e.g., when communicating with a stranger), and silence can be viewed more
negative than by Americas (Hasegawa & Gudykunst, 1998).

Language Styles

Eastern high-context cultures are well known for the value which they place on the
status of an individual in social relationships and people's strong group orientation.
Because of this, for people in these societies, the appropriate language style and the
correct choice of linguistic code are very important. For them, status similarity or
difference is more important for their communication than intimacy (close social
distance) (Hijirida & Sohn, 1986). This appears to be reflected even in their use of
language. The Japanese and Korean languages have a rich system of marking status.
For instance, the detailed analysis of Japanese language (Goldstein & Tamura,
1975) has revealed the two essential linguistic characteristics: status-markedness
and group-orientedness, which distinguish it from American English.

Asians tend to distinguish between the *private linguistic code* (language used
when no third parties are present) and the *public linguistic code* (language used in
presence of others) (Goldstein & Tamura, 1975). Koreans have even more complex
differentiation—five different styles of language in terms of formality and respect:
"formal one-down, informal one-down, one-across, formal one-up, and informal
one-up" Lim, 2003, p.62). Different inflectional endings, address terms, pronouns,
lexical items, honorific prefixes and suffixes, particles, and others are used in
these styles.

In East Asian cultures, relationships are more important than actions, and styles
are more important than contents. Maintaining the relationship using culturally
mandated styles or showing good deeds is more important than accomplishing the
current task or reasoning of evidence in support of informational contents. Asians
are more concerned with the overall quality of the interaction rather than with the
meaning of particular words or sentences. They rely on the long run relationships
more than on the words (Gudykunst & Kim, 1984, p. 142).

Japanese are also perceived through the lens of embedded connectedness in relationships. Again, the language manifests this aspect of their culture. When Japanese
make linguistic code-choices, they care very much about group identities.

Correspondingly, Japanese linguistic structures connect the individual and group and separate both from the outside (Goldstein & Tamura, 1975).

Japanese and Korean languages, representing *collectivistic* and *high-context cultures*, carefully consider not separating the other from self. In Japanese and Korean, communicators avoid focusing on individual identities during the conversation when they rarely use personal pronoun *you*. It seems they can communicate well without use pronouns. When the subject of a sentence is a pronoun, it is usually omitted. They also do not feel awkward when they do not remember the other's name (Goldstein & Tamura, 1975).

The use of first-person singular pronouns may signal the locus of individual responsibility. In English, for example, the use of subject pronouns is obligatory: a speaker must mention "*I*" or "*you*" in a sentence, even if the referent is unambiguous (Kashima & Kashima, 1998). In other languages (e.g., Spanish, Chinese, and Japanese), representing *collectivistic* and *high-context cultures*; however, a speaker can choose to drop subject pronouns (or subjects) from of a grammatical sentence. Personal pronouns are not required in these cases because the verb inflections, the grammatical rule of subject–verb agreement, or other way, indicate the referents. In Japanese and Chinese, pronouns can also be omitted (Kashima & Kashima, 1998).

Expressive Behavior

In *high-context cultures*, people ascribe high importance to the physical and relationship context of a situation paying less attention to the explicit information that a communication bears (Hall, 1976). They prefer to set the context and setting to convey the message, without referring directly to the feeling. The meanings are internalized with large emphasis on nonverbal codes (Lustig & Koester, 1999). People rely on indirectness in communication and believe that persons can reach truth and understanding without rationality—through nonlinear thinking. With such circular thinking of people in high-context cultures, their communication can move back and forth, leaving out details and assuming that two speakers implicitly understand each other (Choe, 2001; Hall & Hall, 1990; Würtz, 2005). A person is expected to be able to read "between the lines" and understand the untold message.

People usually speak one after another in a linear way, so the speaker is rarely interrupted. Individuals extensively use nonverbal strategies for conveying meanings and communicate with messages using behavioral language, gestures, silence, proximity, and other paraverbal cues Hall (1976, 1990; Kim, Pan, & Park, 1998; Würtz, 2005). Nonverbal aspects of communication are more important than verbal aspects.

Persons in *high-context cultures* are cautious in initial interactions; they disclose and develop a relationship slowly, compared to people in low-context cultures, yet the established relationships are quite deep and stable. Strong behavioral norms, well-structured social hierarchy, and closeness of human relationships influence their communication style (Gudykunst, 1983; Nishimura, Nevgi, & Tella, 2008).

People from *high-context cultures* are taciturn and sparse in their words, value pauses, and silence in communication. They may be perceived as sneaky, nondisclosing, and mysterious (Andersen, 2000). People in *high-context cultures* do not place emphasis on verbal communication in their social perception. Elliot et al. (1981) found that less verbal people were perceived as more attractive in Korea, a *high-context culture*. People in *high-context cultures* are sensitive to the various aspects of nonverbal communication, in particular, to contextual cues. Location and speed of interaction, posture, body movements, and facial expressions have for them more meaning. People in *high-context cultures* expect communicators to understand unarticulated moods, subtle gestures, and environmental clues that people from *low-context cultures* simply do not process (Andersen, Hecht, Hoobler, & Smallwood, 2003; Hall, 1976).

2.5.3   Interpersonal Communication in Low-Context Cultures

Values of Verbal Communication

North Americans and northern Europeans (e.g., Swiss, Germans, Danes, Swedish, and Norwegians) tend to compartmentalize their personal relationships and other aspects of daily life not paying attention to intricate details (Hall & Hall, 1990). Therefore, every time when they communicate they need the detailed elaboration of a message. This aspect of their interaction affects many situations and relationships of their life. Their culture of communication is low-context. Low-context people can be confused and lost when people from high-context cultures do not provide them enough information in a message. When there is too little information, people can feel left out. People in Western cultures consider a pause and the absence of sound in a conversation, when they last long, as conversationally uneasy and awkward (Hasegawa & Gudykunst, 1998; Morsbach, 1976; Oliver, 1971).

There are differences among European cultures in this regard. The Mediterranean, Spanish, Italian, and French people are much higher on the context scale than the Germans and the other northern Europeans.

Generally, the Western cultures have their origins in the ancient Greek and Roman cultures (e.g., Aristotle, Plato, Socrates), thus, it is expected that they are *low-context* cultures. They subscribe to the principle of the universal meanings and the importance of reasoning. This Western cultural tradition of analytic and rational thinking suggests expressing the thoughts and ideas logically, clearly, and persuasively (Gudykunst & Kim, 1984 p. 140).

Language Styles

Many Western societies consider social distance as more important for the quality of relationships than status relationships, probably due to their historic egalitarian movement. Therefore, in their choice of linguistic code, social distance (in terms of degree of intimacy) plays a higher role than people's status (Brown & Gilman, 1960). Because of this, Indo-European languages, representing mostly *individualistic* and *low-context cultures*, do not have the diversity of forms, comparable to Japanese or Korean, to mark status differences (some pronouns, address terms, and speech acts, see for review, Lim, 2003, p.62).

In terms of connectedness in relationships, British and Americans have priorities in clear individual boundaries, autonomy and separateness in relationships. British English linguistic norms reflect this. In the same vein, American English links individual to individual by name and nonreciprocal pronoun usage (Lim, 2003; Tamura & Lau, 1992). Certainly, the loyalty to some groups in Western societies also exists, and their vocabularies reflect this binding of an individual to group. However, linguistic structures on the whole do not (Lim, 2003).

English speakers want to highlight the individual identity of a speaker and other person. The use of first-person singular pronouns may signal the locus of individual responsibility. In English, it is impossible to maintain a conversation without pronouns or without reference to the name of other, which one speaks to (Goldstein & Tamura, 1975). The use of subject pronouns is obligatory: a speaker must mention "*I*" or "*you*" in a sentence, even if the referent is unambiguous (Kashima & Kashima, 1998).

Researchers (Kashima & Kashima, 1998) theorized that the linguistic practice of pronoun drop (the omission of the first-person singular pronoun as "*I*" in English) is related to the psychological differentiation among a speaker, a conversational partner, and the context of speech. English speakers want to highlight the individual identity of a speaker and other person. The use of first-person singular pronouns signals the locus of individual responsibility. An explicit use of "*I*" in English intends to separate the individual identity of the person and the partner from the context—reflecting individualistic cultures, while an omission of "*I*" in Spanish, Japanese, and Chinese reduces the prominence of the speaker's person from the conversational partner and the context—reflecting collectivistic cultures. Authors explored the use of first- and second-person singular pronouns (e.g., *I* and *you*) across 39 languages spoken in 71 cultures and found that cultures with "non-pronoun-drop languages" tend to be more individualistic than those with "pronoun-drop languages" (Kashima & Kashima, 1998).

Another related observation is the tendency of Americans to call a new communicator with their first name. Some scholars (Hall & Hall, 1990) view this as an artificial way to make communication high-contextualized. This manner often offends people from other cultures who consider the use of first names acceptable only in close relationship. They prefer using a formal practice of address until the other person indicates when familiarity is acceptable.

Expressive Behavior

People in *low-context cultures*, such as in the United States and countries of northern Europe, attribute more importance to the meanings that the behaviors of others and their messages explicitly convey (Hall, 1976; Lustig & Koester, 1999). They prefer to communicate through explicit messages in speech and text, relying more on the content than on the context of communication. The meaning depends more on content of spoken words. The communicative messages clearly and unambiguously construct information with a high degree of specificity. People in these cultures view the specific details and precise time schedules as very important things, at the expense of context of interaction (Hall, 1984).

People in low-context cultures communicate consistently with their feelings. They use direct and explicit messages to ensure that a partner understands them correctly. They rely on directedness in communication and emphasize logic, assuming that partners can reach truth and understanding through linear rational thinking. Conversation evolves from information and arguments that are already stated to next ones. When something remains unclear, partners usually expect explanations. Conversations are less physically animated (Choe, 2001; Hall & Hall, 1990; Nishimura, Nevgi, & Tella, 2008; Würtz, 2005).

People in *low-context cultures* substantially rely on verbal communication. They are frequently perceived as excessively talkative, elaborative in excessive details, sometimes too obvious and redundant. People in *low-context cultures* value verbal communication in their social perception. Elliot et al. (1981) found that people in the United States perceived more verbal people as more attractive. People, especially men, in the *low-context cultures* are less sensitive to perceive nonverbal communication paying less attention to the circumstances of interaction, tension, movements, and facial expressions. People in *low-context cultures* simply do not process such subtle aspects of communication as understand unarticulated moods, subtle gestures, and environmental clues (Andersen, Hecht, Hoobler, & Smallwood, 2003; Hall, 1976).

2.5.4 Construct of Context Differentiation

Context Differentiation at Cultural and Individual Levels

Matsumoto and his colleagues (Matsumoto, Yoo, & Fontaine, 2009) proposed a new construct *context differentiation* (CD) that describes the relative consistency or inconsistency of behavior across context and differentiate behaviors that people follow across contexts. Some cultures encourage individuals to highly differentiate their behaviors across contexts, while others discourage such differentiation. On the cultural level, the cultures of *high context differentiation* encourage the differentiation of behavior in different contexts. Thus, inconsistency in behavior across contexts may be a cultural norm. The cultures of *low context differentiation* encourage the less differentiation of behavior in different contexts. Thus, consistency would be the cultural norm (Matsumoto, Yoo, & Fontaine, 2009).

The construct *context differentiation* is different from Hall's dimension of *high-context versus low-context cultures,* yet I believe they are closely related and may have similar influence on individual behavior and emotional life. It is also reasonably to expect that the cultural norms of *high-context cultures* (in Hall's, 1976, 2000, construct) should suggest *high context differentiation* (in Matsumoto et al.'s, 2009, construct)—differentiation of behavior and emotions in different contexts. While the Halls' construct is a *culture level dimension*, the Matsumoto et al.'s construct is applicable to *both individual and cultural level* of analysis.

Individual Measures of Context Differentiation

Context differentiation is "the degree to which individuals differentiate their thoughts, feelings, or actions according to the specific context in which they are in" (Matsumoto, et al., 2009, p. 253). People, which are *high in context differentiation,* tend to behave, think, and feel in a particular way in one context and behave in another way in another context. People, which are *low in context differentiation,* tend to act, think, and feel more consistently across contexts. Large ranges of individual differences in this dimension are possible within cultures, as well between cultures.

The advantage of *context differentiation* construct is that authors (Matsumoto, et al., 2009) proposed a measure of context differentiation based on display rules, which can operate on individual level. It assesses behaviors and feelings of individuals within culture, as well as across cultures in different contexts. Thus, implications of this construct and measure for the study of cultural models of emotions are quite beneficial.

2.6 Temporal Pattern of Life as a Cultural Parameter

2.6.1 Time and Psychology

Concept of Time

The modern Western scientific tradition in understanding time stems from the Newton's mathematical theory of *absolute time*. According to Newton (1643–1727), the absolute time is an objective reality that progresses at a consistent pace of seconds, minutes, days, weeks, months, and years; it is imperceptible—existing independently of any perceiver. People are able to perceive time only in *relative terms*—measured by the motion of perceivable objects: Sun and shadows, Moon and stars on the sky. Time is characterized by a *sequence of events,* perceptions, cognitions, and emotions, *rhythm* as a repeated pattern of events, perceptions, cognitions, and emotions, the *speed* as the flow of time—slow, medium, or fast, *duration* as the time that an event lasts, and the *synchrony* of individuals' times attuned to each other. For psychology, the most important thing is this individual and group time and how people experience it.

In personal, family, community, and social realities, individuals perceive time in relative terms: (1) in relation to the events, which occur in their individual and community life, and (2) in relation to the images, thoughts and emotions, which pass by in their mind. Temporal aspects of human activity reflect on such psychological processes of everyday life as *time perception, pace of life, time orientation, and time use* (McGrath & Tschan, 2004).

Circular Regime of Time Passage

A traditional and natural *regime of time* flows circularly, repeating itself in a cycle of events: from morning to night every day, from day to day every week, from one season to another every year, from one year to another in every human life. This was a typical time passage from ancient agricultural eras for majority of commoners. This is the way how many people have routinely experienced their time for centuries. This is a quite typical cultural pattern of time passage in the life of people, families, and small communities in many traditional and modern cultures. I call this individual flow of time as a *circular regime of time*. This kind of time is missing in the typology of Hall and Hall (1990) because they studied the time flow of business people.

It is nonlinear time in terms of an individual life, yet it is still linear for historians since historical events—from one king to another, from one war to another—evolve in a sequence and according to their importance. Geometrically, *circular regime of time* is represented in circular figures (e.g., sequence of similar circles and squares), while *linear regime of time* is usually depicted on a straight line stretching from the left (past) to the right (future), as a sequence of relatively related events, with an arrow at the end indicating the direction of the time flow. In most cultures of the world, people represent linear time spatially from left to right (or in some cases from right to left, or from back to front) with respect to the body (e.g., Boroditsky & Gaby, 2010; Fuhrman & Boroditsky, 2010). However, people in Pormpuraaw—a remote Australian Aboriginal community—represent time differently (Boroditsky & Gaby, 2010) That is, time flows left to right when one is facing south, from right to left when one is facing north, away from the body when one's facing west, and toward the body when one is facing east.

Monochronic (Linear) Regime of Time Passage

In modern economic and social era, a *linear regime of time* is widespread among people in many modernized cultures. Spatially, it is cognitively represented in people's minds in the forms of calendars that mark events and appointments in the compartmentalized time locations—hours, days, weeks, and so on. I call this concept as *linear time regime* sequentially evolving as a series of events leading from the beginning toward something else: every day, every week, every season, every year, and so on. This also can be called as *monochronic time* (Hall & Hall, 1990) since it flows on one line (*mono*) from the past to the future (*chronic*). Brislin and Kim (2003) called it a clock-time since for people in clock-time cultures (e.g., the United States) it is very important to adhere to punctuality and schedules.

Monochromic time is experienced in a *linear* way, being naturally divided into time segments, like a road is divided into space segments. The time is scheduled and timed. The calendar, agenda, and guidelines are more important than people and things, which are involved. A person tends to concentrate on one thing at a time. Since a person in the *monochromic time regime* concentrates on one thing at a time in a linear order, they do not like to be interrupted. The events are valuable in terms of time: *time is money*. It can be spent, wasted, lost, and it has priorities. *Monochromic people* take commitments seriously as obligations with deadlines and emphasize promptness. They are committed to the job and follow the plans strictly. They are *low-context people* and, therefore, need additional information for completion of tasks. Short-term relationships seem natural in many cases. *Monochromic individuals* concern about privacy, private property, and rarely borrow things from others. They avoid distracting other people (Hall & Hall, 1990, p.15).

Nowadays, *monochronic time regime* appears as natural and logical; it is experienced as a common time passage in modern economic and social life in the United States, "with whistles and bells counting off the hours" (Hall & Hall, 1990, p. 14). It is typical in the Great Britain, Germany, the Netherlands, Sweden, Norway, Switzerland, and others. Generally saying, western *low-context cultures* have a tendency to be *monochromic*. It should be noted, however, that *monochromic time regime* is not natural; it violates many innate rhythms of humans.

Polychromic Regime of Time Passage

Polychromic time regime (Hall & Hall, 1990) is drastically different from monochromic one because the events in people's subjective experience do not occur in a strict sequence. It seems they are happening at the same time. The polychronic time is compared to "a single point than to a road" (p.14). The events—the things and people involved—are more important than schedule. Brislin and Kim (2003) called it an *event time* since for people in *event-time cultures* (e.g., Latin America) prefer the natural flow of social events. *Polychromic* people are highly distractible and prone to interruptions. They borrow things often and easily. They understand commitments as the goals to be attained, if possible.

Polychronic are *high-context people*. An emphasis is on completion of human transactions, not on the holding of schedules. They change plans easily and often. They are more committed to people having strong tendency to build and rely on lifetime relationships. For instance, two Latins in polychromic time regime, which are natural for them, are conversing on a street corner. They likely prefer to come late for their next meeting than interrupt the current conversation until it naturally concludes. Another polychromic person waiting for him understands the late arrival unsurprisingly, while a complaint from a monochromic person about lateness is perceived as an offense. The examples of such time-flexible cultures are Latin American and Mediterranean peoples. Generally saying, *high-context* cultures such as those in the Middle East, southern Europe, and Central and South America have the tendency to be *polychronic*.

Since its introduction by Hall (1983; Hall & Hall, 1990), several studies have been conducted in the management area. Researchers have been developed the instruments to measure this construct on the individual level as a time personality: Attitude Index and Orientation Scale (Bluedorn, Kaufman, & Lane, 1992), The Inventory of Polychronic Values (IPV, Bluedorn, Kalliath, Strube, & Martin, 1999), and Polychronic–Monochronic Tendency Scale (PMTS, Lindquist, & Kaufman-Scarborough, 2007). The studies have been mostly conducted in the United States, as those cited above, or in Spain (Adams, & van Eerde, 2010). Even though, according to the earlier expectation, in Spain, as Mediterranean culture, polychromic style should be prevalent; the results obtained among managers in Madrid showed that they are monochromic people. Unfortunately, not many empirical cross-cultural studies have been conducted so far (e.g., Nonis, Teng, & Ford, 2005).

Regimes of Time and Emotions

Regarding the effect of *passage time regimes* on emotional life of people, they have different influence. *Circular time regime* is routine and therefore, it is relatively relaxed with calm emotions of small joys and small disappointments. *Circular time regime* assumes permanent or recurrent relationships, where people meet periodically by their wish or by necessity. These relationships can be tensed or relaxed.

Monochronic time regime is full of new events, the need for progression from bad to better, from good to the best, and therefore, it is more condensed with intense emotions of happiness of achievements and frustrations of failures. *Monochronic time regime* intensifies some relationships, while loosens others. Being compartmentalized, time resembles a room where some people have access to, while others have a limited admission.

Successful switching from *circular time regime* in personal life to *monochromic time regime* in business life (and back) is important for modern people. Then, they will be able to avoid the routine of life, which might be boring for some of them, and still avoid the overloading with intense business emotions, being able to relax in their personal life. *Polychromic time regime* seems combine the emotional benefits of both circular and monochromic and gives more flexibility for people in their relationships. Unfortunately, no studies have explored so far the effect of these time regimes on emotional life and close relationship of the people.

2.6.2   Time Orientation of Cultures

Short-Term Versus Long-Term Orientation

Another cultural dimension in time perception that differentiates among cultures is short-term versus long-term orientation. People in short-term cultures act and think more in the immediate present and short-term perspective, while in long-term cultures people act and think more about the future, capable of delayed gratification of social, material, and emotional needs (Hofstede & Minkov, 2010; Minkov & Hofstede, 2012a).

Hofstede (2001) conducted the large-scale cross-cultural study asking respondents across 36 countries of the world about their perceptions of time. The results showed that those countries of *short-term oriented* are Ghana, Nigeria, Sierra Leone, Philippines, Spain, Canada, Botswana, Malawi, Gambia, Zimbabwe, United States, and New Zealand, while those of *long-term oriented* are Norway, Denmark, Hungary, Thailand, Czech Republic, India, Brazil South Korea, Japan, Taiwan, Hong Kong, and China. *The medium-term oriented countries* are Australia, Austria, Germany, Poland, Sweden, Italy, Belgium, France, Switzerland, Finland, and Netherlands.

Researchers found that life in the cultures with *long-term orientations* is associated with culturally specific types of interpersonal relationships. They are characterized by unequal status relationships, hierarchical organization, and horizontal cooperation. People believe that humility is a great human virtue and focus on building long-term relationships. In families, they differentiate more between elders and youngers, as well as between brother and sisters. All these factors presumably cause a stable society (Hofstede, 2001).

Hofstede (2001) also found that among 22 countries, which he studied, the societies with a *short-term orientation* (most Western countries) tend to endorse the values of future-oriented rewards, such as perseverance and thrift. On the other side, the countries with a *long-term orientation* (such as China and Taiwan) tend to endorse and respect the values of tradition, such as fulfilling social obligations and preservation of "face." The long-term orientation is associated with other societal characteristics.

A meta-analysis of studies conducted across 26 countries (Van Hemert, Poortinga, & van de Vijver, 2007) showed that *long-term orientation* is significantly related to emotional expression.

Past Versus Future Orientation

Past, present, future… where do people live, spend their time most? Individual and typological differences in this regard are evident. Some people love to dream about future; other to recall their past memories, yet the others prefer to live in a current moment of their life span.

This internal time location is certainly a subjective experience. Objectively, the absolute time continues passing by evenly and in one direction—from the past to the future, but subjectively individuals experience it differently. The time orientation—a largely unconscious cognitive process—sets up a focus and relative emphasis of personal experiences in temporal categories of past, present, and future (Goldrich, 1967; Kluckhohn & Strodtbeck, 1961; Lee, Liu, & Hu, 2017).

The parameter of *time orientation* ranges in the continuum from a category of past to present and to future indicating the category to which a person gives cognitive attention. This orientation places relative rather than exclusive emphasis on the temporal continuum (Shipp, Edwards, & Lambert, 2009; Zimbardo & Boyd, 1999).

Zimbardo Time Perspective Inventory (ZTPI, Zimbardo & Boyd, 1999) is an individual level measure of five temporal orientations: Past Positive (PP), Past Negative (PN), Present Hedonistic (PH), Present Fatalistic (PF), and Future (F). The instrument has shown cross-cultural validity in more than 20 countries (see for review, Sircova et al., 2014), and it was used in a comprehensive cross-cultural comparison. The results of the recent study that included 12,200 participants across 26 samples from 24 countries confirmed the five temporal orientations across many countries with diverse cultural traditions. Authors, however, do not report cross-cultural differences in those variables (Sircova et al., 2014).

Research with this *Time Perspective Inventory* has revealed several associations of the scores on subscales with mental health problems, self-esteem, spiritual growth, psychological well-being, life satisfaction, positive, and more satisfactory relations with others (see for review, (Sircova et al., 2014). Thus, it is reasonably to expect that time perspective and time orientation can have its effect on emotional life and relationships of people in cultural contexts.

Do countries have past versus future orientations? Although the time orientation is an individual psychological parameter, yet cultural background plays its role in setting up individual preferences (Gonzalez & Zimbardo, 1985; Hill, Block, & Buggie, 2000; Levine, 2008). There are cultural variations in time orientation. Cultures can also be categorized with future, present, and past time orientations. For examples, people from future-oriented cultures tend to store information relevant for the future, think, and communicate about future more than those from present- or past-oriented cultures.

Anthropologists Hall and Hall (1990) suggested that India and Iran are past-oriented countries; the urban United States is oriented to the present and short-term future, while countries of Latin America are both past and present oriented. Authors, however, did not provide a measure of the time orientation, which they took into account.

The dimension of *future orientation* received substantial research attention on both individual and cultural level (see for review, Ashkanasy, Gupta, Mayfield, & Trevor-Roberts, 2004).

Individual future orientation as a dimension reflects the subjective experience of time oriented to the goals and event, which happen in the future (Trommsdorff, 1983). *Cultural future orientation* reflects the extent to which a society encourages such future-oriented behaviors as expectation of delayed gratification and planning

(House et al., 1999). The dimension is considered as a basic value orientation of all cultures (see for detailed review, Ashkanasy, Gupta, Mayfield, & Trevor-Roberts, 2004; Kluckhohn & Strodtbeck, 1961).

A recent rigorous (in terms of methodology) and comprehensive (in terms of global coverage) studies brought a systematic view on this concept. Analysis of the data from the Global Leadership and Organizational Behavior Effectiveness (GLOBE) Research Project, which included 62 countries (Ashkanasy, Gupta, Mayfield, & Trevor-Roberts, 2004) showed that people in North European and North American countries are higher in their *future orientation*, whereas in Eastern European, Latin European, Arab, and Latin American countries are lower in their *future orientation*. The scores of respondents from Asian countries are largely distributed across the whole spectrum.

It should be noted, however, that Western countries are not homogeneous in this variable. There is diversity between countries as well as within multiracial or multiethnic countries. Authors (Ashkanasy, Gupta, Mayfield, & Trevor-Roberts, 2004) also found that within Europe, people in Northern countries (e.g., Germany, the Netherlands, and Austria) are more future oriented than those in the Mediterranean countries (e.g., Italy and Greece). In the United States, European Americans have higher future orientation than African Americans and Hispanics (Brown & Segal, 1996; Graham, 1981; Marin & Marin 1991). Asian Americans are more future-oriented than Blacks (Steinberg et al., 2009). In New Zealand, people of European descent are more future-oriented compared to Māori—the indigenous Polynesian people of New Zealand (Bray, 1970).

2.6.3 The Pace of Life as Cultural Dimension

The Pace of Acting and Communication

Pace of life is the speed of people's everyday activities. What is the speed of walking, working, eating, and speaking? Can this be considered as a cultural dimension related with emotional life and relationship of individuals in a culture?

Levine and his colleagues conducted a series of cross-cultural studies with objective measures (Levine, Lynch, Miyake, & Lucia, 1989; Levine & Norenzayan, 1999). In one study (Levine & Norenzayan, 1999), researchers observed how people walked a 60-foot distance in downtown areas of major cities, the speed of transactions in post office, and accuracy of clocks in 31 countries. Authors found that the pace of life, according to these measures, was fastest in Italy, Ireland, Germany, Switzerland, Japan, and while slowest in Brazil, El Salvador, Mexico, Indonesia, and Syria.

Several ecological and cultural variables correlated with this pace of life (Levine & Norenzayan, 1999). In terms of temperatures, inhabitants of hotter places were slower than those in cooler places. Residents of big cities were faster than those of small towns. People in the countries with vibrant and active economies were faster.

People in individualistic cultures were also faster. Interesting findings were about the effect of pace of life on health and happiness. People in faster places generally have worse health, yet greater happiness.

Temporal norms of life vary among regions, ethnic, and socio-economic subcultures within one country. For example, in the United States, people in the Northeastern states are fast-paced, while people in the West (mostly California) are more relaxed. Northeasterners walk faster, talk faster, work faster, and more often wear watches, compared to people in other American cities.

As for ethnic and socio-economic cultures, American Indians say that they "live on Indian time." Mexican-Americans distinguish the actual time on the clock (*hora inglesa*) and the more casual time (*hora mexicana*). African Americans frequently separate the sense of time of their own culture from the sense of time of European Americans. Their prevailing tempo is very slow, and time is not organized, compared to typically fast and well-scheduled European Americans. Yet, they can speed up their tempos when circumstances call for it. They can be on time when they care to be and are not on time when they do not want to be (Levine, 2008).

A geography of time (Levin, 2008) provides many cross-cultural examples of how people perceive, interpret, behave in time perspective, and how these aspects of their life affect their wealth, health, and happiness. Generally, people living in fast societies and cities are wealthier. Yet, in their lives they experience many stresses which put them at risk in cardiovascular health: they are more likely to suffer coronary heart disease. People in the fast cities are more likely to have higher life satisfaction.

The Pace of Communication

The speed and pace with which people communicate are their typological features that depend on their temperaments and characters. Some people can code, pronounce quickly, and decode the others' messages promptly. They may prefer short or long sentences, simple or complex grammatical and stylistic structures, simple or complex word. Taking into account all these characteristics of communication, their messages might be slow or fast. This can also refer to the way how quickly people develop their relationships.

The dimension of the *message speed* can also characterize the typical patterns of communication prevalent in a society along with the spectrum of slow-fast message speed. According to the cultural dimension of *message speed* (Hall & Hall, 1990), people in *high message speed* cultures prefer fast messages (typical for *low-context cultures*). Such messages are quickly and easily delivered and decoded. They include, for example, prose, headlines, propaganda, TV commercials, simple emotions, and easy relationship familiarity. In the cultures of high-speed messages (e.g., the United States), people are eager to make quick contacts. They tend to disclose and develop relationships rapidly, yet the relationships may be quite shallow. Americans are unbelievably friendly, informal, and compassionate, yet their communication typically does not involve an exchange of deep emotions and confidences (Hall & Hall, 1990). This type of communication and relationship might be viewed as superficial by the people from high-context, slow-message cultures, yet it might be considered as the respect of privacy and confidentiality by the people from low-context, fast-speed cultures.

People in *slow message speed* cultures prefer slow messages (typical for *high-context cultures*). It takes more time and a little more effort to deliver and decode them. The examples include poetry, art, TV documentaries, complex emotions, and deep relationships. In the cultures of slow speed messages, it takes more time to get to know someone well. In these cultures (e.g., many European and Arab countries), people disclose their emotions and launch relationships gradually, yet the established relationships are deep-rooted and long lasting. Therefore, personal relationships and friendships are highly valued (Hall & Hall, 1990). This type of communication and relationship might be viewed as deep and sincere by the people from high-context, slow-message cultures, yet it might be considered as intrusive and indiscreet by the people from low-context, fast-speed cultures.

Within cultures, there are definite individual and typological differences in the preferences of slow and fast speed messages. Yet, the typical cultural patterns, to which some individuals conform better than others, are still evident.

A study (Lee & Boster, 1992) found that speech rate may have different effect on enhancing one's credibility in different cultures. Rapid speech delivery is an effective means to bring more credibility of American speakers (both men and women), as well as of Korean female speakers. However, slow delivery is more effective to increase the credibility of Korean male speakers.

The pace of communication also includes the pace of information flow through a network. How fast or slow? How long does it take a message to come through to reach its addressee? Cultural misunderstanding of the process of information flow often hinders adequate cross-cultural communication. Hall and Hall (1990) provide interesting observations in this regard.

In such *low-context* cultures as Switzerland, Germany, the United States, information cannot flow freely. It is much focused and compartmentalized and therefore, it is slow in transition. Information is used as an instrument to control and command. Different from this, in such *high-context cultures* as the France, Spain, and Japan, information moves rapidly, people live in a sea of information. Interpersonal contact with each other is more important than anything else; information flows freely. People stay in constant contact, stay in touch and to keep up to date. "Because these cultures are also characteristically high-information-flow cultures, being out of touch means to cease to exist as a viable human being" (Hall & Hall, 1990, p. 23).

2.7 Reaction to Ambiguity and Uncertainty as a Cultural Parameter

2.7.1 Personal Tolerance of Ambiguity

Ambiguity tolerance, as a personality trait, determines the way how a person "perceives and processes information about ambiguous situations or stimuli when confronted by an array of unfamiliar, complex, or incongruent clues" (Furnham &

Ribchester, 1995, p.179). This is exactly the situations that a lover frequently meets in his/her love adventures.

Person with low tolerance of ambiguity experiences stress, reacts prematurely, and avoids ambiguous stimuli. At the other extreme of the scale, however, a person with high tolerance for ambiguity perceives ambiguous situations/stimuli as desirable, challenging, and interesting and neither denies nor distorts their complexity of incongruity (Furnham & Ribchester, 1995 p.179).

Ambiguity tolerance, or intolerance, is a personality variable that includes emotional and perceptual components. A person can welcome (or at least accept) or deny emotional ambivalence. A person can tolerate, or be intolerant of cognitive ambiguity.

In recent several decades, researchers have extensively investigated the variable of ambiguity intolerance as a personality trait. They also explored this variable among different groups and countries, correlating it with diverse array of social, political, and religious variables (see for review, Furnham & Ribchester, 1995).

Uncertainty and *ambiguity* of various situations can put tension on people in deciding what to do and how to behave. In some societies, the living in such risky, uncertain, and ambiguous circumstances is typical and normal in life. People adapt to those and, therefore, do not make efforts to avoid them. Some can even enjoy such situations, while the others tolerate. In other societies, the life in risky and ambiguous conditions seems uncomfortable and intolerable. Therefore, people have a strong desire to reduce a chance of uncertainty avoiding such situations.

2.7.2 Culturally Typical Reaction to Uncertainty

Uncertainty Avoidance as a Cultural Dimension

Hofstede's concept of *uncertainty avoidance* as a cultural dimension is similar to the person's *tolerance of ambiguity* as an individual characteristic. They are different. Not being synonymous, they are still related. Avoidance of uncertainty is more wide ranging than intolerance of ambiguity, which implies known alternatives.

This cultural dimension was proposed by Hofstede (1980/1984; Hofstede & Bond, 1984) to describe the attitudes that people have toward ambiguous situations and the beliefs they create to avoid these. Hofstede looked at the distribution of individual differences in societies and found that countries on average vary in their avoidance and tolerance of uncertainty. People in *high uncertainty avoidance cultures* tend to avoid uncertainty more than members of *low uncertainty avoidance cultures*.

How People and Cultures React to the Life with Uncertainty

How people and cultures react to the life that creates uncertainty, stress, and anxiety? Some may seek to increase rules of normative behavior and, thus, avoid uncertainty, while others are better capable to tolerate uncertainty without excess anxiety and stress. Among the countries, which are most likely to be intolerant of ambiguity and avoid uncertainty, are Portugal, Greece, Spain, Belgium, France, Japan, Peru, Chile, and Argentina. Among the countries, which are most tolerant of ambiguity and lowest in uncertainty avoidance, are Ireland, England, Denmark, Sweden, Hong Kong, Singapore, the Philippines, India, and the United States (Hofstede, 1984). There can also be a within-country's cultural variation. For instance, Andersen et al. (1990) revealed that in the United States , intolerance for ambiguity is much higher in southern states than in northern states.

Hofstede (1980/1984) contends that societies deal with various uncertainties, which are caused by nature, social groups, organizations, and other people that cannot be controlled. The cultures of high uncertainty avoidance strive to structure actions, to be more task-oriented and ritualized. He demonstrated how the uncertainty avoidance is related to the studies on national differences concerned with such things as anxiety, achievement, motivation, and values. Individuals and cultures with tendency for *high uncertainty avoidance* tend to avoid risk taking and experience fear of failure, while those with *low uncertainty avoidance* take the risk as it is, without feel fear (Hofstede, 1980/1984; Hofstede, 2001). People in the cultures with high uncertainty avoidance tend to think that "what is different is dangerous," but people in the cultures with low uncertainty avoidance tend to think that "what is different is curious" (Hofstede, 1984, p. 119).

Uncertainty Avoidance and Emotional Life

How does *uncertainty avoidance* as a cultural dimension can affect emotional life of people in different cultural contexts? Some studies (e.g., Hofstede, 1984; Fernandez et al., 2000; Lynn & Martin, 1995; Schimmack, 1996) found that *uncertainty avoidance* in a society is greatly associated with emotionality.

According to Hofstede (1984), the cultures with *strong uncertainty avoidance* (i.e., Greece) tend to be more active and emotional, while in the cultures with *weak uncertainty avoidance* (i.e., Denmark) people are less emotional and relaxed. Some other studies (Arrindell et al., 1997) found that people in the cultures with *strong uncertainty avoidance* experience more negative emotions, higher anxiety, and low subjective well-being. In these cultures, the frequency of anger, fear, and sadness is higher.

The prevalence *of uncertainty avoidance dimension* is associated with cultural variations in the experience of positive or negative emotions—the topic of our primary interest in this book. People in cultures with *high uncertainty avoidance* experience negative emotions more often and experience positive emotions less often than *low uncertainty avoidance* cultures. People in the countries with *high uncertainty avoidance* tend to display more emotions. They adequately recognize such emotions as sadness and fear, compared to the countries with low in uncertainty avoidance (Hofstede, 1984; Schimmack, 1996). They experience high emotional intensity (Basabe et al., 2000).

A study of 21 thousands of respondents (*M* age = 30.2 year) in 48 countries in three time periods of 1980–2000s (Steel, Taras, Uggerslev, & Bosco, 2018) revealed that across its measures in that study, the uncertainty avoidance and subjective well-being do not correlate at the individual level. Nevertheless, happy nations on average have low uncertainty avoidance. Although the effect of uncertainty avoidance on subjective well-being is related to political and economic institutes, yet it is still partially independent from those parameters.

In cultures with *high uncertainty avoidance*, there is a strong desire for consensus. People view deviant behavior as not acceptable. They tend to display emotions more than the individuals from *low uncertainty avoidance* cultures. They openly show their emotions, in particular, expressing more emotion in relationships (Gudykunst, & Matsumoto, 1996).

2.8   The Cultural Values of Survival and Self-Expression

2.8.1   Traditional and Modern Societies

The Theory of Modernization

Modernization theory considers societies based on their economic, social, political, and cultural characteristics and distinguish them along the spectrum between *traditional* and *modern* ones (Inglehart 1997, Inglehart & Baker, 2000; Inglehart & Welzel, 2005). It proposes that two bipolar dimensions differentiate societies: materialism-postmaterialism and modernization- postmodernization. Societies, which are high on materialism scale, highly value survival and security (e.g., economic growth and stable economy), whereas societies, which are high postmaterialism scale, highly value self-expression and tolerance of minorities (e.g., social participation, freedom, and humane society). The *survival values* stress physical and economical security (Inglehart & Baker, 2000), whereas the *self-expression values* focus on quality of life and subjective well-being (Inglehart, 1997, p. 349). Both groups of values influence emotion expression and interpersonal relationship accordingly. Inglehart and his colleagues (Inglehart, 1997; Inglehart & Baker, 2000; Inglehart & Welzel 2005) proposed the term *modernization*—the transition from the societies with prevalence of *survival values* to the societies with prevalence of *self-expression values*.

As for the two essential dimensions of interpersonal relationships—social distance (intimacy vs. social distance) and power status (high vs. low power status), traditional societies put higher value on *power status* over *social distance*, while modern societies put higher value on *social distance* over *power distance*.

Socioeconomic factors play a crucial role in modernization of societies. In their analysis of data from World Value Survey (from 60 countries, 75% of the global population), Inglehart and Baker (2000) demonstrated that socioeconomic parameters largely explain the evolution of countries (1) from cultural values emphasizing survival to the values emphasizing self-expression and (2) from traditional values to secular and rational ones.

Historical religions seem also play its role in modernization, may be in association with current socioeconomic status. The countries originated from Protestant culture highly appreciate self-expression values, while the countries originated from Orthodox culture have low appreciation of these values.

Modernization of Societies and Emotions

Modernization affects many aspects of social behavior and relationship. In particular, as studies discovered (Karandashev et al., 2019) that people's preferences in mating differ in traditional and modern cultures.

> The stable biologically and evolutionarily determined characteristics of physical appearance, such as *smell, skin, body*, etc., are important for one's sensory preferences in romantic attraction in less modernized societies, which are characterized by greater Power Distance, lower Individualism, Indulgence, and Emancipative values. On the other hand, the characteristics of romantic partner's appearance, which are more flexible and easier to change, such as *expressive behavior, dress, dance*, etc., are more important in more modernized societies with lower Power Distance, high value of Individualism, Indulgence, and Emancipation.

The study of association of emotions with life satisfaction in 46 nations (Kuppens et al., 2008) found that despite general tendency that positive emotions were stronger linked to life satisfaction than negative emotions, this positive effect of positive emotions on life satisfaction was bigger in the more modernized countries valuing self-expression (e.g., the United States, Canada, Australia, and the Netherlands) than in countries valuing survival (e.g., Zimbabwe, China, Hungary, and Russia).

Based on the distinction of survival values (prevalent in traditional societies) and self-expressive values (prevalent in modernized societies), the two cultural models of emotions can be proposed: evolutionary-based and self-expressive models. Several studies cited above shed the light on possible profiles of their emotional patterns, yet much more research is needed to elaborate those.

2.8.2   The Modern Cultural Change Toward Modernization of Societies

Multicultural Transformation of Societies

The modern world became immensely multicultural and integrated—"Westernized" in many cases. Mobility and migration take place much more commonly than ever before. Different cultures absorb and acquire similar values in the process of modernization (Hatfield & Rapson, 1996; Leung & Iwawaki, 1988).

The former division between Western and Eastern cultures seems obsolete. Modern societies amalgamate different cultural characteristics. For example, Finland holds some features of both Western and Eastern cultures. It shares values of North European low-context societies—democracy, equality for women, human rights, and ecology, yet their communication style is closer Eastern high-context cultures—introverted, modest, quite, silent, reluctant to interrupt, priority of diplomacy over truth, little body, and facial expressiveness (Nishimura, et al., 2008).

Modernization Shift

Modern Finland reveals a Janus face—one looking forward and another looking backward, as the Roman deity Janus. It resembles a high context culture in many regards, yet throughout recent times it has been changing and acquiring the features of modern lower context societies. People more often use first names, interrupt partners, ask more questions, and practice small talks more convincingly. It is true at least for communication style of the younger generation (Nishimura, Nevgi, & Tella, 2008). So, is the silent Finn reality or a myth? As Salo-Lee (2007), Finish professor of communication believes, it is rather a myth. It is well known by Finns and foreigners, yet the myth is gradually fading away even as a stereotype.

The modern Indian culture has become more westernized. It is rapidly moving toward a modern low-context culture due to travel, trade, television, and technology (Lewis, 1996, 2003; Sen, 2005). Now, they tend to be more dialogue-oriented and favor direct communication. However, the differences between American and Indian styles of communication still remain. A recent cross-cultural study (Kapor, et al., 2003) demonstrated that Indian students use more indirect communication and more positive perception of conversational silence than Americans do. The results showed that Indian communication style became closer to the low-context culture than it traditionally has been (Kapor, et al., 2003).

2.9   Relational Mobility as a Cultural Parameter

2.9.1   The Concept of Relational Mobility

Concept of Relational Mobility

The concept of *relational mobility* has proposed a socio-ecological factor which can explain how much freedom and opportunity a society provides for individuals to choose and change interpersonal relationships based on their personal preferences (Yuki, & Schug, 2012). The *relational mobility* is "the amount of opportunities people have to select new relationship partners in a given society or social context" (Yuki et al., 2007, p.3). In some societies and communities, individuals are embedded in their social network and, therefore, they have few opportunities to select new interaction partners outside of their current relationships. In other societies and communities, however, individuals have many opportunities to select new partners and form relationships. The relational mobility varies in human societies, countries, regions, and different periods of history (Karandashev, 2017).

Relational Mobility and Personal Choice

The level of intergroup and interpersonal *mobility* explains how group memberships and personal relationships evolve through *personal choice* or *environmental affordance* (Adams, 2005; Chen, Chiu, & Chan, 2009; Oishi, Lun, & Sherman, 2007; Schug et al., 2009; Yamagishi & Yamagishi, 1994; Yuki et al., 2007).

People living in societies high in *relational mobility* have many opportunities to meet new acquaintances, build new relationships, and to abandon the relationships that are not interesting or useful for them anymore. They are in relationships due to their personal choice, not due to external societal, community, or family constraints. Relational mobility is a possibility that a society or community provides for individuals to engage in a new relationship when they encounter a new partner.

2.9.2 Relational Mobility and Emotions in Interpersonal Relationships

Relational Mobility Across Cultures

From a socio-ecological approach to culture, the behavioral tendencies, which an individual adopts to attain the desirable outcomes, depend on the social and ecological settings in which they reside. These adaptive strategies lead to the evolvement of cross-cultural differences (Yuki, & Schug, 2012).

Relational mobility as a societal dimension is *higher in modern cultures*, such as the United States, Canada, western, and northern European countries. They view their relationships as voluntary (Wiseman, 1986), usually belong to the groups with overlapping and permeable boundaries (Triandis, 1995), and have more potential partners for their friendships, romantic relationships, and acquaintances. Americans have broad networks of weak ties (Granovetter, 1973). A comprehensive study of relational mobility in 39 societies found that people in the societies characterized by high relational mobility experience and express more "proactive interpersonal behaviors (e.g., self-disclosure and social support) and psychological tendencies that help them build and retain relationships (e.g., general trust, intimacy and self-esteem)" (p. 7521).

People living in traditional societies that are low in *relational mobility* have few opportunities to meet new acquaintances. Environmental and group affordances build and maintain their relationships, rather than their personal choice. In these social contexts, relationships are generally more stable and resilient to change

(Wiseman, 1986; Yamagishi, Jin, & Miller, 1998). Partners are bound to each other by obligation and social institutions.

Generally, relational mobility has been lower in societies with interdependent subsistence styles, such as farming, and in societies with stronger ecological threats. Nowadays, relational mobility is low in many traditional societies in the world, such as in West Africa and East Asia. People are bound to existing relationships in a community which they perceive as obligatory; they have fewer new acquaintances and potential partners for friendship and mating relationships.

Effects of Relational Mobility on Emotional Life

Relational mobility of a society, or community, where people reside, is related to their thinking, emotions, and behaviors. This cultural dimension influence attention, attribution, passionate love, and commitment (San Martin, Schug, & Maddux, 2019; Yuki, & Schug, 2020). Cross-cultural studies have demonstrated that the *relational mobility* affects several aspects of emotions which people experience in relationships, in particular in comparison between North American and East Asian countries (Yamada, Kito, & Yuki, 2017).

The studies have investigated these variables in the United States, Japan (Tsuji, 2002), China (Ho, 1998a), and Ghana (Adams, 2005). In particular, interpersonal relationships are typically more stable and enduring in Eastern societies. For instance, Japanese move residences less frequently than Americans, (Long, 1991).

For example, relational mobility—usually associated with modern cultures—can have impact on experience and expression of interpersonal emotions. For example, individuals may experience *higher passion* in the societies where freedom to choose and replace their partners is culturally acceptable—*high relational mobility*. On the other hand, individuals may be *less passionate* in the societies where stable relationships are expected to be culturally normative—*low relational mobility*. Researchers found (Yamada, Kito, & Yuki, 2017) that in the United States—a society with high relational mobility—individuals are more passionate, while in Japan—a society with low relational mobility—individuals are less passionate toward their romantic partners. In addition to the national differences, authors (Yamada, Kito, & Yuki, 2017) found that the *perceived relational mobility* in local ecology also affects participants' intensity of passion.

2.10   Cultural Values

2.10.1   Recent Theories of Cultural Values

Conception of Values

Cultural values are the broad and trans-situational goals and desired ideas that a society encourages people to pursue in life. These are the general and abstract conceptions of what is good and right, what is desirable and appropriate. People belonging to one culture implicitly or explicitly share their cultural value priorities. Throughout decades, the studies of values have been very extensive in many social disciplines, such as cultural anthropology, social and cultural psychology.

The general interdisciplinary conception of values, which reflects the views of many scholars, has been specified by Schwartz (1992, 1994) in six main characteristics:

1. Values are beliefs linked inextricably to affect.
2. Values refer to desirable goals that motivate action.
3. Values transcend specific actions and situations.
4. Values serve as standards or criteria.
5. Values are ordered by importance relative to one another.
6. The relative importance of multiple values guides action.

Different values express different types of goals and corresponding motivation. Personal values reflect personal goals, while cultural values express the goals of culture.

Trompenaars Theory of Cultural Values

This theory and method were developed primarily for investigation of cultural values in organizational, corporate, and managerial cultures across the globe. The survey of values in an extensive sample of thousands of respondents (organization employees) in 46 countries (Smith, Peterson, &Wang, 1996; Trompenaars & Hampden-Turner, 1998) identified two country-level dimensions of values: (1) *egalitarian commitment* versus *conservatism* and (2) *utilitarian involvement* versus *loyal involvement*.

The first cultural dimension is *egalitarian commitment* versus *conservatism*. In the cultures encouraging *egalitarian commitment*, people tend to endorse general and abstract principles of what is right and just. They believe that impersonal criteria (e.g., qualifications) rather than a personal relationship should be taken into account in organization. In the cultures encouraging *conservatism*, people usually have the preference of their immediate circle of personal relationships, rather than of outsiders. This value type includes such values as priority of personal or family relationships in business relationships and the loyalty to a boss.

The second cultural dimension is *utilitarian involvement* versus *loyal involvement*. *Utilitarian involvement* means the engagement in an organization based on how it meets the individual goals of a person. *Loyal involvement* means the engagement in an organization based on a long-lasting identification with the organization when its goals are perceived as own personal.

Schwartz Theory of Cultural Values

Schwartz (1992, 1994, 1999, 2003, 2006) has developed and extensively studied two major conceptions of human values:

(1) The theory of basic personal values, which include ten broad personal values (e.g., hedonism, security, self-direction, achievement, conformity, and benevolence).
(2) The theory of cultural values, which include seven cultural values (e.g., embeddedness, autonomy, egalitarianism, mastery, and harmony).

The first theory describes basic values on individual level. These are personality characteristics. The second theory describes values on cultural level. These are normative value orientations characterizing cultures (Schwartz, 2011).

In this chapter, we focus on the cultural values that characterize society, not individuals. These are the cultural parameters of society.

Based on the extensive survey of the value preferences of thousands of respondents (students and teachers) from 63 countries, Schwartz (1992, 1994, 1999) identified seven country-level value orientations.

- *Embeddedness* emphasizes maintaining the status quo, propriety, and restraint of actions or inclinations that might disrupt the solidary group or the traditional order in which people are embedded.
- *Intellectual autonomy* emphasizes the desirability of individuals' pursuing their own ideas and intellectual directions independently.
- *Affective autonomy* emphasizes the desirability of individuals' pursuing affectively positive experience.
- *Hierarchy* emphasizes the legitimacy of an unequal distribution of power, roles, and resources.
- *Egalitarianism* emphasizes transcendence of selfish interests in favor of voluntary commitment to promoting the welfare of others.
- *Mastery* emphasizes getting ahead through active self-assertion.
- *Harmony* emphasizes fitting harmoniously into the environment (quoted in Smith, Peterson, & Schwartz, 2002, p.193).

Further analysis (Schwartz, 1999, 2003, 2006, 2014) concluded in seven country-level types of values, which organized into three dimensions—*embeddedness* versus *autonomy*, *hierarchy* versus *egalitarianism*, and *mastery* versus *harmony*, as a quasi-circumplex structure. Researchers have replicated these culture-level value dimensions and their structure in cultural samples from 60 nations (e.g., Schwartz & Bardi, 2001; Schwartz & Boehnke, 2004).

The dimension *embeddedness* versus *autonomy* describes how society regulates the boundaries between an individual and a larger group.

In cultures high in *autonomy*, societies view individuals as independent (autonomous) from their group. Autonomous individuals are expected to appreciate their own uniqueness, follow their own ideas, preferences, abilities, and express their own internal preferences, motives, and feelings. The theory and research (Schwartz, 1994, 1999, 2006) distinguish two kinds of autonomy: *intellectual* and *affective*.

The society with high cultural value of *intellectual autonomy* motivates people to pursue personal interests and their own ideas. This value inspires independent intellectual aspirations and growth. *Affective autonomy* reflects the value of pleasure, exciting life, and encourages people to pursue their own positive affective experience.

In cultures high in *embeddedness,* individuals are closely embedded in their in-group.

The major value and meaning of individual life are associated with identification of a person with group, social relationships, shared way of life, and pursuing shared goals of the group. This collective orientation of *embeddedness* in society implies respect for social order and tradition, and the maintenance of proper relationships with people in the immediate social environment surrounding a person. This value suggests individuals restraining their dispositions and actions that may disrupt the solidary of group.

The cultural dimension of *hierarchy* versus *egalitarianism* defines how society maintains the social order and how people coordinate with others, consider their welfare, and manage their interdependencies.

In cultures high in *hierarchy,* society is regarded as a hierarchical system of social relationships with ascribed roles. The system of social power functions to ensure the responsible behavior of its members. It is expected that individuals perceive this hierarchical distribution of roles and comply with the obligations associated with their roles. They should accept status differentials in power and unequal resource distribution as legitimate. The values of authority, social power, wealth, and humility are very important in hierarchical societies.

In cultures high in *egalitarianism,* society expects that individuals perceive each other as equals and take responsibility for each other. Individuals are expected to respect equality in interpersonal relationships. The value of *egalitarianism* implies voluntary commitment to cooperate with others and desire to promote the well-being of other members of society. Social justice, honesty, and responsibility are on a high priority.

The dimension of *harmony* versus *mastery* describes the societal values of how individuals regulate the relations with other people and environment.

In cultures high in *harmony,* people are expected to fit in environment or social relationships. In ecological sense, the value of harmony highlights the importance of unity with the environment, adjustment to nature, and self-transcendence. In relationships with others, this value emphasizes the social and interpersonal adjustment. People are motivated to understand and appreciate the things as they are, rather than to direct and change those.

In cultures high in *mastery,* society emphasizes the need for control of situations over the adjustment to social environment. It encourages individuals to master and change the environment. The value of *mastery* highlights the importance of getting ahead. Individuals are motivated to actively pursue personal goals, despite the expense of others. The personal characteristics of a high priority are *self-assertion,* along with competence, daring, ambition, and success.

2.10.2   Influence of Cultural Values on Emotions

Since values are the beliefs that are closely intertwined with affect, it is reasonable to expect that personal and cultural values greatly influence emotional experience and expression of people in a culture. As Schwartz (2012) commented, "When values are activated, they become infused with feeling. People for whom independence is an important value become aroused if their independence is threatened, despair when they are helpless to protect it, and are happy when they can enjoy it" (p.3). The value orientations, which people endorse, should impact their emotional experience and expression by facilitating or discouraging certain emotions.

Cultural values as the emotion-linked beliefs can be the core constituents of cultural models of emotions. *Affective autonomy* is an evident candidate for this role and this country-levels dimension should be associated with people's tendency to more emotional expressiveness. This expectation, however, was not supported; the variables of culture-level values did not explain the differences in effect sizes (Van Hemert, Poortinga, & van de Vijver, 2007).

Cultural values are associated with the complexity of emotions across cultures, according to correlations of Schwartz cultural values with scores of emotions differentiation (Matsumoto et al., 2009). In particular, people in the countries with higher cultural values of Hierarchy and Embeddedness showed higher emotion differentiation. On the other side, people in the countries with lower Affective autonomy and lower Egalitarianism showed higher emotion differentiation.

Researchers found (Wong, Bond, & Rodriguez Mosquera, 2008) that cultural value orientations are associated with the means of the *nonverbal expression of emotions* on the cultural-level. In particular, in the societies with high value of *hierarchy,* people tend to inhibit their nonverbal expression of such negative emotions, as fear, guilt, and shame. In the societies with high value of *autonomy* and low value of *embeddedness*, people are willing to nonverbally express joy to a greater degree than in the societies with high in embeddedness value. In the societies with high value of *mastery,* people talk less during experience of anger—low verbal expression.

Other study, however, found that cultural values are associated with the tendencies to suppress emotions (Matsumoto, Yoo, & Nakagawa, 2008). People tend to suppress their emotions more frequently in the cultures with high value of *embeddedness* and *hierarchy* and low value in *affective autonomy* and *egalitarianism*. Such suppression of emotional expression helps them maintain social order and adapt to hierarchical relationships.

The way how people cope with adaptation to the life in a new country also reflects the emotional experience. A study showed (Bardi, & Guerra, 2011) that cultural value dimensions, such as *embeddedness* versus *autonomy* and *hierarchy* versus *egalitarianism* affect psychological strategies of coping. The sample included 292 international university students in their first year in Britain.

As authors reasonably hypothesized, the participants from the countries *high in embeddedness* would use the coping strategies emphasizing tradition and group interests, while those from countries *high in autonomy*—the coping strategies focused on decision and action.

Authors also expected that students from countries *high in hierarchy,* which are based on fixed hierarchy and roles, would use passive strategies, while those from countries *high in egalitarianism,* which are based on encouragement of personal responsibility and responsible behavior, the active strategies.

Overall, the results of the study showed that participants, who came from the countries high in *embeddedness* and *hierarchy,* more commonly employ *emotion-focused* or *avoidant coping.* However, the research design had the confounding variables, which did not allow identifying whether cultural values or adaptation difficulties affected coping strategies. Researchers interpreted data in light of the greater cultural distance in cultural values in home countries compared to Britain as host country. This causes subsequent difficulties in adaptation to this new country (Bardi, & Guerra, 2011).

References

Aaker, J., Drolet, A., & Griffin, D. (2008). Recalling mixed emotions. *Journal of Consumer Research, 35,* 268–278.

Adams, G. (2005). The cultural grounding of personal relationship: Enemyship in North American and West African worlds. *Journal of Personality and Social Psychology, 88*(6), 948–968.

Adams, S. J., & van Eerde, W. (2010). Time use in Spain: Is polychronicity a cultural phenomenon? *Journal of Managerial Psychology, 25*(7), 764–776.

Aiello, J. R. (1987). Human spatial behavior. In D. Stokols & I. Altman (Eds.), *Handbook of environmental psychology* (pp. 389–504). New York, NY: Wiley.

Almaney, A., & Alwan, A. (1982). *Communicating with the Arabs.* Prospect Heights, IL: Waveland.

Andersen, P. (1988). Explaining intercultural differences in nonverbal communication. In L. A. Samovar & R. E. Porter (Eds.), *Intercultural communication: A reader* (pp. 272–281). Belmont, CA: Wadsworth.

Andersen, P. A. (1985). Nonverbal immediacy in interpersonal communication. In A. W. Siegman & S. Feldstein (Eds.), *Multichannel integrations of nonverbal behavior* (pp. 1–36). Hillsdale, NI: Lawrence Erlbaum.

Andersen, P. A. (1999). *Nonverbal communication: Forms and functions.* Mountain View, CA: Mayfield.

Andersen, P. A. (2000). Explaining intercultural differences in nonverbal communication. In L. A. Samovar & R. E. Porter (Eds.), *Intercultural communication: A reader* (9th ed., pp. 258–279). Belmont, CA: Wadsworth.

Andersen, P. A., & Andersen, J. F. (1984). The exchange of nonverbal communication. In L. A. Samovar & R. E. Porter (Eds.), *Intercultural communication: A reader.* Belmont, CA: Wadsworth.

Andersen, P. A., & Bowman, L. (1999). Positions of power: Nonverbal influence in organizational communication. In L. K. Guerrero, J. A. DeVito, & M. L. Hecht (Eds.), *The nonverbal communication reader: Classic and contemporary readings* (pp. 317–334). Prospect Hetehts, IL: Waveland.

Andersen, P. A., Hecht, M. L., Hoobler, G. D., & Smallwood, M. (2003). Nonverbal communication across cultures. In W. B. Gudykunst (Ed.), *Cross-cultural and intercultural communication* (pp. 73–90). Thousand Oaks, CA: Sage.

Andersen, P. A., Lustig, M. W., & Andersen, J. E. (1990). Changes in latitude, changes in attitude: The relationship between climate and interpersonal communication predispositions. *Communication Quarterly, 38*, 291–311.

Andersen, P. A., Lustig, M. W., & Andersen, J. F. (1987). Regional patterns of communication in the United States: A theoretical perspective. *Communication Monographs, 54*, 128–144.

Arrindell, W. A., Hatzichristou, C., Wensink, J., Rosenberg, E., van Twillert, B., Stedema, J., & Meijer, D. (1997). Dimensions of national culture as predictors of cross-national differences in subjective well-being. *Personality and Individual Differences, 23*, 37–53.

Ashkanasy, N., Gupta, V., Mayfield, M., & Trevor-Roberts, E. (2004). Future orientation. In R. House, P. Changes, M. Javidan, P. Dorfman, & W. Gupta (Eds.), *Culture, leadership, and organizations: The GLOBE study of 62 societies* (pp. 282–342). Thousand Oaks, CA: Sage.

Bardi, A., & Guerra, V. M. (2011). Cultural values predict coping using culture as an individual difference variable in multicultural samples. *Journal of Cross-Cultural Psychology, 42*(6), 908–927.

Barnlund, D. C. (1975). Communicative styles in two cultures: Japan and the United States. In A. Kendon, R. M. Harris, & M. R. Key (Eds.), *Organization of behavior in face-to-face interaction* (pp. 427–456). The Hague, The Netherlands: Mouton.

Basabe, N., Paez, D., Valencia, J., Gonzalez, J. L., Rimé, B., & Diener, E. (2002). Cultural dimensions, socioeconomic development, climate, and hedonic level. *Cognition & Emotion, 16*, 103–125.

Basabe, N., Paez, D., Valencia, J., Rimé, B., Pennebaker, J., Diener, E., & González, J. L. (2000). Sociocultural factors predicting subjective experience of emotion: A collective level analysis. *Psicothema, 12*(Suppl 1), 55–69.

Basabe, N., & Ros, M. (2005). Cultural dimensions and social behavior correlates: Individualism-collectivism and Power distance. *International Review of Social Psychology, 18*(1), 189–225.

Bernstein, B. (1971). *Class, codes and control: Vol. 1. Theoretical studies toward a sociology of language*. London, UK: Roudedge & Kegan Paul.

Bluedorn, A. C., Kalliath, T. J., Strube, M. J., & Martin, G. D. (1999). Polychronicity and the Inventory of Polychronic Values (IPV) the development of an instrument to measure a fundamental dimension of organizational culture. *Journal of Managerial Psychology, 14*(3/4), 205–231.

Bluedorn, A. C., Kaufman, C. F., & Lane, P. M. (1992). How many things do you like to do at once? An introduction to monochronic and polychronic time. *Academy of Management Perspectives, 6*(4), 17–26.

Boiger, M., De Deyne, S., & Mesquita, B. (2013). Emotions in "the world": Cultural practices, products, and meanings of anger and shame in two individualist cultures. *Frontiers in Psychology, 4*: Article 867. https://doi.org/10.3389/fpsyg.2013.00867

Boiger, M., Mesquita, B., Uchida, Y., & Barrett, L. F. (2013). Condoned or condemned: The situational affordance of anger and shame in the US and Japan. *Personality and Social Psychology Bulletin, 39*(4), 540–553.

Bond, M. H. (1993). Emotions and their expression in Chinese culture. *Journal of Nonverbal Behavior, 17*(4), 245–262.

Boroditsky, L., & Gaby, A. (2010). Remembrances of times east: Absolute spatial representations of time in an Australian aboriginal community. *Psychological Science, 21*(11), 1635–1639.

Bray, D. H. (1970). Extent of future time orientation: A cross-ethnic study among New Zealand adolescents. *British Journal of Educational Psychology, 40*, 200–208.

Brewer, M. B., & Chen, Y.-R. (2007). Where (who) are collectives in collectivism? Toward conceptual clarification of individualism and collectivism. *Psychological Review, 114*, 133–151.

Brislin, R. W., & Kim, E. S. (2003). Cultural diversity in people's understanding and use of time. *Applied Psychology: An International Review, 52*, 363–382. https://doi.org/10.1111/1464-0597.00140

Brown, C. M., & Segal, R. (1996). Ethnic differences in temporal orientation and its implications for hypertension management. *Journal of Health and Social Behavior, 37*, 350–361.

Brown, R., & Gilman, A. (1960). The pronouns of power and solidarity. In T. A. Sebeok (Ed.), *Style in language* (pp. 252–276). Cambridge, MA: MIT Press.

Buck, R. (1984). *The communication of emotion.* New York, NY: Guilford Press.

Cambra, R. E., & Klopf, D. W. (1979). *A cross-cultural analysis of interpersonal needs.* Paper presented at the speech association intercultural communication conference, Honolulu, HI.

Chan, D. K. (1994). COLINDEX: A refinement of three collectivism measures. In U. Kim, H. C. Triandis, C. Kagitcibasi, S. Choi, & G. Yoon (Eds.), *Individualism and collectivism: Theory, method, and applications* (pp. 200–210). Thousand Oaks, CA: Sage.

Chen, J., Chiu, C.-y., & Chan, F. S.-F. (2009). The cultural effects of job mobility and the belief in a fixed world. *Journal of Personality and Social Psychology, 97,* 851–865.

Chentsova-Dutton, Y. E., & Tsai, J. L. (2010). Self-focused attention and emotional reactivity: The role of culture. *Journal of Personality and Social Psychology, 98,* 507–519.

Choe, Y. (2001). *Intercultural conflict patterns and intercultural training implications for Koreans.* Paper presented at the 16th Biennal world communication association conference, Cantabria, Spain.

Cline, R. J., & Puhl, C. A. (1984). Gender, culture, md geography: A comparison of seating arrangements in the United States and Taiwan. *International Journal of Intercultural Relations, 8,* 199–219.

Condon, J. C., & Yousef, F. (1983). *An introduction to intercultural communication.* Indianapolis, IN: Bobbs-Merrill.

Diener, E., Diener, M., & Diener, C. (1995). Factors predicting the subjective Well-being of nations. *Journal of Personality and Social Psychology, 69,* 851–864.

Dittmar, H., Bond, R., Hurst, M., & Kasser, T. (2014). The relationship between materialism and personal well-being: A meta-analysis. *Journal of Personality and Social Psychology, 107,* 879–924.

Donohue, W. (1990). *The new freedom: Individualism and collectivism in the social lives of Americans.* New Brunswick, NJ: Transaction Publishers.

Eid, M., & Diener, E. (2001). Norms for experiencing emotions in different cultures: Inter- and intra-national differences. *Journal of Personality and Social Psychology, 81*(5), 869–885.

Elliot, S., Scott, M. D., Jensen, A. D., & McDonough, M. (1981). Perceptions of reticence: A cross-cultural investigation. *Annals of the International Communication Association, 5*(1), 591–602.

Feldman, S., Mont-Reynaud, R., & Rosenthal, D. (1992). When East meets West: The acculturation of values of Chinese adolescents in the U.S. and Australia. *Journal of Research on Adolescence, 2,* 147–173.

Fernandez, I., Carrera, P., Sanchez, F., Paez, D., & Candia, L. (2000). Differences between cultures in emotional verbal and non-verbal reactions. *Psicothema, 12*(Suppl 1), 83–92.

Fiske, A. P. (2002). Using individualism and collectivism to compare cultures—A critique of the validity and measurement of the constructs: Comment on Oyserman et al. (2002). *Psychological Bulletin, 128,* 78–88.

Fitzpatrick, J., Liang, S., Feng, D., Crawford, D., Tsorell, G., & Morgan-Fleming, B. (2006). Social values and self-disclosure: A comparison of Chinese native, Chinese resident (in U.S.) and North American spouses. *Journal of Comparative Family Studies, 37,* 113–127.

Fuhrman, O., & Boroditsky, L. (2010). Cross-cultural differences in mental representations of time: Evidence from an implicit nonlinguistic task. *Cognitive Science: A Multidisciplinary Journal, 34*(8), 1430–1451.

Furnham, A., & Ribchester, T. (1995). Tolerance of ambiguity: A review of the concept, its measurement and applications. *Current Psychology, 14*(3), 179–199.

Furukawa, E., Tangney, J., & Higashibara, F. (2012). Cross-cultural continuities and discontinuities in shame, guilt, and pride: A study of children residing in Japan, Korea and the USA. *Self and Identity, 11,* 90–113.

Gelfand, M., Spurlock, D., Sniezek, J., & Shao, L. (2000). Culture and social prediction: The role of information in enhancing confidence in social predictions in the United States and China. *Journal of Cross-Cultural Psychology, 31,* 498–516.

Gerin-Lajoie, M., Richards, C. L., & McFadyen, B. J. (2006). The circumvention of obstacles during walking in different environmental contexts: A comparison between older and younger adults. *Gait & Posture, 24*, 364–369.

Goldrich, J. M. (1967). A study in time orientation: The relation between memory for past experience and orientation to the future. *Journal of Personality and Social Psychology, 6*(2), 216–221. https://doi.org/10.1037/h0024556

Goldstein, B. Z., & Tamura, K. (1975). *Japan and America: A comparative study in language and culture.* Rutland, VT: Charles E. Turtle.

Gonzalez, A., & Zimbardo, P. G. (1985). Time in perspective. *Psychology Today, 19*(3), 20–26.

Graham, R. J. (1981). The role of perception of time in consumer research. *Journal of Consumer Research, 7*, 335–342.

Granovetter, M. (1973). The strength of weak ties. *American Journal of Sociology, 78*, 1360–1380.

Gudykunst, W. B. (1983). Uncertainty reduction and predictability of behavior in low-and high-context cultures: An exploratory study. *Communication Quarterly, 31*(1), 49–55.

Gudykunst, W. B., & Kim, Y. Y. (1984). *Communicating with strangers: An approach to intercultural communication.* Reading, MA: Addison-Wesley.

Gudykunst, W. B., & Matsumoto, Y. (1996). Cross-cultural variability of communication in personal relationships. In W. B. Gudykunst, S. TingToomey, & T. Nishida (Eds.), *Communication in personal relationships across cultures* (pp. 19–56). Thousand Oaks, CA: Sage.

Hall, E. T. (1966). *The hidden dimension* (2nd ed.). Garden City, NY: Anchor Books/Doubleday.

Hall, E. T. (1976). *Beyond culture.* Garden City, NY: Doubleday/Anchor.

Hall, E. T. (1983). *The dance of life: The other dimension of time.* Garden City, NY: Doubleday.

Hall, E. T. (2000). Context and meaning. In L. A. Samovar & R. E. Porter (Eds.), Intercultural communication: A reader, 9th ed. (pp. 34–43). Belmont, CA: Wadsworth Publishing Co.

Hall, E. T., & Hall, E. T. (1984). *The dance of life: The other dimension of time.* Anchor.

Hall, E. T., & Hall, M. R. (1990). *Understanding cultural differences.* Yarmouth, ME: Intercultural Press.

Halliday, M. (1973). *Explorations in the functions of language.* New York, NY: Elsevier.

Halliday, M. (1978). *Language as social semiotic: The social interpretation of language and meaning.* Baltimore, MD: University Park.

Hamamura, T. (2012). Are cultures becoming individualistic? A cross-temporal comparison of individualism–collectivism in the United States and Japan. *Personality and Social Psychology Review, 16*(1), 3–24.

Hasegawa, T., & Gudykunst, W. B. (1998). Silence in Japan and the United States. *Journal of Cross-Cultural Psychology, 29*, 668–684.

Hatfield, E., & Rapson, R. L. (1996). *Love and sex: Cross-cultural perspectives.* Boston, MA: Allyn and Bacon.

Hijirida, K., & Sohn, H. M. (1986). Cross-cultural patterns of honorifics and sociolinguistic sensitivity to honorific variables: Evidence from English, Japanese, and Korean. *Papers in Linguistics, 19*, 365–401.

Hill, O. W., Block, R. A., & Buggie, S. E. (2000). Culture and beliefs about time: Comparisons among Black Americans, Black Africans, and White Americans. *The Journal of Psychology, 134*, 443–461.

Ho, D. Y. F. (1998a). Interpersonal relationships and relationship dominance: An analysis based on methodological relationism. *Asian Journal of Social Psychology, 1*, 1–16.

Hofstede, G. (1984). *Culture's consequences: International differences in work-related values.* Newbury Park, CA: SAGE. Originally published in 1980.

Hofstede, G. (1991). *Cultures and organizations. Software of the mind.* London, UK: McGraw-Hill.

Hofstede, G. (1998). Attitudes, values and organizational culture: Disentangling the concepts. *Organization Studies, 19*(3), 477–493.

Hofstede, G. (2001). *Culture's consequences: Comparing values, behaviors, institutions, and organizations across nations* (2nd ed.). Thousand Oaks, CA: Sage.

Hofstede, G. (2011). Dimensionalizing cultures: The Hofstede model in context. *Online readings in psychology and culture, 2*(1), 2307–0919.

Hofstede, G., & Bond, M. H. (1984). Hofstede's culture dimensions: An independent validation using Rokeach's value survey. *Journal of Cross-Cultural Psychology, 15*(4), 417–433.

Hofstede, G., & Minkov, M. (2010). Long-versus short-term orientation: New perspectives. *Asia Pacific Business Review, 16*(4), 493–504.

Hong, J., & Lee, A. Y. (2010). Feeling mixed but not torn: The moderating role of construal level in mixed emotions appeals. *Journal of Consumer Research, 37*, 456–472.

Horenstein, V. D. P., & Downey, J. L. (2003). A cross-cultural investigation of self-disclosure. *North American Journal of Psychology, 5*, 373–386.

House, R. J., Ranges, P. J., Ruiz-Quintanilla, S. A., Dorfman, P. W., Javidan, M., Dickson, M., et al. (1999). Cultural influences on leadership and organizations: Project GLOBE. In W. Mobley, J. Gessner, & V. Arnold (Eds.), *Advances in global leadership, 1* (pp. 171–234). Greenwich, CT: JAL.

Hui, C. H., & Triandis, H. C. (1986). Individualism-collectivism: A study of cross-cultural researchers. *Journal of Cross-Cultural Psychology, 17*(2), 225–248.

Hymes, D. H. (1971). Sociolinguistics and the ethnography of speaking. In E. Ardener (Ed.), *Social anthropology and language* (pp. 47–93). London, UK: Tavistock.

IJzerman, H., & Semin, G. R. (2010). Temperature perceptions as a ground for social proximity. *Journal of Experimental Social Psychology, 46*, 867–873.

Inglehart, R. (1997). *Modernization and postmodernization: Cultural, economic, and political change in 43 societies*. Princeton, NJ: Princeton University Press.

Inglehart, R., & Baker, W. E. (2000). Modernization, cultural change, and the persistence of traditional values. *American Sociological Review, 65*(1), 19–51. https://doi.org/10.2307/2657288

Inglehart, R., & Welzel, C. (2005). *Modernization, cultural change, and democracy: The human development sequence*. Cambridge, UK: Cambridge University Press.

Ishii, S. (1973). Characteristics of Japanese nonverbal communication behavior. *Communication, 2*, 163–180.

Kapoor, S., Hughes, P., Baldwin, J. R., & Blue, J. (2003). The relationship of individualism-collectivism in India and the United States. *International Journal of Intercultural Relations, 27*, 683–700.

Karandashev, V. (2017). *Romantic love in cultural contexts*. New York, NY: Springer.

Karandashev, V. , Zarubko, E. Artemeva, V. Evans, M., Morgan, K. A. D., Neto, F., … Purvis, J. (2019). Cross-Cultural Comparison of Sensory Preferences in Romantic Attraction. *Sexuality and Culture*, published online 3 July 2019 https://doi.org/10.1007/s12119-019-09628-0

Kashima, E. S., & Kashima, Y. (1998). Culture and language: The case of cultural dimensions and personal pronoun use. *Journal of Cross-Cultural Psychology, 29*(3), 461–486.

Kashima, Y., Yamaguchi, S., Kim, U., Choi, S., Gelfand, M., & Yuki, M. (1995). Culture, gender, and self: A perspective from individualism-collectivism research. *Journal of Personality and Social Psychology, 69*, 925–937.

Killen, M., & Wainryb, C. (2000). Independence and interdependence in diverse cultural contexts. *New Directions for Child and Adolescent Development, 2000*(87), 5–21.

Kim, D., Pan, Y., & Park, H. S. (1998). High-versus low-context culture: A comparison of Chinese, Korean, and American cultures. *Psychology & Marketing, 15*(6), 507–521.

Kim, J., Seo, M., Yu, H., & Neuendorf, K. (2014). Cultural differences in preference for entertainment messages that induce mixed responses of joy and sorrow. *Human Communication Research, 40*, 530–552.

Kitayama, S., & Markus, H. R. (2000). The pursuit of happiness and the realization of sympathy: Cultural patterns of self, social relations, and well-being. In E. Diener & E. M. Suh (Eds.), *Culture and subjective well-being* (pp. 113–161). Cambridge, MA: MIT Press.

Kitayama, S., Markus, H. R., & Kurokawa, M. (2000). Culture, emotion, and well-being: Good feelings in Japan and the United States. *Cognition and Emotion, 14*, 93–124.

Kitayama, S., Markus, H. R., Matsumoto, H., & Norasakkunkit, V. (1997). Individual and collective process in the construction of the self: Self-enhancement in the United States and self-criticism in Japan. *Journal of Personality and Social Psychology, 72*, 1245–1267.

Kitayama, S., Mesquita, B., & Karasawa, M. (2006). Cultural affordances and emotional experience: Socially engaging and disengaging emotions in Japan and the United States. *Journal of Personality and Social Psychology, 91*(5), 890–903.

Kitayama, S., Park, H., Sevincer, A. T., Karasawa, M., & Uskul, A. K. (2009). A cultural task analysis of implicit independence: Comparing North America, Western Europe, and East Asia. *Journal of Personality and Social Psychology, 97*(2), 236–255. https://doi.org/10.1037/a0015999

Klopf, D. W., & Thompson, C. A. (1991). Nonverbal immediacy differences among Japanese, finish and American university students. *Perceptual and Motor Skills, 73*, 209–210.

Kluckhohn, F. R., & Strodtbeck, F. L. (1961). *Variations in value orientations.* Evanston, IL: Row, Peterson.

Koopmann-Holm, B., & Tsai, J. L. (2014). Focusing on the negative: Cultural differences in expressions of sympathy. *Journal of Personality and Social Psychology, 107*, 1092–1115.

Kuppens, P., Realo, A., & Diener, E. (2008). The role of positive and negative emotions in life satisfaction judgment across nations. *Journal of Personality and Social Psychology, 95*, 66–75.

La France, M., & Mayo, C. (1978). Cultural aspects of nonverbal communication. *International Journal of Intercultural Relations, 2*(1), 71–89.

Lay, C., Fairlie, P., Jackson, S., Ricci, T., Eisenberg, J., Sato, T., … Melamud, A. (1998). Domain-specific allocentrism-idiocentrism: A measure of family connectedness. *Journal of Cross-Cultural Psychology, 29*(3), 434–460.

Lee, H. O., & Boster, F. J. (1992). Collectivism-individualism in perceptions of speech rate: A cross-cultural comparison. *Journal of Cross-Cultural Psychology, 23*(3), 377–388.

Lee, S., Liu, M., & Hu, M. (2017). Relationship between future time orientation and item nonresponse on subjective probability questions: A cross-cultural analysis. *Journal of Cross-Cultural Psychology, 48*(5), 698–717.

Leung, K., & Iwawaki, S. (1988). Cultural collectivism and distributive behavior. *Journal of Cross-Cultural Psychology, 19*, 35–49.

Levine, R. N. (2008). *A geography of time: On tempo, culture, and the pace of life.* New York, NY: Basic Books.

Levine, R. V., Lynch, K., Miyake, K., & Lucia, M. (1989). The type A city: Coronary heart disease and the pace of life. *Journal of Behavioral Medicine, 12*, 509–524.

Levine, R. V., & Norenzayan, A. (1999). The pace of life in 31 countries. *Journal of Cross-Cultural Psychology, 30*, 178–205.

Lewis, R. D. (1996). *When cultures collide. Managing successfully across cultures.* London, UK: Nicholas Brealey Publishing.

Lewis, R. D. (2003). *The intercultural imperative: Global trends in the 21st century.* Yarmouth, ME: Intercultural Press.

Lim, T.-S. (2003). Language and verbal communication across cultures. In W. B. Gudykunst (Ed.), Handbook of international and intercultural communication (pp. 53–71). Thousand Oaks, CA: Sage.

Lindquist, J. D., & Kaufman-Scarborough, C. (2007). The polychronic—Monochronic tendency model: PMTS scale development and validation. *Time & Society, 16*(2–3), 253–285.

Little, K. B. (1968). Cultural variations in social schemata. *Journal of Personality and Social Psychology, 10*, 1–7.

Long, L. (1991). Residential mobility differences among developed countries. *International Regional Science Review, 1*, 133–147.

Lustig, M. W., & Koester, J. (1999). *Intercultural competence: Interpersonal communication across culture* (3rd ed.). New York, NY: Longman.

Lynn, R., & Martin, T. (1995). National differences for thirty-seven nations in extraversion, neuroticism, psychoticism and economic, demographic and other correlates. *Personality and Individual Differences, 19*, 403–406.

Lytle, A. L., Brett, J. M., Barsness, Z. I., Tinsley, C. H., & Janssens, M. (1995). A paradigm for confirmatory cross-cultural research in organizational behavior. *Research in Organizational Behavior, 17*, 167–214.

Marin, G., & Marin, B. V. (1991). *Research with Hispanic populations*. Newbury Park, CA: Sage.

Markus, H. R., & Kitayama, S. (1991). Culture and the self: Implications for cognition, emotion, and motivation. *Psychological Review, 98*, 224–253.

Marsella, A. J., De Vos, G. A., & Hsu, F. L. (Eds.). (1985). *Culture and self: Asian and Western perspectives*. New Yours, NY: Tavistock Publications.

Matsumoto, D. (1991). Cultural influences on facial expressions of emotion. *Southern Communication Journal, 56*, 128–137.

Matsumoto, D., Kudoh, T., & Takeuchi, S. (1996). Changing patterns of individualism and collectivism in the United States and Japan. *Culture & Psychology, 2*(1), 77–107.

Matsumoto, D., & Kupperbusch, C. (2001). Idiocentric and allocentric differences in emotional expression, experience, and the coherence between expression and experience. *Asian Journal of Social Psychology, 4*(2), 113–131.

Matsumoto, D., Takeuchi, S., Andayani, S., Kouznetsova, N., & Krupp, D. (1998). The contribution of individualism vs. collectivism to cross-national differences in display rules. *Asian Journal of Social Psychology, 1*(2), 147–165.

Matsumoto, D., Yoo, S. H., & Fontaine, J. (2009). Hypocrisy or maturity? Culture and context differentiation. *European Journal of Personality, 23*(3), 251–264.

Matsumoto, D., Yoo, S. H., & Nakagawa, S. (2008). Culture, emotion regulation, and adjustment. *Journal of Personality and Social Psychology, 94*(6), 925–937.

McDaniel, E. R., & Andersen, P. A. (1998). Intercultural variations in tactile communication. *Journal of Nonverbal Communication, 22*, 59–75.

McGrath, J. E., & Tschan, F. (2004). *Temporal matters in social psychology: Examining the role of time in the lives of groups and individuals*. Washington, DC: American Psychological Association. https://doi.org/10.1037/10659-000

Mesquita, B., & Leu, J. (2007). The cultural psychology of emotion. In S. Kitayama & D. Cohen (Eds.), *Handbook of cultural psychology* (pp. 734–759). New York, NY: Guilford Press.

Migliore, L. A. (2011). Relation between big five personality traits and Hofstede's cultural dimensions: Samples from the USA and India. *Cross Cultural Management: An International Journal, 18*, 38–54.

Minkov, M., & Hofstede, G. (2012a). Hofstede's fifth dimension: New evidence from the world values survey. *Journal of Cross-Cultural Psychology, 43*(1), 3–14.

Moore, R. L. (2005). Generation ku: Individualism and China's millennial youth. *Ethnology, 44*(4), 357–376.

Morling, B., Kitayama, S., & Miyamoto, Y. (2002). Cultural practices emphasize influence in the United States and adjustment in Japan. *Personality and Social Psychology Bulletin, 28*(3), 311–323.

Morsbach, H. (1976). Aspects of nonverbal communication in Japan. In L. Samovar & R. Porter (Eds.), *Intercultural communication: A reader* (2nd ed.). Belmont, CA: Wadsworth.

Neto, F. (2007). Love styles: A cross-cultural study of British, Indian, and Portuguese college students. *Journal of Comparative Family Studies, 38*(2), 239–254.

Nishimura, S., Nevgi, A., & Tella, S. (2008). Communication style and cultural features in high/low context communication cultures: A case study of Finland, Japan and India. *Teoksessa A. Kallioniemi (toim.), Uudistuva ja kehittyvä ainedidaktiikka*. Ainedidaktinen symposiumi, 8(2008), 783–796.

Nonis, S. A., Teng, J. K., & Ford, C. W. (2005). A cross-cultural investigation of time management practices and job outcomes. *International Journal of Intercultural Relations, 29*(4), 409–428.

Noon, J. M., & Lewis, J. R. (1992). Therapeutic strategies and outcomes: Perspectives from different cultures. *British Journal of Medical Psychology, 65*(2), 107–117.

Oishi, S., Lun, J., & Sherman, G. D. (2007). Residential mobility, self-concept, and positive affect in social interactions. *Journal of Personality and Social Psychology, 93*, 131–141.

Oliver, R. (1971). *Communication and culture in ancient India and China*. Syracuse, NY: Syracuse University Press.

Oyserman, D., Coon, H. M., & Kemmelmeier, M. (2002). Rethinking individualism and collectivism: Evaluation of theoretical assumptions and meta-analyses. *Psychological Bulletin, 128*(1), 3–72.

Ozdemir, A. (2008). Shopping malls: Measuring interpersonal distance under changing conditions and across cultures. *Field Methods, 20*, 226–248.

Paez, D., & Vergara, A. (1995). Culture differences in emotional knowledge. In J. A. Russel, J. M. Fernández-Dols, A. S. R. Manstead, & J. C. Wellenkamp (Eds.), *Everday conceptions of emotion*. Dordrecht, The Netherlands/Boston, MA/London, UK: Kluwer Academic Press.

Palmer, G. B. (1996). *Toward a theory of cultural linguistics*. Austin, TX: University of Texas Press.

Patterson, M. L. (1983). *Nonverbal behavior: A functional perspective*. New York, NY: Springer.

Patterson, M. L., & Edinger, J. A. (1987). A functional analysis of space in social interaction. In A. W. Siegman & S. Feldstein (Eds.), *Nonverbal behavior and communication* (pp. 523–562). Mahwah, NJ: Lawrence Erlbaum Associates.

Philipsen, G. (1992). *Speaking culturally: Explorations in social communication*. Albany, NY: State University of New York Press.

Pimental, E. (2000). Just how do I love thee? Marital relations in urban China. *Journal of Marriage and the Family, 62*, 32–47.

Porter, R. E., & Samovar, L. A. (1998). Cultural differences in emotional expression: Implications for intercultural communication. In P. A. Andersen & L. K. Guerrero (Eds.), *Handbook of communication and emotion: Research, theory, applications, and contexts* (pp. 452–472). San-Diego, CA: Academic.

Potter, S. H. (1988). The cultural construction of emotion in rural Chinese social life. *Ethos, 16*(2), 181–208.

Putnam, R. (2000). *Bowling alone: The collapse and revival of American community*. New York, NY: Simon & Schuster.

Rapp, M. A., & Gutzmann, H. (2000). Invasions of personal space in demented and nondemented elderly persons. *International Psychogeriatrics, 12*, 345–352.

Regan, P. C., Jerry, D., Narvaez, M., & Johnson, D. (1999). Public displays of affection among Asian and Latino heterosexual couples. *Psychological Reports, 84*(Suppl 3), 1201–1202.

Remland, M. S., Jones, T. S., & Brinkman, H. (1991). Proxemic and haptic behavior in three European countries. *Journal of Nonverbal Behavior, 15*, 215–232.

Remland, M. S., Jones, T. S., & Brinkman, H. (1995). Interpersonal distance, body orientation, and touch: Effects of culture, gender, and age. *The Journal of Social Psychology, 135*(3), 281–297.

Ruby, M. B., Falk, C. F., Heine, S. J., Villa, C., & Silberstein, O. (2012). Not all collectivisms are equal: Opposing preferences for ideal affect between East Asians and Mexicans. *Emotion, 12*, 1206–1209.

Safdar, S., Friedlmeier, W., Matsumoto, D., Yoo, S. H., Kwantes, C. T., Kakai, H., & Shigemasu, E. (2009). Variations of emotional display rules within and across cultures: A comparison between Canada, USA, and Japan. *Canadian Journal of Behavioural Science/Revue canadienne des sciences du comportement, 41*(1), 1–10. https://doi.org/10.1037/a0014387

Salo-Lee, L. (2007). *Tämän päivän "suomalaisuus"*. [Today's 'Finnishness']. http://www.kantti.net/luennot/2007/humanismi/03_salo-lee.shtml. (retrieved 11.18.2019). (cited in Nishimura, S., Nevgi, A., & Tella, S. (2008, p. 788).

San Martin, A., Schug, J., & Maddux, W. W. (2019). Relational mobility and cultural differences in analytic and holistic thinking. *Journal of Personality and Social Psychology, 116*(4), 495–518. https://doi.org/10.1037/pspa0000142

Savani, K., Alvarez, A., Mesquita, B., & Markus, H. R. (2013). Feeling close and doing well: The prevalence and motivational effects of interpersonally engaging emotions in Mexican and European American cultural contexts. *International Journal of Psychology, 48*, 682–694.

Scherer, K. R., Matsumoto, D., Wallbott, H. G., & Kudoh, T. (1988). Emotional experience in cultural context: A comparison between Europe, Japan, and the United States. In K. R. Scherer (Ed.), *Facets of emotion: Recent research* (pp. 5–30). Hillsdale, NJ: Lawrence Erlbaum.

Schimmack, U. (1996). Cultural influences on the recognition of emotion by facial expressions: Individualistic or Caucasian cultures? *Journal of Cross-Cultural Psychology, 27*, 37–50.

Schug, J., Yuki, M., Horikawa, H., & Takemura, K. (2009). Similarity attraction and actually selecting similar others: How cross-societal differences in relational mobility affect interpersonal similarity in Japan and the USA. *Asian Journal of Social Psychology, 12*, 95–103.

Schvaneveldt, P., Young, M., & Schvaneveldt, J. (2001). Dual resident marriages in Thailand: A comparison of two cultural groups of women. *Journal of Comparative Family Studies, 32*, 347–360.

Schwartz, S. (2003). Mapping and interpreting cultural differences around the world. In H. Vinken, J. Soeters, & P. Ester (Eds.), *Comparing cultures, dimensions of culture in a comparative perspective* (pp. 43–73). Leiden, The Netherlands: Brill.

Schwartz, S. (2006). A theory of cultural value orientations: Explication and applications. *Comparative Sociology, 5*(2–3), 137–182.

Schwartz, S. H. (1992). Universals in the content and structure of values: Theoretical advances and empirical tests in 20 countries. *Advances in Experimental Social Psychology, 25*, 1–65.

Schwartz, S. H. (1994). Beyond individualism/collectivism: New cultural dimensions of values. In U. Kim, H. C. Triandis, C. Kagitcibasi, S. Choi, & G. Yoon (Eds.), *Individualism and collectivism: Theory, method and applications* (pp. 85–119). Thousands Oaks, CA: Sage.

Schwartz, S. H. (1999). Cultural value differences: Some implications for work. *Applied Psychology: An International Review, 48*, 23–48.

Schwartz, S. H. (2011). Values: Cultural and individual. In F. J. R. van de Vijver, A. Chasiotis, & S. M. Breugelmans (Eds.), *Fundamental questions in cross-cultural psychology* (pp. 463–493). Cambridge, MA: Cambridge University Press. https://doi.org/10.1017/CBO9780511974090.019

Schwartz, S. H. (2012). An overview of the Schwartz theory of basic values. *Online readings in Psychology and Culture, 2*(1), 2307–0919.

Schwartz, S. H. (2014). National culture as value orientations: Consequences of value differences and cultural distance. In *Handbook of the economics of art and culture* (Vol. 2, pp. 547–586). Amsterdam, The Netherlands: Elsevier.

Schwartz, S. H., & Bardi, A. (2001). Value hierarchies across cultures: Taking a similarities perspective. *Journal of Cross-Cultural Psychology, 32*, 268–290.

Schwartz, S. H., & Boehnke, K. (2004). Evaluating the structure of human values with confirmatory factor analysis. *Journal of Research in Personality, 38*, 230–255.

Schwartz, S. H., Cieciuch, J., Vecchione, M., Davidov, E., Fischer, R., Beierlein, C., ... Dirilen-Gumus, O. (2012). Refining the theory of basic individual values. *Journal of Personality and Social Psychology, 103*(4), 663–688.

Schwartz, S. H., & Ros, M. (1995). Values in the west: A theoretical and empirical challenge to the individualism-collectivism cultural dimension. *World Psychology, 1*, 99–122.

Sen, A. (2005). *The argumentative Indian: Writings on Indian history, culture and identity*. London, UK: Penguin Books.

Shipp, A. J., Edwards, J. R., & Lambert, L. S. (2009). Conceptualization and measurement of temporal focus: The subjective experience of the past, present, and future. *Organizational Behavior and Human Decision Processes, 110*(1), 1–22.

Shuter, R. (1976). Proxemics and tactility in Latin America. *Journal of Communication, 26*, 46–62.

Sircova, A., van de Vijver, F. J. R., Osin, E., Milfont, T. L., Fieulaine, N., Kislali-Erginbilgic, A., ... Boyd, J. N. (2014). A global look at time: A 24-country study of the equivalence of the Zimbardo time perspective inventory. *SAGE Open, 4*, 1–12. https://doi.org/10.1177/2158244013515686

Smith, P., & Bond, M. H. (1999). *Social psychology across cultures* (2nd ed.). Needham Heights, MA: Allyn & Bacon.

Smith, P. B., Peterson, M. F., & Schwartz, S. H. (2002). Cultural values, sources of guidance, and their relevance to managerial behavior: A 47-nation study. *Journal of Cross-Cultural Psychology, 33*(2), 188–208.

Smith, P. B., Peterson, M. F., & Wang, Z. M. (1996). The manager as mediator of alternative meanings. *Journal of International Business Studies, 27*, 115–137.

Sorokowska, A., Sorokowski, P., Hilpert, P., Cantarero, K., Frackowiak, T., Ahmadi, K., ... Blumen, S. (2017). Preferred interpersonal distances: a global comparison. *Journal of Cross-Cultural Psychology, 48*(4), 577–592.

Steel, P., Schmidt, J., & Schultz, J. (2008). Refining the relationship between personality and subjective Well-being. *Psychological Bulletin, 134*, 138–161.

Steel, P., Taras, V., Uggerslev, K., & Bosco, F. (2018). The happy culture: A theoretical, meta-analytic, and empirical review of the relationship between culture and wealth and subjective well-being. *Personality and Social Psychology Review, 22*(2), 128–169.

Steinberg, L., Graham, S., O'Brien, L., Woolard, J., Cauffman, E., & Banich, M. (2009). Age differences in future orientation and delay discounting. *Child Development, 80*, 28–44.

Stephan, C. W., Stephan, W. G., Saito, I., & Barnett, S. M. (1998). Emotional expression in Japan and the United States: The nonmonolithic nature of individualism and collectivism. *Journal of Cross-Cultural Psychology, 29*(6), 728–748.

Sussman, N. M., & Rosenfeld, H. M. (1982). Influence of culture, language and sex on conversational distance. *Journal of Personality and Social Psychology, 42*, 66–74.

Tamir, M., Schwartz, S. H., Cieciuch, J., Riediger, M., Torres, C., Scollon, C., … Vishkin, A. (2016). Desired emotions across cultures: A value-based account. *Journal of Personality and Social Psychology, 111*, 67–82.

Tamura, T., & Lau, A. (1992). Connectedness versus separateness: Applicability of family-therapy to Japanese families. *Family Process, 31*, 319–340.

Triandis, H. (1995). *Individualism and collectivism*. San Francisco, CA: Westview Press.

Triandis, H. C. (1994). *Culture and social behaviour*. New York, NY: McGraw-Hill.

Triandis, H. C., Bontempo, R., Villareal, M. J., Asai, M., & Lucca, N. (1988). Individualism and collectivism: Cross-cultural perspectives on self-ingroup relationships. *Journal of Personality and Social Psychology, 54*, 323–338.

Triandis, H. C., Chan, D. K. S., Bhawuk, D. P., Iwao, S., & Sinha, J. B. (1995). Multimethod probes of allocentrism and idiocentrism. *International Journal of Psychology, 30*(4), 461–480.

Triandis, H. C., McCusker, C., & Hui, C. H. (1990). Multimethod probes of individualism and collectivism. *Journal of Personality and Social Psychology, 47*, 1363–1375.

Trommsdorff, G. (1983). Future orientation and socialization. *International Journal of Psychology, 18*, 381–406.

Trompenaars, F., & Hampden-Turner, C. (1998). *Riding the waves of culture: Understanding diversity in global business* (2nd ed.). New York, NY: McGraw Hill.

Tsai, J. L., & Clobert, M. (2019). Cultural influences on emotion: Empirical patterns and emerging trends. In S. Kitayama & D. Cohen (Eds.), *Handbook of cultural psychology* (2nd ed., pp. 292–318). New York, NY: Guilford Press.

Tsai, J. L., Knutson, B., & Fung, H. H. (2006). Cultural variation in affect valuation. *Journal of Personality and Social Psychology, 90*(2), 288–307.

Tsai, J. L., Levenson, R. W., & Carstensen, L. L. (2000). Autonomic, subjective, and expressive responses to emotional films in older and younger Chinese Americans and European Americans. *Psychology and Aging, 15*(4), 684–693.

Tsai, J. L., Miao, F. F., Seppala, E., Fung, H. H., & Yeung, D. Y. (2007). Influence and adjustment goals: Sources of cultural differences in ideal affect. *Journal of Personality and Social Psychology, 92*, 1102–1117.

Tsuji, R. (2002). *Estimating acquaintanceship volume in Japan and US*. Paper presented at the second joint conference of the mathematical sociology in Japan and in America. Vancouver, Canada.

Uchida, Y., & Kitayama, S. (2009). Happiness and unhappiness in east and west: Themes and variations. *Emotion, 9*, 441–456.

Uchida, Y., Norasakkunkit, V., & Kitayama, S. (2004). Cultural constructions of happiness: Theory and empirical evidence. *Journal of Happiness Studies, 5*(3), 223–239.

Uchida, Y., Townsend, S. S. M., Markus, H. R., & Bergsieker, H. B. (2009). Emotions as within or between people? Cultural variation in lay theories of emotion expression and inference. *Personality and Social Psychology Bulletin, 35*, 1427–1439.

Van Hemert, D. A., Poortinga, Y. H., & van de Vijver, F. J. (2007). Emotion and culture: A meta-analysis. *Cognition and Emotion, 21*(5), 913–943.

Vandello, J. A., & Cohen, D. (1999). Patterns of individualism and collectivism across the United States. *Journal of Personality and Social Psychology, 77*, 279–292.

Vrij, A., & Winkel, F. W. (1991). Cultural patterns in Dutch and Surinam nonverbal behavior: An analysis of simulated police/citizens encounters. *Journal of Nonverbal Behavior, 15*, 169–184.

Webb, J. D., & Weber, M. J. (2003). Influence of sensory abilities on the interpersonal distance of the elderly. *Environment and Behavior, 35*, 695–711.

Weisz, J. R., Rothbaum, F. M., & Blackburn, T. C. (1984). Standing out and standing in: The psychology of control in America and Japan. *American Psychologist, 39*(9), 955–969.

Williams, P., & Aaker, J. L. (2002). Can mixed emotions peacefully coexist? *Journal of Consumer Research, 28*(4), 636–649.

Wiseman, J. (1986). Friendship: Bonds and binds in a voluntary relationship. *Journal of Social and Personal Relationships, 3*(2), 191–211.

Wong, S., Bond, M. H., & Rodriguez Mosquera, P. M. (2008). The influence of cultural value orientations on self-reported emotional expression across cultures. *Journal of Cross-Cultural Psychology, 39*(2), 224–229.

Würtz, E. (2005). Intercultural communication on web sites: A cross-cultural analysis of web sites from high-context cultures and low-context cultures. *Journal of Computer-Mediated Communication, 11*(1), 274–299.

Yamada, J., Kito, M., & Yuki, M. (2017). Passion, relational mobility, and proof of commitment: A comparative socio–ecological analysis of an adaptive emotion in a sexual market. *Evolutionary Psychology, 15*(4), 1474704917746056.

Yamagishi, T., & Jin, N.,& Miller, A.S. (1998). In-group favoritism and culture of collectivism. *Asian Journal of Social Psychology, 1*, 315–328.

Yamagishi, T., & Yamagishi, M. (1994). Trust and commitment in the United States and Japan. *Motivation and Emotion, 18*, 129–166.

Yuki, M., & Schug, J. (2012). Relational mobility: A socioecological approach to personal relationships. In O. Gillath, G. Adams, & A. Kunkel (Eds.), *Decade of Behavior 2000– 2010. Relationship Science: Integrating Evolutionary, Neuroscience, and Sociocultural Approaches* (pp. 137–151). Washington, DC: American Psychological Association. https://doi.org/10.1037/13489-007

Yuki, M., & Schug, J. (2020). Psychological consequences of relational mobility. *Current Opinion in Psychology, 32*, 129–132.

Yuki, M., Schug, J., Horikawa, H., Takemura, K., Sato, K., Yokota, K., & Kamaya, K. (2007). *Development of a scale to measure perceptions of relational mobility in society.* CERSS working paper 75, Center for Experimental Research in Social Sciences, Hokkaido University.

Yum, J. O. (1988). The impact of Confucianism on interpersonal relationships and communication patterns in East Asia. *Communication Monographs, 55*, 374–388.

Zimbardo, P. G., & Boyd, J. N. (1999). Putting time in perspective: A valid, reliable individual-differences metric. *Journal of Personality and Social Psychology, 77*, 1271–1288.

Chapter 3
Theories, Examples of Cultural Models, and Methods to Explore Those

3.1 Theories and Examples of Cultural Models

3.1.1 Conception of Cultural Models

Cultural Models in Multidisciplinary Research

Throughout recent decades, the theories and research of *cultural models* have become popular in humanities, behavioral, and social disciplines. The concept of *cultural model* attracts interest of anthropology (e.g., Bennardo, 2018a, 2018b; Bennardo & De Munck, 2014; Kronenfeld, 2008; Plaut, 2002; Strauss, 1992), linguistics (e.g., Geeraerts, 2003; Holland & Quinn, 1987; Kristiansen & Dirven, 2008; White, 1987), medical science (e.g., Angel & Williams, 2000; Garro, 1994; Kirmayer & Sartorius, 2007; Weiss, 1988), cognitive science (Bruner, 1986, 1990; Nisbett & Miyamoto, 2005; Shore, 1996), developmental psychology (e.g., Keller, 2003; Keller et al., 2006; Lamm & Keller, 2007; Suizzo, 2002), the psychology of self (e.g., Cross & Gore, 2003; Vignoles et al., 2016) and emotions (e.g., Bachen & Illouz, 1996; Wong & Tsai, 2007) as a framework for explanation of cultural phenomena. Various definitions are quite similar or overlapping.

Conceptual Definition of Cultural Model

Cultural models are the *cognitive schemas* or *mental models* of worlds that are collectively shared by the members of a society and organize knowledge into systemic units of meaning. They are relatively simple or complex units of the core knowledge. The concept of *cultural model* is deemed to advance the basic units of analysis that goes beyond dimensional analysis. The *cultural model* is represented as a structure consisting of core and peripheral components depicted as the nodes with certain values. Cultural concepts, their features, ideal emotions, culturally important events can be the units of analysis represented in the structure. The model is a cognitive structure containing cultural knowledge shared by people in a cultural community.

The *cultural model* might have intellectual and pragmatic knowledge of how to think, feel, and behave (Kronenfeld, 2008). It serves as a repository of cultural knowledge and motivates behavior (D'Andrade, 1992; De Munck, 2019; Holland & Quinn, 1987; Kronenfeld, 2008; Strauss, 1992). Individuals are agents and subjects of socially constructed and imposed cultural worlds (Holland, Lachicotte, Skinner, & Cain, 1998). According to *Cultural Model Theory* (Bennardo, 2018a, 2018b; Bennardo & de Munck, 2020), culture is mental knowledge shared by people in a particular community. The theory (Bennardo, 2018a, 2018b) assumes that the *locus of culture* is the *minds of individuals*. The communities may be territorially based within countries, geographic regions, or not. It may also be any social group that acknowledges itself as a culture, in which individuals share their identity. The latest examples of cultures might be the various Internet-based groups. This knowledge, which constitutes cultures, is structured as a set of *mental models*, or *cultural models* that are shared by individuals as the components of culture. Some scholars (e.g., Lowe, 2019), however, comment that *cultural models* reflect not only the knowledge shared by a group of individuals, but also the *shared knowledge*, which have origins in *culturally mediated experiences*.

Cultural model is collectively held knowledge, yet individual members of a cultural community have their personal representations of this collective knowledge. Therefore, cultural models can be studied both on cultural and individual levels. Even though in many studies the concept of cultural model is used to represent an ideal model of how people in a culture understand it, yet it is possible to employ the concept of cultural model to represent the typical model of real behavior, thought, and feelings.

Research of Cultural Models in Anthropology and Psychology

Cultural models have become a popular theoretical framework and methodology of research in anthropology (e.g., Bennardo, 2018a, 2018b; Bennardo & De Munck, 2014; De Munck & Bennardo, 2019; De Munck & Kronenfeld, 2016; Holland et al., 1998; Kronenfeld, 2008, 2018) and psychology (e.g., Fehr, 1994; Fehr & Russell, 1984, 1991). Anthropologists have used the term *cultural model* to describe patterns of ideas and practices associated with specific social, cultural, and psychological phenomena. For example, a recent survey administered in populations of Europeans, North Americans, Latino- and Native-Americans, South Asians, South-East Asians, Africans, and Pacific Islanders provided empirically based typology of cultural models (Bennardo & De Munck, 2014).

The growing popularity of the *Cultural Model Theory* in *cultural anthropology* for exploring different aspects of cultural reality was reflected in a number of recent publications on the topic (see for review e.g., Bennardo, 2018a, 2018b; De Munck

& Bennardo, 2019), and particularly in the publication of a special issue of the *Journal of Cultural Cognitive Science* (Bennardo & de Munck, 2020).

The concept of *cultural models* also developed in psychology and communication studies, especially in application to affective science. Mesquita and Leu (2007) describe *cultural models* as the *meanings* and *practices* that emotions accommodate within social and cultural contexts. Specific meanings and practices of *self* and *relationships* in these *contexts* are of special importance. *Cultural models* provide frameworks for socialization reflecting the demands of socioeconomic structure of a society, type of community, social and cultural environment, and human ecology (Karandashev, 2017; Keller et al., 2006).

Cultural models describe how thoughts, emotions, and actions occur in everyday life of a society. *Cultural models* in the context of this book are the *typical patterns of behaviors, beliefs, thoughts, and emotions*, which many people in a culture share with each other due to common cultural background learned from their upbringing.

Cultural Models of Emotions as the Typologies of Emotional Life

The concept of *emotional style* that was proposed in anthropology (Middleton, 1989), for example, sounds like the definition of *cultural model of emotions*. It is "the normative organization of emotions, their indigenous classification, form of communication, intensities of expression, contexts of expression, and patterns of linkage with each other and with other domains of culture" (p. 188). Emotional style describes the cultural ordering of emotions in societies. The eight elements of emotional style (constitutive and regulative rules, communication, linkage, salience, dynamics, dissonance, distancing) which author proposed essentially identify the *dimensions of emotions* as *sociocultural constructions*.

Cultural models in many respects resemble cultural *types* and *styles* and can be used in certain contexts as synonymous.

3.1.2 Examples of Cultural Models in Social Science

Cultural Models of Context Differentiation

Here are several examples of the cultural models that scholars have developed so far. *Cultural models of context differentiation* were useful in cognitive psychology, while the models of the self were useful in developmental psychology and psychology of emotions.

Research has demonstrated that cultural factors influence human perceptual processes (see for review, Nisbett & Miyamoto, 2005). The *cultural model of perceptual processes* of people in Western cultures is *context-independent* and *analytic* concentrating on a salient object *independently* of its context. The *cultural model of perceptual processes* of people in Asian cultures is *context-dependent* and *holistic*, taking into account the relationship between the object and the context in which the object is located. Authors have presented an abundance of research on mechanisms that cause such differences in perception that is not cross-culturally universal (Nisbett & Miyamoto, 2005). Although authors did not explicitly call these two types of perception as cultural models, yet essentially they are. A set of perceptual characteristics serves as the criteria for differentiation of those.

Cultural Models of Psychological Development

Three cultural models of development were proposed in psychology: the model of *independence*, the model of *interdependence*, and the model of *autonomous relatedness* (Kagitçibasi, 1996, 2005). Two dimensions—(1) the dimension of interpersonal distance with the poles of relatedness and separateness and (2) the dimension of agency with the poles of autonomy and heteronomy—were used to construct these models. The combinations of the poles of two underlying independent dimensions created corresponding models. Three cultural models were characterized as follow:

> The model of independence prioritizes the perception of the individual as separate, autonomous, bounded, and self-contained. Socialization strategies focus on mental states and personal qualities to support self-enhancement and self-maximization. The model of independence characterizes urban, educated families in industrialized and post-industrialized information societies.
> The model of interdependence prioritizes the individual as interrelated with others and heteronomous (coagent). Socialization strategies focus on the acceptance of norms and hierarchies to contribute to the harmonic functioning of the social unit, in particular, the family. The model of interdependence characterizes rural, subsistence-based, mainly farming families.
> The model of autonomous relatedness combines interpersonal relatedness with autonomous functioning. Socialization strategies focus on both harmonic integration into the family and autonomy as an agent. The model of autonomous relatedness portrays the urban, educated, middle-class families in societies with an interrelated cultural heritage. (Keller et al., 2006, p. 156)

As one can see, the typological analysis based on combination of two cultural dimensions was used in creating these models.

Cultural Models of Attachment

Several other models have been developed in a similar way, as a combination of two dimensions. For example, the typology of attachment was constructed as a combination of the two dimensions—anxiety and avoidance, and included the following styles (1) *secure attachment,* (2) *anxious-ambivalent attachment,* (3) *anxious-avoidant attachment,* and (4) *disorganized attachment* (e.g., Bartholomew & Horowitz, 1991; Brennan, Clark, & Shaver, 1998; Keller, 2018). The European American and West European studies of attachment in children have dominated this area of research and considered *secure attachment* as a *normative model*. Multiple cross-cultural studies of 1980–1990s (see for review Keller, 2013; van IJzendoorn & Kroonenberg, 1988; van IJzendoorn & Sagi-Schwartz, 2008) compared the distribution of these types of attachments in many cultural samples in attempts to find cultural patterns. However, the meta-analyses of cross-cultural data obtained in those studies revealed that *intracultural variation* of attachment styles is much larger in comparison with *intercultural variation* (van IJzendoorn & Kroonenberg, 1988). Thus, results diminished the role of culture.

The problem was, however, that the attachment theory was methodologically ethnocentric and did not take into account culturally different childrearing philosophies and socialization strategies. Definition of attachment and its measurement reflected the Western middle-class cultural *concept of psychological autonomy*. These cultural views and values of many non-Western and in particular rural social and ecological environments considerably differ from this conception. Researchers (see for review Keller, 2013, 2018; Quinn & Mageo, 2013) have expressed their critiques questioning *categorization of attachment* as *secure* versus *insecure* and *measurement* of this dimension as cross-culturally applicable. Authors also argued that the concepts related to the category of *insecure attachment* and the experimental design of *Strange Situation* measuring it are *ethnocentric* (Quinn & Mageo, 2013).

As for cross-cultural development, Keller (2013, 2018) proposed to go beyond the traditional conceptions and methodology of *attachment* and *stranger anxiety* research, which assumed *psychological autonomy* as a cultural value. She conceptualized the attachment theory in a culture-sensitive framework that incorporates the cultural values of non-Western and rural cultures. Author (Keller, 2013) proposed a strategy and an empirical cross-cultural research program that takes into account evolutionary as well as cultural foundations of attachment, including such cultural practices as culturally specific socialization, multiple caregiving arrangements. Thus, models of infancy varying across cultural contexts determine the diverse cultural models of attachment (Keller, 2003, 2007).

Cultural Models for Understanding Illness

Cultural models for understanding illness can include several types depending on the criteria which medical researchers employ in each case:

1. Explanatory models, which make causal attributions and impute specific mechanisms or processes of pathophysiology
2. Prototypes, which are salient images or exemplars drawn from personal experience, family, friends, mass media, and popular culture that are used to reason analogically about one's own condition
3. Implicit models and procedural knowledge that may be difficult to articulate because they are embedded in body practices and ways of experiencing distress (Kirmayer & Sartorius, 2007, p. 832).

Kirmayer and Sartorius (2007) suggest that explanations and attributions of symptoms can amplify those symptoms, and therefore give rise to culture-specific types of hypochondriacal worry, panic disorder, and medically unexplained symptoms. Authors maintain that *cultural models* influence how people experience and report their symptoms, how they reflect psychophysiology, which symptoms they pay attention to, how they attribute and interpret the symptoms, what kind of coping and treatment they seek. Depending on cultural explanations, unique symptoms and concerns may rise. Cultural explanatory models also illuminate the prevalence and significance of clinical presentations of symptoms and syndromes and determine whether the symptoms cause rise of anxiety, help-seeking, and disability. Cultural models also contribute to psychopathological processes.

Authors (Kirmayer & Sartorius, 2007) provide the examples of how cultural models of explanation can affect not only experience of symptoms, but also their associations with somatic syndromes. For example,

losing semen in the urine is associated with "*dhat* syndrome" in India, based on the notion that semen concentrates vital energy;
    epigastric burning is associated with *hwa-byung* in Korea ("fire illness"), based on the notion of an imbalance of "fire" as a basic constituent of the body;
    heat in the head is a nonspecific symptom commonly reported in equatorial Africa, based on notions of the importance of central heat in the constitution of the person (Kirmayer & Sartorius, 2007, p. 835).

The symptoms are more prevalent in some cultures because they constitute a part of an illness prototype. For example, loss of consciousness was reported more frequently in the Puerto Rico than in other parts of North America because of the influence of the cultural template for *ataque de nervios*, an "attack of nerves" that is associated with such symptoms as crying, shouting, and dissociative behavior, which includes loss of consciousness (Kirmayer & Sartorius, 2007, p. 835).

In this case, the amplification of certain symptoms—due to their culturally specific explanations and attributions, and culturally prototypical associations of those symptoms with some syndromes serve as a complex set of primary criteria in the definitions of these cultural models of illness. The cultural beliefs prevalent in a culture determine the development of these models.

3.1.3 Pan-Cultural and Cultural Approaches to Study Cultural Models of Emotions

Etic Approach in Cultural Studies

Cross-cultural research distinguishes the *etic* and *emic* approach to the studies. Researchers following the *etic approach* describe and explore emotions in terms of the constructs, which are developed in a general theoretical framework assuming that this frame is cross-culturally universal. From this assumption of universality, studies investigate cultural similarities and differences in the constructs. These pancultural constructs and dimensions differ in the degree and relative positioning across cultures (Ronen & Shenkar, 1985). It is largely a quantitative type of research.

These cultural studies assume that Western constructs and instruments have the same meanings in other cultures. Therefore, they employed them in non-Western societies for comparison. Such a comparative method demonstrated ethnocentrism (Nisbet, 1971).

The *etic approach* has been extensively present in research of emotions in psychology, sociology, and communication studies. Anthropology and linguistics employ this approach less frequently. Abundance of studies from this approach is dispersed through the chapters of this book.

Adaptation of research instruments developed in one culture to other cultural settings is a typical example of etic methodology. In this case, scholars assume that emotional constructs are cross-culturally universal in their nature and conceptions, yet differ in their degree across cultures. Conceptual equivalence implies measurement equivalence.

Several analytical techniques have been used to explore measurement equivalence (Hui & Triandis, 1985). Among those, *multi-group confirmatory factor analysis* has been applied especially frequently (Steenkamp & Baumgartner, 1998; Vandenberg & Lance, 2000). In factor analysis, researchers utilize a correlation/covariance matrix as an input.

Conceptually similar, yet different method is a *multi-group latent class factor analysis* (Clogg & Goodman, 1985; Hagenaars, 1990; Morren, Gelissen, & Vermunt, 2011; Vermunt & Magidson, 2005). This method runs as a concurrent factor analysis in several groups. The multiple group approach uses the comparison of measurement models that are different on the level of heterogeneity (inequivalence), which is caused by some exogenous (grouping) variable (McCutcheon, 1987, 2002). The method analyzes the cross-classification of the responses on scale items. In latent-class models, researchers treat indicators and latent variables as categorical variables. (Hagenaars, 1990; McCutcheon, 1987, 2002). Normal distribution, homogeneity of variances, linear relationship, or other traditional modelling assumptions are not expected (Magidson & Vermunt, 2004). The *latent-class factor analysis* (LCFA) also allows detecting and controlling the extreme *response bias* in the cross-cultural data set (Kankarash & Moors, 2011; Moors, 2003; Morren et al., 2011).

Emic Approach in Cultural Studies

Researchers following the *emic approach* describe and explore emotions in terms of the constructs, which are developed in a culturally specific frame and are presumably culturally different from other cultures. This approach highlights cultural differences, cultural relativism, and demonstrates that behavior is qualitatively distinctive across cultures. It is largely a qualitative type of research (Karandashev, 2017; Karandashev et al., 2019). Emic approach strives to understand and describe the observations and interpretations of situations, behavior, and mental processes from participants' views.

This approach is quite typical for such disciplines exploring emotions in different cultural contexts, as anthropology, psycholinguistics, sociology, and literary studies (see for detailed and diverse review, Karandashev, 2017; Karandashev et al., 2019). Abundance of anthropological and linguistic studies from this approach is scattered through the chapters of this book.

Psychology and communication studies have employed this approach less frequently so far. The main challenge in *emic approach* is to ensure the *construct equivalence,* as it is represented across cultures, when similar, yet differing constructs converge (Campbell, 1986; Werner & Campbell, 1970).

For example, researchers may develop a construct and generate items for an instrument concurrently in several cultures. The items common across cultures are retained for the comparative purposes, while item specifics or culturally specific items are removed. Then researchers adopt this common set of items for preparation of test versions in the local languages. The remaining items can be reserved for the culturally specific versions.

This approach favoring such *emic methodology* in development of instrument was illustrated in a study (Boehnke et al., 2014) that explored the relationship between *paternal warmth* and *trust* in five cultural samples (German, Moldova–Russian, Togo–French, Zambia–English, and Zimbabwe–Shona). Researchers from those cultures created items independently. In the study, they verified the structural and measurement equivalence of items which are differently worded in different language versions.

Another possible emic strategy is to elaborate a construct independently and develop an instrument within cultures. Then all instruments are administered in all cultures. This approach allows revealing universal as well as culturally specific aspects of a construct. The process, however, is time consuming.

Balance of Etic and Emic Approaches

The emic approach does not reject the etic approach. The *etic approach* identifies constructs characterizing human behavior, mental and emotional processes, which are common across cultures. The *emic approach* is more culturally sensitive to indigenous psychologies. It explores manifestations of these general constructs and develops other concepts that complement the general conceptual structure of culturally knowledge (Chiu & Hong, 2006; He & van de Vijver, 2012; Ho, 1998b; Poortinga, 1999; Triandis, 2000).

Even though the *etic* and *emic approaches* are distinctively different, yet the both can be balanced in a study. One way to implement such a balance is to start from *etic* and incorporate *emic* concepts. This is *derived etics,* instead of *imposed etics* (Berry, 1969, 1989). In this way, researchers accumulate emic knowledge of similar constructs in cultural contexts. They take into account how culturally appropriate the constructs and measures are. They develop improved instruments and run their cross-cultural validation. Another way to reach a balance of *etic* and *emic* aspects in research is to begin from *emic concepts*, culturally specific, and then apply those concepts to other cultures (He & van de Vijver, 2012).

The three research approaches in cross-cultural research—the *universalist, contextualist*, or *integrationist*—are in use. However, some scholars advocate the integrationist approaches: either the *derived etics approach* or the *indigenous psychologies approach* (Berry, 1969, 1989; Kim, Park, & Park, 2000). The *indigenous psychologies approach* distinguishes monocultural indigenous psychologies and cross-cultural indigenous psychologies. Their convergence can promise the balanced cultural psychology (Yang, 2000).

Anyway, clear conceptual and operational definition of emotional concepts, which are culturally sensitive and open to culturally different cultural meanings, experience, and expression of emotions, is the foundation of an adequate and valid cultural model of emotions. Multiple studies of relations between emotion and culture from both *etic* and *emic*, in some cases, from balanced *etic-emic* approaches are presented in the following chapters. The book itself, I believe, presents an example of such balanced and interdisciplinary approach to the study of cultural models of emotions.

3.1.4 Typology of Cultural Models of Emotional Life

Top-Down and Bottom-Up Approaches Constructing Cultural Models

It is reasonable to consider *cultural models* as the *types* or *styles* of emotional life prescribed, preferred, or prevalent in cultures. A variety of criteria and emotional domains can be used to construct such models. The dimensions of culture are core or anchor parameters, which explain the typical patterns of emotional life in the cultures ranging along these dimensions. The emotional domains, which can be included in the description of the cultural models of emotions, are the representation and interpretation of emotional phenomena, values of emotions, typical appraisals, the typical experience of basic and complex emotions, the typical valence and intensity of emotional experience, the typical expressions of emotions, and so on.

Two major ways to construct cultural models are possible. The first one I would call the *top-down method*. Researchers start from *top*—the theoretical postulation and foundation of a cultural dimension as independent parameters (variable) and then go *down*—to theoretical explanation, selection of available findings, and empirical exploration of emotional parameters (variables), which the cultural dimension entails. In this approach, the ANOVA and Regression analysis are among the typical statistical methods that apply to empirical data to reveal the *cultural patterns of emotions*. The *cultural models of self and relating*, which are described in the following sections, are the examples of this *top-down method*.

The second one I would call the *bottom-up method*. Researchers start from *bottom*—the selection of available findings, empirical investigation, and description of emotional patters typical for certain cultures and then go to *top*—the theoretical explanation of what cultural dimensions typical for selected cultures can explain these culturally-specific patterns of emotions. In this approach, *multidimensional scaling, factor analysis, cluster analysis* are the typical statistical methods applied to reveal cultural models. The *cultural models of guilt and shame*, which are described in the following sections, are the examples of this *bottom-up method*.

The two methods—the *top-down* and *bottom-up*—do not exclude each other and can be used within the same study and research design when researchers tackle the problem from two ends: *top* and *bottom*.

Cultural Models of Emotions Based on Cultural and Social Parameters

The *top-down method* of constructing the models of emotions are based *on cultural and social dimensions*. These can be *the models of emotional life* in *the cultures with independent self-construal and interdependent self-construal*, the *models of emotions* in *high-contact* and *low-contact cultures,* the *models of emotions* in the *cultures with rigid gender roles* and *flexible gender roles*.

The *models of self and relating* (Mesquita & Leu, 2007) is the only one of this kind well-elaborated so far. Any of the cultural dimensions presented in the sections above (Chap. 2) can be the anchors and foundations for constructing this type of cultural models. Among those models, which reflect the dimensions of cultures, are such as

- Individualistic and collectivistic models
- The models of high-power distance and low power distance models
- The models of cultures with rigid gender roles and flexible gender roles
- The models of high-contact and low-contact cultures
- The models of high context differentiation and low context differentiation
- The models of past, present, and future time orientation
- The models of slow and fast pace of time
- The models of uncertainty avoidance and uncertainty acceptance
- The traditional models of survival (biological and social) and modern self-expressive models
- The models of low and high relational mobility, and so on.

Essentially, *any cultural dimensions*, which were reviewed in previous sections or others, can be the basis for constructing a cultural model if researchers have a sufficient theoretical and empirical evidence of how these cultural dimensions are associated with cultural norms of emotions, the people's emotional experience and expression in a given culture. This way, many cultural dimensions—not only traditionally and extensively explored individualism and collectivism, or independent and interdependent self-construal—can be independent variables to construct a cultural model of emotions. *Multidimensional models*, which include more than one cultural dimension, can also be developed and bring more complex models.

The sections of the Chap. 2 have compiled the possible piecemeal drafts of such cultural models. In each section, I have defined a cultural dimension, described the societies characterized by different value on the dimension, and then reviewed theoretical and empirical studies of how this cultural dimension affect or can affect patterns of emotional life. Some of those dimensions have been extensively investigated and therefore, they have plenty of facts and findings about emotional experience and expression associated with them, the others have been explored much less. Further research is needed.

The high correlation between several cultural dimensions is another compounding complication in the construction of these types of cultural models. For example, as I cited above, *individualism-collectivism* and *low-high power distance* (as well as some others) highly correlate with each other in many societies. Researchers have traditionally explained many differences in emotional patterns prevalent in some countries with the norms of individualistic and collectivistic societies. However, a later study showed that actually the dimension of *power-distance* is more important to explain these cultural differences.

The *cultural dimension approach* characterizing societies assumes that a certain dimension is *present more or less across all societies*. However, in the construction of other cultural models of emotions using regional, national, religious, socioeconomic parameters, this approach is not always applicable. A region or nation may have a certain parameter being *present,* while the others have it *absent*. And this explains only why the culturally-specific experience or expression of emotion is present in that culture. For example, many cultural differences in emotions between Americans and Japanese are explained with *individualism* versus *collectivism, independent* versus *interdependent self-construal*. However, some culturally-specific patterns of emotional experience and expression in Japan can be explained by influence of *Zen-Buddhism*, rather than cultural dimension of collectivism. As one can see in the following sections, Mexican culture is also collectivistic, but Mexicans are substantially different from Japanese in their patterns of experience and expression of emotions. The similar way, the Chinese features of emotional experience and expression can be explained by influence of *Confucianism*, rather than their collectivistic nature. Zen-Buddhism and Confucianism are regionally specific factors, but not cultural dimensions in their traditional understanding.

Geographic and Ethnic Models

The *top-down method* of constructing the models of emotions can also be based on the regional, national, ethnic, religious, socioeconomic, or urban versus rural parameters of population. The possible drafts of these models are presented in the sections of Chap. 1. For example, a researcher can select Finnish and Japanese societies as national cultures and comprehensively explore and describe their similarities and differences using multiple cultural, societal, and local features of their life. These could be *Finish* and *Japanese cultural models of emotions*. These would be two descriptive models, which would be compared with each other, rather than placed on the global scale of cultural dimensions. The *religious models of emotions* can be constructed the similar way based on the religious teachings about emotions, as well as experience and expression of emotions in different religions or religious denominations.

Cultural models can be large and overarching several cultures, for example, Eastern culture vs. Western culture. They can be regional, for example, *east-European* vs *west-European cultural models*. They can be national, for example, *American* and. *Japanese cultural models*.

Cultural models can characterize emotional patterns of some ethnic groups within a culture, for example, *African-American* and *Chinese-American cultural models*. The latter can combine the features of a *general American model* and typical *Chinese ethnic model of love*. The *Chinese-Chinese and American-Chinese models may differ*, having common features, yet some differences. Various combinations of cultural ethnic models of emotion are also possible within a country.

Cultural Models of Emotions Based on Characteristics of Societies

It is worth to note that within cultures, there are gender, age, and social class variations of emotional experience and expression. However, there are not many studies exploring these variables so far (see for a brief review, Tsai & Clobert, 2019). Nevertheless, the cultural models of emotions characterizing these cultural subgroups are also possible. Other societal dimensions can be in foundation of cultural models of emotions. These might be:

- The emotional models of cultures of low, middle, and high socioeconomic status
- The models of traditional and modernized societies (modernization in this case can be considered both as a cultural and societal characteristic)
- The models of urban and rural cultures
- The models of societies with gender equality and gender inequality
- The masculine and feminine models of emotions
- The societal models of emotions youth, middle age, and older generations

Cultural Models Based on Typical Patterns of Emotions

The *bottom-up method* of constructing the models of emotions can be based *on the typical patterns of emotional experiences and expressions*. The components of these patterns can be the *meanings and cultural norms of emotions, appraisals* of events and situations, *valence* and *intensity of emotional experience, salience, prevalence,* or *cultural value* of certain emotions, the *quality* and *intensity* of emotional expression. The drafts of these models are presented in the following chapters.

For example, based on the meaning of emotions and appraisals, these are the *intrapersonal* and *interactive models of emotions*, the *models of emotions* elicited by *controllable* and *uncontrollable events*, the models of *self-focused* and *relationship-focused* appraisals.

Based on the *intensity of emotional experience*, these are *passionate* or *dispassionate models* of emotions.

Based on the preferred *valence of emotional experience*, these are *positive, negative,* or *balanced models of emotions*.

Based on the *salience of particular emotions*, these are *cultural models of joy, pride, guilt, shame,* or *honor*.

Based on the norms and actual ways of *emotional expression*, these are *expressive* or *not expressive cultural models, the models of direct* or *nondirect expression of emotions*.

The *models of emotions* can also describe the *cultural norms of emotions* (e.g., focal or ideal affect) or the *real occurrences of emotional experience and expression*.

In the following chapters, I have compiled the data and findings from many studies to describe and support the *culturally typical patterns of emotional experiences and expressions*. Those studies also explored the cultural and social parameters that are associated with these emotional patterns, thus making the moves of *bottom-up*. Those studies are also cited in the Chaps. 1 and 2, where the *top-down approach* is presented. This way, both approaches merge each other from different ends creating the more comprehensive descriptions of cultural models.

Some of these models may look like fragmentary and covering only part of human emotional life. Therefore, including more than one of the parameters listed above can produce more complex models of emotions. In this *bottom-up method* of constructing the models of emotions, identification of the typical patterns of emotions goes first, while exploration of the cultural and societal parameters that determine these patterns of emotional life goes second.

Variety of the Cultural Patterns of Emotional Life

Researchers explore and identify the *patterns of emotional life* based on different *components, domains, and criteria* of *emotional experience and expression*. Among those are

1. *Conceptions of emotions* overall and the *meanings of particular emotions*. This domain of emotional patterns was extensively explored in psycholinguistics and anthropology demonstrating, for instance, the different meanings and attitudes toward *anger*.
2. *Cultural norms of emotions (focal emotions, desired emotions, ideal affect)*. This domain of emotional patterns was extensively explored in sociology and cultural psychology demonstrating, for example, difference in such *norms in individualistic and collectivistic cultures*.
3. *Appraisals* of events and situations, eliciting emotions. This domain was especially explored in cultural psychology demonstrating, for example, that the event can be appraised as *controllable*, or *uncontrollable*, as *ego-focused* or *relationship-focused*. These are the patterns of appraisals more or less typical in some cultures.

4. *The preferred and prevalent valence* and *intensity* of emotional experience. These domains were especially explored in psychology and communication studies. The studies have demonstrated, for example, that *experience of positive emotions* and *high intensity of emotions* are the two patterns of emotional life prevalent and preferred among European Americans, while experience of *balanced positive and negative emotions* and *low intensity of emotions* are the two patterns of emotional life prevalent and preferred among East Asians.

5. The *quality* and *intensity* of emotional expressions. The studies have demonstrated the various ways of expressing emotions depending on their valence, type, and cultural value. For instance, the two patterns of emotional expressiveness are evidently distinguished: highly-expressive (prevalent and preferred among European Americans) and low-expressive (prevalent and preferred among East Asians).

6. *Representativeness and ranking of emotions* in terms of their value or prevalence in emotional experience. These aspects of patterns were investigated in various disciplines studying emotions. These types of emotional patterns are characterized by the emotions which are the more or less representative, the more or less prototypical in the culturally normative or real emotional life of people in a culture. Sometimes, they are so salient that they become the central themes of cultural models of emotions (Mesquita & Ellsworth, 2001; Mesquita & Frijda, 1992). These are the *cultural pattern of pride*, the *cultural pattern of honor*, the *cultural pattern of guilt and shame*.

7. *Composition of elements and the types of relations between elements* within a cultural model. The relationships between elements in the structure may vary in type: descriptive, logical, taxonomic, propositional, part-whole relations, evaluative, sequential, procedural, causal, and so on (Bennardo, 2018a, 2018b; de Munck, 2019). These *structural patterns of emotions* describe how many elements and what types of elements (*meanings, appraisals, experience of an emotion, its valence, intensity, power, expression of an emotion*, etc.) are included, how close or distant the elements are from each other. They may describe sequential and temporal relations between elements.

Investigation and description of these and other patterns of emotions within certain cultural, geographic regions and countries, ethnic or societal groups, can produce west-European, north-European, East Asian, Middle-East, European-American, German, French, Greek, Chinese, and Japanese national models, or Samoan, Tongan, Utku Eskimos cultural models of emotions, as well as many others. Some cultural dimensions and the dimensions of emotions can be salient in certain cultural groups and societies, but not others, while others can be muted.

Cultural Models in Reality of Normative Emotions, Emotional Experience, and Expression

Cultural models of emotion, however, can exist in different modes. The same way as Morris and his colleagues (2015) considered that cultural norms can exist in different realities, we should admit that *cultural models of emotions* also can represent different aspects of normative reality. In particular, cultural models (the same way as the norms) are presented in a culture as institutionalized practices, rules, patterns of sanctioning and behavioral regularities—as the *objective cultural environment*. Besides, cultural models of emotions may reflect subjective perceptions, assumptions, and individual expectations in the forms of *perceived descriptive norms* (interpretive frames that shape how people perceive their society's norms), *perceived injunctive norms* (the patterns of behavior that evoke social approval or disapproval), and *personal norms* (self-expectations). The distinction of all these types of cultural models of emotions is important from methodological standpoint to make the findings from different studies comparable.

Cultural models can represent an *ideal model*—how it should be ideally—or *real model*—how it is in reality of everyday life. For instance, cultural anthropologist (Swidler, 2002) discovered that romantic love as an ideal model of love inspires and motivates young men and women in their search of soul partner for life. It makes male–female *romantic* relationships bright and attractive. It brings men and women hope in possibility for a partner's personal transformation and development. Yet, in real life they tend to prefer practical aspects of love and value a partner for mating purposes.

The distinction of *actual affect* and *ideal affect* (Tsai, 2007; Tsai, Knutson et al., 2006) is important in this regard. The study of *actual affect* is focused on people's actual experience of emotion in response to a particular situation or in general. *Actual affect* assumes the evaluation of emotion as positive or negative. Different from this, *ideal affect* assumes that individuals in a society ideally want to feel certain emotions in a certain way, which are desirable to others. The ideal affect functions like norms of emotional experience, along with some differences, which distinguish those.

The affect valuation index (AVI) allows assessing both actual and ideal affect (Tsai, Knutson, & Fung, 2006). To assess *actual affect*, the AVI asks participants to rate how often they actually feel certain emotions. To assess *ideal affect*, the AVI asks participants to rate how often they would ideally like to feel a variety of states. I would like to highlight this methodological distinction for the future studies of cultural models of emotions.

3.2 Methodology of Emotion Research and Cultural Models

3.2.1 Categorical Approach to the Study of Emotions

Categorical Paradigm in Emotion Research

Two major approaches have dominated the area of cross-cultural research of emotions: categorical and dimensional. I review their contributions to the construction of cultural models of emotional life in this and the following sections. These two approaches complement each other in their structuring of emotional life.

Researchers working in *categorical paradigm* conceptualize emotions as the categories separate from each other, which can be described by certain physiological and neural characteristics, specific subjective experiences, and featured in behavioral and facial expressions. Emotions are multifaceted units. In *categorical approach* to the study of emotions, descriptive and qualitative methods prevail over comparative and quantitative ones.

Emotions can be organized in a prototypical, ranking, or hierarchical structure. They can be arranged according to valence (positive versus negative) or intensity (arousal). Thus, this approach may include the elements of dimensional one.

Theories and Research of Basic Emotions

The theories and research of basic emotions represent a *categorical approach* to the study of emotion. Categorical approach assumes that emotional life consists of a number of discrete emotions, which are qualitatively different from each other in terms of antecedents, physiological processes, emotional experience, and behavioral expression (e.g., Ekman, 1999; Oatley & Johnson-Laird, 1990).

It is assumed that a certain fixed number of discrete emotions and their mixtures describe a diverse range of human emotions. The theories propose that basic emotions are qualitatively different from each other. They have separate, specific, and unique response patterns in physiological and neural systems, in subjective experience, in behavioral and facial expression (Collet, Vernet-Maury, Delhomme, & Dittmar, 1997; Ekman, 1972).

The number of *basic emotions* varies from one theory to another. Ekman (1972, 1992) proposed six basic emotions (anger, disgust, fear, happiness, sadness, and surprise), Plutchik (Plutchik, 2001; Plutchik, Kellerman, & Conte, 1979) proposed eight (joy-sadness, anger-fear, trust-distrust, surprise-anticipation), Izard (1977, 1992, 2007) identified ten, Jack and colleagues (Jack, Sun, Delis, Garrod, & Schyns, 2016) recognized four irreducible emotions (happiness, sadness, anger, and fear). These findings were typically based on experimental research of facial expression of emotions. Cross-cultural studies from this approach attempt to investigate whether certain emotions (e.g., anger, guilt, shame) are experienced by people in different cultures or can be adequately recognized. For example, Jack et al. (2016) followed the classical methodology of experimental design exploring facial expressions of emotion regardless of sociocultural influences. When authors modeled the facial expressions of 60 emotions across two cultures, they found that the four latent facial expression patterns, which are common in both cultures, produce over 60 cross-culturally valid facial expressions. Thus, the sets of simple expressive patterns lay in foundation of more complex facial expressions. Some emotions are displayed with the same facial response. For instance, it turned out that surprise and fear involved the same facial muscles and, therefore, could represent one, rather than two emotions. The similar facts the researchers found for some other emotions (disgust and anger or excitement and shock).

Basic Emotions Across Cultures

These basic emotions are cross-culturally universal and can be compared across cultures in terms of meaning, experience, expression, and recognition (Ekman, 1992, 1999). Happiness, surprise, sadness, disgust, fear, and anger are common discrete emotions widely acknowledged in cross-cultural research. Cross-cultural studies have shown that people in many literate and preliterate societies are able to display and recognize facial expressions of these basic emotions (e.g., Ekman, Sorenson, & Friesen, 1969; Izard, 1971), as well as recognize nonverbal emotional vocalizations (e.g., laughs and screams), expressing these emotions (Sauter, Eisner, Ekman, & Scott, 2010).

The *categorical approach* considers emotion as a matter of presence or absence in a culture. Presence or absence of the words for an emotion in a culture (as in cognitive linguistics), the ability of people to recognize an emotion in facial expressions (as in experimental psychology), and detecting separate neural systems engaged in experience of basic emotions, are the typical examples of this methodological approach. From a categorical approach, the question of research interest is whether people in a culture do or do not experience, for example, a categorical emotion of guilt.

Basic and Complex Emotions

A basic premise of the conception of basic emotions is that these emotions serve as building blocks for complex emotions (e.g., embarrassment, disgust, envy, shame, guilt, jealousy, gratitude, pride), which are the mixtures of basic ones. For example, in the Ekman's theory, the mixture of anger and disgust creates a complex emotion of contempt, whereas anger, fear, and disgust blend in hate. The attempts to construct a comprehensive theory and conduct empirical research following this conceptual idea have been moderately successful. It has not fully succeeded so far. It appears challenging to deconstruct many complex emotions into basic ones. The similar way, in Plutchik's theory, eight basic emotions mix with each other as hues in a color wheel. The basic emotional "colors" fuse creating complementary and secondary emotional "colors." This theory considers *optimism* is a result of *anticipation* and *joy*, whereas *awe* is a mixture of *fear* and *surprise*.

Structure of Basic Emotions

Basic emotions can also be the central points in the layout describing the structure of emotions, in which each basic emotion serves as a central and prototypical label for a set of similar emotions (Harmon-Jones, Harmon-Jones, & Summerell, 2017). For example, when in a study (Shaver, Schwartz, Kirson, & O'Connor, 1987) participants were asked to sort emotion words "bitterness," "irritation," "frustration," and "rage," they grouped them semantically close to each other with the underlying prototype of "anger." The same way, using emotional lexicon of English, Italian, Basque, and Indonesian languages, Shaver and colleagues (Alonso-Arbiol et al., 2006; Shaver et al., 1987; Shaver, Morgan, & Wu, 1996; Shaver, Murdaya, & Fraley, 2001; Shaver, Wu, & Schwartz, 1992) found that the *words of emotional domain* in those cultural contexts are structured around several basic emotions. The words of basic emotions are the central points, while other emotion words convey similar, but different meanings.

Cultural Models Based on Categorical Approach to Emotions

According to *categorical approach*, various types of cultural models of emotions can be constructed. One type of models is based on general *cultural conceptions of emotions* evolved from philosophical cultural traditions. Examples of such models are presented in the following sections. Among those are (1) *intrapersonal, interpersonal, interactive*, and *objectivized* models, (2) *dualistic* and *monistic* models.

Other type of models characterizes similarities and differences in the *cultural meaning of a particular emotion*. The *cultural models of anger* and *happiness*, described in the following sections, can serve as the examples.

Other type of models characterizes *the salience of a particular emotion* among other in a given culture. The *cultural models of honor*, *shame*, and *guilt*, described in the following sections, can serve as the examples.

The studies from *categorical approach* may also classify emotions according to the proposed characteristics: affective valence, motivational direction, and arousal. Therefore, some of these cultural models may use both categorical and dimensional approaches.

3.2.2   Emotional Lexicon as a Source of Knowledge About Cultural Models of Emotions

Cultural models based on categorical approach are quite typical in psycholinguistics (e.g., Athanasiadou & Tabakowska, 1998; Goddard, 1995; Kovecses, 2000, 2002; Wierzbicka, 1992, 1999) and cultural anthropology (e.g., Abu-Lughod, 1986/2000; Briggs, 1970; Levy, 1973; Lutz, 1982, 1988; Potter, 1988).

Many researchers use emotion words as a way to understand people's experience of emotion. They employ emotion words in their experiments and surveys as independent variables (stimuli) or as dependent variables (behavioral choice). Traditionally, Western scholarship has used English, French, and German words for the categorization and description of the emotions in cross-cultural comparison for quite a long time (Lutz, 1988; Russell, 1991). The *lexicons of emotion* across languages are quite similar in terms of meanings. So, researchers just translated original, let us say English, emotion terms into other languages, assuring adequacy of back translation. However, the emotion words in these languages might be not the most representative for the emotion domain in other cultures (Russell, 1991). Classification of emotions and vocabularies are still different. And it is difficult to translate the exact meaning of emotion words across languages (Goddard, 1997; Wierzbicka, 1999).

Some English words for emotions have no equivalents in other languages and vice versa (Wierzbicka, 1986, 1999). For instance, such emotion words as the *schadenfreude* in German (Boecker, Likowski, Pauli, & Weyers, 2015; Leach, Spears, Branscombe, & Doosje, 2003; Leach, Spears, & Manstead, 2015), *saudade* in Portuguese (Farrell, 2006; Neto & Mullet, 2014; Silva, 2012), *amae* in Japanese (Morsbach & Tyler, 1986; Niiya, Ellsworth, & Yamaguchi, 2006; Yamaguchi, 2004), *dapdaphada* and *uulhada* in Korean (Schmidt-Atzert & Park, 1999) are commonly used in their cultures, but have no equivalent in English.

One could argue that even though the cross-cultural analysis of emotion lexicon is valuable for linguistics, yet it may not reveal the reality of emotional life in cultures. Nevertheless, many psycholinguistic and psychological studies assume and assert that emotional lexicon substantially reflects the underlying emotional phenomena (e.g., Kovecses, 2000, 2002; Wierzbicka, 1992, 1999). Wierzbicka (1999) concludes that the prevailing *emotion words* are generally associated with societal values and *cultural models of emotions*, at least in historical origins.

These associations, however, are not simple and straight. As research has demonstrated, the differences in emotion lexicon across cultures do not necessarily mean that associated emotion processes are also different (e.g., Breugelmans & Poortinga, 2006; Frijda, Markam, Sato, & Wiers, 1995; Russell, 1991; Sabini & Silver, 2005). Universalist orientation in research of emotions maintains that despite some differences in emotion lexicons emotion processes are similar across cultures (e.g., Ekman, 1994; Scherer & Wallbott, 1994). The same emotional phenomena and experience can be expressed in various verbal and nonverbal ways.

3.2.3 Dimensional Approach to the Study of Emotions

What Is Dimensional Paradigm?

Researchers working in *dimensional paradigm* consider emotions as the fragments of emotional experience that can be adjacent to each other or overlap. Emotions are the facets of subjective experience that are described and arranged in a structure around a certain number of dimensions. Researchers conceptualize emotions using these underlying dimensions, which are presumably common for all emotions, yet differ in the degree of presence. This approach also suggests that all emotions have a common and interrelated neurophysiological basis.

As one can see in the following sections, the theories and empirical research have identified a various number of emotional dimensions. The two dimensions, *valence (pleasantness, hedonic tone)* and *intensity (arousal)*, – with some variation of terminology in different theories – are widely used. Some scholars have revealed such dimensions as *evaluation/pleasantness, potency-control, activation-arousal, and unpredictability.* Others found *dominance* as an important dimension.

The deeper exploration of dimensionality of positive emotions recognized such dimensions as *absorption, potency, altruistic, spiritual* (Argyle & Crossland, 1987). Investigation of more complex emotions brought more complex classifications of emotions (see the following chapters).

Two-Dimensional Theories of Emotions

The dimensional approach represents appraisals, emotional experience, and emotional expression in a psychometric space arranged around certain dimensions. For several decades of research, emotion scholars have explored the dimensions that can be sufficient to describe diverse emotional experience. Two-dimensional *psychometric space* including *valence (pleasantness)* and *intensity (arousal)* has been the most popular and frequently used. It is understandable because two-dimensional *psychometric space* is simpler to comprehend. It can be easily represented and imagined in two-dimensional *physical space.* Some researchers have proposed three or four dimensions. Some of these dimensional models of emotions are validated in cross-cultural samples. Let us briefly summarize these and other examples of dimensional models of emotions.

Two-dimensional space is the widely used dimensional structure of emotional experience. Different emotions take different positions depending on the measures of underlying dimensions (e.g., Russell, 1980; Russell & Feldman Barrett, 1999 ; Watson, 2000). Researchers may differ in their interpretation of the nature of these two dimensions. Some researchers define these dimensions as *positive affect* and *negative affect* (e.g., Watson, 2000; Watson & Tellegen, 1985), others as *pleasantness-unpleasantness* and *arousal-sleepiness* (Russell, 1980, 2003). Nerveless, the dimensions in these two theories are more or less equivalent. Their pairs are rotated versions of one another (Russell & Feldman Barrett, 1999; Watson, 2000).

The *circumplex model of emotion* is an example of dimensional approach (Feldman Barrett & Russell, 1998; Russell, 1980; Russell & Feldman Barrett, 1999). This model proposes two dimensions—*valence* and *arousal*—that are laid out in circular space where emotions are distributed. The horizontal axis represents *valence*, the vertical axis represents *arousal*, and the crossing of these lines signifies a neutral valence and a medium level of arousal. Emotions are represented in this two-dimensional space according to their level of valence and arousal. For example, pride has high pleasantness and high arousal, sadness has low pleasantness and low arousal, anger has low pleasantness and high arousal.

Another dimensional theory is described in the model of *positive activation—negative activation* (PANA). It suggests that *positive affect* and *negative affect* are the two dimensions that are separate and relatively independent. The horizontal axis denotes low-to-high negative affect and the vertical axis denotes low-to-high positive affect (Watson & Tellegen, 1985; Watson, Wiese, Vaidya, & Tellegen, 1999, see also Rubin & Talarico, 2009). The PANA model can be considered (see Watson & Tellegen, 1985) as a 45-degree rotation of the *circumplex model* defined by two primary axes.

According to other dimensional theory, the *vector model of emotion* (Bradley, Greenwald, Petry, & Lang, 1992), two variables—a dimension of *arousal* and a binary choice of *valence*—determine two vectors starting at zero arousal and neutral valence and proceeding as straight lines. One runs in a positive valence direction, and another runs in a negative valence direction.

Three-Dimensional Theories of Emotions

Plutchik's theory (Plutchik, 2001; Plutchik et al., 1979), described above as *categorical*, can be also considered as a *three-dimensional model of emotions*. It combines the features of both *categorical* and *dimensional* approaches. Emotions are depicted in concentric circles. Inner circles represent basic, while outer circles represent complex emotions. The inner circles of emotions blend to form outer circles of emotions. Emotional words are plotted in this space based on similarity. The emotions appearing in different intensities are combined to form emotional "dyads" of emotions.

One more example of dimensional approach is the PAD emotional state model (Mehrabian, 1996), which proposed three dimensions to represent emotions: *pleasure, arousal,* and *dominance.* The *pleasure-displeasure* dimension characterizes how pleasant an emotion is. The *arousal-nonarousal* dimension characterizes the intensity of the emotion. The *dominance-submissiveness* dimension characterizes the controlling function of the emotion.

Based on the extensive studies of *Semantic Differential,* Osgood and his colleagues (Osgood, May, & Mirron, 1975) proposed three parameters of affective meanings: *evaluation* (such as "good/bad"), *potency* (such as "strong/weak"), and *activity* (such as "passive/active") and found that they are cross-culturally universal.

Later studies further confirmed cross-cultural validity of these dimensions of emotions. MacKinnon and Keating (1989) found applicability of these three dimensions of the *semantic differential* to compare the structure of emotions of Canadians and the US Americans. Shaver and colleagues (Alonso-Arbiol et al., 2006; Shaver et al., 1987, 1992, 1996, 2001) were able to identify *evaluation, potency,* and *activity* as cross-culturally similar dimensions of emotions in four languages (English, Italian, Basque, and Indonesian).

Four-Dimensional Structures of Emotions

Based on a theoretically driven approach, Fontaine, Scherer and colleagues (Fontaine, Scherer, Roesch, & Ellsworth, 2007) have revealed four-dimensional structure of emotional life. They explored "the six components of emotions: (a) appraisals of events, (b) psychophysiological changes, (c) motor expressions, (d) action tendencies, (e) subjective experiences, and (f) emotion regulation" (Fontaine et al., 2007, p. 1050) in English, Dutch, and French languages. Authors found that 144 features of emotions are applicable to 24 emotion terms and can satisfactorily represent similarities and differences in the meaning of emotion words in these three languages. In order of their importance, they are *evaluation/pleasantness, potency-control, activation-arousal,* and *unpredictability.*

The Prototype Theory of Emotions

The *prototype methodological approach* to the study of emotions presents the convergence of *categorical* and *dimensional paradigms.* It is categorical because it treats emotions, or emotional episodes as the units of analysis without their further dissecting. It is dimensional because it arranges those units in ranked order and structures.

In prototypical theory and empirical research (Fehr & Russell, 1984; Russell & Feldman Barrett, 1999), the emotions (e.g., joy, surprise, anger, fear) or emotional episodes (complex processes and subevents unfolding emotion over time) are considered as more or less representative (prototypical) members of the family of *emotion.* The concept of emotion has an internal structure, in which different kinds of emotions differ from each other in a matter of degree—how close they are to the head of family that is called *emotion.* These emotions have fuzzy, but not clear-cut boundaries, which separate them from each other.

Following the *prototype perspective*, researchers found that the emotions of happiness, respect, awe, love, fear, envy, anger, and other categories of emotions constitute their relations as the members of *emotion* family. People are capable to order them from poorer to better examples of emotion, from being the most prototypical to peripheral in terms of ranking (Fehr & Russell, 1984; Russell, 1991; Russell & Feldman Barrett, 1999).

It should be noted, that in this research design, each particular emotion is ranked in prototypical relations of closeness to the concept of emotion. The relation between the particular emotions with each other is not the subject of direct investigation. However, following this prototype view, researchers can use such a prototype analysis to explore the prototypical relations of such specific emotions as fear, anger, love, and commitment with others (e.g., Fehr, 1988; Fehr & Russell, 1991; Russell & Fehr, 1994).

Comparison in Dimensional Approach

The *dimensional approach* considers emotion as a matter of degree (not presence or absence as in categorical approach), as a matter of underlying dimensions and associations, which the emotion has in a culture.

A dimensional approach, such as using several characteristics from various emotion components, may be suitable for the study of how similar and how different emotion processes are across cultures (Mesquita, Frijda, & Scherer, 1997). This approach, rather than comparison of categorical emotion labels, can be beneficial, especially for research of emotions which do not have words in a culture (Breugelmans & Poortinga, 2006).

Researchers, which follow a *dimensional approach*, measure emotions utilizing a set of characteristics (dimensions) on several emotion components. As *stimuli* in the studies, they employed body sensations (Breugelmans et al., 2005; Scherer & Wallbott, 1994), cognitive appraisals (Roseman, Antoniou, & Jose, 1996; Scherer, 1997a, 1997b), and action tendencies (Frijda, Kuipers, & ter Schure, 1989). This approach allows comparing emotion processes across cultures, even in the cases when the emotion lexicon differs (Frijda et al., 1995). Besides, compared to single-item measurement, using multiple indicators to measure emotions makes cross-cultural studies less prone to cultural item bias (Fontaine, Poortinga, Setiadi, & Markam, 2002).

From a dimensional approach, a question of research interest is whether characteristics of emotion associated with a category of guilt co-occur similarly among people in a culture, distinctively from characteristics of shame. For instance, following the dimensional approach, researchers (Breugelmans & Poortinga, 2006) asked participants in two rural, culturally different samples to describe the emotions of *shame* and *guilt* using 29 descriptive characteristics (dimensions). People in those two cultures were able to differentiate these two emotions, even though the lexicon in one culture (the Rarámuri Indians in Mexico) use one and the same word for both *guilt* and *shame*, while in another culture (Javanese) – two different words.

Cultural Models Based on the Dimensional Approach to Emotions

Dimensional approach to emotions allows constructing the *cultural models of emotions* based on various dimensions of appraisal, emotional experience, and expression. *Measurement, approximate measurement*, or *quasi-measurement* of selected emotional dimensions serves as the criteria for such models.

For example, the *cultural attitude to regulation of emotions* differs across cultures. Some societies endorse free experience and open expression of emotion, while other suggest to control, and even suppress the experience and expression of emotions. Subsequently, the *cultural models of emotional regulation* can be developed. The results of the studies in support of such models are presented in the following chapters.

The cultural dimension *locus of control*, when emotions are deemed as *controllable* or *uncontrollable* by an individual appraising an event in their life, sets the criterion for another typology of models. The studies presented in the following sections provide empirical evidence that these models can be applicable to compare cultures.

The dimension of *intensity of emotional experience* allows to categorize cultures according to *passionate* and *dispassionate models of emotions*. Cross-cultural research, which is extensively reviewed in the following sections, brings the convincing findings in support of this division of models.

As for the expression of emotions, a large number of studies in psychology and communication research suggest the importance to distinguish between *expressive* and *nonexpressive cultural models of emotions*, as well as those with tendency for *direct* versus *indirect expression of emotions*.

3.2.4 Conceptual Equivalence of Emotional Constructs Across Cultures

Concept of Cross-Cultural Equivalence

Exploration and construction of cultural models of emotions require ensuring that the results obtained in different cultural samples are equivalent. The concept of *equivalence* characterizes weather it is adequate to compare scores obtained with a measurement instruments in different samples (Fontaine, 2004; Van de Vijver & Tanzer, 2004).

The three levels of equivalence should be taken into account: (1) construct equivalence, (2) measurement unit equivalence, and (3) full score equivalence (He & van de Vijver, 2012; Van de Vijver & Leung, 1997; Van de Vijver & Tanzer, 2004).

Construct equivalence, or *structural equivalence*, implies that researchers in different cultures measure the same construct. This type of equivalence characterizes the identity of constructs in studies across cultural samples. A quantitative scale of measurement is not necessary the same in this case. The methods to investigate and assess the construct equivalence are various types of structural analyses (e.g., *exploratory* or *confirmatory factor analysis, multidimensional scaling*, and *cluster analysis*).

Measurement unit equivalence, or *metric equivalence*, implies that researchers in different cultures measure the construct using the same measurement unit (at interval or ratio level), but different origins. This type of equivalence characterizes *identity of measurement unit* in studies across cultural samples. Such *metric equivalence* allows comparing scores within cultural samples. For example, the differences between men and women, between people of various ages can be compared in each cultural group. The correlations and typical patterns of means across cultural samples can also be compared. However, researchers cannot directly compare the scores across cultural groups. Unless the conversion of the measurements to the same origin has been made, a valid cross-cultural comparison is impossible.

Full score equivalence, or *scalar equivalence*, implies that researchers in different cultures measure the construct using scales with the same measurement unit and origins. This type of equivalence characterizes *identity of measurement unit and scale origin* in studies across cultural samples. In this case, researchers can directly compare the scores in cultural samples. At this level of equivalence, cross-cultural comparison of means in cultural groups using *t-tests* and *analyses of variance*

(ANOVA) is appropriate to investigate cross-cultural differences (He & van de Vijver, 2012).

Construct Equivalency in Adaptation and Validation of Foreign Measurement Instruments in Other Cultures

For many years, scholars from Western countries (e.g., the United States) developed the emotional constructs and the instruments to measure those. Then researchers from other countries translated and validated those constructs in their own cultures (e.g., German, Italian, Russian, and Japanese). The main purpose of such foreign validation has been to ensure that the *translated instruments measure the same constructs*, which their western colleagues had in mind. The goals of cross-cultural studies have been to compare how similar or different the constructs measured in new cultural samples, compared that one which measured in the original western sample. Thus, these studies have been presumably western-centric because the results in western sample were considered as a benchmark. An alternative interpretation is that these constructs are cross-culturally universal. It is assumed that the western authors of emotional measures scientifically elaborate their constructs, and their foreign colleagues have to validate their translated version as close to the original one as possible. If some items of the measure do not comply with original construct, then researchers attempt to revise those making them closer to the original. The *back translation of a measure* is one of the frequently used steps to reach this *construct equivalency*. Researchers have proposed the guidelines to reach the adequate item equivalency in cross-cultural research (Behling & Law, 2000; Cha, Kim, & Erlen, 2007; Hambleton & Zenisky, 2010; Van de Vijver & Hambleton, 1996).

In this process of foreign adaptation of an instrument, *the comparability of the construct across cultures increases, while the local cultural validity decreases* (He & van de Vijver, 2012). In this case, the compilation of a new instrument is the path to improve the cultural suitability *of the construct* and *validity of the instrument*. For development of the instruments, which are not completely equivalent across cultures, the *structural equation modeling* and *item response analysis* can be used as statistical methods (Van de Vijver & Leung, 1997).

Core and Peripheral Components in the Content of Construct Equivalency

The modern science of emotions, as it is shown with a plenty of evidence in the following chapters, begins to realize that the same or similar emotional constructs (e.g., anger, happiness) may have different meanings across cultures. Even though the core meaning of a construct can be cross-culturally universal, despite the differences in words, yet the particular cultural connotations and the content of the construct may be different. Therefore, the modern interpretation of *construct equivalency* should admit that an emotional construct can have the core content, which is cross-culturally equivalent, while peripheral components can have culturally-specific content, which is not equivalent across cultures.

For example, the study of Schwartz and Sagiv (1995) on values presents an example of such approach. Investigating values in 88 samples from 40 countries, the authors proposed criteria for identifying what is cross-culturally universal and what is culture-specific in value meanings and structure. Test-retest and randomly split sample analyses reveal that some one third of deviations represent culture-specific characteristics. Authors found that 44 (out of 57) values are highly consistent in their meaning, whereas the remaining 13 are not consistent across samples. Therefore, the latter value items cannot be compared between cultures in terms of their means, while they can be analyzed qualitatively within a particular culture and qualitatively with other cultures.

Many emotion studies have been actively engaged in cross-cultural comparison of means for emotions across cultures, or searched for correlations between cultural and emotional variables. Then, they were more interested in establishing cross-cultural equivalency of emotional constructs and their measurements, paying less attention to culturally specific. This accent in research interest, however, varied across disciplines. For instance, anthropology has been always interested in cultural features and uniqueness of emotions.

The recent interest of social sciences to *indigenous conceptions of culture* and *emotions* is promising and can be productive. The deficit of appropriate statistical methods to capture these more complex structures is one of the obstacles in this path. It is important to develop the appropriate statistical methods, which can analyze the complex structures of constructs. *Factor analysis, Cluster analysis, Latent class analysis* and their extensions that I briefly describes in other section of this book is the examples of such methodology suitable for structural examination of cross-cultural similarities and differences.

Cultural Sensitivity in Definitions of Constructs

Cross-cultural studies should be sensitive to the way how emotional constructs are defined and described in other cultures. This can be illustrated by observations of researchers about the development of prosocial behavior and empathy in young children (Friedlmeier, Corapci, & Benga, 2015). German and Japanese mothers described their reactions and emotions in the situations of conflict with their child.

> German mothers described their own emotional reaction as becoming angry, empathic, and (im)patient. In contrast, Japanese mothers used neither an emotion term nor sentences to express an inherently emotional state but gave rather general behavioral descriptions when asked about their emotional reaction (e.g. "I let her still continue for a while" or "I tell her that we need to leave as others expect us home"). However, when the project colleague from Japan coded the statements, he could identify emotions in these answers. After a discussion within the project team, these statements were presented to several Japanese exchange students, as well as to German students, and asked them to evaluate the emotional content. The result was surprising: the German students did not recognize much emotional content, whereas the Japanese students agreed strongly about the same emotions behind each statement. (Friedlmeier et al., 2015, p. 128)

These observations indicate that the emotional constructs can be defined and described in culturally specific ways, and cross-cultural studies can benefit if researchers work closely with colleagues in the respective cultures (Jensen, 2012). It is important to apply qualitative methods to discover culture-specific phenomena to avoid the "risk of using culturally biased conceptual categories and explaining the categories from our familiar cultural position" (Saarni, 1998, p. 651).

3.2.5 Cultural Samples in Emotion Research

The Size and Representativeness of Cultural Samples

The cultural and cross-cultural research of emotions in *anthropology* have been traditionally conducted as the field studies exploring the diversity of emotional life and the meaning of emotions in the societies, which are relatively isolated from the mainstream cultures. It is a great advantage. Such studies have brought interesting and productive insights into the cultural diversity of emotional conceptions, experiences, expressions, and cultural models of emotions in those cultures. They substantially deepened the scholarly knowledge about relations between culture and emotions. They bring to scholarly arena the valuable case studies of possible cultural models of emotions, which are extensively reviewed in the following sections. Yet, the *sample size of these studies is relatively small*. For instance, how can we be sure that 28 individuals from two countries are well representative for the cultural models typical or prevalent in those countries? Thus, *anthropology* is great in description of cultural models as case studies, yet it is less convincing in answering the question how representative this model is for a particular society.

The *studies of emotions in psychology and communication* have generally used *larger cultural samples* than in anthropology. The sample size, however, varies depending on the research design: less number of participants—in experimental studies and more participants—in survey studies. The previously raised question— how representative those cultural samples are, however, remains.

In sociology, the survey studies of emotions across cultures have used even *larger samples of respondents*. Yet, we never know how many participants should be to be representative for a culture. Then, researchers use assumptions, inductive reasoning, approximation, and appropriate statistical methods for this purpose. Replication of results in other study with other culturally similar samples is a good way to confirm that a cultural model of emotion is representative for a particular society. However, many academic journals are unwilling to publish replication studies, therefore diminishing the cumulative nature of cross-cultural findings.

Sample size and *representativeness of samples* are important parameters of research to obtain valid and reliable results about cultural similarities and differences. The sample size should guarantee adequate *statistical power* to detect a genuine cultural effect. The size of samples, however, does not guarantee their representativeness. So, the description of the variables of interest in cross-cultural study and how well samples represent those is important.

Unfortunately, as one can see in the following chapters, many cross-cultural studies of emotions have had a relatively modest sample size. Therefore, replication studies and meta-analyses are valuable to validate and consolidate the existing findings. A recent review and discussion of many cross-cultural studies expressed the concerns about replicability and addressed the replication as a long-term strategy in cross-cultural research (Milfont & Klein, 2018).

The expectations of *replicability*, however, may differ in the disciplines studying culture. For instance, cross-cultural psychology and communication science are aware and expect to obtain the cross-cultural findings, which would be replicable (despite the lack of replication studies). Cultural anthropology does not have such expectations; anthropologists explore the unique cultures and challenge our stereotypes. Accent on unique characteristics of a culture under study is the most important.

Profiles of Cultural Samples

Many cross-cultural studies have been conducted with the samples of university students in western European countries and North America and for contrast—in Japan and China. The research findings that are reviewed in the following chapters have demonstrated that comparison of conventionally called *Western* and *Eastern cultures* is interesting, productive, and surprising in many regards because the cultural models of emotions in those cultures are very different and contrasting with each other.

However, after initial fascination with this cultural discovery, scholars of emotions started to realize that *Western* and *Eastern cultures* are fairly diverse. *Western-Eastern* comparison might be too global, overgeneralizing, and therefore not sufficiently adequate to reflect the cultural diversity within each of these global regions. *Western American culture* is different in several respects from many *Western European cultures*, as it is shown in the results of the studies reviewed in this book. Thus, referring to Western culture, when participants of a study are from the United States or/and Netherlands, is not quite adequate. It admits too far extension and generalization. It may be good if researchers are cautious in interpretation of their results, preferably being more specific.

Western Europe is still a pretty vague concept—more specific definition is needed. It is not always clear whether researchers include northern European countries when they refer to western Europe. What about southern European countries? Spain and Portugal, for example, are among those, which can be categorized in both ways. The cultural division of European societies should be more justified based on several cultural dimensions, not just individualism. Which cultural group do Lithuania, Poland, Czech Republic, and Hungary belong to? Researchers measure the place of many countries on the scale of several cultural dimensions, yet the multidimensional cultural typology is not well established.

Western American society is also diverse and multicultural. Therefore, it seems not adequate to call the participants of a study as *Americans* since the sample may consist of people with different cultural backgrounds, despite the fact that American society presumably has some common general characteristics and values. Yet, it is multicultural, and it is not always clear where the cultural divisions and boundaries are. It may be adequate to some extent to name participants as European Americans and Asian Americans since these global regional cultural groups are distinctly different from each other. Nevertheless, as the studies reviewed in the chapters of this book show, they are still different within these global regions. Therefore, in many studies of emotions, it makes sense to be more specific: not just European Americans, but rather French Americans, German Americans, Dutch Americans, Italian Americans; and not just Asian Americans, but rather Japanese Americans, Chinese Americans, Pilipino Americans, Indian Americans (don't confuse with Native Indigenous Americans).

Researchers in the United States have regularly used these American cultural groups as the representatives of the cultures of their origins obtaining interesting cross-cultural results. This approach, however, may have a methodological caveat when participants are at the different degree of acculturation. The averaging of this cultural variation can make comparison of cultures less convincing. So, it is important for researchers to use an acculturation measure to make these studies really worthwhile. Self-identification of their ethnic origins by the participants may be not a valid variable of their cultural identity if they have lived in the country for many years, or if they are immigrants in second generation.

Eastern countries are even more diverse and multicultural. East Asian and west-Asian cultures substantially differ from each other, as well as many countries within these cultural regions do. Again, it is better if researchers are more specific in naming the cultural background of participants. The cultures of Japan, China, India, and others in East- and South-Asia are different. Some Asian countries, such as India, are also very multicultural. Therefore, despite some common cultural mentality of Indians, it may be not quite adequate to extrapolate the results from one cultural region of India to all others, or to average the data obtained in different cultural samples across India.

The studies conducted with convenience samples of countries and participants within countries extend and deepen our knowledge of cultural models of emotions. They reveal the role of specific cultural dimensions, and compare experience and expression of emotions prevalent in particular cultural contexts. Yet, they often do not provide sufficient data for the construction of comprehensive multidimensional and typological cultural models. Because of piecemeal data available in many countries, it is challenging to depict the *regional* or *national cultural models of emotions*.

The Samples of Participants with Mixed Cultural Identity

Modernization of many countries blurs the cultural differences between them, which were distinct in the past. So, the modern world is gradually, yet increasingly, losing its cultural diversity on the national level. The cultural difference between nations seems to be decreasing.

The other trend, however, is the increasing cultural diversity of population within many modern countries, due to more extensive migration than before, due to acculturation or cultural amalgamation of immigrants, and due to growing number of intercultural families. All these processes complicate the definitions of *culture* and *cultural identity*. The *mixed cultures* and *mixed cultural identities* are more frequent realities now than before. Multicultural individuals may have more complex and multifaceted cognitions, emotions, and personalities (Benet-Martinez & Haritatos, 2005; Hong, Morris, Chiu, & Benet-Martinez, 2000; Phinney & Alipuria, 2006).

In the light of these developments, cultural studies encounter new challenges when participants have mixed cultural identities. And the population of those who have a mixed identity, which is challenging to define due to their mixed culturally-diverse genetic history, is growing in many countries. Shall the cultural backgrounds be identified based on demographic questionnaires and nationality—current or former—of parents or grandparents? Which culture does Brian belong, if he was born and lived for many years in England, moved as adult in Japan, and lived there for 40 years? There are even more complicated stories of multicultural life. Methodological issue in cross-cultural research of emotion is how to identify the culture of participants, which they belong to. This is especially challenging in the modern time of migration and intercultural marriages.

Many mixed cultures and cultural identities have been extensively investigated in cross-cultural psychology of emotions as *acculturation*—transition from one culture to another and acquisition of another culture. However, in many cases this process may be not transition, but rather *amalgamation*. Individuals may prefer to live in a mixed culture and merge their cultural identity. Thus, the modern concepts of culture and cultural identity are becoming more complex and even complicated, as it was shown in earlier chapters. In the context of this chapter, the question is how to compile the cultural samples taking into account all these complications caused by multiculturalism, migration, and acculturation. The samples become less homogeneous and more differentiated.

Cultural Samples Are Diverse in Other Societal Parameters

Undergraduate students from a small number of universities from several countries do represent certain communities of cultures. Cross-cultural variation in other societal parameters and confounding variables can make characteristics of cultural samples incomparable. These can be the differences in education levels, in urban or rural residency, in affiliation to religious groups. As Boer, Hanke, and He (2018) noted, many cross-cultural studies recruit only two samples. Therefore, researchers should be cautious in their generalizations.

Undergraduate students are quite typical participants of many cross-cultural studies of emotions. From the practical point of accessibility, it is understandable due to restraints in resources and accessibility. Even though it is implicitly expected that samples of university students in different cultures match, yet this assumption may be not valid. Several factors may contribute to this. Among those are different age ranges, quality of education, and enrollment rates in developing and developed countries.

University students mostly reflect the opinions, values, attitudes, experience, and expression of emotions of young middle-class population. Therefore, these participants' pool may not fully reflect the cultural models of other segments of societies. The extending of cultural knowledge of emotions beyond these limitations is really worthwhile.

In the Chap. 1 above, I extensively reviewed the scholarship and studies that have demonstrated that the cultures of people of middle, high, and low socioeconomic status, the religious and regional cultures can substantially differ within the same national culture. The cultural models of emotions can vary within countries accordingly.

In recent decades, researchers have extended the samples of their cross-cultural investigation of emotions reaching out other cultural categories of participants. They more often included in their studies the participants with different models of emotions and from other cultures (Chentsova-Dutton & Lyons, 2016).

The three *strategies of sampling* are frequently employed in cross-cultural studies: *random, convenience (nonsystematic),* and *purposive.* Each sampling approach has certain implications for analysis at the cultural and the individual levels, and can be used appropriately depending on the goals of the studies (Boehnke, Lietz, Schreier, & Wilhelm, 2011). *Random selection* of cultural samples and representative samples of participants within each culture is the ideal strategy. However, the deficits of accessibility to participants' pool and other resources often limit a possibility to achieve this goal. *Convenience samples* are more practical and therefore more frequently used in cross-cultural studies. Researchers, however, should be cautious in generalization of their results. *Purposive samples* are selected based on the parameters, which can be associated with the research goals and variables under study.

When the samples do not match to each other in some parameters relevant to a study, then researchers may need to control for those parameters using statistical corrections for those confounding differences. Generally, an optimal sampling should be guided by research goals and the distribution of the target variables (He & van de Vijver, 2012).

3.2.6 Adequacy in Cultural Measurement of Emotion

The Concepts of Measurement Equivalence and Bias

The *constructs,* such as attitudes, values, and attributes, are *latent variables* (e.g., factors) that cannot be measured directly. Therefore, measurement instruments, such as surveys, questionnaires, psychometric scales, inventories, assess these latent constructs (variables) with items as indicators of these latent variables (Milfont & Fischer, 2010). When a researcher compares a *latent construct* across samples, it is expected that each item—observed indicator—must be similarly related to the latent variable in all samples. Overall, *measurement invariance* of the whole measurement instrument means that all items—observed indicators—are associated with the *latent construct* (variable) in the same way in every sample. Comparing empirical relations between the *latent variable* and the *indicators* across samples, researchers test *measurement equivalence*. Once these relationships are similar, the measurement is equivalent.

Thus, *measurement invariance* implies that the *measurement structure* of the *latent factor* and the items in the measurement instrument should be *stable* and *invariant*. The association between the items (scale scores) and the latent factors (latent constructs) of respondents should be the same in different groups and measurement times (Mellenbergh, 1989; Van De Schoot, Schmidt, De Beuckelaer, Lek, & Zondervan-Zwijnenburg, 2015).

The concept of *measurement equivalence* means the comparability of constructs (values, attitudes, dimensions), which are measured with a measurement instrument in different groups. The concept of *measurement invariance* is frequently used as synonymous to the *measurement equivalence*. It refers to statistical property of the measurement instrument to measure the construct (opinion, beliefs, values, etc.) in the equivalent way across groups of respondents (see for review Davidov, Meuleman, Cieciuch, Schmidt, & Billiet, 2014; Johnson, 1998; Van de Vijver & Leung, 2011; Vandenberg & Lance, 2000).

Measurement Equivalence and Bias in Cross-Cultural Research

The issue of *measurement equivalence* refers mostly to the studies of participants from different cultural groups and countries. Nevertheless, there are many other cases of comparison when it can be important (e.g., in various social categories, multicultural communities, different time points). People from different socioeconomic and educational groups may understand certain concepts differently. Some regional societies and communities are multilingual and multicultural—a challenge for cross-cultural comparison that I discussed in other sections of this book. The fluency, lexical, and stylistic competency of individuals in an official language may vary substantially. Therefore, even within countries, the use and translation of measurement instruments can distort their equivalence (see for review Davidov et al., 2014).

Many studies showed (see for review Van De Schoot et al., 2015) that the assumption of *measurement invariance* is difficult to meet in survey scales. The results when parameters of measurement are exactly the same across groups are rare. Because of this, many researchers just disregard the issues of *measurement invariance* and compare the means of latent factors in groups without psychometric basis (see for review Van De Schoot et al., 2015). This is a source of *measurement bias*.

When *measurement invariance* is not confirmed, it is possible that respondents have different meanings concerning the items of instrument. And the validity of comparisons between *latent factor means* is compromised. *Measurement equivalence* is a precondition for comparison of variables between groups.

Different factor loadings may indicate that respondents understand constructs differently, and different intercepts may indicate that they use a scale differently (Davidov et al., 2014, p. 65). Nevertheless, the problem with *measurement equivalence* should not inevitably discourage from comparisons between countries. Davidov et al. (2014) summarized the strategies that researchers can apply to deal with *measurement nonequivalence* in cross-country comparisons:

1. Look for subgroups of countries or concepts where measurement equivalence holds and continue with cross-country comparisons of these concepts across this set or these sets of countries.
2. Determine how severe the violation of measurement equivalence is and whether it may still allow meaningful comparisons across countries. In case of doubt, drop noninvariant items.
3. Try to explain the individual, societal, or historical sources of measurement nonequivalence (p. 65).

To assess equivalence of measurements, multidimensional scaling, principal component analysis, exploratory factor analysis, confirmatory factor analysis can be used (Milfont & Fischer, 2010). In cross-cultural psychology, to test *measurement invariance,* researchers widely utilize *multi-group confirmatory factor analysis.* To explore measurement invariance, they run a sequence of increasingly constrained structural equation models and test whether these models differ significantly (see Cheung & Rensvold, 2002; Van de Schoot, Lugtig, & Hox, 2012). Davidov and colleagues (Davidov et al., 2014) also suggested employing some new approaches and statistical methods to test for measurement equivalence, such as exploratory structural equation modeling (ESEM), Bayesian structural equation modeling (BSEM), and alignment.

Bias

Bias is a particular aspect of research design or method, which distorts the results of a study making them less valid than researchers expected. Any *systematic measurement errors* can compromise the validity of cross-cultural comparison and inferences about cultural variability. In cross-cultural research, bias causes the results obtained in different samples not equivalent to each other and misrepresents similarities and differences. The differences in the scores as the indicators of a construct may not truly represent the real differences in the construct (Van de Vijver & Tanzer, 2004). And this problem may be more widespread in studies than emotions researchers believe.

For example, Van Hemert, Poortinga, and van de Vijver (2007) conducted a meta-analysis of 190 cross-cultural emotion studies, published between 1967 and 2000, to assess whether the cross-cultural differences in emotion variables are "valid (substantive factors) or as method-related (statistical artefacts, cultural bias)."

Results have shown that "a correction for statistical artefacts and method-related factors reduced the observed cross-cultural effect sizes considerably." (p. 913).

The content analysis (Boer et al., 2018) of many quantitative cross-cultural studies conducted during recent years has shown a rather low number of cases when researchers tested *measurement equivalence (invariance)*. Few studies use the statistical methods to rule out effects of the measurement biases. Analysis of equivalence is rarely reported in current cross-cultural research. Authors demonstrated the techniques and methods for *invariance testing*, which are currently available and can help to assess and reduce biases in cross-cultural research.

Construct and Instrument Bias

Construct bias implies that researchers measure the construct that does not have the same definition in different cultures. This can happen when the construct only partially overlaps in meaning in different cultures. This can also occur when researchers omit or improperly measure the relevant behavioral and response variables related to the construct in each cultural sample (Van de Vijver & Poortinga, 1997). For example, as I will show in the following chapters, the construct of *happiness* has different meanings in Western and East Asian cultures (Uchida, Norasakkunkit, & Kitayama, 2004). The concept of happiness is not universal and contains several culturally-specific aspects. The construct may only partially overlap across culture. Therefore, the measurement of happiness has to take into consideration the possible common as well as varying cultural meaning of happiness.

The fault of *construct bias* may occur if researchers in cultural samples administer not the same, but only partially overlapping set of instruments, or different versions of the same instrument, which presumably measure the same construct. However, practically the *construct bias* is more likely when researchers use the same instrument in different cultural contexts without cultural validation that it measures the same construct. Cross-cultural research requires using culture-sensitive measures.

Writing of explicit and comprehensive *conceptual* and *operational definition of constructs* under study is the best way to avoid the *construct bias*. This requirement is not always followed in emotion research. For example, some scholars may use the words, like anger, love, shame, and guilt as independent (or dependent) variables. First, they do not define those constructs conceptually because throughout the years of emotions scholarship "everyone knows" what the anger is. Second, they do not define those constructs operationally displaying the words as stimuli. However, the research presented in the following chapters shows that the meaning of emotional words can be interpreted differently. Participants—individually and culturally—may have specific connotations or points of reference related to these emotions. They may think of different situations and circumstances, the real, desired, normative experience, or just a cultural idea of an emotion in mind. Therefore, explicit conceptual and operational definitions, as well as explicitly written instructions to participants can help avoid a possible *construct bias*.

Item Bias

Item bias takes place when a statement, question, word, picture, or any other stimulus may have different meanings in other cultures. Item bias partially compromises the equivalency of instrument, or some of its scale. Different understanding of the item (independent variable) makes response (dependent variable) not adequately comparable.

Item bias can occur due to its poor translation into other language, ambiguous or ambivalent connotations in different cultures, or particular association that a statement or word has for people in one culture, but not in other. Some words and expressions are culturally specific and may not have equivalent words in other languages. The English "I feel blue," or "I feel the chemistry between us" are not well translatable. Therefore, the use of culturally-specific metaphors in measurement instruments makes them vulnerable to the item bias. My best advice would be to use plain language and vocabulary of low-educated (or at least moderately educated) person in the construction of measurement instruments. Misunderstanding of a sentence, question, or word by a native speaker can also be a source of item bias.

Exact translation of items (questions, words, statements) of a measurement instrument may be desirable, yet the *adequate and culturally sensitive translation of their meaning* is more important. Despite these efforts of perfect translation, however, participants in different cultural samples can still interpret the items not the same way. Besides, some items applicable in one culture may be not applicable in another. For instance, the questions about gender roles in house and driving car are not applicable in some countries where many participants do not live in houses and do not have cars.

Despite the requirement of linguistic equivalence for the measurement of a construct across cultures, some authors (Boehnke et al., 2014) propose loosening this requirement. Instead of using identically worded items in different language versions of an instrument, they suggest to follow an emic methodology. Developing the instrument, researchers within cultures should generate items independently and then investigate structural and measurement equivalence of the instrument.

Response Style Bias

Individuals or groups of participants may have a systematic tendency to use particular categories of answers, or certain points on rating scales, when they evaluate any target construct. Regardless of the content of question in a survey, they tend to respond in certain ways (Paulhus, 1991a, 1991b; Van Vaerenbergh & Thomas, 2013). The *response styles* can be driven by participants' emotional states, personality traits, and cultural factors.

The corrections for the biased response styles may be important to identify the real cross-cultural differences in the constructs under study, instead of cultural differences in response styles. However, researchers should approach such correction and adjustment carefully. If the scores in cultural samples are due to both response styles and genuine differences between groups, then adjustment for response styles may remove genuine cross-cultural differences (He & van de Vijver, 2012; Van Vaerenbergh & Thomas, 2013). Let us consider some of the *response style biases*.

Acquiescence is a tendency to agree ("yea-saying") rather than to disagree with statements, regardless of their content. *Acquiescence bias* is displayed when participants agree with majority of questions, statements, or items, and reluctant to disagree. The number of points in Likert rating scale can affect *acquiescence bias* (e.g., Hui & Triandis, 1989; Weijters, Cabooter, & Schillewaert, 2010). In particular, in case when a scale has a midpoint as a response anchor, the *acquiescence* is higher (Weijters et al., 2010).

People with such characteristics of cognitive style as cognitive simplicity, rigid mental organization, and intolerance of alternatives tend to exhibit more *acquiescence* in their responses than those with social concern and socially desirable responding (Knowles & Nathan, 1997). *Acquiescence* is more prevalent in responses among participants of low socioeconomic status and of collectivistic cultures (Harzing, 2006; Rammstedt, Kemper, & Borg, 2013; Smith & Fischer, 2008).

Another kind of response bias is *hallo effect*. This is a consistent tendency of participants to rely on general impression in their ratings of the attitudes toward a target person or object.

General positive or negative evaluation of a person changes (or adjusts) evaluations of the person's traits, which are rated positively or negatively accordingly, regardless other available or insufficient information (Berscheid & Walster, 1972; Cooper, 1981; Dion, Berscheid, & Walster, 1972; Nisbett & Wilson, 1977). What is beautiful is good. What is good is good in all respects.

The halo effect can substantially alter the rating of an object or person in case of highly positive or negative emotions. When people are happy, they believe they are happy in all regards. Happiness embraces all aspects of life. When a man or woman passionately loves, they love everything in their beloved.

Demand characteristics may also have certain effects on participants' behavior and responses altering the results as artifact of research design (Orne, 1962; Rosnow, 2002; Rosnow & Rosenthal, 1997). The term *demand characteristics* stands for the idea that participants may be aware of what findings a researcher anticipates and what behavior is expected from participants (McCambridge, De Bruin, & Witton, 2012).

For example, this may occur when participants interpret the implicit assumption of "*being a good research participant*" in a specific way. In particular, they exhibit particular behaviors or answer questions with certain personal bias. This way they attempt to serve as a *good subject* to meet researcher's expectations (Nichols & Maner, 2008).

The *bias of "being a good research participant"* can compromise the results of study, making them not adequately comparable between cultural groups. Instead of an implied instruction "be yourself, and act as if you were alone," participants in some cultures may try to "maintain a good impression regardless of how you really feel." The desire to make an impression on researchers can substantially skew the results. I should admit, however, that no studies investigating this effect in cross-cultural settings have been conducted so far.

Extreme response bias is a tendency of participants to respond questions or rate items in the extreme way. They tend to answer with the extreme responses rather than with those in the middle. Rating of their attitudes with 5 out of 5, or 1 out of 5, on majority of statements brings a clear evidence of extremity style.

It is important to note that *extreme response bias* affects descriptive and inferential statistics, and therefore, compromise validity of the cross-cultural comparisons (Cheung & Rensvold, 2000). The differences in extreme response bias in cultural samples may cause wrong and invalid conclusions about real differences between cultures. Cultures differ in the tendency toward *extreme response bias* (Arce-Ferrer, 2006; Greenleaf, 1992; Hui & Triandis, 1989; Smith & Fischer, 2008). For instance, compared to other cultures, participants from Mediterranean and Latin American countries, African Americans and Latino Americans in the United States, have higher tendency to use extreme responses (Cheung & Rensvold, 2000).

The Methods to Detect Measurement Biases

Measurement inequivalence and *response bias* can distort the results of comparison of attitudes among cultural groups (Kankarash & Moors, 2011; Morren et al., 2011; Van de Vijver & Leung, 2011).

Statistical corrections and adjustments are useful on the stage of data analysis. Neglecting to apply those may result in development of invalid or inadequate models of emotions. Mean scores and correlations, or some more complex statistical methods deriving from them are the most typical in construction of cultural models. Researchers proposed various analytic methods of bias detection and verification of equivalence. Among those methods are exploratory factor analysis (EFA), confirmatory factor analysis (CFA), differential item functioning analysis (DIF) (He & van de Vijver, 2012).

Researchers can use the *frequency* of particular responses, the *means* and *standard deviations* of scores in individuals and cultural groups to control for these response tendencies (Fischer, 2004). Let us consider some examples.

Correlations between the scores corrected based on within-cultural (or within-individual) standardization of the raw scores can indicate the degree to which the response style influences the scores. Differences in the size of correlations show how salient the response style is in the data set (He & van de Vijver, 2012).

Here is another approach to detection of biased response styles. First, researchers run regression analysis, in which standardized scores are used to predict the raw scores. Second, they compare the raw scores with the predicted scores in *t* tests. This analysis allows detecting the cultural groups, which exhibit biased response styles (Hanges, 2004).

One more method to detect and treat a response style is to compute the response style scores. This can be the proportion of items that are endorsed as a *measure of acquiescence.* Or this can be the proportion of extreme responses as a *measure of extremity* scoring (Van Dijk, Datema, Piggen, Welten, & Van de Vijver, 2009).

The Rating of Emotions Referenced to Self or Cultural Group

In *self-referenced rating approach*, researchers ask participants to self-report and rate their preference, experience, and expression of emotions. It is a common methodology in cross-cultural emotion research. Introspections of own thoughts, feelings, attitudes, and the reflection of own behavior convey indicators for investigation. *Self-referenced rating* reveals individual preferences and differences. It should be noted that such self-rating may be biased for the study of objective cultural differences because participants may be not typical representatives of their culture; they can be more in favor or opposed to the norms of their cultural group.

The norms, experience, and expression of emotions at the level of culture and at the level of individual may differ. These differences can be due to the extent to which an individual within a culture has internalized the cultural values. Because of this, some individuals are more representative of the cultural type than others. The differences can also be due to individual and typological variety of individuals within the society. Averaging the individual self-ratings, we can say that the American culture is extraverted and self-asserted, yet very many individuals in that society are introverted, shy, and timid.

These could be the reasons why many studies (see for review Fischer, 2006) have demonstrated that self- and culture-referenced ratings have little congruence in a number of cultural and psychological dimensions. Several scholars have also commented on the possible problems of measuring and comparing participants' self-ratings as indicators of culture (e.g., Heine, Lehman, Peng, & Greenholtz, 2002; Oyserman, Coon, & Kemmelmeier, 2002; Peng, Nisbett, & Wong, 1997). For instance, studies showed (Heine et al., 2002) that due to *reference-group effect*, social-comparison processes can complicate cross-cultural comparison and make self-ratings confounding and ambiguous. When participants rate themselves in one cultural sample, they may have in mind one set of standards for comparison than participants in another cultural sample do. Therefore, the data obtained in cross-cultural research using subjective Likert scales can be compromised because of different reference groups.

In a *group-referenced rating approach*, researchers ask participants to rate the typical behavior of others—members of their cultural group. Such methodology reveals the social perceptions, descriptive norms, and experiences of a cultural group. This *group-referenced rating* reflects the norms shared within a group. The *group-referenced rating* can be a valuable alternative to the self-ratings.

The studies have revealed that self-rating and group-referenced rating may not overlap, or partially overlap, or have more complex relations (e.g., Fischer, 2006; House, Hanges, Javidan, Dorfman, & Gupta, 2003; Peng et al., 1997; Terracciano et al., 2005). For example, whereas "cultural experts agreed that East Asians are more collectivistic than North Americans, cross-cultural comparisons of trait and attitude measures failed to reveal such a pattern" (Heine et al., 2002, p. 903).

Generalization about cultural differences needs taking into account the different *referents of ratings* (Fischer, 2006). Research of cultural norms, values, and behaviors should ask individuals to rate these aspects of culture in *reference to their society*, rather than in reference to their personal views and preferences. This rating is more valid if these cultural phenomena are observable and normative. If research aims to explore how cultural norms and values influence the individual level variables of participants, then *self-referent rating* is suitable.

Ratings Versus Ranking in Construction of Cultural Models

The earlier sections of this chapter showed that the *procedure of rating* in *self-report research design* is vulnerable to such response biases, as acquiescence, extreme responses, hallo effect, and alike. This may create a challenge for researchers in the discovery of the real differential value of emotions and the real experience and expression of emotions. It seems that wanting everything and at once is natural tendency. When participants feel elation, they tend to rate everything as great. Culture still can moderate this tendency. These difficulties with *rating response biases* can obscure factor analysis and hide real cultural differences in emotions.

The *ranking* as the *forced-choice procedure* can help achieve goals in some cases of cross-cultural research. The results of studies in different fields demonstrate the similar findings between rating and ranking, or ranking shows better validity (e.g., Moors, Vriens, Gelissen, & Vermunt, 2016; Moore, 1975; Rankin & Grube, 1980; Van Herk & van de Velden, 2007).

For example, researchers (Harzing et al., 2009) have investigated the problem with response style differences and proposed a solution. The results of their study showed that even though the simple response format of 7-point Likert scale has advantages, compared to traditional 5-point Likert scales, yet ranking is a better solution. When these response formats are used, the findings bring the better validity of cross-national differences.

The study of Russell and Gray (1994) showed that both rating and ranking may have their respective merits. Generally, the data obtained with two methods correlate. There are some factors that affect their validity and reliability, which are worthwhile to know for emotion researchers. In particular, participants who show a larger spread of their ratings have good correspondence between their ratings and ranks. Under the *relative instruction,* participants' ratings have larger spread that their ratings guided by the absolute instruction. A ranking procedure has its advantages in case where the items are highly discriminable. In case when ranking is not suitable, a rating procedure with *relative* instructions is a good option (Russell & Gray, 1994, p. 79).

Researchers have occasionally used the ranking response format as an alternative to rating in the studies of values (e.g., McCarty & Shrum, 2000; Moore, 1975; Rankin & Grube, 1980), and some scholars found that "ranking and ratings do produce results that are more similar than often thought" (Moors et al., 2016, p. 15).

The *ranking procedure* can be used in construction of *cultural models of emotion* when scholars are interested to explore the *relative values of specific emotions or dimensions* in a culture, or compare the value structures of emotions across cultures.

3.3   Exploring Scientific Constructs and Dimensions for the Construction of Cultural Models of Emotions

3.3.1   Descriptive Methodology of Cultural Models of Emotions

Descriptive Approach to Cultural Models of Emotions in Anthropology

This approach is quite typical in anthropology and linguistics and relies largely on qualitative description of emotional life, emotional conceptions, or emotional phenomena in a particular cultural context. Measurement and quantitative methods may be used, but not necessarily. The cultural model of this type describes emotional life of people in a culture as a unique cultural construction. In this approach, comparison with emotional life in other cultures is limited and is mostly descriptive and qualitative, rather than quantitative. The anthropological models of anger, presented in the following sections, are the examples of such descriptive models.

These models are the case studies of cultural diversity that expand our views on emotions as cultural phenomena and their multiple connections with other aspects of culturally-specific life. As Nelson and Jankowiak (2021, p. 41) noted, "A principle objective of anthropology is to challenge cultural stereotypes…" For instance, Lutz (1982, 1988) explored the *culture of Ifaluk*, Gerber (1975)—the *Samoans' culture*, (White, 1985)—the *culture of Solomon Islands*, Myers (1979)—the *culture of Pintupi Aborigines of Australia*, Abu-Lughod (1986/2000)—the *culture of a Bedouin tribe in Egypt*, Briggs (1970)—the culture of *Utku Inuits of Northern Canada*. These anthropologists showed that many indigenous *views on emotions* in those cultures are drastically different from *American view*, thus challenging American ethnocentric opinion in this regard. This and many other examples, presented in the following chapters of this book illustrate this point.

Among the methods, which cultural anthropologists use in their research are participant observations, structured and unstructured interviews, free listing, pile sorting, questionnaires, scaling, consensus analysis, (Bernard, 2006; Bernard & Gravlee, 2014; De Munck, 2009; Ember & Ember, 2009). In extension of traditional methods of cultural anthropology, Chrisomalis (2006) suggested a comparative perspective with diachronic methods. In this approach, events and processes in their temporal perspective are the units of analysis that are compared with one another allowing a direct comparison of cultural change over time.

Descriptive Approach to Cultural Models of Emotions in Psycholinguistics

Psycholinguistic studies compare the *lexicon of emotions* in different languages that may reflect prevailing *emotionology* (Wierzbicka, 1999) and cultural models of emotions (e.g., Athanasiadou & Tabakowska, 1998; Goddard, 1995; Ljung, 2010; Wierzbicka, 1991, 1992, 1999, 2003, 2004a).

Emotional experience is substantially expressed in metaphors, metonymies, and related concepts. These lexical units have many cross-culturally similarity, yet reveal cultural differences (Boers, 2003; Kövecses, 2003, 2005, 2006). Idioms, proverbs, and figurative compounds, being compared in cross-cultural perspective also discover important knowledge of emotions across language and cultures (Dobrovolskij & Piirainen, 2005).

Descriptive Approach to Cultural Models of Emotions in Psychology

Cross-cultural psychology also employs descriptive methods in field work and case studies (see for review, Berry, Poortinga, & Pandey, 1997; Lonner & Berry, 1986). Cultural psychologists also employ qualitative descriptive research designs, which include the extended work of researcher in the field. This approach is well suited for in-depth and detailed descriptions of a phenomenon that is little known (Karasz & Singelis, 2009).

Descriptive Approach to Cultural Models of Emotions in Personal Observations

Other useful sources of cultural knowledge are personal observations of people who have lived in those cultural contexts. These may be the notes of travelers, immigrants, journalists, or people temporarily living in other country as professionals. This also can be the expert opinions of local scholars. When documented in books, magazines, and media forums, and compiled together in a systematic way, they can present the data from observers' perspective (e.g., Daun, 1995; Davies & Ikeno, 2011; Ferguson, 2016; Flippo, 2018; Hendry, 2019). Although they may be patchy and fragmentary, they can still be considered as "case studies." Even being anecdotal, when they coincide from independent sources, they can confirm their validity. In their cumulative amount and range, they may serve as convincing evidence, which are good to supplement other data collected with rigorous scientific methodology.

3.3.2 Comparative Methodology of Cultural Models of Emotions

Quantitative Comparative Approach to Cultural Models of Emotions

This approach is more typical for psychology, sociology, and communication sciences (e.g., Berry et al., 1997; Cohen, 2007; Davidov, Schmidt, & Billiet, 2018; Matsumoto & Van de Vijver, 2010; Van de Vijver & Leung, 1997; Zhu, 2016).

It is less frequently employed in anthropology and linguistics (e.g., De Munck, 2009; Jakobovits, 1966; Kovecses, 2006; Wierzbicka, 1999). In many studies (see for review, Bernard, 2006; Bernard & Gravlee, 2014; De Munck, 2009; Ember & Ember, 2009; Johnson, 1978), cultural anthropologists employ quantitative methods of data collection (e.g., scaling, free listing, pile sorting, structured questionnaires) and analysis (univariate, bivariate, and multivariate analyses). In addition to qualitative conceptual and operational descriptions of emotions, their experiences and expressions, researchers attempt to quantify their similarities and differences.

If emotions are *qualitatively equivalent*, they can be compared *quantitatively*. For example, the dimensions of valence (positive vs. negative) and intensity (high vs. low) appeared to be equivalent across many cultures. Therefore, researchers compared the people's preferences and experience of positive, negative, or balanced emotions investigating how similar or different cultures are in this regard. Based on typicality of these similarities and differences, it is possible to construct corresponding cultural models of emotions, which are described in the following chapters. The same way, based on typicality of the emotions of high or low intensity, the models of passionate and dispassionate emotions are described later in the book. This *comparative paradigm* has been probably the most typical throughout recent decades and provided abundance of knowledge for the construction of cultural models of emotions. For instance, Western and Eastern cultures, American and Japanese countries have been compared on a number of emotions, their experiences and expressions.

Following this approach, researchers measure several specially selected emotional variables in purposely (or conveniently) selected cultural samples. Then they run *analysis of variance* (ANOVA) of these variables between categorically different groups and interpret similarities and differences in light of knowledge available about those cultures. For example, categorization of Japanese (or Chinese) sample as belonging to collectivistic culture, while American (actually European American) sample as belonging to individualistic culture was sufficient explanatory framework in many studies. Later this framework was developed deeper with introduction of the conception of independent and interdependent self-construal (see details in the previous and following chapters).

Alternatively, researchers correlate these emotional variables (their means or patterns of means) with cultural variables (e.g., individualism and collectivism) in a number of cultural samples. Multiple studies conducted in such research designs have provided the extensive knowledge to construct individualistic and collectivistic models of emotions, with independent and interdependent self-construal as explanatory framework.

If emotions are *qualitatively not equivalent* in different cultures, they can be compared only *qualitatively* with description of similarity and difference, or with a measure of presence or absence—as in *categorical descriptive approach*, see above.

Multidimensional Approach to Cultural Models of Emotions

In multifaceted cases, emotions can be compared with more complex multidimensional, multilevel, or structural methods. The main purpose of categorical and dimensional approaches in construction of cultural models is to find similarities and differences in samples and associate those with some cultural factors and dimensions, which likely affect those. The number of emotional and cultural variables, which researchers are able to measure, has substantially extended throughout recent decades. And the number of studies from categorical and dimensional approaches continues to grow, accumulating more and more knowledge about emotions in different countries.

However, the single and even multiple comparisons of nations in emotional variables with one statistics (such as the mean value, or correlation) can disguise the cultural complexity of emotional life (Eid & Diener, 2001). Multidimensional approach to emotion research and corresponding methods take into account the descriptive statistics (e.g., means and standard deviations) of several emotional variables comparing those with several cultural variables at once. Analysis of variance of single variables (among the others) from an emotional group and comparing this variance with the variance of single variables (among the others) from a cultural group are the essentials of this multidimensional comparative methodology. The single variables on the one side are compared with the single variables on the other side. ANOVA and Pierson correlation, or their derivatives, are the typical statistical tools.

The purpose of truly *multidimensional methodology* is to analyze several emotional variables (or cultural variables) at once and create typologies of their combinations.

Discovering (1) the *emotional typologies* as the *typical combinations of emotions* and *their dimensions*—emotional patterns of means and standard deviations—and (2) *relations of these patterns with cultural dimensions* are the steps toward real multidimensionality in cultural models of emotions. This is the *bottom-up approach*, as described above.

The same way, discovering (1) the *cultural typology* as the typical *patterns of cultural dimensions* and (2) identification of the *single emotions*, or *emotional patterns* typical for those types of culture are the steps toward another multidimensionality of cultural models of emotions. This is the *top-down approach*.

Several multivariate statistics, such as multivariate analysis of variance (MANOVA), multivariate analysis of covariance (MANCOVA), multivariate regression, discriminant analysis, and cluster analysis are useful to achieve this goal. They allow comparing the complex cultural patterns of meaning, experience, and expression of emotions.

3.3.3 Structural Methodology of Cultural Models of Emotions

Exploring the Relationships Between Constructs and Their Structures

Researchers are also interested in exploration of *relationships between emotional variables* in different cultural contexts. These are the relations of covariance, semantic similarity, causation, and others.

Correlations between variables demonstrate their association and correlational structure of emotional processes, experience, expression, and then allow comparing these structures across cultures. This still looks like *comparative approach,* yet it is integrated with *multidimensional* and *structural approaches.*

Various statistical methods, such as canonical correlation analysis, principal component analysis, structural equation modeling, factor analysis, multidimensional scaling, discriminant analysis, and cluster analysis allow identifying the typical structures of relations (correlational or semantic) between emotional variables in a given culture. Then researchers compare these structures in various cultures to evaluate their structural similarity, and sometimes differences.

Structural equation modeling (SEM) is an approach to statistical analysis of data that include several methods, techniques, and extensions. Its main purpose is to explore the structure of relations among *observed measures* and *latent variables.* The SEM approach has many advantages for the studies of *conceptual structures,* compared to correlation that is traditionally used in the behavioral and social sciences (Hoyle, 1995; Kline, 2015). *Confirmatory factor analysis* (CFA) is probably the most promising SEM method for development of *cultural models of emotions* and therefore, is reviewed in more details below.

Overall, cross-cultural psychology has developed many methods of data collection and statistical analyses (e.g., Davidov et al., 2018; Matsumoto & Van de Vijver, 2010; Van de Vijver & Leung, 1997), which can be used for development of *structural cultural models of emotions.* Some of them are briefly reviewed in the following sections.

Multiple-Group Confirmatory Factor Analysis

Factor analysis aims to identify the factors that account for the variation and covariation among the indicators of an instrument. A *factor* (*latent variable*) is a variable that is associated with indicators (*observed measures*), such as survey responses, ratings of items, behavioral ratings. This *latent variable* (*factor*) accounts for the correlations between these *observed measures.* That means that the *observed measures* correlate with each other because of the latent variable as a common cause, due to the influence of the same underlying construct. These structures of relations are the latent variable measurement models. Such a measurement model offers a simpler understanding of the covariation between indicators. It reduces the number of measured variables to the fewer number of factors (Brown, 2015; Thompson, 2004).

Confirmatory factor analysis (CFA) is widely employed for the purpose of measurement scale development and validation across groups. It is useful when researchers want to verify their theoretical structure of a construct. CFA explores *measurement models* as the *typical structures of relationships* between (a) *indicators (observable measures)* and (b) *latent variables (factors)*, such as the instrument total score, subscale scores, which are the variables measuring the construct.

Multiple-group confirmatory factor analysis (MG-CFA) is an extension of *structural equation modeling* (SEM). The method has become typical for many studies which investigate invariance of structures and measures across groups (Chen, 2008; Hirschfeld & Von Brachel, 2014). MG-CFA compares "latent variable means, variances, and covariances across groups while holding measurement parameters invariant" (Asparouhov & Muthén, 2014, p. 495).

Multiple-group confirmatory factor analysis is especially useful to explore the *measurement invariance* in cross-cultural psychology. The method can be very valuable for the development of *structural cultural models of emotions* that are *cross-culturally similar*. If researchers theorize that their *structural model of emotions* should be the same across certain cultural groups—due to some cultural factors—the *multiple-group confirmatory factor analysis* would be a good option.

The method, however, is not sensitive to the possibly different relations between those variables in other cultures. It seeks to make the structure of relations between emotional variable in different cultural samples equivalent to each other. The method can also inform researchers that *structural model of emotion* in one culture is different from others. Yet, to compare the two models is another and separate task.

The *alignment method* as a new method for *multiple-group confirmatory factor analysis* (MG-CFA) is used "to estimate group-specific factor means and variances without requiring exact measurement invariance" (Asparouhov & Muthén, 2014, p. 495). The method is able to estimate models for several groups and can be a valuable alternative to MG-CFA methods, which estimate *measurement invariance* manually (with modification indices). The *alignment method* automates and simplifies the analysis of measurement invariance.

Multiple factor analysis (MFA) can be another alternative method (Abdi & Valentin, 2007; Abdi, Williams, & Valentin, 2013; Pagès, 2014) for investigation of structures of constructs in cross-cultural research. MFA is an extension of principal component analysis (PCA), which allows analyzing "a set of observations described by several groups of variables" (Abdi & Valentin, 2007, p. 658). MFA explores the common structures, which are present in all or some of these groups.

> *First* it computes a PCA of each data table and 'normalizes' each data table by dividing all its elements by the first singular value obtained from its PCA. *Second*, all the normalized data tables are aggregated into a grand data table that is analyzed via a (non-normalized) PCA that gives a set of factor scores for the observations and loadings for the variables. (Abdi et al., 2013, p. 149)

To reveal communalities and discrepancies, the different data sets are projected on the global analysis. Every data table displays a set of partial factor scores for the observations. This information reveals the specific "view-point" of this data table

(Abdi et al., 2013). Researchers in different domains of science employ MFA. I believe that cross-cultural research of emotions can also benefit from its use when dealing with cultural groups in attempt to identify commonalities as well as differences in the structures of constructs.

Multidimensional Scaling and Cultural Models of Emotions

Multidimensional scaling (MDS) is a statistical *method* of *data reduction* that analyzes the structure in a set of distance measures between objects (e.g., emotions, individuals, cultures). The input for analysis is *distance-like data*, such as quantitative measures of similarities, dissimilarities, distances, or proximities between pairs of objects. The data sets may include ratings of similarities between emotions, individuals, cultures, as well as intercorrelations between measurement items. Subjective ratings of similarity or dissimilarity between objects (e.g., emotions, individuals, cultures), attributes (e.g., dimensions), or scripts of events and behaviors can be examined with MDS. The method can analyze several data sets obtained from several respondents, raters, or cultural samples (Borg & Groenen, 2005; Borg, Groenen, & Mair, 2012).

MDS analyzes the data and locate objects as the points in a geometrical conceptual space. The distances between the points depict similarities and dissimilarities between objects in Euclidean space. The similar objects are shown by the points that are close to each other, whereas the dissimilar objects are shown by the points that are far apart (Borg & Groenen, 2005; Borg, Groenen, & Mair, 2012; Young, 2013).

The structure of relationship between objects is represented as a *two-* or *three-dimensional scatterplot*, which help better understand the dimensional structure of data. The conceptual space may be non-Euclidean and may have more dimensions.

Multidimensional scaling (MDS) has been used in emotion research, including cross-cultural comparisons. For example, researchers explored how people across cultures and languages perceive similarity and differences in the meaning between feelings described by words, in the feelings expressed by facial expressions (Herrmann & Raybeck, 1981; Katsikitis, 1997; Russell, 1994); Russell, Lewicka, & Niit, 1989), in the features of vocal patterns of emotions (Van Bezooijen, Otto, & Heenan, 1983), and in the emotional scripts (Panayiotou, 2008). Cross-cultural scholars can effectively employ the MDS for development of *cultural models of emotions*.

Latent Class Analysis and Cultural Models of Emotions

Latent class analysis is a statistical technique that allows exploring the *measurement model,* in which individuals can be classified into latent classes. Such classification is usually based on the typical patterns of multivariate categorical data, such as participants' responses. *Simultaneous latent-class analysis across groups* presents an especially interesting and perspective method for investigation of measurement equivalence (invariance) in cross-cultural research (Kankaraš, Moors, & Vermunt, 2010; Kankaraš & Vermunt, 2014). It is beneficial for comparison of the latent structures between multiple cultural groups.

Eid and colleagues (e.g., Eid & Diener, 2001; Eid, Langeheine, & Diener, 2003; Kim-Prieto & Eid, 2004) have proposed to use the *latent class analysis* as methodology to explore and evaluate *typological structures of emotion*. Authors describe several benefits of this methodological approach. *Latent class analysis* allows studying "(a) categorical response variables, (b) intra- and international differences in individual profiles, and (c) universal and culture-specific norm types." (Eid & Diener, 2001, p. 883).

Due to these advantages, the method is well suitable for the cross-cultural comparison of emotional experience and expression. It also gives the analytical capability to construct *structural cultural models of emotions* by measuring the equivalence of structures across cultures. In particular, even though the analysis rejected the strong assumption of measurement invariance for the total cross-cultural sample, nevertheless authors (Eid & Diener, 2001) were able to identify those groups of individuals, which are equivalent across countries, and those groups of individuals, which are culturally specific. Their model with universal and culture-specific classes has shown the structural equivalence and structural diversity of the norms of emotions between cultures. *Latent class analysis* is capable to separate universal from culture-specific patterns of emotion. The method also allows to identify different classes corresponding to patterns of different cultures, as well as variations of patterns within cultures (Eid & Diener, 2001). Thus, the method uses a typological approach that is more informative and productive than a dimensional approach for construction of cultural models of emotions.

Cluster Analysis for Development of Cultural Models of Emotions

Cluster analysis is a statistical methodology for analyzing multivariate data with a main objective to classify a sample of cases (e.g., objects, individuals, groups) into subsets, which are homogeneous and well separated from each other. This *classification* is made based on the value of several variables of research interest (e.g., attitudes, actions, emotions). The cases with the same subset resemble one another and on the basis of this similarity constitute a homogeneous subset—*cluster*. These cases within the cluster are separated and differ from those in other clusters.

Thus, cluster analysis determines multidimensional distances between cases using similarities and differences between those in corresponding variables. Researchers pick out the clusters of cases, which have the relatively small distances. The hidden patterns of similarities and differences between cases in their variables create a structure of cases, their taxonomy, or typology.

Among several clustering techniques, *nonhierarchical* and *hierarchical clustering* are the commonly used (Bezdek, 2017; Kaufman & Rousseeuw, 2009; Kettenring, 2006; Maxwell, Pryor, & Smith, 2002).

The *nonhierarchical clustering* separates the cases in a number of clusters minimizing intracluster variance and maximizing intercluster variance using an iterative algorithm. The *two-step clustering* technique compares the values of model choice criteria in different clustering solutions and automatically chooses what the optimum number of clusters is.

The *k-means clustering* allows selecting the number of clusters that the algorithm generates. For example, when researchers hypothesize to obtain four clusters, they select 4 in the *k-means* option. Then, the algorithm of cluster analysis separates the cases in four clusters with minimum of intracluster variance and maximum of intercluster variance. The quality and meaning of clusters are interpreted in terms of cluster centroids, the relative sizes of clusters, and meaningful explanation in light of theoretical conception.

The *hierarchical clustering* uses a step-wise process merging several closest cases at each step. This hierarchical procedure develops a tree-like structure (dendrogram) where each case is a leaf at the top of the tree, while all of the cases comprise a single group at the bottom.

Although these clustering methods are productive in social science studies, they may be not as effective dealing with the data where clusters are ambiguous, or overlap with each other. In this case, *fuzzy clustering* can be a flexible option to the other clustering methods. The method allows for a case to belong to more than one cluster simultaneously (Bolin, Edwards, Finch, & Cassady, 2014; De Oliveira & Pedrycz, 2007; Höppner, Klawonn, Kruse, & Runkler, 1999).

Many studies employ cluster analysis to classify cases (objects, individuals, social groups) based on the observed variables measuring those. However, it is also possible to use cluster analysis for dimension reduction—thus clustering variables (Farrelly et al., 2017; Revelle, 1979, 2019; Tryon, 1958). For instance, hierarchical cluster analysis (HCA) can be a useful nonparametric method for psychometric analysis of survey data. A study (Farrelly et al., 2017) has demonstrated that HCA have several advantages compared to EFA. The graphics of HCA, such as dendrograms, means plots, heat maps are very helpful. When hierarchical clustering is used to validate factorially designed measures, it shows more stable and consistent results.

Methods of *cluster analysis* have found their applications in various fields, such as marketing, business, social sciences, biology, medicine (see for review, Fonseca, 2013; Hennig, Meila, Murtagh, & Rocci, 2015; Kaufman & Rousseeuw, 2009; Kettenring, 2006; Maxwell et al., 2002) since they are useful for various tasks of classifications.

For example, in sociology *cluster analysis* was used to create a fivefold typology of welfare state regimes (Bambra, 2007), to structure intergenerational exchanges in American families, to identify family types (Henry, Tolan, & Gorman-Smith, 2005), to classify casino gamblers (Lee, Lee, Bernhard, & Yoon, 2006).

Cross-cultural research has actively utilized cluster analysis to classify countries based on some cultural parameters (e.g., Ladwig, Richter, Ringle, & Heitger, 2012; Maleki & de Jong, 2014; Merritt, 2000; Minkov & Hofstede, 2014; Ronen &

Shenkar, 1985; Widmer, Treas, & Newcomb, 1998), such cultural dimensions, values, socioeconomic variables of societies, and personality traits.

In emotion research, researchers (e.g., Stephens, Christie, & Friedman, 2010) used cluster analysis to investigate the specificity of basic emotions in terms of autonomic nervous system (ANS) variables, as well as to identify the distinct clusters of individuals based on their individual response tendencies (these are extreme alpha-adrenergic, extreme beta-adrenergic, or relatively nonreactive). Researchers used clustering to explore taxonomy of the vocabulary of emotions (Storm & Storm, 1987). Cluster analysis was also used for clustering of emotions in cultural and cross-cultural perspective (Dietze, 1963; Scollon, Diener, Oishi, & Biswas-Diener, 2004; Toivonen et al., 2012).

Latent cluster analysis (LCA) is another statistical technique of clustering to explore typologies. It is based on *dichotomous variables* and identifies latent classes based on the patterns of responses (Clogg, 1995; Hagenaars & Halman, 1989; Lazarsfeld & Henry, 1968).

These capabilities and statistical techniques, summarized above, make cluster analysis a very perspective statistical method to create cultural models of emotions as the typologies of emotional patterns across cultures. Its advantages are in possibilities to classify cases and variables.

On individual level of study (see next section), researchers can treat individual participants as cases and classify those based on the variables of emotional meanings, experiences, and expressions. It might be worthwhile to include the participants from all cultural samples at once, or run cluster analysis on each sample separately, depending on the task at hand. Compiling the groups of participants who are similar within clusters and different from those in other cluster opens various opportunities for further analysis. This is a better approach than just averaging the emotional variables for a whole cultural sample with unverified assumption of its homogeneity. It might be likely that the cultural sample is heterogeneous and need more differentiated further analysis. The division between cultural models of emotions may be not on the "borders" of cultural samples, but even within those samples. The similar kind of analysis was conducted with latent class factor analysis (Eid et al., 2003; Eid & Diener, 2001).

On cultural level of study (see next section), cultures can also be the cases for cluster analysis, as in some recent studies (Minkov & Hofstede, 2012b; Minkov & Hofstede, 2014), if the sample of cultures is sufficient and have corresponding variables of emotions.

As I commented above, cluster analysis can also be employed for dimension reduction, thus classifying variables. Whereas factor analysis runs the dimension reduction based on correlation/covariance, the cluster analysis runs the dimension reduction based on similarities and dissimilarities between variables. The nature of relations between latent variables of emotions in both types of analysis may overlap, yet differ. In factor analysis, observed measures (items) can correlate and co-vary due to different reasons, for example, causation, third variable association, semantic similarities. And researchers may not know the nature of this covariance between items. Therefore, they call that latent variable with a very general term "factor." If researchers want to classify items in groups based on their similarity, then cluster analysis is more preferable method. The cluster analysis of variables (items), as indicators of emotions, can help identify the typical patterns of emotional experience and expression in different cultures. Thus, *clustering of cases,* or *variables,* or strategic *combination of both approaches,* according to the aim of study, can bring several possibilities to create cultural models of emotions.

Multilevel Methodology of Cultural Models

Multilevel methodology implies that psychological parameters can be analyzed on the country level or individual level. For example, Triandis and colleagues (Triandis et al., 2001) investigated how the variables of culture, personality, deception, and emotions are related in international management negotiation. Authors applied *multilevel analysis* and found different relations between collectivism and the use of "deception in negotiations, and to greater emotional reactions (i.e. guilt, shame, and disgust) after the use of deception" at the cultural and individual levels (p. 73).

Cultural models can describe and analyze variables at any of these levels using corresponding sets of variables: individualism of society, power distance, context differentiation, or relational mobility—at the country level, whereas idiocentrism (psychological variable of individualism), personality traits, prevalent emotional valence, intensity, or expressivity—at the individual level.

It is also possible to derive the variables of one level from the variables of another level by aggregation or disaggregation of scores (Van de Vijver, van Hermert, & Poortinga, 2008). For example, in case of aggregation, the culture-level scores for variables of personality traits are obtained by aggregation of individual scores on these variables when a researcher calculate the sample means in national samples (Fischer & Poortinga, 2018; Smith, Fischer, Vignoles, & Bond, 2013). The pitfall of such aggregation is that all participants from the United States, for instance, – an average extraverted country—obtain the high extraversion score, despite the fact that many Americans are introverts. These aggregated individual variables should be interpreted cautiously to avoid the methodological fallacy, which I call "an average temperature of human bodies among patients in the hospital." We can calculate the latter variable, but it would be meaningless for research. The country-level individual variables conceal and mask the real individual diversity of people within country.

In case of disaggregation, individual-level scores of individualism are simply attributed to individual participants based on their nation-level variables (Fischer & Poortinga, 2018). The pitfall of disaggregation is that participants from the United States are assumed to be individualistic because they reside in an individualist country, whereas those from an East Asian country are assumed to be collectivistic. This assumption is obscure and may be not adequate. As I commented in earlier section, it is not obvious whether the fact where individuals are raised, or where they live, and how long is more important. The matter of individual variations within a society should also be taken into account.

The explicit tests to verify such ambiguous assumptions may be useful to avoid confusions. The good examples of studies are when researchers included the measure of cultural identity in their research design (e.g., Nguyen & Benet-Martínez, 2013; Tsai, Chentsova-Dutton, Freire-Bebeau, & Przymus, 2002).

Researchers using various techniques of multilevel analysis (Hox, 2010; Muthén & Muthén, 1998–2017) can explore the data at any level and the relationships between levels. Statistical analyses of interactions between variables of higher level (countries) and variables of lower level (individuals nested within these countries) are possible (Fischer & Poortinga, 2018).

For example, *multilevel component analysis* (MLCA) analyzes nested data (Kuppens, Ceulmans, Timmerman, Diener, & Kim-Prieto, 2006). That is quite typical in research design of cross-cultural studies, where participants are nested in cultures, while those cultures, in turn, may be nested in larger cultures (up to universal). Generally, the method can be used for various tasks of cross-cultural analysis of the structures of numerical data, such as structural equivalence of measurement instruments, or structural equivalence of a specific class of variables.

In case of emotion research, the *societal norms* of experience and expression of emotions are the *variables of cultural level*, while the *real experience and expression* of emotions are the *variables of individual level*. Researchers can investigate the cultural models of emotions in a society at any of these levels, or in interactions of both.

In this context, it is important to distinguish the variable of *internal subjective perspective* and the variables of *external objective perspective* on emotions. *Internal perspective* is a variable of interest when a researcher asks, "How/when *do you* experience this emotion...," or "How/when *do you* display this emotion..." in certain social context. On the other side, *external perspective* is a variable of interest when a research asks, "How/when *do people in your country* experience their emotion..." or "How *do people in your country* display their emotion..." in certain social context. The first perspective reflects the *variable of individual level*, while the second perspective reflects the *variable of country level*. The first type of variables can be self-biased, self-defensive, with tendency to self-identify with a culture (i.e., people of that culture) or oppose to it. The second type of variables is also subjective and may be biased due to self-identification with or opposition to the culture, but once it is generalized across individual opinions, it represents an objective picture of cultural life. It is a worthwhile research design to explore the interaction of these two levels to construct a comprehensive and multilevel cultural model of emotions.

Methodological differentiation of *self-referenced rating* versus *group-referenced rating,* which is discussed in earlier sections, is pertinent here. These two types of response format reflect, respectively, the individual-level variables (*self-referenced rating)* and country-level variables (*group-referenced rating).*

Many multilevel analyses in cross-cultural research are traditionally focused on two levels: *culture (country, or population) level* and *individual level.* Nevertheless, it is possible and might be interesting to explore cultural models that include three levels: (1) culture as a country, (2) culture as ethic community, (3) individual levels. This type of research design can be useful in light of multifaceted concept of culture and diversity of types of culture that are presented in the earlier sections.

References

Abdi, H., & Valentin, D. (2007). Multiple factor analysis (MFA). In N. J. Salkind (Ed.), *Encyclopedia of measurement and statistics* (pp. 657–663). Thousand Oaks, CA: Sage.

Abdi, H., Williams, L. J., & Valentin, D. (2013). Multiple factor analysis: Principal component analysis for multitable and multiblock data sets. *Wiley Interdisciplinary Reviews: Computational Statistics, 5*(2), 149–179.

Abu-Lughod, L. (2000). *Veiled sentiments: Honor and poetry in a Bedouin society*. Berkeley, CA: University of California Press. (Original work published 1986).

Alonso-Arbiol, I., Shaver, P. R., Fraley, R. C., Oronoz, B., Unzurrunzaga, E., & Urizar, R. (2006). Structure of the Basque emotion lexicon. *Cognition and Emotion, 20*(6), 836–865.

Angel, R. J., & Williams, K. (2000). Cultural models of health and illness. In *Handbook of multicultural mental health* (pp. 25–44). Cambridge, MA: Academic.

Arce-Ferrer, A. J. (2006). An investigation into the factors influencing extreme-response style. *Educational and Psychological Measurement, 66*(3), 374–392.

Argyle, M., & Crossland, J. (1987). The dimensions of positive emotions. *British Journal of Social Psychology, 26*(2), 127–137.

Asparouhov, T., & Muthén, B. (2014). Multiple-group factor analysis alignment. *Structural Equation Modeling: A Multidisciplinary Journal, 21*(4), 495–508.

Athanasiadou, A., & Tabakowska, E. (Eds.). (1998). *Speaking of emotions: Conceptualisation and expression*. Berlin, Germany: Mouton de Gruyter.

Bachen, C. M., & Illouz, E. (1996). Imagining romance: Young people's cultural models of romance and love. *Critical Studies in Media Communication, 13*(4), 279–308.

Bambra, C. (2007). Defamilisation and welfare state regimes: A cluster analysis. *International Journal of Social Welfare, 16*(4), 326–338.

Bartholomew, K., & Horowitz, L. M. (1991). Attachment styles among young adults: A test of a four-category model. *Journal of Personality and Social Psychology, 61*, 226–244.

Behling, O., & Law, K. S. (2000). *Translating questionnaires and other research instruments: Problems and solutions*. Thousand Oaks, CA: Sage.

Benet-Martínez, V., & Haritatos, J. (2005). Bicultural identity integration (BII): Components and psychological antecedents. *Journal of Personality, 73*, 1015–1050.

Bennardo, G. (2018a). Cultural models theory. *Anthropology Newsletter, 59*(4), e139–e142.

Bennardo, G. (2018b, July 17). Cultural models theory. *Anthropology News website*. https://doi.org/10.1111/AN.919.

Bennardo, G., & de Munck, V. (2020). Cultural model theory in cognitive anthropology: Recent developments and applications. *Journal of Cultural Cognitive Science., 4*, 1–2. https://doi.org/10.1007/s41809-020-00055-4

Bennardo, G., & De Munck, V. C. D. (2014). *Cultural models: Genesis, methods, and experiences*. Oxford, UK: Oxford University Press.

Bernard, H. R. (2006). *Research methods in anthropology: Qualitative and quantitative approaches* (4th ed.). Lanham, MD: Rowman & Littlefield.

Bernard, H. R., & Gravlee, C. C. (Eds.). (2014). *Handbook of methods in cultural anthropology* (2nd ed.). Lanham, MD: Rowman & Littlefield.

Berry, J. W. (1969). On cross-cultural comparability. *International Journal of Psychology, 4*, 119–128.

Berry, J. W. (1989). Imposed etics-emics-derived etics: The operationalization of a compelling idea. *International Journal of Psychology, 24*, 721–735.

Berry, J. W., Poortinga, Y. H., & Pandey, J. (Eds.). (1997). *Handbook of cross-cultural psychology. Vol. 1: Theory and method*. Boston, MA: Allyn & Bacon.

Berscheid, E., & Walster, E. (1972). Beauty and the best. *Psychology Today, 5*, 42–46.

Bezdek, J. C. (2017). *A primer on cluster analysis: 4 basic methods that (usually) work*. Sarasota, FL: Design Publication.

Boecker, L., Likowski, K. U., Pauli, P., & Weyers, P. (2015). The face of schadenfreude: Differentiation of joy and schadenfreude by electromyography. *Cognition and Emotion, 29*(6), 1117–1125.

Boehnke, K., Arnaut, C., Bremer, T., Chinyemba, R., Kiewitt, Y., Koudadjey, A. K., ... Neubert, L. (2014). Toward emically informed cross-cultural comparisons: A suggestion. *Journal of Cross-Cultural Psychology, 45*(10), 1655–1670.

Boehnke, K., Lietz, P., Schreier, M., & Wilhelm, A. (2011). Sampling: The selection of cases for culturally comparative psychological research. In D. Matsumoto & F. J. R. van de Vijver (Eds.), *Culture and psychology. Cross-cultural research methods in psychology* (pp. 101–129). New York, NY: Cambridge University Press.

Boer, D., Hanke, K., & He, J. (2018). On detecting systematic measurement error in cross-cultural research: A review and critical reflection on equivalence and invariance tests. *Journal of Cross-Cultural Psychology, 49*, 713–734.

Boers, F. (2003). Applied linguistics perspectives on cross-cultural variation in conceptual metaphor. *Metaphor and Symbol, 18*(4), 231–238.

Bolin, J. H., Edwards, J. M., Finch, W. H., & Cassady, J. C. (2014). Applications of cluster analysis to the creation of perfectionism profiles: A comparison of two clustering approaches. *Frontiers in Psychology, 5*, 343.

Borg, I., & Groenen, P. J. (2005). *Modern multidimensional scaling: Theory and applications.* New York, NY: Springer.

Borg, I., Groenen, P. J., & Mair, P. (2012). *Applied multidimensional scaling.* Cham, Switzerland: Springer.

Bradley, M. M., Greenwald, M. K., Petry, M., & Lang, P. J. (1992). Remembering pictures: Pleasure and arousal in memory. *Journal of Experimental Psychology: Learning, Memory, & Cognition, 18*, 379–390.

Brennan, K. A., Clark, C. L., & Shaver, P. R. (1998). Self-report measurement of adult attachment: An integrative overview. In J. A. Simpson & W. S. Rholes (Eds.), *Attachment theory and close relationships* (pp. 46–76). New York, NY: Guilford Press.

Breugelmans, S. M., Ambadar, Z., Vaca, J. B., Poortinga, Y. H., Setiadi, B., Widiyanto, P., & Philippot, P. (2005). Body sensations associated with emotions in Rarámuri Indians, rural Javanese, and three student samples. *Emotion, 5*(2), 166–175.

Breugelmans, S. M., & Poortinga, Y. H. (2006). Emotion without a word: Shame and guilt among Rarámuri Indians and rural Javanese. *Journal of Personality and Social Psychology, 91*(6), 1111–1122.

Briggs, J. L. (1970). *Never in anger: Portrait of an Eskimo family.* Cambridge, MA: Harvard University Press.

Brown, T. A. (2015). *Confirmatory factor analysis for applied research* (2nd ed.). New York, NY: Guilford Press.

Bruner, J. (1986). *Actual minds, possible worlds.* New York, NY: Plenum Press.

Bruner, J. (1990). *Acts of meaning.* Cambridge, MA: Harvard University Press.

Campbell, D. T. (1986). Science's social system of validity-enhancing collective belief change and the problems of the social sciences. In D. W. Fiske & R. A. Shweder (Eds.), *Metatheory in social science: Pluralities and subjectivities* (pp. 108–135). Chicago, IL: University of Chicago Press.

Cha, E. S., Kim, K. H., & Erlen, J. A. (2007). *Translation of scales in cross-cultural research: Issues and techniques. Journal of Advanced Nursing, 58*(4), 386–395.

Chen, F. F. (2008). What happens if we compare chopsticks with forks? The impact of making inappropriate comparisons in cross-cultural research. *Journal of Personality and Social Psychology, 95*(5), 1005–1018. https://doi.org/10.1037/a0013193

Chentsova-Dutton, Y. E., & Lyons, S. H. (2016). Different ways of measuring emotions cross-culturally. In H. L. Meiselman (Ed.), *Emotion Measurement* (pp. 601–628). Cambridge, UK: Woodhead Publishing.

Cheung, G. W., & Rensvold, R. B. (2000). Assessing extreme and acquiescence response sets in cross-cultural research using structural equations Modeling. *Journal of Cross-Cultural Psychology, 31*, 187–212.

Cheung, G. W., & Rensvold, R. B. (2002). Evaluating goodness-of-fit indexes for testing measure-ment invariance. *Structural Equation Modeling, 9*(2), 233–255.

Chiu, C.-Y., & Hong, Y.-Y. (2006). *Social psychology of culture*. New York, NY: Psychology Press.

Chrisomalis, S. (2006). Comparing cultures and comparing processes: Diachronic methods in cross-cultural anthropology. *Cross-Cultural Research, 40*(4), 377–404.

Clogg, C. C. (1995). Latent class models. In G. Arminger, C. C. Clogg, & M. E. Sobel (Eds.), *Handbook of statistical modeling for the social and behavioral sciences* (pp. 311–359). New York, NY: Plenum.

Clogg, C. C., & Goodman, L. A. (1985). Simultaneous latent structure analysis in several groups. *Sociological Methodology, 15*, 81–110.

Cohen, D. (2007). Methods in cultural psychology. In S. Kitayama & D. Cohen (Eds.), *Handbook of cultural psychology* (pp. 196–236). New York, NY: Guilford Press.

Collet, C., Vernet-Maury, E., Delhomme, G., & Dittmar, A. (1997). Autonomic nervous system response patterns specificity to basic emotions. *Journal of the Autonomic Nervous System, 62*(1–2), 45–57.

Cooper, W. H. (1981). Ubiquitous halo. *Psychological Bulletin, 90*(2), 218–244. https://doi.org/10.1037/0033-2909.90.2.218

Cross, S. E., & Gore, J. S. (2003). Cultural models of the self. In M. R. Leary & J. P. Tangney (Eds.), *Handbook of self and identity* (pp. 536–564). New York, NY: Guilford Press.

D'Andrade, R. G. (1992). Cultural models and motivations. In R. D'Andrade & C. Strauss (Eds.), *Human motives and cultural models* (pp. 23–44). Cambridge, UK: Cambridge University Press.

Daun, A. (1995). *Swedish mentality*. University Park, PA: Penn State University Press.

Davidov, E., Meuleman, B., Cieciuch, J., Schmidt, P., & Billiet, J. (2014). Measurement equiva-lence in cross-national research. *Annual Review of Sociology, 40*, 55–75.

Davidov, E., Schmidt, P., & Billiet, J. (Eds.). (2018). *Cross-cultural analysis: Methods and appli-cations* (2nd ed.). New York, NY: Routledge.

Davies, R. J., & Ikeno, O. (2011). *Japanese mind: Understanding contemporary Japanese culture*. Rutland, VT: Tuttle Publishing.

De Munck, V. C. (2009). *Research design and methods for studying cultures*. Lanham, MD: Rowman Altamira.

De Munck, V. C. (2019). *Romantic love in America: straight, gay, polyarmourous*. Washington, DC: The Rowman & Littlefield.

De Munck, V. C., & Bennardo, G. (2019). Disciplining culture: A sociocognitive approach. *Current Anthropology, 60*(2), 174–193.

De Munck, V. C., & Kronenfeld, D. B. (2016). Romantic love in the United States: Applying cul-tural models theory and methods. *SAGE Open, 6*(1), 2158244015622797.

De Oliveira, J. V., & Pedrycz, W. (Eds.). (2007). *Advances in fuzzy clustering and its applications*. New York, NY: Wiley.

Dietze, A. G. (1963). Types of emotions or dimensions of emotion? A comparison of typal analysis with factor analysis. *The Journal of Psychology, 56*(1), 143–159.

Dion, K., Berscheid, E., & Walster, E. (1972). What is beautiful is good. *Journal of Personality and Social Psychology, 24*, 285–290.

Dobrovolskij, D., & Piirainen, E. (2005). *Figurative language. Cross-cultural and Cross-linguistic perspectives*. Amsterdam, The Netherlands: Elsevier.

Eid, M., & Diener, E. (2001). Norms for experiencing emotions in different cultures: Inter- and intra-national differences. *Journal of Personality and Social Psychology, 81*(5), 869–885.

Eid, M., Langeheine, R., & Diener, E. (2003). Comparing typological structures across cultures by multigroup latent class analysis: A primer. *Journal of Cross-Cultural Psychology, 34*(2), 195–210.

Ekman, P. (1972). Universals and cultural differences in facial expressions of emotion. In J. Cole (Ed.), *Nebraska Symposium Motivation, 1971* (Vol. 19, pp. 207–282). Lincoln, NE: University of Nebraska Press.

Ekman, P. (1992). Are there basic emotions? *Psychological Review, 99*, 550–553.

Ekman, P. (1994). Moods, emotions, and traits. In P. Ekman & R. Davidson (Eds.), *The nature of emotion: Fundamental questions* (pp. 56–58). New York, NY: Oxford University Press.

Ekman, P. (1999). Basic emotions. In T. Dalgleish & T. Power (Eds.), *The handbook of cognition and emotion* (pp. 45–60). Sussex, UK: Wiley.

Ekman, P., Sorenson, E. R., & Friesen, W. V. (1969). Pancultural elements in facial displays of emotion. *Science, 164*, 86–88.

Ember, C. R., & Ember, M. (2009). *Cross-cultural research methods* (2nd ed.). Lanham, MD: AltaMira Press.

Farrell, P. (2006). Portuguese saudade and other emotions of absence and longing. In B. Peeters (Ed.), *Semantic primes and universal grammar: Empirical evidence from the romance languages* (pp. 235–258). Amsterdam, The Netherlands: John Benjamins.

Farrelly, C. M., Schwartz, S. J., Amodeo, A. L., Feaster, D. J., Steinley, D. L., Meca, A., & Picariello, S. (2017). The analysis of bridging constructs with hierarchical clustering methods: An application to identity. *Journal of Research in Personality, 70*, 93–106.

Fehr, B. (1988). Prototype analysis of the concepts of love and commitment. *Journal of Personality and Social Psychology, 55*, 557.

Fehr, B. (1994). Prototype-based assessment of laypeople's views of love. *Personal Relationships, 1*, 309–331.

Fehr, B., & Russell, J. A. (1984). The concept of emotion viewed from a prototype perspective. *Journal of Experimental Psychology: General, 113*(3), 464–486.

Fehr, B., & Russell, J. A. (1991). The concept of love viewed from a prototype perspective. *Journal of Personality and Social Psychology, 60*(3), 425–438.

Feldman Barrett, L., & Russell, J. A. (1998). Independence and bipolarity in the structure of current affect. *Journal of Personality and Social Psychology, 74*(4), 967–984. https://doi.org/10.1037/0022-3514.74.4.967

Ferguson, R. (2016). *Scandinavians: In search of the soul of the North*. London, UK: Head of Zeus.

Fischer, R. (2004). Standardization to account for cross-cultural response bias: A classification of score adjustment procedures and review of research in JCCP. *Journal of Cross-Cultural Psychology, 35*, 263–282. https://doi.org/10.1177/0022022104264122

Fischer, R. (2006). Congruence and functions of personal and cultural values: Do my values reflect my culture's values? *Personality and Social Psychology Bulletin, 32*(11), 1419–1431.

Fischer, R., & Poortinga, Y. H. (2018). Addressing methodological challenges in culture-comparative research. *Journal of Cross-Cultural Psychology, 49*(5), 691–712.

Flippo, H. (2018). *When in Germany, do as the Germans do: The clued-in guide to German life, language, and culture* (2nd ed.). Chicago, IL: McGraw-Hill.

Fonseca, J. R. (2013). Clustering in the field of social sciences: That is your choice. *International Journal of Social Research Methodology, 16*(5), 403–428.

Fontaine, J. R. J. (2004). Equivalence. In K. Kempf-Leonard (Ed.), *Encyclopedia of social measurement* (Vol. 1, pp. 803–813). New York, NY: Academic.

Fontaine, J. R. J., Poortinga, Y. H., Setiadi, B., & Markam, S. S. (2002). Cognitive structure of emotion terms in Indonesia and The Netherlands. *Cognition & Emotion, 16*, 61–86. https://doi.org/10.1080/02699933014000130

Fontaine, J. R. J., Scherer, K. R., Roesch, E. B., & Ellsworth, P. (2007). The world of emotion is not two-dimensional. *Psychological Science, 18*(12), 1050–1057. https://doi.org/10.1111/j.1467-9280.2007.02024.x

Friedlmeier, W., Corapci, F., & Benga, O. (2015). Early emotional development in cultural perspective. In L. Jensen (Ed.), *Oxford handbook of human development and culture: An interdisciplinary perspective* (pp. 127–148). New York, NY: Oxford University Press. https://doi.org/10.1093/oxfordhb/9780199948550.013.9

Frijda, N. H., Kuipers, P., & ter Schure, E. (1989). Relations among emotion, appraisal, and emotional action readiness. *Journal of Personality and Social Psychology, 57*(2), 212–228. https://doi.org/10.1037/0022-3514.57.2.212

Frijda, N. H., Markam, S. S., Sato, K., & Wiers, R. (1995). Emotions and emotion words. In J. A. Russell, A. J. R. Manstead, J. C. Wellenkamp, & J. M. Fernandez-Dols (Eds.), *Everyday conceptions of emotions: An introduction to the psychology, anthropology, and linguistics of emotions* (pp. 121–143). Dordrecht, The Netherlands: Kluwer Academic.

Garro, L. C. (1994). Narrative representations of chronic illness experience: Cultural models of illness, mind, and body in stories concerning the temporomandibular joint (TMJ). *Social Science & Medicine, 38*(6), 775–788.

Geeraerts, D. (2003). Cultural models of linguistic standardization. In R. Dirven, R. Frank, & M. Pütz (Eds.), *Cognitive models in language and thought: Ideology, metaphors and meanings* (pp. 25–68). Berlin, Germany: Mouton de Gruyter.

Gerber, E. R. (1975). *The cultural patterning of emotions in Samoa.* San Diego, CA: University of California.

Goddard, C. (1995). Conceptual and cultural issues in emotion research. *Culture & Psychology, 1*(2), 289–298.

Goddard, C. (1997). Cultural values and "cultural scripts" of Malay (Bahasa Melayu). *Journal of Pragmatics, 27*, 183–201.

Greenleaf, E. A. (1992). Measuring extreme response style. *Public Opinion Quarterly, 56*, 323–351.

Hagenaars, J. A. (1990). *Categorical longitudinal data: Log-linear panel, trend, and cohort analysis.* Newbury Park, CA: Sage.

Hagenaars, J. A., & Halman, L. C. (1989). Searching for ideal types: The potentialities of latent class analysis. *European Sociological Review, 5*(1), 81–96.

Hanges, P. (2004). Response bias correction procedure used in GLOBE. In R. J. House, P. I. Hanges, M. Javidan, P. J. Dorfman, & Gupta (Eds.), Culture, leadership, and organizations: The GLOBE study of 62 culture (pp. 737–752). Thousand Oaks, CA: Sage.

Harmon-Jones, E., Harmon-Jones, C., & Summerell, E. (2017). On the importance of both dimensional and discrete models of emotion. *Behavioral Sciences, 7*(4), 66.

Harzing, A.-W. (2006). Response styles in cross-national survey research: A 26-country study. *International Journal of Cross Cultural Management, 6*, 243–266. https://doi.org/10.1177/1470595806066332

Harzing, A. W., Baldueza, J., Barner-Rasmussen, W., Barzantny, C., Canabal, A., Davila, A., … Liang, Y. K. (2009). Rating versus ranking: What is the best way to reduce response and language bias in cross-national research? *International Business Review, 18*(4), 417–432.

He, J., & van de Vijver, F. (2012). Bias and equivalence in cross-cultural Research. *Online Readings in Psychology and Culture, 2*(2). https://doi.org/10.9707/2307-0919.1111

Heine, S. J., Lehman, D. R., Peng, K., & Greenholtz, J. (2002). What's wrong with cross-cultural comparisons of subjective Likert scales? The reference-group effect. *Journal of Personality and Social Psychology, 82*, 903–918.

Hendry, J. (2019). *Understanding Japanese society* (5th ed.). Abingdon, UK: Routledge.

Hennig, C., Meila, M., Murtagh, F., & Rocci, R. (Eds.). (2015). *Handbook of cluster analysis.* Boca Raton, FL: CRC Press.

Henry, D. B., Tolan, P. H., & Gorman-Smith, D. (2005). Cluster analysis in family psychology research. *Journal of Family Psychology, 19*(1), 121.

Herrmann, D. J., & Raybeck, D. (1981). Similarities and differences in meaning in six cultures. *Journal of Cross-Cultural Psychology, 12*(2), 194–206.

Hirschfeld, G., & Von Brachel, R. (2014). Improving multiple-group confirmatory factor analysis in R–A tutorial in measurement invariance with continuous and ordinal indicators. *Practical Assessment, Research, and Evaluation, 19*(1), 7.

Ho, D. Y. F. (1998b). Indigenous psychologies: Asian perspectives. *Journal of Cross-Cultural Psychology, 29*, 88–103.

Holland, D., Lachicotte, W., Jr., Skinner, D., & Cain, C. (1998). *Identity and agency in cultural worlds.* Cambridge, MA: Harvard University Press.

Holland, D., & Quinn, N. (Eds.). (1987). *Cultural models in language and thought.* New York, NY: Cambridge University Press.

Hong, Y. Y., Morris, M. W., Chiu, C. Y., & Benet-Martinez, V. (2000). Multicultural minds: A dynamic constructivist approach to culture and cognition. *American Psychologist, 55*(7), 709–720.

Höppner, F., Klawonn, F., Kruse, R., & Runkler, T. (1999). *Fuzzy cluster analysis: Methods for classification, data analysis and image recognition.* New York, NY: Wiley.

House, R. J., Hanges, P. J., Javidan, M., Dorfman, P., & Gupta, V. (Eds.). (2003). *GLOBE, cultures, leadership, and organizations: GLOBE study of 62 societies.* Thousand Oaks, CA: Sage.

Hox, J. J. (2010). *Multilevel analysis: Techniques and applications* (2nd ed.). New York, NY: Routledge.

Hoyle, R. H. (1995). The structural equation modeling approach: Basic concepts and fundamental issues. In R. H. Hoyle (Ed.), *Structural equation modeling: Concepts, issues, and applications* (pp. 1–15). Thousand Oaks, CA: Sage.

Hui, C. H., & Triandis, H. C. (1985). Measurement in cross-cultural psychology: A review and comparison of strategies. *Journal of Cross-Cultural Psychology, 16*(2), 131–152.

Hui, C. H., & Triandis, H. C. (1989). Effects of culture and response format on extreme response style. *Journal of Cross-Cultural Psychology, 20*, 296–309. https://doi.org/10.1177/0022022189203004

Izard, C. E. (1971). *The face of emotion.* East Norwalk, CT: Appleton-Century-Crofts.

Izard, C. E. (1977). *Human emotions.* New York, NY: Plenum Press.

Izard, C. E. (1992). Basic emotions, relations among emotions, and emotion-cognition relations. *Psychological Review, 99*(3), 561–565. https://doi.org/10.1037/0033-295X.99.3.561

Izard, C. E. (2007). Basic emotions, natural kinds, emotion schemas, and a new paradigm. *Perspectives on Psychological Science, 2*(3), 260–280.

Jack, R. E., Sun, W., Delis, I., Garrod, O. G., & Schyns, P. G. (2016). Four not six: Revealing culturally common facial expressions of emotion. *Journal of Experimental Psychology: General, 145*(6), 708–730.

Jakobovits, L. A. (1966). Comparative psycholinguistics in the study of cultures. *International Journal of Psychology, 1*(1), 15–37.

Jensen, L. A. (2012). Bridging universal and cultural perspectives: A vision for developmental psychology in a global world. *Child Development Perspectives, 6*, 98–104. https://doi.org/10.1111/j.1750-8606.2011.00213.x

Johnson, A. (1978). *Quantification in anthropology.* Stanford, CA: Stanford University Press.

Johnson, T. P. (1998). Approaches to equivalence in cross-cultural and cross-national survey research. In J. A. Harkness (Ed.), *Cross-cultural survey equivalence* (pp. 1–40). Mannheim, Germany: Zentrum für Umfragen, Methoden und Analysen.

Kagitçibasi, C. (1996). *Family and human development across countries: A view from the other side.* Hillsdale, NJ: Lawrence Erlbaum.

Kagitçibasi, C. (2005). Autonomy and relatedness in cultural context: Implications for family, parenting, and human development. *Journal of Cross-Cultural Psychology, 36*(4), 403–422.

Kankaraš, M., Moors, G., & Vermunt, J. K. (2010). Testing for measurement invariance with latent class analysis. In E. Davidov, P. Schmidt, & J. Billiet (Eds.), *Cross-cultural analysis: Methods and applications* (pp. 359–384). New York, UK: Routledge.

Kankaraš, M., & Vermunt, J. K. (2014). Simultaneous latent class analysis across groups. In A. C. Michalos (Ed.), *Encyclopedia of quality of life and well-being research* (pp. 5969–5974). Heidelberg, Germany: Springer.

Kankarash, M., & Moors, G. (2011). Measurement equivalence and extreme response bias in the comparison of attitudes across Europe: A multigroup latent-class factor approach. *Methodology: European Journal of Research Methods for the Behavioral and Social Sciences, 7*, 68–80. https://doi.org/10.1027/1614-2241/a000024

Karandashev, V. (2017). *Romantic love in cultural contexts.* New York, NY: Springer.

Karandashev, V., Zarubko, E., Artemeva, V., Evans, M., Morgan, K. A. D., Neto, F., … Purvis, J. (2019). Cross-Cultural Comparison of Sensory Preferences in Romantic Attraction. *Sexuality and Culture*, published online 3 July 2019 https://doi.org/10.1007/s12119-019-09628-0

Karasz, A., & Singelis, T. M. (2009). Qualitative and mixed-methods research in cross-cultural psychology. *Journal of Cross-Cultural Psychology, 40*, 909–916.

Katsikitis, M. (1997). The classification of facial expressions of emotion: A multidimensional-scaling approach. *Perception, 26*(5), 613–626.

Kaufman, L., & Rousseeuw, P. J. (2009). *Finding groups in data: An introduction to cluster analysis*. New York, NY: Wiley.

Keller, H. (2003). Socialization for competence: Cultural models of infancy. *Human Development, 46*(5), 288–311. https://doi.org/10.1159/000071937

Keller, H. (2007). *Cultures of infancy*. Mahwah, NJ: Lawrence Erlbaum.

Keller, H. (2013). Attachment and culture. *Journal of Cross-Cultural Psychology, 44*(2), 175–194.

Keller, H. (2018). Universality claim of attachment theory: Children's socioemotional development across cultures. *Proceedings of the National Academy of Sciences, 115*(45), 11414–11419.

Keller, H., Lamm, B., Abels, M., Yovsi, R., Borke, J., Jensen, H., … Su, Y. (2006). Cultural models, socialization goals, and parenting ethnotheories: A multicultural analysis. *Journal of Cross-Cultural Psychology, 37*(2), 155–172.

Kettenring, J. R. (2006). The practice of cluster analysis. *Journal of Classification, 23*(1), 3–30.

Kim, U., Park, Y. S., & Park, D. (2000). The challenge of cross-cultural psychology: The role of the indigenous psychologies. *Journal of Cross-Cultural Psychology, 31*(1), 63–75.

Kim-Prieto, C., & Eid, M. (2004). Norms for experiencing emotions. *Journal of Happiness Studies, 5*(3), 241–268.

Kirmayer, L. J., & Sartorius, N. (2007). Cultural models and somatic syndromes. *Psychosomatic Medicine, 69*(9), 832–840.

Kline, R. B. (2015). *Principles and practice of structural equation modeling*. New York, NY: Guilford Press.

Knowles, E. S., & Nathan, K. T. (1997). Acquiescent responding in self-reports: Cognitive style or social concern? *Journal of Research in Personality, 31*(2), 293–301.

Kovecses, Z. (2000). *Metaphor and emotion: Language, culture, and body in human feeling.* Cambridge, UK: Cambridge University Press.

Kövecses, Z. (2002). Emotion concepts: Social constructionism and cognitive linguistics. In S. R. Fussell (Ed.), *The verbal communication of emotions* (pp. 117–132). Mahwah, NJ: L. Erlbaum Associates.

Kövecses, Z. (2003). *Metaphor and emotion: Language, culture, and body in human feeling.* Cambridge, UK: Cambridge University Press.

Kövecses, Z. (2005). *Metaphor in culture: Universality and variation.* Cambridge, UK: Cambridge University Press.

Kovecses, Z. (2006). *Language, mind, and culture: A practical introduction.* Oxford, UK: Oxford University Press.

Kristiansen, G., & Dirven, R. (Eds.). (2008). *Cognitive sociolinguistics: Language variation, cultural models, social systems.* Berlin, Germany: Walter de Gruyter.

Kronenfeld, D. (2008). Cultural Models. *Intercultural Pragmatics, 5*(1), 67–74.

Kronenfeld, D. B. (2018). Cultural models. In *The International Encyclopedia of Anthropology, 1–8.* Hoboken, NJ: Wiley.

Kuppens, P., Ceulmans, E., Timmerman, M. E., Diener, E., & Kim-Prieto, C. (2006). Universal intracultural and intercultural dimensions of the recalled frequency of emotional experience. *Journal of Cross-Cultural Psychology, 37*(5), 491–515.

Ladwig, T., Richter, N., Ringle, C. M., & Heitger, N. (2012). Cultural hybrid personalities? Clustering nations according to the big five personality traits. *Clustering Nations According to the Big Five Personality Traits (November 22, 2012). Hamburg University of Technology (TUHH) Research Paper*, (009).

Lamm, B., & Keller, H. (2007). Understanding cultural models of parenting: The role of intracultural variation and response style. *Journal of Cross-Cultural Psychology, 38*(1), 50–57.

Lazarsfeld, P. F., & Henry, N. W. (1968). *Latent structure analysis.* New York, NY: Houghton Mifflin.

Leach, C. W., Spears, R., Branscombe, N. R., & Doosje, B. (2003). Malicious pleasure: Schadenfreude at the suffering of another group. *Journal of Personality and Social Psychology, 84*(5), 932–943. https://doi.org/10.1037/0022-3514.84.5.932

Leach, C. W., Spears, R., & Manstead, A. S. R. (2015). Parsing (malicious) pleasures: Schadenfreude and gloating at others' adversity. *Frontiers in Psychology, 6,* Article 201.

Lee, C. K., Lee, Y. K., Bernhard, B. J., & Yoon, Y. S. (2006). Segmenting casino gamblers by motivation: A cluster analysis of Korean gamblers. *Tourism Management, 27*(5), 856–866.

Levy, R. I. (1973). *Tahitians.* Chicago, IL: University of Chicago Press.

Ljung, M. (2010). *Swearing: A cross-cultural linguistic study.* New York, NY: Palgrave Macmillan.

Lonner, W., & Berry, J. (1986). *Field methods in cross-cultural research.* Newbury Park, CA: Sage.

Lowe, E. D. (2019). Are shared models always cultural models? A study of the cultural model of affect and emotion in Chuuk. *Journal of Cultural Cognitive Science, 4,* 1–13.

Lutz, C. (1982). The domain of emotion words on Ifaluk. *American Ethnologist, 9*(1), 113–128.

Lutz, C. (1988). *Unnatural emotions: Everyday sentiments on a Micronesian atoll and their challenge to Western theory.* Chicago, IL: University of Chicago Press.

MacKinnon, N. J., & Keating, L. J. (1989). The structure of emotions: Canada-United States comparisons. *Social Psychology Quarterly, 52,* 70–83.

Magidson, J., & Vermunt, J. K. (2004). Latent class models. In D. Kaplan (Ed.), *The Sage handbook of quantitative methodology for the social sciences* (pp. 175–198). Thousand Oaks, CA: Sage.

Maleki, A., & de Jong, M. (2014). A proposal for clustering the dimensions of national culture. *Cross-Cultural Research, 48*(2), 107–143.

Matsumoto, D., & Van de Vijver, F. J. (Eds.). (2010). *Cross-cultural research methods in psychology.* Cambridge, UK: Cambridge University Press.

Maxwell, B. A., Pryor, F. L., & Smith, C. (2002). Cluster analysis in cross-cultural research. *World Cultures, 13*(1), 22–38.

McCambridge, J., De Bruin, M., & Witton, J. (2012). The effects of demand characteristics on research participant behaviours in non-laboratory settings: A systematic review. *PLoS One, 7*(6), e39116.

McCarty, J. A., & Shrum, L. J. (2000). The measurement of personal values in survey research: A test of alternative rating procedures. *Public Opinion Quarterly, 64*(3), 271–298.

McCutcheon, A.L. (1987). Latent class analysis. Beverly Hills, CA: Sage.

McCutcheon, A. L. (2002). Basic concepts and procedures in single- and multiple-group latent class analysis. In J. A. Hagenaars & A. L. McCutcheon (Eds.), *Applied latent class analysis* (pp. 56–85). Cambridge, UK: Cambridge University Press.

Mehrabian, A. (1996). Pleasure-arousal-dominance: A general framework for describing and measuring individual differences in temperament. *Current Psychology, 14*(4), 261–292.

Mellenbergh, G. J. (1989). Item bias and item response theory. *International Journal of Educational Research, 13*(2), 127–143.

Merritt, A. (2000). Culture in the cockpit Do Hofstede's dimensions replicate? *Journal of Cross-Cultural Psychology, 31,* 283–301.

Mesquita, B., & Ellsworth, P. C. (2001). The role of culture in appraisal. In K. R. Scherer & A. Schorr (Eds.), *Appraisal processes in emotion: Theory, methods, Research* (p. 233248). New York, NY: Oxford University Press.

Mesquita, B., & Frijda, N. H. (1992). Cultural variations in emotions: A review. *Psychological Bulletin, 112*(2), 179–204. https://doi.org/10.1037/0033-2909.112.2.179

Mesquita, B., Frijda, N. H., & Scherer, K. R. (1997). Culture and emotion. In P. Dasen & T. S. Saraswathi (Eds.), *Handbook of cross-cultural psychology. Basic processes and human development* (Vol. 2, pp. 255–297). Boston, MA: Allyn & Bacon.

Mesquita, B., & Leu, J. (2007). The cultural psychology of emotion. In S. Kitayama & D. Cohen (Eds.), *Handbook of cultural psychology* (pp. 734–759). New York, NY: Guilford Press.

Middleton, D. R. (1989). Emotional style: The cultural ordering of emotions. *Ethos, 17*(2), 187–201.

Milfont, T., & Klein, R. (2018). Replication and reproducibility in cross-cultural psychology. *Journal of Cross-Cultural Psychology, 49,* 735–750.

Milfont, T. L., & Fischer, R. (2010). Testing measurement invariance across groups: Applications in cross-cultural research. *International Journal of Psychological Research, 3*(1), 111–130.

Minkov, M., & Hofstede, G. (2012b). Is national culture a meaningful concept? Cultural values delineate homogeneous national clusters of in-country regions. *Cross-Cultural Research, 46*(2), 133–159.

Minkov, M., & Hofstede, G. (2014). Clustering of 316 European regions on measures of values: Do Europe's countries have national cultures? *Cross-Cultural Research, 48*(2), 144–176.

Moore, M. (1975). Rating versus ranking in the Rokeach value survey: An Israeli comparison. *European Journal of Social Psychology, 5*(3), 405–408. https://doi.org/10.1002/ejsp.2420050313

Moors, G. (2003). Diagnosing response style behavior by means of a Latent-class factor approach: Socio-demographic correlates of gender role attitudes and perceptions of ethnic discrimination reexamined. *Quality and Quantity, 37*, 277–302.

Moors, G., Vriens, I., Gelissen, J., & Vermunt, J. (2016). Two of a kind. Similarities between ranking and rating data in measuring values. *Survey Research Methods, 10*(1), 15–33.

Morren, M., Gelissen, J. P., & Vermunt, J. K. (2011). Dealing with extreme response style in cross-cultural research: A restricted latent class factor analysis approach. *Sociological Methodology, 41*(1), 13–47.

Morris, M. W., Hong, Y., Chiu, C., & Liu, Z. (2015). Normology: Integrating insights about social norms to understand cultural dynamics. Organizational Behavior and Human Decision Processes, 129, 1–13. https://doi.org/10.1016/j.obhdp.2015.03.001

Morsbach, H., & Tyler, W. J. (1986). A Japanese emotion: Amae. In R. Harre (Ed.), *The social construction of emotions* (pp. 289–307). New York, NY: Basil Blackwell.

Muthén, L. K., & Muthén, B. O. (1998–2017). *Mplus User's Guide* (7th ed.). Los Angeles, CA: Muthén &Muthén.

Myers, F. R. (1979). Emotions and the self: A theory of personhood and political order among Pintupi aborigines. *Ethos, 7*(4), 343–370.

Nelson, A., & Jankowiak, W. (2021). Love's ethnographic record: Beyond the love/arranged marriage dichotomy and other false essentialisms. In C. Mayer & E. Vanderheiden (Eds.), *International Handbook of Love: Transcultural and Transdisciplinary Perspectives* (pp. 41–57). Cham, CH: Springer.

Neto, F., & Mullet, E. (2014). A prototype analysis of the Portuguese concept of saudade. *Journal of Cross-Cultural Psychology, 45*(4), 660–670.

Nguyen, A. M. D., & Benet-Martínez, V. (2013). Biculturalism and adjustment: A meta-analysis. *Journal of Cross-Cultural Psychology, 44*(1), 122–159.

Nichols, A. L., & Maner, J. K. (2008). The good-subject effect: Investigating participant demand characteristics. *The Journal of General Psychology, 135*(2), 151–166.

Niiya, Y., Ellsworth, P. C., & Yamaguchi, S. (2006). Amae in Japan and the United States: An exploration of a "culturally unique" emotion. *Emotion, 6*(2), 279–295.

Nisbet, R. (1971). Ethnocentrism and the comparative method. In A. Desai (Ed.), *Essays on modernization of underdeveloped societies* (Vol. 1, pp. 95–114). Bombay, India: Thacker.

Nisbett, R. E., & Miyamoto, Y. (2005). The influence of culture: Holistic versus analytic perception. *Trends in Cognitive Sciences, 9*(10), 467–473.

Nisbett, R. E., & Wilson, T. D. (1977). The halo effect: Evidence for unconscious alteration of judgments. *Journal of Personality and Social Psychology, 35*(4), 250–256. https://doi.org/10.1037/0022-3514.35.4.250

Oatley, K., & Johnson-Laird, P. N. (1990). Semantic primitives for emotions: A reply to Ortony and Clore. *Cognition and Emotion, 4*(2), 129–143.

Orne, M. T. (1962). On the social psychology of the psychological experiment: With particular reference to demand characteristics and their implications. *American Psychologist, 17*, 776–783.

Osgood, C. E., May, W. H., & Mirron, M. S. (1975). *Cross-cultural universals of affective meanings.* Urbana, IL: University of Illinois Press.

Oyserman, D., Coon, H. M., & Kemmelmeier, M. (2002). Rethinking individualism and collectivism: Evaluation of theoretical assumptions and meta-analyses. *Psychological Bulletin, 128*(1), 3–72.

Pagès, J. (2014). *Multiple factor analysis by example using R*. Boca Raton, FA: CRC Press.

Panayiotou, G. (2008). Emotional dimensions reflected in ratings of affective scripts. *Personality and Individual Differences, 44*(8), 1795–1806.

Paulhus, D. L. (1991a). Measures of personality and social psychological attitudes. In J. P. Robinson & R. P. Shaver (Eds.), *Measures of social psychological attitudes series* (Vol. 1, pp. 17–59). San Diego, CA: Academic.

Paulhus, D. L. (1991b). Measurement and control of response bias. In J. P. Robinson, P. R. Shaver, & L. S. Wrightsman (Eds.), *Measure of personality and social psychological attitudes* (pp. 17–59). San Diego, CA: Academic.

Peng, K., Nisbett, R., & Wong, N. (1997). Validity problems comparing value across cultures and possible solutions. *Psychological Methods, 2*, 329–344.

Phinney, J., & Alipuria, L. (2006). Multiple social categorisation and identity among multiracial, multi-ethnic and multicultural individuals: Processes and implications. In R. Crisp & M. Hewstone (Eds.), *Multiple Social categorisation: Processes, models and applications* (pp. 211–238). New York, NY: Psychology Press.

Plaut, V. C. (2002). Cultural models of diversity in American: The psychology of difference and inclusion. In R. A. Shweder, M. Minow, & H. R. Markus (Eds.), *Engaging cultural differences: The multicultural challenge in liberal democracies* (pp. 365–395). New York, NY: Russell Sage Foundation.

Plutchik, R. (2001). The nature of emotions: Human emotions have deep evolutionary roots, a fact that may explain their complexity and provide tools for clinical practice. *American Scientist, 89*(4), 344–350.

Plutchik, R., Kellerman, H., & Conte, H. R. (1979). A structural theory of ego defenses and emotions. In *Emotions in personality and psychopathology* (pp. 227–257). Boston, MA: Springer.

Poortinga, Y. H. (1999). Do differences in behaviour imply a need for different psychologies? *Applied Psychology, 48*, 419–432.

Potter, S. H. (1988). The cultural construction of emotion in rural Chinese social life. *Ethos, 16*(2), 181–208.

Quinn, N., & Mageo, J. (Eds.). (2013). *Attachment reconsidered: Cultural perspectives on a Western theory*. New York, NY: Springer.

Rammstedt, B., Kemper, C. J., & Borg, I. (2013). Correcting big five personality measurements for acquiescence: An 18-country cross-cultural study. *European Journal of Personality, 27*(1), 71–81.

Rankin, W. L., & Grube, J. W. (1980). A comparison of ranking and rating procedures for value system measurement. *European Journal of Social Psychology, 10*(3), 233–246.

Revelle, W. (1979). Hierarchical cluster analysis and the internal structure of tests. *Multivariate Behavioral Research, 14*(1), 57–74.

Revelle, W. (2019). *An introduction to the psych package: Part II Scale construction and psychometrics*. Available at: https://cran.r-project.org/web/packages/psychTools/vignettes/overview.pdf

Ronen, S., & Shenkar, O. (1985). Clustering countries on attitudinal dimensions: A review and synthesis. *Academy of Management Review, 10*, 435–454.

Roseman, I. J., Antoniou, A. A., & Jose, P. E. (1996). Appraisal determinants of emotions: Constructing a more accurate and comprehensive theory. *Cognition and Emotion, 10*, 241–277.

Rosnow, R., & Rosenthal, R. (1997). *People studying people: Artifacts and ethics in behavioral research*. New York, NY: Freeman.

Rosnow, R. L. (2002). The nature and role of demand characteristics in scientific inquiry. *Prevention & Treatment, 5*(1), 37.

Rubin, D. C., & Talarico, J. M. (2009). A comparison of dimensional models of emotion: Evidence from emotions, prototypical events, autobiographical memories, and words. *Memory, 17*(8), 802–808.

Russell, J. A. (1980). A circumplex model of affect. *Journal of Personality and Social Psychology, 39*(6), 1161–1178. https://doi.org/10.1037/h0077714

Russell, J. A. (1991). Culture and the categorization of emotions. *Psychological Bulletin, 110*, 426–450.

Russell, J. A. (1994). Is there universal recognition of emotion from facial expression? A review of the cross-cultural studies. *Psychological Bulletin, 115*(1), 102–141. https://doi.org/10.1037/0033-2909.115.1.102

Russell, J. A. (2003). Core affect and the psychological construction of emotion. *Psychological Review, 110*, 145–172.

Russell, J. A., & Fehr, B. (1994). Fuzzy concepts in a fuzzy hierarchy: Varieties of anger. *Journal of Personality and Social Psychology, 67*, 186–205.

Russell, J. A., & Feldman Barrett, L. (1999). Core affect, prototypical emotional episodes, and other things called emotion: Dissecting the elephant. *Journal of Personality and Social Psychology, 76*, 805–819.

Russell, J. A., Lewicka, M., & Niit, T. (1989). A cross-cultural study of a circumplex model of affect. *Journal of Personality and Social Psychology, 57*, 848–856.

Russell, P. A., & Gray, C. D. (1994). Ranking or rating? Some data and their implications for the measurement of evaluative response. *British Journal of Psychology, 85*(1), 79–92.

Saarni, C. (1998). Issues of cultural meaningfulness in emotional development. *Developmental Psychology, 34*, 647–652. https://doi.org/10.1037/0012-1649.34.4.647

Sabini, J., & Silver, M. (2005). Why emotion names and experiences don't neatly pair. *Psychological Inquiry, 16*(1), 1–10.

Sauter, D. A., Eisner, F., Ekman, P., & Scott, S. K. (2010). Cross-cultural recognition of basic emotions through nonverbal emotional vocalizations. *Proceedings of the National Academy of Sciences, 107*(6), 2408–2412.

Scherer, K. R. (1997a). Profiles of emotion-antecedent appraisal: Testing theoretical predictions across cultures. *Cognition and Emotion, 11*(2), 113–150.

Scherer, K. R. (1997b). The role of culture in emotion-antecedent appraisal. *Journal of Personality and Social Psychology, 73*(4), 902–922.

Scherer, K. R., & Wallbott, H. G. (1994). Evidence for universality and cultural variation of differential emotion response patterning. *Journal of Personality and Social Psychology, 66*(2), 310–328.

Schmidt-Atzert, L., & Park, H.-S. (1999). The Korean concepts of Dapdaphada and Uulhada: A cross-cultural study of the meaning of emotions. *Journal of Cross-Cultural Psychology, 30*(5), 646–654.

Schwartz, S. H., & Sagiv, L. (1995). Identifying culture-specifics in the content and structure of values. *Journal of Cross-Cultural Psychology, 26*, 92–116.

Scollon, C. N., Diener, E., Oishi, S., & Biswas-Diener, R. (2004). Emotions across cultures and methods. *Journal of Cross-Cultural Psychology, 35*(3), 304–326.

Shaver, P., Schwartz, J., Kirson, D., & O'Connor, C. (1987). Emotion knowledge: Further exploration of a prototype approach. *Journal of Personality and Social Psychology, 52*, 1061–1086. https://doi.org/10.1037/0022-3514.52.6.1061

Shaver, P. R., Morgan, H. J., & Wu, S. (1996). Is love a "basic" emotion? *Personal Relationships, 3*, 81–96. https://doi.org/10.1111/j.1475-6811.1996.tb00105.x

Shaver, P. R., Murdaya, U., & Fraley, R. C. (2001). Structure of the Indonesian emotion lexicon. *Asian Journal of Social Psychology, 4*, 201–224.

Shaver, P. R., Wu, S., & Schwartz, J. C. (1992). Cross-cultural similarities and differences in emotion and its representation. In M. S. Clark (Ed.), *Review of personality and social psychology* (Vol. 13, pp. 175–212). Thousand Oaks, CA: Sage.

Shore, B. (1996). *Culture in mind: Cognition, culture, and the problem of meaning.* New York, NY: Oxford University Press.

Silva, Z. B. (2012). Saudade–a key Portuguese emotion. *Emotion Review, 4*(2), 203–211.

Smith, P. B., & Fischer, R. (2008). Acquiescence, extreme response bias and culture: A multilevel analysis. In F. J. R. Van de Vijver, D. A. van Hemert, & Y. H. Poortinga (Eds.), *Multilevel analysis of individuals and cultures* (pp. 285–314). New York, NY: Taylor & Francis /Lawrence Erlbaum.

Smith, P. B., Fischer, R., Vignoles, V., & Bond, M. H. (2013). *Understanding social psychology across cultures: Engaging with others in a changing world* (2nd ed.). London, UK: Sage.

Steenkamp, J. E. M., & Baumgartner, H. (1998). Assessing measurement invariance in cross-national consumer Research. *Journal of Consumer Research, 25,* 78–90.

Stephens, C. L., Christie, I. C., & Friedman, B. H. (2010). Autonomic specificity of basic emotions: Evidence from pattern classification and cluster analysis. *Biological Psychology, 84*(3), 463–473.

Storm, C., & Storm, T. (1987). A taxonomic study of the vocabulary of emotions. *Journal of Personality and Social Psychology, 53*(4), 805–816.

Strauss, C. (1992). Models and motives. In R. D'Andrade & C. Strauss (Eds.), *Human motives and cultural models* (pp. 1–20). New York, NY: Cambridge University Press.

Suizzo, M. A. (2002). French parents' cultural models and childrearing beliefs. *International Journal of Behavioral Development, 26*(4), 297–307.

Swidler, A. (2002). *Talk of love: How culture matters.* Chicago, IL: University of Chicago Press.

Terracciano, A., Abdel-Khalek, N., Ádám, L., Adamovová, C. K., Ahn, H. N., Ahn, B., et al. (2005). National character does not reflect mean personality trait levels in 49 cultures. *Science, 310,* 96–100.

Thompson, B. (2004). *Exploratory and confirmatory factor analysis.* Washington, DC: American Psychological Association.

Toivonen, R., Kivelä, M., Saramäki, J., Viinikainen, M., Vanhatalo, M., & Sams, M. (2012). Networks of emotion concepts. *PLoS One, 7*(1), e28883.

Triandis, H. C. (2000). Dialectics between cultural and cross-cultural psychology. *Asian Journal of Social Psychology, 3,* 185–195.

Triandis, H. C., Carnevale, P., Gelfand, M., Robert, C., Wasti, S. A., Probst, T., … Kim, U. (2001). Culture and deception in business negotiations: A multilevel analysis. *International Journal of Cross Cultural Management, 1*(1), 73–90.

Tryon, R. C. (1958). General dimensions of individual differences: Cluster analysis vs. multiple factor analysis. *Educational and Psychological Measurement, 18*(3), 477–495.

Tsai, J. L. (2007). Ideal affect: Cultural causes and behavioral consequences. *Perspectives on Psychological Science, 2*(3), 242–259.

Tsai, J. L., Chentsova-Dutton, Y., Freire-Bebeau, L., & Przymus, D. E. (2002). Emotional expression and physiology in European Americans and Hmong Americans. *Emotion, 2*(4), 380–397.

Tsai, J. L., & Clobert, M. (2019). Cultural influences on emotion: Empirical patterns and emerging trends. In S. Kitayama & D. Cohen (Eds.), *Handbook of cultural psychology* (2nd ed., pp. 292–318). New York, NY: Guilford Press.

Tsai, J. L., Knutson, B., & Fung, H. H. (2006). Cultural variation in affect valuation. *Journal of Personality and Social Psychology, 90*(2), 288–307.

Uchida, Y., Norasakkunkit, V., & Kitayama, S. (2004). Cultural constructions of happiness: Theory and empirical evidence. *Journal of Happiness Studies, 5*(3), 223–239.

Van Bezooijen, R., Otto, S. A., & Heenan, T. A. (1983). Recognition of vocal expressions of emotion: A three-nation study to identify universal characteristics. *Journal of Cross-Cultural Psychology, 14*(4), 387–406.

Van de Schoot, R., Lugtig, P., & Hox, J. (2012). A checklist for testing measurement invariance. *European Journal of Developmental Psychology, 9*(4), 486–492.

Van De Schoot, R., Schmidt, P., De Beuckelaer, A., Lek, K., & Zondervan-Zwijnenburg, M. (2015). Editorial: Measurement Invariance. *Frontiers in Psychology, 6,* 1064. https://doi.org/10.3389/fpsyg.2015.01064

Van de Vijver, F., & Hambleton, R. K. (1996). *Translating tests. European Psychologist, 1*(2), 89–99.

Van de Vijver, F., & Tanzer, N. K. (2004). Bias and equivalence in cross-cultural assessment: An overview. *Revue Européenne de Psychologie Appliquée/European Review of Applied Psychology, 54*(2), 119–135.

Van de Vijver, F., van Hermert, D. A., & Poortinga, Y. H. (Eds.). (2008). *Multilevel analysis of individuals and cultures.* New York, NY: Lawrence Erlbaum.

Van de Vijver, F. J. R., & Leung, K. (1997). *Methods and data-analysis for cross-cultural research.* Thousand Oaks, CA: Sage.

Van de Vijver, F. J. R., & Leung, K. (2011). Equivalence and bias: A review of concepts, models, and data analytic procedures. In D. Matsumoto & F. J. R. Van de Vijver (Eds.), *Cross-cultural research methods in psychology* (pp. 17–45). New York, NY: Cambridge University Press.

Van de Vijver, F. J. R., & Poortinga, Y. H. (1997). Towards an integrated analysis of bias in cross-cultural assessment. *European Journal of Psychological Assessment, 13*, 29–37. https://doi.org/10.1027/1015-5759.13.1.29

Van Dijk, T. K., Datema, F., Piggen, A.-L. J. H. F., Welten, S. C. M., & Van de Vijver, F. J. R. (2009). Acquiescence and extremity in cross-national surveys: Domain dependence and country-level correlates. In A. Gari & K. Mylonas (Eds.), *Quod erat demonstrandum: From Herodotus' ethnographic journeys to cross-cultural research* (pp. 149–158). Athens, Greece: Pedio Books.

Van Hemert, D. A., Poortinga, Y. H., & van de Vijver, F. J. (2007). Emotion and culture: A meta-analysis. *Cognition and Emotion, 21*(5), 913–943.

Van Herk, H., & van de Velden, M. (2007). Insight into the relative merits of rating and ranking in a cross-national context using three-way correspondence analysis. *Food Quality and Preference, 18*(8), 1096–1105.

Van IJzendoorn, M. H., & Kroonenberg, P. M. (1988). Cross-cultural patterns of attachment: A meta-analysis of the strange situation. *Child Development, 59*, 147–156.

Van IJzendoorn, M. H., & Sagi-Schwartz, A. (2008). Cross-cultural patterns of attachment: Universal and contextual dimensions. In J. Cassidy & P. R. Shaver (Eds.), *Handbook of attachment: Theory, research and clinical applications* (pp. 713–734). New York, NY: Guilford Press.

Van Vaerenbergh, Y., & Thomas, T. D. (2013). Response styles in survey research: A literature review of antecedents, consequences, and remedies. *International Journal of Public Opinion Research, 25*(2), 195–217.

Vandenberg, R. J., & Lance, C. E. (2000). A review and synthesis of the measurements invariance literature: Suggestions, practices, and recommendations for organizational research. *Organizational Research Methods, 3*, 4–69.

Vermunt, J. K., & Magidson, J. (2005). Factor analysis with categorical indicators: A comparison between traditional and latent class approaches. In A. Van der Ark, M. A. Croon, & K. Sijtsma (Eds.), *New developments in categorical data analysis for the social and Behavioral sciences* (pp. 41–62). Mahwah, NJ: Erlbaum.

Vignoles, V. L., Owe, E., Becker, M., Smith, P. B., Easterbrook, M. J., Brown, R., … Lay, S. (2016). Beyond the 'east–west' dichotomy: Global variation in cultural models of selfhood. *Journal of Experimental Psychology: General, 145*(8), 966–1000.

Watson, D. (2000). *Mood and temperament.* New York, NY: Guilford Press.

Watson, D., & Tellegen, A. (1985). Toward a consensual structure of mood. *Psychological Bulletin, 98*(2), 219–235. https://doi.org/10.1037/0033-2909.98.2.219

Watson, D., Wiese, D., Vaidya, J., & Tellegen, A. (1999). The two general activation systems of affect: Structural findings, evolutionary considerations, and psychobiological evidence. *Journal of Personality and Social Psychology, 76*(5), 820–838. https://doi.org/10.1037/0022-3514.76.5.820

Weijters, B., Cabooter, E., & Schillewaert, N. (2010). The effect of rating scale format on response styles: The number of response categories and response category labels. *International Journal of Research in Marketing, 27*, 236–247. https://doi.org/10.1016/j.ijresmar.2010.02.004

Weiss, M. G. (1988). Cultural models of diarrheal illness: Conceptual framework and review. *Social Science & Medicine, 27*(1), 5–16.

Werner, O., & Campbell, D. T. (1970). Translating, working through interpreters, and the problem of decentering. In R. Naroll & R. Cohen (Eds.), *A handbook of cultural anthropology* (pp. 398–419). New York, NY: American Museum of National History.

White, G. M. (1985). Premises and purposes in a Solomon Islands ethnopsychology. In G. M. White & J. Kirkpatrick (Eds.), *Person, self, and experience: Exploring Pacific ethnopsychologies* (pp. 328–366). Berkeley, CA: University of California Press.

White, G. M. (1987). Proverbs and cultural models: An American psychology of problem solving. In D. Holland & N. Quinn (Eds.), *Cultural models in language and thought* (pp. 151–172). Cambridge, UK: Cambridge University Press.

Widmer, E. D., Treas, J., & Newcomb, R. (1998). Attitudes toward nonmarital sex in 24 countries. *Journal of Sex Research, 35*(4), 349–358.

Wierzbicka, A. (1986). Human emotions: Universal or culture-specific? *American Anthropologist, 88*(3), 584–594.

Wierzbicka, A. (1991). *Cross-cultural pragmatics: The semantics of human interaction.* Berlin, Germany: Mouton de Gruyter.

Wierzbicka, A. (1992). *Semantics, culture and cognition: Universal human concepts in culture-specific configurations.* New York, NY: Oxford University Press.

Wierzbicka, A. (1999). *Emotions across languages and cultures: Diversity and universals.* Cambridge, UK: Cambridge University Press.

Wierzbicka, A. (2003). *Cross-cultural pragmatics.* Berlin, Germany: Mouton de Gruyter.

Wierzbicka, A. (2004a). 'Happiness' in cross-linguistic & cross-cultural perspective. *Daedalus, 133*(2), 34–43.

Wong, Y., & Tsai, J. (2007). Cultural models of shame and guilt. In J. L. Tracy, R. W. Robins, & J. P. Tangney (Eds.), *The self-conscious emotions: Theory and research* (pp. 209–223). New York, NY: Guilford Press.

Yamaguchi, S. (2004). Further clarifications of the concept of amae in relation to dependence and attachment. *Human Development, 47*, 28–33.

Yang, K. S. (2000). Monocultural and cross-cultural indigenous approaches: The royal road to the development of a balanced global psychology. *Asian Journal of Social Psychology, 3*(3), 241–263.

Young, F. W. (2013). *Multidimensional scaling: History, theory, and applications.* New York: Psychology Press.

Zhu, H. (Ed.). (2016). *Research methods in intercultural communication: A practical guide.* New York, NY: Wiley Blackwell.

Chapter 4
Emotional Processes in Cultural Contexts

4.1 Construction of Emotional Life

4.1.1 Basic Emotional Phenomena and Processes

Basic Emotional Phenomena

Four most typical terms—*feeling, emotion, affective state*, and *mood*—are used in scholarly literature to describe emotional phenomena, such as neural and physiological processes, subjective experience, expression, and behavior. They are quite often used interchangeably, yet with slightly different meaning.

The *feeling* is a vague term, which is not well-defined in modern psychology, so it is used in various contexts. *Feeling* is understood as a fleeting experience that embodies physiological processes, body sensations, and subtle subjective aspects of emotions, such as feeling cold, feeling warm, feeling hot, heart beats faster, breathing changes, lump in the throat, blushing, sweating, gooseflesh, stomach sensations, the racing heart of fear, the lightness in limbs and body of joy, weak in the knees, the flushed face of shame, and hot in the eye (Breugelmans et al., 2005; Cromby, 2007). In many contexts of scholarly writing, however, the *word feeling* is often used as a synonym of *emotion*.

Emotion is a complex of the *internal, short-lived*, and *arousing bio-psychosocial responses* that may involve mental or behavioral actions (Ekman, 1994; Matsumoto & Hwang, 2012). Fear, disgust, and anger are examples of such responses. Emotions are faster than cognitive information processing. Therefore, they help evaluate a situation. Such a quick appraisal allows acting promptly and requires minimal conscious involvement (Tooby & Cosmides, 2008).

Affective state (or affect) defines an emotional experience in terms of arousal—high to low—and valence—positive to negative (Feldman Barrett & Russell, 1999; Larsen & Diener, 1992). The terms *affect* and *affective state* have been used in scholarship in quite broad spectrum of meanings.

© The Author(s), under exclusive license to Springer Nature Switzerland AG 2021   159
V. Karandashev, *Cultural Models of Emotions*,
https://doi.org/10.1007/978-3-030-58438-2_4

Mood describes a less specific and less intense emotional state that is not evidently activated by a particular event or stimulus. Emotions are short-lived states lasting for a few seconds or minutes, while mood lasts a few days (Davidson, 1994; Watson & Clark, 1994).

All these emotional concepts—feelings, emotions, affective states, moods, and others—are emotional phenomena, which are collectively called emotional experiences. Some of them do not perfectly fit into the emotional categories considered above (e.g., feelings of hunger, tiredness, calmness, superiority, respect, and friendly feelings).

The processes of appraisal, awareness, and interpretation of feelings—physiological and psychosomatic—transform the feelings into emotions, affective states, and moods. Subjective perception of body sensation, conscious or unconscious reflections of neuroendocrine, skeletomuscular, and autonomic nervous systems trigger emotional processing (Levenson, 2003). Certain patterns of feelings become emotions via awareness and appraisal.

Cultural differences in emotions have been found in antecedent events, appraisals, subjective feelings, behavioral components (e.g., Matsumoto, Kudoh, Scherer, & Wallbott, 1988; Mesquita & Walker, 2003; Scherer, Matsumoto, Wallbott, & Kudoh, 1988), structure of emotions (Fontaine, Poortinga, Setiadi, & Markam, 2002; Scollon, Diener, Oishi, & Biswas-Diener, 2004).

Classifications of Emotions

There are several groups of emotions that researchers have explored in recent decades. Among those are *basic emotions*, such as anger, sadness, disgust, fear, and surprise (Ekman, 1992, 1999; Izard, 2007), *positive emotions*, such as joy, hope, gratitude, pride, inspiration, and love (Fredrickson, 2001; Fredrickson & Cohn, 2008; Fredrickson & Losada, 2005), *prosocial emotions*, such as regret, joy, empathy, sympathy, and compassion (McCullough, Bono, & Root, 2007; Stürmer, Snyder, & Omoto, 2005), *self-conscious emotions*, such as guilt, shame, embarrassment, and pride (Lewis, 2008; Prinz & Nichols, 2010; Tangney & Fischer, 1995; Tracy & Robins, 2004), and *moral emotions*, such as contempt, disgust, anger, embarrassment, shame, guilt, compassion, and gratitude (Haidt, 2003; Tangney, 1999; Tangney, Stuewig, & Mashek, 2007). These groups are not exclusive of each other, but rather overlapping. Some of them are more biologically driven, while others are rather culturally driven (see for review Matsumoto & Hwang, 2012; Russell, 1991).

Emotions as Bio-Psycho-Social Processes

Emotions engage several components, such as physiological reactions, feelings and sensations, subjective experiences and emotions, expressive behaviors, and action tendencies. Emotions are *bio-psycho-social processes* (Matsumoto & Hwang, 2012) because they engage:

1. The patterns of *physiological reactions* taking place in autonomic and central nervous systems.
2. The constellations of *mental activities* necessary to elicit, regulate, and maintain the emotional responses.
3. The *social processes* that influence the *social meaning* of emotions and determine how emotions evolve in a particular social context.

The Componential-Processing Approach to the Study of Emotional Life

The componential-dynamic approach became popular in research of emotions. It considers emotions as the processes that expand over time in ongoing interactions with environment and other people. Emotions are launched with an evaluation of emotion cues, which then activate a synchronized set of responses: physiological, experiential, and behavioral (Ellsworth, 1991; Frijda, 1986; Gross & John, 1998, 2003; Lazarus, 1991; Scherer, 1984).

According to *appraisal theories* of emotion, these components depend on cognitive appraisals (Scherer & Fontaine, 2019)—the associated interpretation of a situation and event (Barrett, Mesquita, Ochsner, & Gross, 2007; Lazarus, 1991; Ortony & Turner, 1990). For instance, the experience of anger evolves from the *appraisal* that the event is negative in valence, it is unjust and might be frustrating, and a person can blame an offender for it. The appraisal of novelty is among the key triggers of emotions (Ellsworth, 2013).

Appraisals are similar to emotion responses (Roseman, Dhawan, Rettek, Naidu, & Thapa, 1995), while cultural norms, interpretive schemes, and frameworks serve as the criteria for appraisal processes, thus mediating emotional experience (Markus & Kitayama, 1991; Shweder, 1993). Thus, they are in turn dependent on cultural context, in which they occur. Cultural settings trigger the ways how people make sense of the world and react to situations and events. They determine and frame people's emotional experiences and behaviors in a culture.

Emotions as the bio-psycho-social reactions to the events potentially require actions and interactions (Barrett et al., 2007; Lazarus, 1991; Ortony & Turner, 1990). Experience of emotion also engages *action tendency*—the readiness to act upon the situation and event. For instance, experience of anger may consist of the tendency to control the situation, confront the offender, or retaliate.

During the course of interaction, emotions involve the reactions to previous events, as well as anticipation of the further development of the interactions. They include physiological reactions, body sensations, feelings, appraisals, expressions, and action tendencies as the components of the emotional processes (Matsumoto & Hwang, 2012; Mesquita & Frijda, 1992; Scherer & Fontaine, 2019).

These responses, however, are not necessarily expressed as visible. An output filter, which functions as emotional regulation, controls how the responses are expressed behaviorally. Thus, the activation of the emotional responses and their modulation affect emotional expressivity (Gross & John, 1998, 2003).

Universality of Basic Emotional Processes

The large-scale cross-cultural survey studies exploring emotional responses (Cosnier, Dols, & Fernandez, 1986; Scherer & Wallbott, 1994; Wallbott, Ricci-Bitti, & Banninger-Huber, 1986) were able to identify the cross-culturally common patterns of the simple nonverbal expressions for several emotions. However, the emotional expressive behaviors for more complex emotions and emotional complexes were culturally diverse.

In the same vein, the conception of *psychological universalism* suggests that while basic emotional processes may be similar across cultures, yet the manifestations of these processes are culturally different (Berry, Poortinga, Segall, & Dasen, 2002; Poortinga & Soudijn, 2002). The findings from the study of *shame* and *guilt* (Breugelmans & Poortinga, 2006) in two culturally different rural samples, compared with student samples, are in support of this idea of *psychological universalism* concerning these modal emotions. Authors found that people in those cultures are able to differentiate 29 emotion characteristics in the descriptions of these two emotions, even though in one culture (Rarámuri—a group of indigenous people in Mexico), people use only one word for both emotions of *guilt* and *shame*, while in other (Javanese), people use two different words (Breugelmans & Poortinga, 2006).

The data from linguistics are also in agreement with this conclusion. There are definitely the universals in language use for communicative expression. Comparative linguistic studies demonstrate some similarities among cultures, which are evident at the general atomic and semantic, but not at specific molecular and episodic levels, which are more culturally affected. Thus, linguistic universals of expression appear more valid on semantic primitives and basic semantic elements, whereas cultural differences are more evident in specific uses of language and pragmatics (Lim, 2003). Lim contended that Anglocentrism continues to be the dominant paradigm of today's cross-cultural studies in pragmatics as a field of linguistics exploring the practical use of signs, words, and sentences. However, it is important to compare pragmatic features in expression across many languages to gain really valid cross-cultural generalization. Researchers have already found many interesting culturally specific differences (see for review, Lim, 2003, p. 67).

4.1.2 Cultural Conceptions of Emotion

Cultural Meanings of Emotions

The construction of emotions depends on the sociocultural contexts, in which they occur (Boiger & Mesquita, 2014). For example, the cultures that emphasize the autonomy of individuals and self-promotion may welcome the expression of anger because these emotions allow people to express their desires and adjust their relationships. Therefore, the emotions of anger in such culture are common. Different from those, cultures that accentuate relational interdependence and modesty discourage the expression of anger, perceiving it as immature.

The meanings of the same emotions may be different across cultures (e.g., Russell, 1991; Trommsdorff & Cole, 2011; Uchida & Kitayama, 2009).

Cultural differences in emotional patterns occur because cultural contexts constrain certain types of appraisals, or promote others, according to their values. The connotations and content of specific emotions adjust to fit norms and practices, which help pursue cultural goals and values. For example, American cultural values tend to emphasize the importance of autonomy, compared to Eskimo or Japanese cultural values highlighting the maintenance of harmony and adjustment to others.

Because of this, American people tend to easily experience and express *anger* in case of personal frustration, while Eskimo or Japanese generally ignore expressions of *anger*, and it is likely to de-escalate situation (Briggs, 1970; Markus & Kitayama, 1991). As for culturally specific coping strategies, Americans tend to cope externalizing their emotion of *anger* into aggressive behavior. Japanese prefer to cope with *anger* via transcendental reappraisal and self-improvement (Uchida & Kitayama, 2009).

For European Americans, the meaning of *happiness* is associated with positive hedonic experience and personal achievement, while for Japanese, *happiness* is associated with social harmony. In North American culture, *happiness* is a hedonic experience which signals personal success and helps achieve it. In Japanese culture *happiness* contains certain social ambivalence—it is more conducive for harmony-focused relationships (Uchida & Kitayama, 2009).

American Conception of Emotion

In American culture, similar to several Western European cultures, a basic unit of society is an individual, and the privacy of emotional life is a major value orientation. Therefore, emotions are situated within an individual's self and people know about these emotions and feelings through their introspection. Therefore, the primary referents of emotions are an individual's internal feelings and affective states. Because of this, the terms for emotions commonly denote people's internal subjective states, which they convey to others. These feelings are more important than social appraisal for their experience and expression of emotions (Lutz, 1982, 1988).

For Americans, the important aspects of their culture are a possibility to declare internal feelings and express their individual emotional experience. The self and individual experiences are in the roots of social actions. Personal emotion and emotional experience have a definite priority legitimizing social action (Potter, 1988, p. 182).

American culture endorses open expression of emotion, rather than keeping those under control of reason. Nevertheless, cultural beliefs tend to devaluate emotions in the face of reason, admitting gender differences. Traditionally, men are viewed of being more capable for reasoning than women, and women are deemed to be more emotional than men (Lynch, 1990).

Chinese Conception of Emotion

Chinese cultural perspective on understanding emotions is different from American one. People are aware of their emotions. For them, however, the somatic and interpersonal processes associated with the experience of emotions are the primary referents. Emotion is not sufficient rationale for important social actions and relationships.

For the Chinese, a person acquires social meaning of life more from social context than from an individual's emotional experience. The emotions, being present within individuals, are just concomitant phenomena of social life, not central ones. They are logically secondary and do not substantially influence social relationships. The social life takes place independently of any emotion. The social order exists independently of internal subjective feelings (Potter, 1988). From these cultural norms, a Chinese person considers their emotions as unrelated to their social relationship.

Indian Conception of Emotions

Indian conceptions of emotion have their cultural specifics. Sanskrit and Bengali languages of India have no single concept of *emotion*, but rather several related words.

The old spiritual traditions in India, such as Āyurveda, Brahmanism, Vedanta, and Yoga, suggested an ideal of emotionlessness that an individual can achieve controlling their senses, mind, and emotions. This ideal of emotionlessness created a stereotypical view of Indian conception of emotion in the West (Bilimoria & Wenta, 2015; McDaniel, 1995). These traditions, however, are not widely present in modern India. The modern devotional and aesthetic traditions differ from those old schools of thoughts (McDaniel, 1995). It is worth noting that Indian approach to emotions distinguishes between notions of *bhava* as a personal emotion and *rasa* as an impersonal emotion, in which an individual is distanced as an observer. Cultural value suggests intensifying emotion of *bhakti* until it becomes overwhelming and powerful. *Rasa*, as a depersonalized emotion, is valued higher than a personal emotion. A person experiences and appreciates *rasa* emotions as through a glass window. This allows keeping unpleasant feelings out of internal experience and observing those as an object of art. In this case, emotions are viewed not as passions and disturbances, but rather as aesthetic objects. Emotion becomes an active response engaging meaning and beauty, rather than a passive reaction to an event (McDaniel, 1995).

4.1.3 Cultural Influences on Emotional Life

Biological Versus Cultural Factors of Emotions

The role of biological and social factors in formation of emotions has been discussed throughout decades. Recently, many emotions researchers follow the theoretical position that both biological and social (cultural) parameters determine how emotion processes evolve. Accordingly, emotions can be *cross-culturally universal* and *cross-culturally different* (e.g., Ekman, 1972; Ekman et al., 1987; Matsumoto & Hwang, 2012; Mesquita, 2003; Mesquita & Frijda, 1992). The meanings, experiences, and expressions of emotions may substantially differ across cultures, despite similarities (Mesquita, 2003; Shweder, Haidt, Horton, & Joseph, 2008).

However, the extent, to which such cultural influence may occur, depends on specific aspects of emotional life. The matter is in a relative contribution of biological and cultural factors. Matsumoto and Hwang (2012) proposed that *"the relative contribution of biological and cultural factors to emotion depends on what emotion is being studied and the specific domain of emotion assessed"* (p. 92).

Throughout recent decades, extensive studies have investigated various domains of emotions, such as *physiological reactions, facial expressions, vocal utterances, subjective experiences,* the *meanings of emotions,* their descriptors, features, and concepts of emotion (see for detailed review, Matsumoto & Hwang, 2012).

According to a comprehensive review of the *cultural variations in emotions* (Mesquita & Frijda, 1992), cultural similarities and differences exist in many components of the emotion process, including *antecedent events eliciting emotions, appraisals of the events, patterns of physiological responses, experience of emotions, action readiness, emotional behavior,* and *emotional regulation.*

Domains of Emotional Life and Culture

Matsumoto and Hwang (2012) suggested that emotional life of individuals consists of several emotional domains, which are affected by cultural influences to a different extent: (1) priming reactions (cognitive gating, expressive behavior, and physiological responses), (2) subjective experience (affect, feelings, and self-reports), (3) emotion meaning (beliefs about emotion, values about emotion, and attitudes about emotions).

Priming reactions are the prompt responses to an event or stimulus. The contribution of culture in these responses is low. *Subjective experiences* include self-reported experiences, internal labeling of emotion, and its interpretations, which are more influenced by culture through the appraisal. *Attitudes, beliefs, and values* represent the meaning of emotions. They are apparently and highly influenced by culture (Matsumoto & Hwang, 2012).

While priming reactions and subjective experiences are the momentary constructions and patterns of emotions emerging in interactions and within relationships, the cultural attitudes, beliefs, and values tend to be quite stable affordances for the construction of emotion. Cultural contexts emphasize certain values and practices and prescribe a person how to act and relate to others. All cultures include scripts, prototypical actions, attitudes, rules, beliefs, and values, representing emotions. These components can be less differentiated; they form the emotional complexity of an individual and a society.

Social Functions of Emotions

Cultural regulation of people's *emotions* plays an important *role* in life of societies. Therefore, various cultures develop their norms regarding *experience* and *expression* of emotions.

Since emotions serve as the primary motivators of behavior, they fulfill certain social functions. They encourage adhering to norms and creating sanctions against their breach and violation (Keltner & Haidt, 1999; Tomkins, 1962, 1963). They are capable to regulate, facilitate, and coordinate social relationships. They help groups function effectively. Through the norms regulating emotions, cultures make certain that behaviors of individuals and groups comply with cultural scripts, which assist to increase social coordination and decrease social chaos (Matsumoto & Hwang, 2012).

Social functions of many emotions are recognized similarly across cultures, yet their meaning depends on cultural norms, goals, and ideals that Mesquita called *cultural mandates* since they serve their social functions (Mesquita, 2003; Mesquita, Boiger, & De Leersnyder, 2017). In their light, some emotions, which are beneficial to the socially desirable outcomes, are valued, while others are devalued and, therefore, suppressed or avoided. As a consequence, the emotions that coincide with the *cultural mandates* are experienced and expressed intensely and frequently in the people's everyday life, while emotions that do not coincide with those—less intensely and infrequently (Mesquita, 2003). The ubiquity of *shame* in a Bedouin tribe in Egypt (Abu-Lughod, 1986/2000) and the *anger* avoidance among the Utku Inuits of Northern Canada (Briggs, 1970) are the two frequently referred examples in this regard.

Interpersonal processes in cultural contexts promote and afford those emotions, which are consistent with their cultural mandates. Accordingly, individuals tend to associate some situations with certain emotions and encounter them frequently. Cultures also have equivalent language representations and produce corresponding children's books, while people hold more detailed and elaborate interpersonal scripts for the emotions that correspond to the cultural mandate, such as shame in Japan and anger in Germany (Mesquita et al., 2017). As another example of comparison, according to the Taiwanese cultural norms of adjusting to others, the storybooks for children tend to depict rather calmer than excited smiles, while in accordance with North American cultural norms of influencing environments, storybooks usually display their main characters with excited rather than calm smiles (Tsai, Louie, Chen, & Uchida, 2007).

Affiliative and Distancing Function of Emotions

People in various cultural contexts tend to interpret emotions in terms of their *affiliative and distancing functions* (Kitayama, Markus, & Kurokawa, 2000). The dimension of *social engagement* ranges from socially engaging (affiliative) to socially disengaging (distancing) emotions. It is viewed as a dimension different from *approach* and *avoidance*.

These tendencies are evident since culturally normative emotions are the subject of interpersonal and cultural regulation. Researchers (Mesquita et al., 2017) demonstrated this in cross-cultural studies using the samples of Japanese, Turkish, Belgian, and American participants.

Comparing the occurrence of *socially engaging* and *disengaging emotions* in the samples of North American and Japanese students, researchers (Kitayama, Mesquita, & Karasawa, 2006) found that people experience the emotions which are conducive to achieve a cultural mandate at the higher intensity, while those emotions which violate a cultural mandate at the lower intensity.

Results demonstrated that North Americans experienced more positive disengaging emotions (e.g., pride), compared to positive engaging emotions (e.g., friendly feelings). Japanese, on the other hand, experienced more positive engaging emotions, compared to positive disengaging emotions. As for comparison between cultures, Americans experienced more positive disengaging emotions (e.g., pride), compared to Japanese, yet Japanese and Americans were not different in their reporting of positive engaging emotions (e.g., friendly feelings). Furthermore, Americans experienced negative disengaging emotions (e.g., anger) stronger than Japanese. However, Japanese experienced negative engaging emotions (e.g., shame) stronger than Americans.

These results are generally in accordance with authors' theory that "disengaging emotions (such as pride and anger) are more prevalent in North American contexts where the *cultural mandate* is one of independence, because emotions with distancing functions can be thought of as expressing and achieving independence..." Different from this, "socially engaging emotions (friendly feelings, shame) are more prevalent in Japanese contexts where the cultural mandate is one of interdependence, because emotions that serve affiliative function are consistent with this Japanese mandate" (Mesquita et al., 2017, p. 103).

Based on a series of studies, authors conclude that individuals shape their emotional experience in a situation to better match the *cultural mandates*, which guide their behavior. They actively create the meaning in the situation and the emotions that they experience. Societies actively and passively shape the cultural patterns of emotional experience. People tend to experience and express more commonly those emotions that help them to be a good person in their culture (Barrett, 2012, 2017; Boiger & Mesquita, 2014; Mesquita, Boiger, & De Leersnyder, 2016). Moreover, the research suggests that following culturally normative emotions in the ways, which are culturally fitting, allows better individual's adjustment and well-being (see for review, Mesquita et al., 2017).

Emotional Affordances in Cultures

Emotions are the dynamic processes, which evolve at a small time-scale during moment-to-moment interactions with events, situations, and other people (Boiger & Mesquita, 2014). How individuals experience these emotions depends on *emotional affordances*—the range of emotions, which are likely to occur in a particular culture, relationship, and circumstance. Emotional affordances during short or long interactions determine experience (or not experience) and expression (or not expression) of emotions that evolve differently from moment-to-moment interactions depending on the input of others. Friends, lovers, and acquaintances pick up the emotional behavior of their partners and rely on their emotional reactions, especially when they appraise ambiguous situations.

How Culture Regulates Emotions

Cultures regulate emotions in various ways. They can calibrate biological emotions to culturally available events. Because of this, people absorb the cultural standards of what they should be emotional about. Cultures regulate priming reactions. This way, people acquire the knowledge of what kinds of emotional reactions they should have when an emotion is elicited. They also learn what the acceptable behaviors are, when certain emotions arise. Through appraisal, cultures can define the quality of subjective experience of emotions and regulate the intensity of emotional experiences. Through cultural knowledge, cultures prompt the emergence of social and other human emotions. Cultures define emotional meanings, values, attitudes, and beliefs about emotions in societies (Matsumoto & Hwang, 2012).

Emotions in the Context of Relationships

Quality and intensity of emotions in social interaction also depend on the context of ongoing relationships with others. Family and other kinship bonds, close relationships can restrain the possible and likely emotions and the ways when and how these emotions are expressed.

For example, in romantic and marital relationships, partners experience synchronized emotional time-dynamics (Butler, 2011; Butner, Diamond, & Hicks, 2007). Emotions of partners in a couple co-vary with each other. They become mutually dependent in their emotional lives: being in a relationship makes them to adjust the possible emotions that they experience on daily basis: if one partner feels happy, so does the other.

Emotional synchrony between partners can be also manifested in physiological parameters associated with emotions (Larson & Almeida, 1999; Levenson & Gottman, 1983; Saxbe & Repetti, 2010). In particular, physiological patterns of partners during emotionally intense interactions become interconnected in such parameters as heart rate, skin conductance, and salivary cortisol. It is worth to note that couples in strained and unstable relationships exhibit more such physiological links. Negative affect and associated physiological changes seem transmit easier (possibly unconsciously, through mimicry, Hatfield, Cacioppo, & Rapson, 1994), while positive affect is less affected (Larson & Almeida, 1999; Levenson & Gottman).

4.1.4 Cultural Models of Self and Relating and Models of Emotions

The Cultural Models of Self and Relating

The first approach, which can be used in the *construction of cultural models of emotions*, is *based on the cultural dimensions of societies* and communities. Following this approach, researchers select an important cultural dimension, classify the societies along this criterion, and then systematically analyze and review the available research findings compiling the comprehensive pictures of how similar or different the emotional patterns constituting emotional life of people in those societies are. *Individualism* and *collectivism* have been among the popular cultural dimensions for the studies of emotions. People in individualistic societies are characterized by *independent model of self*, while people in collectivistic societies are characterizes by interdependent societies by *interdependent model of self* (Markus & Kitayama, 1991; Mesquita & Leu, 2007; Tsai & Clobert, 2019). These models can explain the differences in the patterns of their emotional life. In particular, *self-construals* associated with these cultural differences play an important role in the construction and experience of emotions (Nezlek, Kafetsios, & Smith, 2008; Nezlek, Sorrentino et al., 2008).

Along the same line, much of theoretical and empirical cross-cultural research on emotions in recent decades have compared emotional experience of people in *East Asian, as interdependent cultural context*, and *Western, as independent cultural context*. According to this distinction, Mesquita and Leu (2007) suggested that emotions reflect the *cultural models of self* and *relating*, which constraint and afford certain emotions.

Based on this explanatory framework, Mesquita and Leu (2007) proposed the *cultural models of emotions* that reflect the *cultural models of self* and *relating*. These models developed from the extensive research that contrasted emotions of people in *East Asian, as interdependent cultural context*, and *Western, as independent cultural context*. According to authors (Mesquita & Leu, 2007), the major themes of cultural models, ideal affect, emotional styles are the main factors, which determine emotional lives of people in different cultures. Focal, normative, and ideal emotional representations are also included as the domains of these cultural models. Authors have demonstrated that these *cultural models* affect various components of the emotional experience and expression, such as "the appraisal of the event, action readiness, bodily changes, expressive and instrumental behavior, and conscious regulatory processes" (p. 736).

In this section, I summarize these two models—*cultural model of self* and the *cultural model of relating*, and how they reflect on emotional life of people in those cultures. The details of the studies and corresponding references are presented below and dispersed in the following chapters.

Appraisals in the Cultural Models of Self and Relating

The *cultural model of self* (prevailing in independent cultures) and the *cultural model of relating* (prevailing in interdependent cultures) affect how individuals in those cultures appraise the similar situations. An individual in *independent culture* (e.g., European American) tends to appraise a situation from a standpoint of how *the situation may impact individual goals*, while an individual in *interdependent culture* (e.g., Japanese) appraises from the standpoint of *how the situation may impact relational goals*. These two types of appraisals, according to the two different cultural models, trigger different emotional reactions to the similar situation and cause different emotional experience and expression. Within the framework of the *cultural model of self* (self-focused), a typical appraisal of the situation *when something bad happened* is the *blaming other person* for *their mistake* or *offense* that causes experience of *anger*, as well as its *assertive* and *aggressive* expression. Within the framework of the *cultural model of relating* (other-focused), a typical appraisal of similar situation is the *assuming that other person had their reason* to act this way. Consequently, an individual feels *sympathy with other person*, the *decreased emotional experience* and exhibit those in *doing nothing against that person*.

In a study of emotional experience among Dutch, Turkish, and Surinamese people, Mesquita (2001) found that for the Turkish and Surinamese respondents, their *emotions* are largely *relational phenomena*. This fact reflects interdependent aspect of those cultures. For the Dutch respondents, their emotions are much less focused on the social relations, but they are rather internal phenomena of the individual. This fact reflects independent aspect of that culture.

Inside-Out and Outside-In Perspectives in Cultural Appraisal

The similar aspect of *interdependent cultural model* of emotional experience regarding Japanese culture was highlighted contrasting *outside-in perspective* with *inside-out perspective* (Hamaguchi, 1985). People in *independent cultures* tend to perceive the meaning of social situations eliciting emotions primarily *from their individual perspective*—an *inside-out perspective*. People in *interdependent cultures* perceive the meaning of such situations *from the perspective of other people*—*outside-in perspective* (Hamaguchi, 1985).

Another cross-cultural study (Mesquita & Leu, 2007) found that the appraisals of Japanese participants (a sample of *interdependent culture*), compared to American participants (a sample of *independent culture*), were more focused on awareness of the meaning of the situation to others. When they reported their experience of emotions and behavior in the situations of *humiliation, offense,* or *being valued* in the past, the Japanese participants were able to differentiate the *perspective of others* and *their own perspective*. More than 40% of the Japanese participants described and appraised the situation from an *outside-in perspective*—the viewpoint of a third person. This ability to understand the divergent perspective of other may be the reason why many Japanese responded to offense by doing nothing. Their awareness of the perspective of another person made them less likely to react against the offender. In that study, none of the Americans described and appraised the situations from such an *outside-in perspective*. Taking an *inside-out perspective* made European Americans to act with the assertiveness and aggression.

The similar distinction between the tendency to perceive a situation from *an outside-in perspective* (typical in interdependent cultures) and the tendency to perceive a situation from an *inside-out perspective* (typical in independent cultures) was evident in the study of attribution of emotional experience to others (Cohen & Gunz, 2002). Canadian participants of Eastern descent (interdependent culture) revealed a better ability for implicit awareness of others' perspective compared to Canadians of Western descent.

Thus, several studies have demonstrated that the *perspective of others* is more likely to be included in appraisal of situation in the model of interdependent cultures than in the model of independent cultures.

Experience and Expression of Emotions in the Models of Self and Relating

Another example is the norms of experience and expression of positive and negative emotions according to these two cultural models. People in the cultures with *cultural model of self* and the *cultural model of relating* use the styles of emotional regulation specific for their cultures. According to the first model, people tend to maximize positive emotions and minimize negative emotions. According to the second model, people tend to emphasize moderation of positive and negative emotions.

People in European American culture, which perfectly fits to the concept of *cultural model of self*, admire the elevated and excited positive experience, as well as open expression of *positive emotions*, yet they strive to avoid *negative emotions*. People in that culture are more willing to express and express their happiness to others.

People in Japanese culture, which fits well to the concept of *cultural model of relating*, encourage moderation in experience and expression of *positive emotions* and *negative emotions*. They are more willing to accept the reality of *negative emotions* as a natural part of life, along with *positive emotions*. Japanese are more comfortable than European Americans with a mixture of positive and negative emotional experiences keeping a holistic and dialectic view on emotions. Even happiness they experience and describe as a mixed emotion of positive and negative affect. According to the *cultural model of relating*, people in that culture believe that the excessive expression of happiness may cause dissonance in interpersonal relationships when happiness of one individual is not congruent with unhappy or quiet emotions of other person making them uncomfortable.

Many other studies (e.g., Mesquita, 2001; Mesquita & Karasawa, 2002; Tsai & Clobert, 2019) also found support for this theoretical distinction of emotional experience between the *cultural models of self* and *relating*. For example, Mesquita and Karasawa (2002) investigated daily emotions of American and Japanese students living in the United States, and Japanese students living in Japan. Administering questionnaires four times a day during one-week period, authors found that European Americans experienced their emotional lives as more pleasant than did two Japanese groups. Data showed that *interdependent concerns* are predictive for *emotional experiences of Japanese.* Yet, *independent* as well as *interdependent concerns* are predictive for the emotional experiences of Americans. The latter finding can be explained by a higher cultural diversity of American society, compared to Japanese one.

Diversity of Cultural Models of Self and Relating

Independent and *interdependent* cultures are quite diverse and therefore, distinguishing those two as homogeneous opposites of *Asian* and *Western* societies does not reflect a variety of their emotional experience (Mesquita & Leu, 2007; Tsai & Clobert, 2019). Other cultural dimensions—beyond *independence* and *interdependence*—should be taken into account in cross-cultural studies of emotions (Mesquita & Leu, 2007).

The distinction between independent and interdependent cultures does not bring sufficient understanding of cultural differences in emotional experience. *Independent cultures* include not only European Americans, but also various western European societies. *Interdependent cultures* include not only east Asian, but also non-east Asian interdependent societies. Actually, there are different kinds of interdependent and collectivistic cultural models. In the following sections, the examples of Japanese and Mexican models are described. Both, being *interdependent*, are still substantially different in other dimensions of culture and emotional experience. European American, French, German, Scandinavian models are described. All, being independent, differ from each other in other cultural and emotional dimensions.

These two types of cultural models of emotions—*self* and *relating*—have a more diversity if taking into account other cultural dimensions. Although the opposition of *Western* (*independent*) and *Asian* (*interdependent*) cultures is valid and explains emotional life very well, yet this opposition may be not sufficient in application to many cultures.

4.1.5   Acculturation of Emotions

Concept of Acculturation

An individual can acquire another culture in various ways: via socialization, cultural assimilation or accommodation, and enculturation or acculturation. It is possible that there are more or less sensitive periods for the acquisition of culture, for example, for language learning or for developing of taste and food preferences. After such a sensitive period, an individual cannot fully acquire a culture the same way a native person does. The cultural changes may take different dynamics depending on the types and forms of cultures and how they compatible. During these processes of acculturation, an individual can experience difficulties in coping with an unfamiliar language, different values, beliefs, norms of behavior, and foods of other cultures.

The same way as values, beliefs, norms of behavior, the cultural construction of emotional life is relatively stable and usually changes slowly within its national boundaries, but it can also be dynamic when individuals migrate from one country to another. In the latter case, emotional acculturation takes place. As people move between cultures, they adjust their emotional patterns according to the context, which a new culture affords (Boiger & Mesquita, 2014). Moreover, individuals moving between cultures modify their emotional patterns in accordance with those, which are afforded by their new cultural contexts.

Emotional Acculturation of Immigrants

Once immigrants are exposed to novel situations, which are culturally different, they can sooner or later adjust their meaning systems (Savani, Morris, Naidu, Kumar, & Berlia, 2011). This occurs slower among Americans since they have a cultural value to influence, and faster among Indians since they have cultural value to adjust (Boiger, Mesquita, Tsai, & Markus, 2012; Morling, Kitayama, & Miyamoto, 2002; Roseman et al., 1995; Weisz, Rothbaum, & Blackburn, 1984).

Research has demonstrated emotional acculturation of immigrants in several cultural samples. In the study of emotional patterns of Korean immigrants in America and Turkish immigrants in Belgium, in comparison with the emotional patterns of their respective cultures of settlement, researchers (De Leersnyder, Mesquita, & Kim, 2011, 2013) collected the data on the emotional events that immigrants experienced in their lives and the extent how they felt each of 20 emotions. Then, authors compared an immigrant's profile with the average profile of the respective host culture as the degree of their emotional acculturation. They discovered that those immigrants, who had spent more time in the host culture, exhibited the emotional patterns more similar to the average mainstream pattern. In addition, the immigrants, who interacted with people in a new cultural context more frequently (compared with those who did not), showed emotional patterns more similar to the new culture. They altered their cultural emotional interpretations and adjusted their emotional patterns.

Similar results were obtained in other studies. When Consedine, Chentsova-Dutton, and Krivoshekova (2014) investigated emotional experience of the women who immigrated in the United States of America from the Dominican Republic, Haiti, the English-speaking Caribbean countries, and Eastern Europe, researchers found that the more time immigrants spent in the United States, the greater emotional similarity they had with people of American culture.

Positive Outcome of Emotional Acculturation

It is important to mention that, as studies showed (Consedine et al., 2014; De Leersnyder, Kim, & Mesquita, 2015; De Leersnyder, Mesquita, Kim, Eom, & Choi, 2014), such emotional acculturation has positive outcome for physical and psychological well-being of immigrants. The immigrants with a greater cultural fit of their emotional patterns in the host culture had better relational and psychological well-being. However, these consequences of acculturation had a positive effect only in culturally desirable situations: in the situations promoting autonomy in the United States, in the situations promoting relatedness in Korea, but in both types of situations in Belgium (De Leersnyder et al., 2015).

It is interesting that immigrants can switch their emotional patterns when they are in their native culture at home or when they are in host cultures outside of home. Being bicultural, they tend to change—unconsciously or consciously—their emotional attitudes in these culturally different situations (De Leersnyder, 2017).

4.2 Culture and Control of Emotional Processes

4.2.1 Concepts of Emotional Control and Regulation

Human Ability to Control Emotions

Experience and expression of emotion can be natural occurrences when they flow as they are. This is typical for emotional life among animals. They have adaptive capability—that can be instinctive or learned—to adjust their emotional responses depending on circumstances. However, only people as self-conscious and self-aware humans learn to modify their emotions intentionally depending on their goals.

The human ability to control, adjust, and alter emotional responses to achieve goals and desired outcomes in available context is called *emotion regulation*. Regulation can occur either consciously or subconsciously, intentionally or unintentionally. Boys and girls acquire through early cultural socialization how to express emotions properly and regulate their expression accordingly. For example, girls may express higher levels of happiness in interaction with a stranger than when they are alone, thus up-regulating happy expressions in order to please the stranger. Different from this, boys express lower levels of happiness in interaction with a stranger than when they are alone, thus down-regulating happy expressions in order to look "cool and calm" (Chaplin, 2015).

Children learn how to adjust their expression of emotion depending on interpersonal context. Among American White middle-class participants of the age 7–12 years, Zeman and Garber (1996) found that children reported their expressing negative emotions (e.g., anger, sadness) more frequently when they are alone or in front of a parent than when they are with a peer. As they explained, they anticipated that their parents would accept their emotions while peers would reject. In their interactions with others, children thought of the expectancies of others.

Methods of Emotional Regulation

Emotional regulation can occur on different stages of emotional processes: (1) selection of situation, (2) modification of situation, (3) deployment of attention, (4) cognitive change, or (5) modulation of physiological, experiential, or behavioral responses (Gross, 2001).

Multiple studies (see for review, Matsumoto, 2006b) have demonstrated cultural differences in emotion regulation. In particular, cultures differ in the stimulus selection, appraisals that trigger emotion, in emotional expression, in the display rules governing their modification, in coping, and the processes of cognitive *re-appraisal*.

For instance, *cognitive change* includes *cognitive reappraisal*, when an individual re-construes an emotion-eliciting situation to change its emotional impact (Gross, 1998, 2001; Gross & John, 2003). These emotion regulation processes are affected by cultures. For example, as I showed in the previous sections, cultural views and values trigger certain types of appraisal and reappraisal of situations.

Modulation of response is another example of *emotion regulation.* An individual may focus on *expressive suppression* as the inhibition of ongoing emotional expressive behavior (Gross, 2001; Gross & John, 2003). This suppression regulation strategy may be adaptive, for instance, in the case of anger since an open expression of anger might be threatening to interpersonal relationships. Being generally beneficial for relationship maintenance, suppression of emotion can cause some negative social consequences (Butler et al., 2003; Gross & John, 2003). However, the frequency of *emotional suppression* and its consequences are moderated by cultural values.

Culture and Emotional Regulation

Among the early studies on the topic was an experiment conducted by Friesen (as cited in Ekman, 1972, 1993). The results revealed that Japanese and European participants displayed the same facial expressions while watching an emotional film alone, yet the Japanese participants displayed more positive and less negative expressions in the present of an experimenter. Thus, the Japanese suppressed their emotions more than the Europeans did.

Recent studies revealed (Butler, Lee, & Gross, 2007; Gross & John, 2003) that Asian Americans in the United States have higher frequency of habitual suppression compared to Caucasians. They also tend to perceive discrepancy between inner feelings and outward expressions and use the masking more than do Caucasians (Gross & John, 1998). Asian Americans exhibit greater suppression of distress cues compared to European Americans (Okazaki, 2002). Thus, one can see that Americans holding Asian values suppress emotion more often in their daily life than Americans holding Western European values do.

These differences in use and consequences of emotional suppression can be explained by European American and Asian cultural values.

4.2.2   Emotion Suppression Among European Americans

Negative Perception of Emotional Suppression Among European Americans

European American cultures favor an open expression of emotions. The strategy of *expression of emotions* is valued more than suppression by American and some other Western cultures. According to the Western European values of *self-assertion* and *independence*, open emotion expression is socially endorsed in many situations.

The use of *emotion suppression* among European Americans is reserved mostly for psychological self-protection and withdrawal in the case of social threats (Markus & Kitayama, 1991; Matsumoto, 1990; Oyserman, Coon, & Kemmelmeier, 2002; Tsai & Levenson, 1997) and is accompanied by avoidant attachment, lack of trust in others, and social withdrawal (Gross & John, 2003). Anthropological and linguistic research also showed (Wierzbicka, 1994) that European Americans suppress their emotions in the service of asserting one's will and protecting the self.

Since in European American culture, suppression typically serves the goal of self-protection, it is accompanied by negative emotions (Butler et al., 2003; Gross & John, 2003). Study showed (Butler, Lee, & Gross, 2007) that among Americans with Western European values, regular suppression causes the development of self-protective mechanisms, negative emotion (e.g., fear and anger), negative partner-perceptions, reduced interpersonal responsiveness, and hostile behavior. A high contradictory motivation to express versus inhibit emotions, as an indication of *emotional ambivalence*, leads to lesser life satisfaction among European Americans, but not among Chinese (Suh, Diener, Oishi, & Triandis, 1998) and lesser interpersonal responsiveness (Butler et al., 2007).

Emotion Suppression and Interpersonal Responsiveness

Interpersonal responsiveness is the important provision of appropriate responses to a partner's conversational needs. It facilitates coordination of social interaction and leads to increased rapport, affiliation, and positive relationship. *Low interpersonal responsiveness*, on the other end, is the diminished interest in the partner and wish to withdraw (Berg & Derlega, 1987; Davis, 1982; Laurenceau, Barrett, & Peitromonaco, 1998). This parameter of communication substantially effects emotions and interpersonal relationships, yet being mediated by culture.

Among Americans with Western European values, low responsiveness of an individual occurs as a consequence of suppression (Butler et al., 2007). Then, a partner likely interprets this as indifference, withdrawal, hostility, and respond less friendly and more hostile as well. As a result, the partner will be unwilling to develop a friendship or other type of close relationship (Berg & Derlega, 1987; Davis, 1982; Laurenceau et al., 1998). These negative social consequences have been generally revealed in experimental studies (Butler et al., 2003; Gross, 2002; Gross & John, 2003; John & Gross, 2004).

4.2.3 Emotion Suppression in East Asian Cultures

Suppression of Emotion as a Self-Regulation Strategy

East Asian cultures favor a moderated emotional life. Research showed that the *suppression of emotions* is highly respected regulation strategy in these cultures compared to European American culture (Butler et al., 2007; Ford & Mauss, 2015; Su, Wei, & Tsai, 2014; Wei, Su, Carrera, Lin, & Yi, 2013). East Asian cultures are prevalently collectivistic. They expect that individuals adjust their behavior to the group. These cultures emphasize such values as in-group harmony, conformity, and obedience. To be compliant with these values individuals restrain their emotional expressions that threaten in-group harmony. Due to these values, in Asian culture, suppression is more normative and prosocial (Suh et al., 1998).

According to the Asian values of *interdependence* and *relationship harmony*, people use suppression for prosocial goals and during positive social interactions. Asian cultures encourage suppression of emotions in situations of concern to hurt someone else and in an attempt to preserve relationships (Wierzbicka, 1994).

For people with Asian cultural values, suppression does not have such detrimental effects as for European Americans. Cultural differences in the responsiveness of the suppressors mediated their emotional reactions. Thus, negative social impacts of suppression are moderated by cultural values. Americans with Asian values did not show low responsiveness as a consequence of suppression. Despite suppressing their emotions, they remained socially connected and avoided negative impacts on their social interaction and relationship (Butler et al., 2007).

Differences in Cultures Versus Differences in Personality Traits

The question remains whether *cultural differences* or *average personality traits across countries* determine cross-cultural differences in emotion regulation. Results of a recent study (Matsumoto, 2006b) found differences between the United States and Japan on several aspects of *emotion regulation*. However, data analysis revealed that individual differences in such personality traits as extraversion, neuroticism, and conscientiousness completely mediated the country differences on all emotion regulation variables.

> what appeared to be cultural differences may in fact have been group differences on personality traits that produced the apparent cultural differences. That is, the observed cross-national United States–Japan differences may have occurred not because of anything cultural per se but because Americans are more likely to have personalities that are associated with more reappraisal, whereas the Japanese are more likely to have personalities associated with more suppression. (Matsumoto, 2006b, p. 430)

4.3 Cultural Complexity of Emotions

4.3.1 Complexity of Emotions

Emotion Lexicon and Knowledge About Emotions

Cultures differ in emotion language, conceptual knowledge about emotions, emotion-related values, emotional appraisals of events, feelings rules (norms for subjective experience), and display rules (norms for emotional expression). All domains of emotional life may be more or less differentiated determining the complexity of emotional life (Matsumoto, Yoo, & Fontaine, 2009; Trnka, Šolcová, & Tavel, 2018; Su et al., 2014; Wei et al., 2013).

Multiple linguistic, anthropological, and psychological studies have explored *emotion language* and revealed cross-culturally diversity and complexity of *emotional lexicon* for the basic and complex emotions (Johnson-Laird & Oatley, 1992; Kövecses, 2000, 2002; Russell, 1991; Wierzbicka, 1992, 1999). Many languages across cultures share similarities and still have differences in their *lexicons of emotions* and *basic emotional categories* (see for review Russell, 1991).

People communicating in different languages use a diverse set of concepts with different divisions. Many English categories and words for emotions do not have the same equivalents in other languages, while the languages in other cultural settings have their culturally specific emotion words (see for reviews Karandashev, 2019; Russell, 1991). Different cultures have similar, but varying emotion lexicons that consist of various amounts of emotion words, which may be more or less differentiated. Nevertheless, they can be explained in terms of other concepts and decomposed into simpler lexical units.

The studies of emotion languages have revealed the cross-cultural universals in the constructions of *emotion lexicons*, as well as differentiation in their complexity (Fontaine, Scherer, & Soriano, 2013; Shaver, Morgan, & Wu, 1996; Shaver, Murdaya, & Fraley, 2001; Shaver, Schwartz, Kirson, & O'Connor, 1987; Shaver, Wu, & Schwartz, 1992; Russell, 1991; Wierzbicka, 1986, 1992, 1999).

For example, several cross-cultural studies demonstrated similarities in emotion lexicon across many languages and cultures. Researchers were able to identify similar distinct basic emotions in English, Italian, Basque, and Indonesian languages (Alonso-Arbiol et al., 2006; Shaver et al., 1996; Shaver et al., 2001; Shaver et al., 1987; Shaver et al., 1992), in Filipino emotion lexicon (Church, Katigbak, Reyes, & Jensen, 1999), and in many languages throughout the world (Fehr & Russell, 1991). However, subordinate categories of emotions were more numerous and culturally diverse.

The number of linguistic labels for emotion categories, the number of synonymic words in emotion lexicons, semantic specificity of words for complex emotions, and the frequency of use of emotion words in everyday life defines the complexity of emotion lexicons, and cultures vary in this regard.

Based on a detailed review of emotional lexicon discovered in anthropological and linguistic research across many cultures, Russell (1991) summarized the major findings as follows:

1. basic categories of emotion are pancultural, subordinate categories culture specific;
2. emotional focal points are pancultural, boundaries culture specific;
3. most emotion categories are culture specific but can be defined by pancultural semantic primitives (p. 426).

Analysis of relations between emotion words and structure of emotional lexicon allows revealing complexity of emotional life of people across cultures. Their hierarchical or multidimensional structures can be very productive in the construction of *cultural models of mental representation of emotions*. Several examples will be presented in the following chapters.

Conceptual knowledge about emotions consists of *emotion concepts, conceptual metaphors, metonymies,* and *related concepts* which describe and define emotional knowledge, experience, cultural prototypical scenarios, and scripts. The *conceptual knowledge* and *emotion lexicon* reflect prevailing cultural *emotionology* in terms of values, thoughts, feelings (Kövecses, 2000, 2002; Wierzbicka, 1992, 1999), and can be an important source of information for construction of *cultural models of emotions*.

Emotion-Related Values

Emotion-related values represent preferences for certain kind of emotional experience, expression, and emotional regulation. People in a given culture may embrace or avoid emotions, overtly or covertly express emotions. They may prefer either emotional expression or emotional suppression as the strategies of emotional regulation.

Several empirical studies (see below) have investigated cultural variations in the experience of positive or negative emotions and found that generally,

– East Asians prefer a balance between negative and positive emotions more than Westerners;
– East Asians favor less intense positive emotions more and highly intense positive emotions less than Westerners;
– East Asians and Westerners differ in their emotional complexity and the tendency to experience positive and negative emotion in response to the same situation;
– East Asians choose emotional expression less and suppression more than Westerners.

Let us consider some of these cultural values of emotional life in details below.

Westerners tend to experience either positive or negative emotions toward events and situations. Co-occurrence of positive and negative emotions is relatively rare in their emotional experience, while such experience is more common among East

Asians (Bagozzi, Wong, & Yi, 1999; Schimmack, Oishi, & Diener, 2002). These differences can be explained by the prevalence of culturally dominant *linear* folk epistemology in Western cultures and *dialectical* folk epistemology in East Asian cultures, with their worldview of holism and acceptance of change (Hui, Fok, & Bond, 2009; Kim, Seo, Yu, & Neuendorf, 2014; Spencer-Rodgers, Peng, & Wang, 2010). *Dialectical beliefs* admit the complementarity of opposite emotions and contradictions as they are. Studies of emotional complexity in Western and East Asian samples found cultural differences that are in agreement with such an epistemology-based explanation (Kitayama et al., 2000; Perunovic, Heller, & Rafaeli, 2007; Scollon, Diener, Oishi, & Biswas-Diener, 2005).

Feeling Rules

Feeling rules are a set of regulations that suggest what emotions people should feel or should not feel in certain typical situations. Feeling rules are the societal expectations about how it is appropriate and desirable to feel specific emotions in different contexts (Eid & Diener, 2001). Feeling rules are more specific than emotion-related values and place more emphasis on the suitability of the experience of discrete emotions in specific contexts.

In a cross-cultural study on feeling rules (Eid & Diener, 2001) for joy, affection, pride, contentment, anger, fear, sadness, and guilt that was administered in two collectivistic (China, Taiwan) and two individualistic (United States, Australia) cultures, researchers asked the participants to rate how desirable or appropriate to experience these emotions. The results revealed that in collectivistic cultures *guilt*, while in individualistic cultures *pride*, were viewed as more appropriate emotions. According to the authors' interpretation of these results, collectivistic (Confucian) cultures place high value on self-reflective emotions related to an individual's failures or wrong actions, while individualistic cultures place high value on self-reflective emotions about an individual's successful actions.

Display Rules

Display rules are the cultural norms of how specific emotions should be expressed verbally and nonverbally and modified, if necessary, in social situations and circumstances (Ekman & Friesen, 1969, 1971; Matsumoto, Yoo, Hirayama, & Petrova, 2005; Matsumoto et al., 2009). As it was introduced in previous sections, the construct of *context differentiation* (Matsumoto et al., 2009) describes how differently individuals in a culture behave and express emotions in the context of different situations, in interaction with different people. The cultural norms of some cultures recommend differentiating the behaviors depending on situation and people, with who a person interacts, while other cultures recommend consistency across situations and people.

High context differentiation cultures advise larger differentiations among emotions. This way—differentiating their use of emotional expressions within a context—people can differentiate among contexts. *Low context differentiation* cultures, on the other side, believe that differentiating among emotions is not important in egalitarian society suggesting to express emotions consistently across situations, contexts, and with different people. Thus, people in the cultures of *high context differentiation* should have higher complexity of emotions and their expressions, compared with the cultures of *low context differentiation*.

4.3.2 Emotion Differentiation

Context Differentiation

The proposed *measure of context differentiation* (Matsumoto et al., 2009) allows assessing both individual and the cultural complexity of emotions in display rules. The latter is of special interest for the topic of this book. The Display Rule Assessment Inventory (DRAI) asks participants "what they should do if they felt each of seven emotions towards interactants in two settings—public and private" (p. 255). The *high* versus *low context differentiation* is a variable of emotional complexity in display rules. Some individuals and cultures make few distinctions among emotions and display rules, while others make large distinctions among the emotions. Thus, "an estimate of the variability across emotion for each situation, and then pooled across situations, comprised this measure… Larger variabilities reflect greater differentiation in respondents' expressivity endorsements of the various emotions; smaller variabilities would reflect less" (p. 254).

Differentiation of emotion expressivity in different relationship contexts was demonstrated, for example, in the study of display rules comparing the samples of Japanese, the US American and Canadian students (Safdar et al., 2009). Authors revealed that for powerful emotions (contempt, anger, and disgust), the Japanese differentiate their display rules depending on how close their relationship with partners are more than participants in the US American and Canadian samples do. The display rules for expression of contempt, disgust, and anger toward partners in close relationship (e.g., family members and close friends) are the same in three cultures, but different toward partners in medium (acquaintances and classmates) and distal relationship (professors) (Safdar et al., 2009). Thus, Japanese culture, characterized by *high context differentiation*, compared to American and Canadian cultures, characterized by *low context differentiation*, have revealed greater differentiation in the display rules toward individuals of their close, medium, and distal groups.

According to their cultural display rules, the Japanese considered appropriate to express negative powerful and positive emotions "less to members of the distal than of the medium group and less to members of the medium than of the close group" (p. 8). Thus, in close relationship the Japanese are most expressive in negative powerful (contempt, disgust, and anger) and positive emotions (happiness). As for happiness, the similar differentiation of display rules was revealed in its expression toward individuals of close, medium, and distal groups in American and Canadian samples. For such emotions as sadness, fear, and surprise, authors did not find any significant differentiation in display rules toward individuals of different closeness (Safdar et al., 2009).

Other cross-cultural studies on display rules will be presented in the following sections.

Emotional Complexity and Its Measures

What is emotional complexity and how can we measure it? How can we compare the complexity of emotional life in different cultures? Emotional complexity can be defined and measured as

1. *Emotional differentiation*—the capability of individuals to experience emotions in a differentiated manner, with a variety of discrete emotions, both positive and negative (Grossmann & Ellsworth, 2017; Grossmann, Huynh, & Ellsworth, 2016; Gruhn, Lumley, Diehl, & Labouvie-Vief, 2013).
2. *Emotional dialecticism*—the acceptance of the experience of pleasant and unpleasant emotional states concurrently or successively (Bagozzi et al., 1999; Lindquist & Barrett, 2008).
3. *Emotional granularity*—the ability of individuals to verbally express emotional experiences with specificity and precision (Kashdan, Barrett, & McKnight, 2015; Lindquist & Barrett, 2008).

The studies were able to identify which cultural parameters of societies are associated with emotional complexity. In particular, collectivist, higher power distance, and masculine countries have more differentiated and complex rules for emotional expression especially in the case of negative emotions (Fernandez, Carrera, Sanchez, Paez & Candia, 2000).

Another study (Matsumoto et al., 2009), briefly commented in earlier chapters, found relations of Hofstede dimensions of culture and Schwartz cultural values with scores of emotions differentiation. The higher Hierarchy, Power Distance, and Embeddedness in a country, the higher emotion differentiation on the country level, whereas the lower Individualism (vs. Collectivism), Affective Autonomy (and to some degree lower Egalitarianism), the higher emotion differentiation on the country level. Thus, these cultural dimensions are predictive parameters for the cultural complexity of emotions.

References

Abu-Lughod, L. (2000). *Veiled sentiments: Honor and poetry in a Bedouin society*. Berkeley, CA: University of California Press. (Original work published 1986).
Alonso-Arbiol, I., Shaver, P. R., Fraley, R. C., Oronoz, B., Unzurrunzaga, E., & Urizar, R. (2006). Structure of the Basque emotion lexicon. *Cognition and Emotion, 20*(6), 836–865.

Bagozzi, R. P., Wong, N., & Yi, Y. (1999). The role of culture and gender and the relationship between positive and negative affect. *Cognition and Emotion, 3*, 641–672.

Barrett, L. F. (2012). Emotions are real. *Emotion, 12*, 413–429.

Barrett, L. F. (2017). *How emotions are made: The secret life of the brain.* Boston, MA: Houghton Mifflin.

Barrett, L. F., Mesquita, B., Ochsner, K. N., & Gross, J. J. (2007). The experience of emotion. *Annual Review of Psychology, 58*, 373–403.

Barrett, L. F., & Russell, J. A. (1999). The structure of current affect: Controversies and emerging consensus. *Current Directions in Psychological Science, 8*(1), 10–14.

Berg, J. H., & Derlega, V. J. (1987). *Responsiveness and self-disclosure.* New York, NY: Plenum Press.

Berry, J. W., Poortinga, Y. H., Segall, M. H., & Dasen, P. R. (2002). *Cross-cultural psychology: Research and applications* (2nd ed.). Cambridge, UK: Cambridge University Press.

Bilimoria, P., & Wenta, A. (Eds.). (2015). *Emotions in Indian thought-systems.* New Delhi, India: Routledge.

Boiger, M., & Mesquita, B. (2014). A socio-dynamic perspective on the construction of emotion. In L. F. Barrett & J. A. Russell (Eds.), *The psychological construction of emotion* (pp. 377–398). New York, NY: Guilford Press.

Boiger, M., Mesquita, B., Tsai, A. Y., & Markus, H. R. (2012). Influencing and adjusting in daily emotional situations: A comparison of European and Asian American action styles. *Cognition & Emotion, 26*(2), 332–340.

Breugelmans, S. M., Ambadar, Z., Vaca, J. B., Poortinga, Y. H., Setiadi, B., Widiyanto, P., & Philippot, P. (2005). Body sensations associated with emotions in Rarámuri Indians, rural Javanese, and three student samples. *Emotion, 5*(2), 166–175.

Breugelmans, S. M., & Poortinga, Y. H. (2006). Emotion without a word: Shame and guilt among Rarámuri Indians and rural Javanese. *Journal of Personality and Social Psychology, 91*(6), 1111–1122.

Briggs, J. L. (1970). *Never in anger: Portrait of an Eskimo family.* Cambridge, MA: Harvard University Press.

Butler, E. A. (2011). Temporal interpersonal emotion systems: The "TIES" that form relationships. *Personality and Social Psychology Review, 15*(4), 367–393.

Butler, E. A., Egloff, B., Wilhelm, F. H., Smith, N. C., Erickson, E. A., & Gross, J. J. (2003). The social consequences of expressive suppression. *Emotion, 3*, 48–67.

Butler, E. A., Lee, T. L., & Gross, J. J. (2007). Emotion regulation and culture: Are the social consequences of emotion suppression culture-specific? *Emotion, 7*(1), 30–48.

Butner, J., Diamond, L. M., & Hicks, A. M. (2007). Attachment style and two forms of affect coregulation between romantic partners. *Personal Relationships, 14*, 431–455.

Chaplin, T. M. (2015). Gender and emotion expression: A developmental contextual perspective. *Emotion Review, 7*(1), 14–21. https://doi.org/10.1177/1754073914544408

Church, A. T., Katigbak, M. S., Reyes, J. A., & Jensen, S. M. (1999). The structure of affect in a non-Western culture: Evidence for cross-cultural comparability. *Journal of Personality, 67*(3), 505–534.

Cohen, D., & Gunz, A. (2002). As seen by the other…: Perspectives on the self in the memories and emotional perceptions of Easterners and Westerners. *Psychological Science, 13*(1), 55–59.

Consedine, N. S., Chentsova-Dutton, Y. E., & Krivoshekova, Y. S. (2014). Emotional acculturation predicts better somatic health: Experiential and expressive acculturation among immigrant women from four ethnic groups. *Journal of Social and Clinical Psychology, 33*(10), 867–889.

Cosnier, J., Dols, J. M. F., & Fernandez, A. J. (1986). The verbalization of emotional experiences. In K. R. Scherer, H. G. Wallbott, & A. B. Summerfield (Eds.), *Experiencing emotion: A cross-cultural study* (pp. 117–128). Cambridge, UK: Cambridge University Press.

Cromby, J. (2007). Toward a psychology of feeling. *International Journal of Critical Psychology, 21*(94), 94–118.

Davidson, R. J. (1994). On emotion, mood, and related affective constructs. In P. Ekman & R. J. Davidson (Eds.), *The nature of emotion: Fundamental questions* (pp. 51–55). New York, NY: Oxford University Press.

Davis, D. (1982). Determinants of responsiveness in dyadic interactions. In W. Ickes & E. G. Knowles (Eds.), *Personality, roles and social behavior* (pp. 85–140). New York, NY: Springer.

De Leersnyder, J. (2017). Emotional acculturation: A first review. *Current Opinion in Psychology, 17*, 67–73.

De Leersnyder, J., Kim, H., & Mesquita, B. (2015). Feeling right is feeling good: Psychological well-being and emotional fit with culture in autonomy- versus relatedness-promoting situations. *Frontiers in Psychology, 6*: Article 630. https://doi.org/10.3389/fpsyg.2015.00630

De Leersnyder, J., Mesquita, B., & Kim, H. (2013). Emotional acculturation. In D. Hermans, B. Mesquita, & B. Rime (Eds.), *Changing emotions* (pp. 127–133). Hove, UK: Psychology Press.

De Leersnyder, J., Mesquita, B., & Kim, H. S. (2011). Where do my emotions belong? A study of immigrants' emotional acculturation. *Personality and Social Psychology Bulletin, 37*(4), 451–463.

De Leersnyder, J., Mesquita, B., Kim, H. S., Eom, K., & Choi, H. (2014). Emotional fit with culture: A predictor of individual differences in relational well-being. *Emotion, 14*, 241–245.

Eid, M., & Diener, E. (2001). Norms for experiencing emotions in different cultures: Inter- and intra-national differences. *Journal of Personality and Social Psychology, 81*(5), 869–885.

Ekman, P. (1972). Universals and cultural differences in facial expressions of emotion. In J. Cole (Ed.), *Nebraska Symposium Motivation, 1971* (Vol. 19, pp. 207–282). Lincoln, NE: University of Nebraska Press.

Ekman, P. (1992). Are there basic emotions? *Psychological Review, 99*, 550–553.

Ekman, P. (1993). Facial expression and emotion. *American Psychologist, 48*(4), 384–392. https://doi.org/10.1037/0003-066X.48.4.384

Ekman, P. (1994). Moods, emotions, and traits. In P. Ekman & R. Davidson (Eds.), *The nature of emotion: Fundamental questions* (pp. 56–58). New York, NY: Oxford University Press.

Ekman, P. (1999). Basic emotions. In T. Dalgleish & T. Power (Eds.), *The handbook of cognition and emotion* (pp. 45–60). Sussex, UK: Wiley.

Ekman, P., & Friesen, W. (1969). The repertoire of nonverbal behavior: Categories, origins, usage, and coding. *Semiotica, 1*, 49–98.

Ekman, P., & Friesen, W. V. (1971). Constants across cultures in the face and emotion. *Journal of Personality and Social Psychology, 17*, 124–129.

Ekman, P., Friesen, W. V., O'Sullivan, M., Chan, A., Diacoyanni-Tarlatzis, I., Heider, K., … Tzavaras, A. (1987). Universals and cultural differences in the judgments of facial expressions of emotion. *Journal of Personality and Social Psychology, 53*(4), 712–717. https://doi.org/10.1037/0022-3514.53.4.712

Ellsworth, P. C. (1991). Some implications of cognitive appraisal theories of emotion. In K. Strongman (Ed.), *International review of studies on emotion* (pp. 143–161). New York, NY: Wiley.

Ellsworth, P. C. (2013). Appraisal theory: Old and new questions. *Emotion Review, 5*, 125–131. https://doi.org/10.1177/1754073912463617

Fehr, B., & Russell, J. A. (1991). The concept of love viewed from a prototype perspective. *Journal of Personality and Social Psychology, 60*(3), 425–438.

Fernandez, I., Carrera, P., Sanchez, F., Paez, D., & Candia, L. (2000). Differences between cultures in emotional verbal and non-verbal reactions. *Psicothema, 12*(Suppl 1), 83–92.

Fontaine, J. R. J., Poortinga, Y. H., Setiadi, B., & Markam, S. S. (2002). Cognitive structure of emotion terms in Indonesia and The Netherlands. *Cognition & Emotion, 16*, 61–86. https://doi.org/10.1080/02699933014000130

Fontaine, J. R. J., Scherer, K. R., & Soriano, C. (Eds.). (2013). *Components of emotional meaning: A sourcebook*. Oxford, UK: Oxford University Press.

Ford, B. Q., & Mauss, I. B. (2015). Culture and emotion regulation. *Current Opinion in Psychology, 3*, 1–5.

Fredrickson, B. (2001). The role of positive emotions in positive psychology: The broaden-and-build theory of positive emotions. *American Psychologist, 56*(3), 218–226.

Fredrickson, B., & Losada, M. F. (2005). Positive affect and the complex dynamics of human flourishing. *American Psychologist, 60*(7), 678–686.

Fredrickson, B. L., & Cohn, M. A. (2008). Positive emotions. In M. Lewis, J. M. Haviland-Jones, & L. F. Barrett (Eds.), *Handbook of emotions* (pp. 777–796). New York, NY: Guilford Press.

Frijda, N. H. (1986). *The emotions.* Cambridge, UK: Cambridge University Press.

Gross, J. J. (1998). Antecedent-and response-focused emotion regulation: Divergent consequences for experience, expression, and physiology. *Journal of Personality and Social Psychology, 74*(1), 224–237.

Gross, J. J. (2001). Emotion regulation in adulthood: Timing is everything. *Current Directions in Psychological Science, 10*, 214–219.

Gross, J. J. (2002). Emotion regulation: Affective, cognitive, and social consequences. *Psychophysiology, 39*, 281–291.

Gross, J. J., & John, O. P. (1998). Mapping the domain of expressivity: Multimethod evidence for a hierarchical model. *Journal of Personality and Social Psychology, 74*, 170–191.

Gross, J. J., & John, O. P. (2003). Individual differences in two emotion regulation processes: Implication for affect, relationships, and well-being. *Journal of Personality and Social Psychology, 85*, 348–362.

Grossmann, I., & Ellsworth, P. C. (2017). What are mixed emotions and what conditions foster them? Life-span experiences, culture and social awareness. *Current Opinion in Behavioral Sciences, 15*, 1–5.

Grossmann, I., Huynh, A. C., & Ellsworth, P. C. (2016). Emotional complexity: Clarifying definitions and cultural correlates. *Journal of Personality and Social Psychology, 111*(6), 895–916. https://doi.org/10.1037/pspp0000084

Gruhn, D., Lumley, M. A., Diehl, M., & Labouvie-Vief, G. (2013). Time-based indicators of emotional complexity: Interrelations and correlates. *Emotion, 13*(2), 226–237.

Haidt, J. (2003). The moral emotions. In R. J. Davidson, K. R. Scherer, & H. H. Goldsmith (Eds.), *Series in affective science. Handbook of affective sciences* (pp. 852–870). Oxford, UK: Oxford University Press.

Hamaguchi, F. (1985). A contextual model of the Japanese: Towards a methodological innovation in Japanese studies. *Journal of Japanese Studies, 11*, 289–321.

Hatfield, E., Cacioppo, J. T., & Rapson, R. L. (1994). *Emotional contagion.* New York, NY: Cambridge University Press.

Hui, C. M., Fok, H. K., & Bond, M. H. (2009). Who feels more ambivalence? Linking dialectical thinking to mixed emotions. *Personality and Individual Differences, 46*, 493–498.

Izard, C. E. (2007). Basic emotions, natural kinds, emotion schemas, and a new paradigm. *Perspectives on Psychological Science, 2*(3), 260–280.

John, O. P., & Gross, J. J. (2004). Healthy and unhealthy emotion regulation personality processes, individual differences, and life span development. *Journal of Personality, 72*, 1301–1333.

Johnson-Laird, P. N., & Oatley, K. (1992). Basic emotions, rationality, and folk theory. *Cognition & Emotion, 6*(3–4), 201–223.

Karandashev, V. (2019). *Cross-cultural perspectives on the experience and expression of love.* New York, NY: Springer.

Kashdan, T. B., Barrett, L. F., & McKnight, P. E. (2015). Unpacking emotion differentiation: Transforming unpleasant experience by perceiving distinctions in negativity. *Current Directions in Psychological Science, 24*(1), 10–16.

Keltner, D., & Haidt, J. (1999). Social functions of emotion at four levels of analysis. *Cognition and Emotion, 13*(5), 505–521.

Kim, J., Seo, M., Yu, H., & Neuendorf, K. (2014). Cultural differences in preference for entertainment messages that induce mixed responses of joy and sorrow. *Human Communication Research, 40*, 530–552.

Kitayama, S., Markus, H. R., & Kurokawa, M. (2000). Culture, emotion, and well-being: Good feelings in Japan and the United States. *Cognition and Emotion, 14*, 93–124.

Kitayama, S., Mesquita, B., & Karasawa, M. (2006). Cultural affordances and emotional experience: Socially engaging and disengaging emotions in Japan and the United States. *Journal of Personality and Social Psychology, 91*(5), 890–903.

Kovecses, Z. (2000). *Metaphor and emotion: Language, culture, and body in human feeling.* Cambridge, UK: Cambridge University Press.

Kövecses, Z. (2002). Emotion concepts: Social constructionism and cognitive linguistics. In S. R. Fussell (Ed.), *The verbal communication of emotions* (pp. 117–132). Mahwah, NJ: L. Erlbaum Associates.

Larsen, R. J., & Diener, E. (1992). Promises and problems with the circumplex model of emotion. In M. S. Clark (Ed.), *Review of personality and social psychology: Emotion* (pp. 25–59). Newbury Park, CA: Sage.

Larson, R., & Almeida, D. (1999). Emotional transmission in the daily lives of families: A new paradigm for studying family process. *Journal of Marriage and the Family, 61*, 5–20.

Laurenceau, J., Barrett, L. F., & Peitromonaco, P. R. (1998). Intimacy as an interpersonal process: The importance of self-disclosure and partner disclosure, and perceived partner responsiveness in interpersonal exchanges. *Journal of Personality and Social Psychology, 74*, 1238–1251.

Lazarus, R. S. (1991). *Emotion and adaptation.* New York, NY: Oxford University Press.

Levenson, R. W. (2003). Blood, sweat, and fears: The autonomic architecture of emotion. *Annals of the New York Academy of Sciences, 1000*(1), 348–366.

Levenson, R. W., & Gottman, J. M. (1983). Marital interaction: Physiological linkage and affective exchange. *Journal of Personality and Social Psychology, 45*(3), 587–597.

Lewis, M. (2008). Self-conscious emotions: Embarrassment, pride, shame, and guilt. In M. Lewis, J. M. Haviland-Jones, & L. F. Barrett (Eds.), *Handbook of emotions* (pp. 742–756). New York, NY: Guilford Press.

Lim, T.-S. (2003). Language and verbal communication across cultures. In W. B. Gudykunst (Ed.), *Handbook of international and intercultural communication* (pp. 53–71). Thousand Oaks, CA: Sage.

Lindquist, K. A., & Barrett, L. F. (2008). Emotional complexity. In M. Lewis, J. M. Haviland-Jones, & L. F. Barrett (Eds.), *The handbook of emotions* (pp. 513–530). New York, NY: Guilford Press.

Lutz, C. (1982). The domain of emotion words on Ifaluk. *American Ethnologist, 9*(1), 113–128.

Lutz, C. (1988). *Unnatural emotions: Everyday sentiments on a Micronesian atoll and their challenge to Western theory.* Chicago, IL: University of Chicago Press.

Lynch, O. M. (1990). *Divine passions.* Berkeley, CA: University of California Press.

Markus, H. R., & Kitayama, S. (1991). Culture and the self: Implications for cognition, emotion, and motivation. *Psychological Review, 98*, 224–253.

Matsumoto, D. (1990). Cultural similarities and differences in display rules. *Motivation and Emotion, 14*(3), 195–214.

Matsumoto, D. (2006b). Are cultural differences in emotion regulation mediated by personality traits? *Journal of Cross-Cultural Psychology, 37*(4), 421–437.

Matsumoto, D., & Hwang, H. S. (2012). Culture and emotion: The integration of biological and cultural contributions. *Journal of Cross-Cultural Psychology, 43*(1), 91–118.

Matsumoto, D., Kudoh, T., Scherer, K. R., & Wallbott, H. (1988). Antecedents of and reactions to emotions in the United States and Japan. *Journal of Cross- Cultural Psychology, 19*(3), 267–286.

Matsumoto, D., Yoo, S. H., & Fontaine, J. (2009). Hypocrisy or maturity? Culture and context differentiation. *European Journal of Personality, 23*(3), 251–264.

Matsumoto, D., Yoo, S. H., Hirayama, S., & Petrova, G. (2005). Development and validation of a measure of display rule knowledge: The display rule assessment inventory. *Emotion, 5*(1), 23–40.

McCullough, M. E., Bono, G., & Root, L. M. (2007). Rumination, emotion, and forgiveness: Three longitudinal studies. *Journal of Personality and Social Psychology, 92*(3), 490–505.

McDaniel, J. (1995). Emotion in Bengali religious thought: Substance and metaphor. In J. Marks & R. T. Ames (Eds.), *Emotions in Asian thought* (pp. 39–63). Albany, NY: SUNY Press.

Mesquita, B. (2001). Emotions in collectivist and individualist contexts. *Journal of Personality and Social Psychology, 80*(1), 68–74.

Mesquita, B. (2003). Emotions as dynamic cultural phenomena. In R. Davidson, H. Goldsmith, & K. R. Scherer (Eds.), *The handbook of affective sciences* (pp. 871–890). New York, NY: Oxford University Press.

Mesquita, B., Boiger, M., & De Leersnyder, J. (2016). The cultural construction of emotions. *Current Opinion in Psychology, 8*, 31–36.

Mesquita, B., Boiger, M., & De Leersnyder, J. (2017). Doing emotions: The role of culture in everyday emotions. *European Review of Social Psychology, 28*(1), 95–133.

Mesquita, B., & Frijda, N. H. (1992). Cultural variations in emotions: A review. *Psychological Bulletin, 112*(2), 179–204. https://doi.org/10.1037/0033-2909.112.2.179

Mesquita, B., & Karasawa, M. (2002). Different emotional lives. *Cognition & Emotion, 16*(1), 127–141.

Mesquita, B., & Leu, J. (2007). The cultural psychology of emotion. In S. Kitayama & D. Cohen (Eds.), *Handbook of cultural psychology* (pp. 734–759). New York, NY: Guilford Press.

Mesquita, B., & Walker, R. (2003). Cultural differences in emotions: A context for interpreting emotional experiences. *Behaviour Research and Therapy, 41*(7), 777–793.

Morling, B., Kitayama, S., & Miyamoto, Y. (2002). Cultural practices emphasize influence in the United States and adjustment in Japan. *Personality and Social Psychology Bulletin, 28*(3), 311–323.

Nezlek, J. B., Kafetsios, K., & Smith, C. V. (2008). Emotions in everyday social encounters: Correspondence between culture and self-construal. *Journal of Cross-Cultural Psychology, 39*(4), 366–372.

Nezlek, J. B., Sorrentino, R. M., Yasunaga, S., Otsubo, Y., Allen, M., Kouhara, S., & Shuper, P. A. (2008). Cross-cultural differences in reactions to daily events as indicators of cross-cultural differences in self-construction and affect. *Journal of Cross-Cultural Psychology, 39*(6), 685–702.

Okazaki, S. (2002). Self-other agreement on affective distress scales in Asian Americans and White Americans. *Journal of Counseling Psychology, 49*, 428–437.

Ortony, A., & Turner, J. H. (1990). What's basic about basic emotions. *Psychological Review, 97*, 315–331.

Oyserman, D., Coon, H. M., & Kemmelmeier, M. (2002). Rethinking individualism and collectivism: Evaluation of theoretical assumptions and meta-analyses. *Psychological Bulletin, 128*(1), 3–72.

Perunovic, W. Q. E., Heller, D., & Rafaeli, E. (2007). Within-person changes in the structure of emotion: The role of cultural identification and language. *Psychological Science, 18*(7), 607–613.

Poortinga, Y. H., & Soudijn, K. (2002). Behaviour– Culture relationships and ontogenetic development. In H. Keller, Y. H. Poortinga, & A. Schölmerich (Eds.), *Between culture and biology: Perspectives on ontogenetic development* (pp. 320–340). Cambridge, UK: Cambridge University Press.

Potter, S. H. (1988). The cultural construction of emotion in rural Chinese social life. *Ethos, 16*(2), 181–208.

Prinz, J. J., & Nichols, S. (2010). Moral emotions. In J. M. Doris & The Moral Psychology Research Group (Eds.), *The moral psychology handbook* (pp. 111–146). Oxford, UK: Oxford University Press.

Roseman, I. J., Dhawan, N., Rettek, S. L., Naidu, R. K., & Thapa, K. (1995). Cultural differences and cross-cultural similarities in appraisals and emotional responses. *Journal of Cross-Cultural Psychology, 26*, 23–48.

Russell, J. A. (1991). Culture and the categorization of emotions. *Psychological Bulletin, 110*, 426–450.

Safdar, S., Friedlmeier, W., Matsumoto, D., Yoo, S. H., Kwantes, C. T., Kakai, H., & Shigemasu, E. (2009). Variations of emotional display rules within and across cultures: A comparison between Canada, USA, and Japan. *Canadian Journal of Behavioural Science/Revue canadienne des sciences du comportement, 41*(1), 1–10. https://doi.org/10.1037/a0014387

Savani, K., Morris, M. W., Naidu, N. V. R., Kumar, S., & Berlia, N. V. (2011). Cultural conditioning: Understanding interpersonal accommodation in India and the United States in terms of the
modal characteristics of interpersonal influence situations. *Journal of Personality and Social
Psychology, 100*(1), 84–102.

Saxbe, D., & Repetti, R. L. (2010). For better or worse? Coregulation of couples' cortisol levels
and mood states. *Journal of Personality and Social Psychology, 98*(1), 92–103.

Scherer, K. R. (1984). Emotion as a multicomponent process: A model and some cross-cultural
data. In P. Shaver (Ed.), *Review of personality and social psychology* (Vol. 5, pp. 37–63).
Beverly Hills, CA: Sage.

Scherer, K. R., & Fontaine, J. R. (2019). The semantic structure of emotion words across languages is consistent with componential appraisal models of emotion. *Cognition and Emotion,
33*(4), 673–682.

Scherer, K. R., Matsumoto, D., Wallbott, H. G., & Kudoh, T. (1988). Emotional experience in
cultural context: A comparison between Europe, Japan, and the United States. In K. R. Scherer
(Ed.), *Facets of emotion: Recent research* (pp. 5–30). Hillsdale, NJ: Lawrence Erlbaum.

Scherer, K. R., & Wallbott, H. G. (1994). Evidence for universality and cultural variation of differential emotion response patterning. *Journal of Personality and Social Psychology, 66*(2),
310–328.

Schimmack, U., Oishi, S., & Diener, E. (2002). Cultural influences on the relation between pleasant emotions and unpleasant emotions: Asian dialectic philosophies or individualism-collectivism? *Cognition and Emotion, 76*(6), 705–719.

Scollon, C. N., Diener, E., Oishi, S., & Biswas-Diener, R. (2004). Emotions across cultures and
methods. *Journal of Cross-Cultural Psychology, 35*(3), 304–326.

Scollon, C. N., Diener, E., Oishi, S., & Biswas-Diener, R. (2005). An experience sampling and
cross-cultural investigation of the relation between pleasant and unpleasant affect. *Cognition
and Emotion, 19*(1), 27–52.

Shaver, P., Schwartz, J., Kirson, D., & O'Connor, C. (1987). Emotion knowledge: Further exploration of a prototype approach. *Journal of Personality and Social Psychology, 52*, 1061–1086.
https://doi.org/10.1037/0022-3514.52.6.1061

Shaver, P. R., Morgan, H. J., & Wu, S. (1996). Is love a "basic" emotion? *Personal Relationships,
3*, 81–96. https://doi.org/10.1111/j.1475-6811.1996.tb00105.x

Shaver, P. R., Murdaya, U., & Fraley, R. C. (2001). Structure of the Indonesian emotion lexicon.
Asian Journal of Social Psychology, 4, 201–224.

Shaver, P. R., Wu, S., & Schwartz, J. C. (1992). Cross-cultural similarities and differences in emotion and its representation. In M. S. Clark (Ed.), *Review of personality and social psychology*
(Vol. 13, pp. 175–212). Thousand Oaks, CA: Sage.

Shweder, R. A. (1993). The cultural psychology of emotions. In M. Lewis & J. Hovland (Eds.),
Handbook of emotions (pp. 417–437). New York, NY: Guilford Press.

Shweder, R. A., Haidt, J., Horton, R., & Joseph, C. (2008). The cultural psychology of the emotions: Ancient and renewed. In M. Lewis, J. M. Haviland-Jones, & L. Feldman Barrett (Eds.),
Handbook of emotions (pp. 409–427). New York, NY: Guilford Press.

Spencer-Rodgers, J., Peng, K., & Wang, L. (2010). Dialecticism and the co-occurrence of positive
and negative emotions across cultures. *Journal of Cross-Cultural Psychology, 41*, 109–115.

Stürmer, S., Snyder, M., & Omoto, A. M. (2005). Prosocial emotions and helping: The moderating role of group membership. *Journal of Personality and Social Psychology, 88*(3), 532–546.
https://doi.org/10.1037/0022-3514.88.3.532

Su, J. C., Wei, M., & Tsai, H. T. (2014). Running away from unwanted feelings: Culture matters.
Cognition and Emotion, 28(7), 1313–1327.

Suh, E., Diener, E., Oishi, S., & Triandis, H. C. (1998). The shifting basis of life satisfaction judgements across cultures: Emotions versus norms. *Journal of Personality and Social Psychology,
74*, 482–493.

Tangney, J. P. (1999). The self-conscious emotions: Shame, guilt, embarrassment and pride. In T.
Dalgleish & M. J. Power (Eds.), *Handbook of cognition and emotion* (p. 541–568). John Wiley
& Sons. https://doi.org/10.1002/0470013494.ch26

Tangney, J. P., & Fischer, K. (Eds.). (1995). *Self-conscious emotions: The psychology of shame, guilt, embarrassment, and pride*. New York, NY: Guilford Press.

Tangney, J. P., Stuewig, J., & Mashek, D. J. (2007). Moral emotions and moral behavior. *Annual Review of Psychology, 58*, 345–372.

Tomkins, S. S. (1962). *Affect, imagery, and consciousness (Vol. 1: The positive affects)*. New York, NY: Springer.

Tomkins, S. S. (1963). *Affect, imagery, and consciousness (Vol. 2: The negative affects)*. New York, NY: Springer.

Tooby, J., & Cosmides, L. (2008). The evolutionary psychology of the emotions and their relationship to internal regulatory variables. In M. Lewis, J. M. Haviland-Jones, & L. Feldman Barrett (Eds.), *Handbook of emotions* (3rd ed., pp. 114–137). New York, NY: Guilford Press.

Tracy, J. L., & Robins, R. W. (2004). Putting the self into self-conscious emotions: A theoretical model. *Psychological Inquiry, 15*(2), 103–125.

Trnka, R., Šolcová, I. P., & Tavel, P. (2018). Components of cultural complexity relating to emotions: A conceptual framework. *New Ideas in Psychology, 51*, 27–33.

Trommsdorff, G., & Cole, P. M. (2011). Emotion, self-regulation, and social behaviour in cultural contexts. In X. Chen & K. H. Rubin (Eds.), *Socioemotional development in cultural context* (pp. 131–163). New York, NY: Guilford Press.

Tsai, J. L., & Clobert, M. (2019). Cultural influences on emotion: Empirical patterns and emerging trends. In S. Kitayama & D. Cohen (Eds.), *Handbook of cultural psychology* (2nd ed., pp. 292–318). New York, NY: Guilford Press.

Tsai, J. L., & Levenson, R. W. (1997). Cultural influences on emotional responding: Chinese American and European American dating couples during interpersonal conflict. *Journal of Cross-Cultural Psychology, 28*(5), 600–625.

Tsai, J.L., Louie, J.Y., Chen, E.E, & Uchida, Y (2007). Learning what feelings to desire: Socialization of ideal affect through children's storybooks. Personality and Social Psychology Bulletin, 3, 17–30.

Uchida, Y., & Kitayama, S. (2009). Happiness and unhappiness in east and west: Themes and variations. *Emotion, 9*, 441–456.

Wallbott, H. G., Ricci-Bitti, P., & Banninger-Huber, E. (1986). Non-verbal reactions to emotional experiences. In K. R. Scherer, H. G. Wallbott, & A. B. Summerfield (Eds.), *Experiencing emotion: A cross-cultural study* (pp. 98–116). Cambridge, UK: Cambridge University Press.

Watson, D., & Clark, L. A. (1994). Emotions, moods, traits, and temperaments: Conceptual distinctions and empirical findings. In P. Ekman & R. J. Davidson (Eds.), *The nature of emotion: Fundamental questions* (pp. 89–93). New York, NY: Oxford University Press.

Wei, M., Su, J. C., Carrera, S., Lin, S.-P., & Yi, F. (2013). Suppression and interpersonal harmony: A cross-cultural comparison between Chinese and European Americans. *Journal of Counseling Psychology, 60*, 625–633.

Weisz, J. R., Rothbaum, F. M., & Blackburn, T. C. (1984). Standing out and standing in: The psychology of control in America and Japan. *American Psychologist, 39*(9), 955–969.

Wierzbicka, A. (1986). Human emotions: Universal or culture-specific? *American Anthropologist, 88*(3), 584–594.

Wierzbicka, A. (1992). *Semantics, culture and cognition: Universal human concepts in culture-specific configurations*. New York, NY: Oxford University Press.

Wierzbicka, A. (1994). Emotion, language, and cultural scripts. In S. Kitayama & H. R. Markus (Eds.), *Emotion and culture* (pp. 133–196). Washington, DC: American Psychological Association.

Wierzbicka, A. (1999). *Emotions across languages and cultures: Diversity and universals*. Cambridge, UK: Cambridge University Press.

Zeman, J., & Garber, J. (1996). Display rules for anger, sadness, and pain: It depends on who is watching. *Child Development, 67*(3), 957–973.

Chapter 5
Cultural Models of Emotional Experience

5.1 Diversity of Emotional Experience

5.1.1 What Is Emotional Experience?

Sources of Knowledge About Emotional Experience

Subjective emotional experience emerges from several sources: physiological changes and body sensations, awareness of these changes, perception of an event eliciting emotion, and its appraisal. Being biologically based in its roots, the experience of emotions may still be influenced by cultural factors through appraisal, interpretation, and labeling, which in turn depend on the culture-specific meaning of the event (Matsumoto & Hwang, 2012; Scherer et al. 1988).

To explore people's emotional experience, researchers collect the data, which include the diverse set of variables in different circumstances and events. They ask participants about their attitudes toward cultural norms of emotional experience. They retrospectively assess their self-reported frequency of real emotional experience, or episodic memories of emotional events, which they personally experienced. This may be semantic knowledge of general emotional events (e.g., wedding), or autobiographical memory of an episode of being angry (Rubin & Talarico, 2009; Watson, Clark, & Tellegen, 1988). In experimental situations, researchers may use such stimuli as emotional facial expressions, emotion words, picture stimuli, or affective states.

© The Author(s), under exclusive license to Springer Nature Switzerland AG 2021   191
V. Karandashev, *Cultural Models of Emotions*,
https://doi.org/10.1007/978-3-030-58438-2_5

Parameters of Emotional Experience for Construction of Cultural Models of Emotions

In the context of this chapter, I highlight and review several aspects of emotional experience, which can be used to construct the cultural models of emotions. I present the empirical evidence in support from several disciplines. In this section, I briefly summarize some key points, which are more extensively analyzed in the following section. Therefore, I omit the corresponding references to the sources and studies.

First, people with different cultural background mentally conceptualize emotions differently and focus their attention during experience of emotions on their

- *internal subjective experiences*
- *social relationships*, or
- *the relations between the person and the event.*

Throughout recent decades, many theoretical and empirical studies in psychology, sociology, communication studies, and anthropology have demonstrated the presence of these culturally different models of emotions: *intrapersonal, interpersonal, interactive. Objectified model of emotions* probably belongs to the third group, yet it is so unique with origins from Indian culture that I describe it in a separate section.

Second, even though the basic patterns of physiological and neural activities associated with emotional experience are cross-culturally universal, yet people may have the culturally developed abilities to modify their experience of emotions. This can be driven, for example, by the cultural norms of self-regulation, by meditation or suppression. The same can be said about body sensations associated with emotions. Even though they are substantially similar across cultures, yet later studies revealed some differences. Many of these differences can be explained by the different view on the relations between *heart* (emotional part) and *mind* (rational part) of mental life. According to the *dualistic* view—typical of Western cultures, *mind* (*rational*) and *heart* (*emotional*) are in dichotomous relations. People may be guided by their emotions (*heart*), or by their reasoning (*mind*). In the *monistic* view—typical of East Asian cultures, cultural beliefs integrate the *rational* and *emotional* parts of mental life. In light of these worldview differences, it is possible to think about *dualistic* and *monistic models* of mental life and how they reflect on experience of emotions.

Third, across cultures, universal and specific appraisals of events and interpretation of situations are the important factors affecting people's experience of emotions. There are certain *cultural patterns of appraisals*, which depend on cultural values (e.g., honor, autonomy, relatedness), self-construals, and so on. Accordingly, it is possible to think about *patterns of self-focused and other-focused appraisals*, which can be characteristic for *independent* and *interdependent models of culture*, and how these models affect emotional experience.

Fourth, cultures differ in their cultural norms and real experience of basic and complex emotions, such as anger, happiness, pride, honor, shame, guilt, and others.

These emotions may have culturally determined meaning and be salient in cultural beliefs and people's minds. In this regard, it is possible to talk about *the culture of pride*, the *culture of honor*, the *culture of shame*, and so on, or about *different cultural models of happiness*.

Fifth, there is plenty of empirical evidence (presented in the following sections) that cultures vary in the value and prevalence of positive, negative, or balanced valence of emotions, as well as in the value of high versus low emotional intensity. Therefore, it is reasonable to construct the *cultural models* of *positive*, *negative*, or *balanced* experience of emotions. In the same way, the *cultural models* of *passionate* and *dispassionate* life are based on the value and prevalence of high or low arousal affective states.

5.1.2   How to Describe Emotional Experience

Analogies of Physical Space that Describe Emotional Experience

The feelings associated with emotions are challenging to define and, therefore, to describe these feelings well and adequately people frequently use words, metaphors, and phrases referring to physical space and analogies in their emotional descriptions. It is easier to understand emotions in other simpler and more tangible terms.

Mental and emotional space seems intangible to grasp the reality of subjective emotional experience. Therefore, people employ the physical space of their body to visualize and imagine their emotions. One can say that emotional concepts emerge from bodily activity through appraisal and metaphorical projection. People frequently use spatial perceptions and imaginations as mapping metaphors for understanding of emotion concepts. Since emotions reflect the constellations of psychosomatic feelings, which are appraised and interpreted, then body sensation words and metaphors referring to emotions seem natural (see for review, Karandashev, 2019, p.11).

Metaphors of emotion, affect, and mood are widely used in colloquial English (Averill, 1990; Schnall, 2014). Being "red" is generally associated with being angry, "white"—with being fearful, "blue"—with being sad. Anger is "exploding," despair is "crushing," and joy is "bursting." Metaphoric expressions, such as "cold feet," "butterflies in the stomach," "heartbroken," "a shiver down our spine," and so on are commonly used when people speak of emotion.

Research has demonstrated (Glenberg et al., 2008; Niedenthal, Barsalou, Winkielman, Krauth-Gruber, & Ric, 2005; Wilson & Gibbs Jr, 2007) that the understanding of subjective and abstract words, which refer to emotions, activates sensory and motor systems. This is why people frequently use special analogies to describe their emotional experience. In particular, they mentally associate emotion concepts with spatial coordinates on the horizontal plane and the vertical plane.

Positive and Negative Affective States in Imaginary Physical Space

On the horizontal plane, right-handers and left-handers allocate positive and negative concepts differently. Experimental studies (Casasanto, 2009) found that right-handers associate positive concepts with their rightward space, while negative concepts with their leftward space. Left-handers revealed the contrasting pattern: they associated rightward space with negative concepts and leftward with positive concepts. The embodiment interpretation that author suggests for these opposite mental connotations for valence is that "right- and left-handers implicitly associated positive valence more strongly with the side of space on which they could act more fluently with their dominant hands" (Casasanto, 2009, p.351). Neuroscience studies further confirmed such differentiation on the horizontal plane: the left hemisphere is associated with the processing of positive concepts, whereas the right hemisphere is associated with the processing of negative concepts (Davidson, 1992; Gadea, Espert, Salvador, & Martí-Bonmatí, 2011).

Location of the positive and negative concepts on the vertical plane is not contingent on handedness: people associate the "up" spatial location with positive concepts, whereas the "down" spatial location with negative concepts (Marmolejo-Ramos, Elosúa, Yamada, Hamm, & Noguchi, 2013; Schnall, 2014). As for positive and negative emotional states, one may say "I'm on top of the world," or "feeling up," or in contrast, "I'm down in the dumps," or "fell into a depression." Another example, an upright, relaxed posture of a person when he or she feels happy and a slumped, drooping posture when he or she feels depressed (Schnall, 2014, p. 3).

The vertical plane is salient in people's mind over the horizontal plane in their mental association with valences of emotional concepts. This finding is valid for Australian as well as for Japanese participants, even though they differ in their cultural, linguistic backgrounds, and they use different writing axes: the Australians write along the horizontal axis (rightward), while the Japanese write along the vertical one (downward) (Marmolejo-Ramos et al., 2013).

Bodily Lexicon Referring to Emotional Experience

Bodily metaphors are widespread in people's everyday talk. Some of them are more typical than others (Kovecses, 2000; Schnall, 2014, see also Karandashev, 2019, p.5). Head and heart are the terms, which are most commonly used in metaphorical descriptions of mental and emotional life. In Western tradition, the *head* is considered as the locus for rational thought, whereas the *heart* as the locus of emotions (e.g., Berendt & Tanita, 2011). "Listen to your heart" (assuming "not your head") means listen to your emotions (assuming "not reasoning"). The *heart as a container of emotions* is among the typical metaphors for *emotion* (Kovecses, 2000). Many languages have the *heart metaphor* of emotion (see for review Karandashev, 2019).

Some cultures and languages embody emotions in other parts of body. For Tahitians, emotions are situated in the intestines (Levy, 1973), for Japanese—in the abdomen, belly, stomach, gut, and intestines (Berendt & Tanita, 2011), for Nigerians, the Akan ethnic group of Ghana, and people in the central and eastern part of Cote d'Ivoire—in the belly (Agyekum, 2015), for Malay indigenous people—in the liver (Howell, 1981). The cultural metaphors of emotions express such notions when people say they feel their intestines "boiling with anger" (Kovecses, 2000), or their liver "jumping with fright" (Lutz, 1988), or "My liver, my soul" (Pérez, 2008). Such cultural variations are associated with corresponding indigenous conceptions of bodily and mental functioning, as well as with polysemy of the words denoting various parts of body (Agyekum, 2015, see also Karandashev, 2019).

Is it adequate to explore emotional experience via emotion words and metaphors? Are they the descriptions of experience or expression of emotions? The key point to answer these questions is that expression and experience of emotion interact with each other. The expression of emotions helps individuals to better understand their subjective emotional experience. Expression of emotion serves as an objectification of their subjective experience.

Dimensional Structure of Emotional Experience

The *two-dimensional model of emotion* initially revealed with English-speaking student sample, included valence (pleasure–displeasure) and arousal (arousal–sleepiness) (Russell, 1980). It was further validated in cross-cultural research (Russell, Lewicka, & Niit, 1989) with Greek, Polish, Estonian, and Chinese participants. Some researchers proposed the third dimension: *power* (Fontaine, Poortinga, Setiadi, & Markam, 2002; Shaver, Schwartz, Kirson, & O'Connor, 1987; Shaver, Wu, & Schwartz, 1992), others—even fourth dimension *novelty* (Fontaine, Scherer, Roesch, & Ellsworth, 2007; Fontaine, Scherer, & Soriano, 2013).

A recent componential approach to the research on emotions, as reflected in emotion terms across languages and cultures, has revealed that *four dimensions* parsimoniously represent the semantic space of the emotion life: *valence, arousal, power, novelty* (Fontaine et al., 2007; Fontaine et al., 2013). A cross-linguistic and cross-cultural study using the extensive set of data (34 samples from 27 countries in 23 languages, Fontaine et al., 2007, 2013) were able to reliable identify these dimensions. The later study using a larger and more representative list of emotion terms successfully replicated these findings with a variety of emotion terms describing many emotion features representing the appraisal, bodily reaction, action tendency, feeling, and expression components of the emotion process (Gillioz, Fontaine, Soriano, & Scherer, 2016).

The *valence dimension* characterizes *hedonic tone* of emotional experience and differentiates pleasant and unpleasant emotions. The *arousal dimension* characterizes *intensity of emotional experience* and differentiates high arousal emotions (such as anguish and love) and low arousal emotions (such as compassion and depression). The *power dimension* differentiates powerful emotions (such as anger) and powerless emotions (such as sadness and fear). The *novelty dimension* differentiates the emotions of high novelty (such as surprise and joy) and the emotions of little novelty (such as guilt and fear). The novelty dimension is important in differentiating between "predictable emotions (like those caused by one's own actions) and the more unpredictable ones, elicited by sudden external events that fully capture the person's attention either in a positive" (Gillioz et al., 2016, p. 144). It is characterized by "appraisals of unpredictability and suddenness, and by facial expressions such as jaw drop and widely open eyes" (p. 141).

These studies explored the semantic dimensionality of emotions. The question remains whether these dimensions reflect the actual emotional experience of people. According to the studies (Larsen & Diener, 1992; Russell, 1980; Thayer, 1989; Watson & Tellegen, 1985) asking people to evaluate how certain emotions describe their emotional states, the two dimensions of emotions—valence and arousal—are the most salient. No studies were conducted so far which would explore whether the four dimensions—valence, arousal, power, and novelty—might better represent people's emotional experience.

5.1.3   The Cultural Models Based on the Locus of Emotions

Intrapersonal Model of Emotions: The Cases of the United States and Western European Cultures

The intrapersonal model largely prevails in Western cultures and considers emotions as more intrapersonal and less interpersonal focused phenomena. In Western scientific tradition, internal subjective states of an individual are the primary referents of emotion concepts (e.g., Bockover, 1995; Lutz, 1982). Hence, the words of emotional lexicon denote an individual's internal states.

Such an *intrapersonal model of emotion* is reflected in the words describing emotions. The modern conceptualization and even the term of *emotion* in Western science are closely associated with its English meaning (Danzinger, 1997). The Latin *emovere* ("to move out," "move away") coined the term *emotion* in the early nineteenth century (Bilimoria & Wenta, 2015); many other world languages have no single words, which are equivalent to the English word *emotion* (Solomon, 1995; Wierzbicka, 2004b). Since emotions are private and natural physiological experience, the English emotion lexicon mostly refers to internal feeling states and their physiological descriptions (Lutz, 1982).

The prevailing cultures of the United States and Western Europe consider *emotions* as unique *individual experiences*. Emotions are person-specific and, therefore, they are worthwhile to experience and express openly (Friedlmeier, Corapci, & Benga, 2015). In the Western cultural values, it is expected that people "support the social order by reference to inner feelings" (Potter, 1988, p. 194).

The studies of lay-people's theories of emotions (Uchida, Townsend, Markus, & Bergsieker, 2009) have demonstrated that Americans understand and experience emotions as phenomena that take place within an individual. Americans highlight the importance of an individual and believe that their feelings are essential to their experience of emotions. The origins of meaningful emotional experience are in the self. The privacy of emotional life is a highly important value. Expressive individualism is an essential aspect of American culture – expressing their feelings, individuals communicate with others. Their personal emotions are a definite priority (Lutz, 1988).

Thus, in *intrapersonal model*, emotions are considered as *internal individual states*. The implicit assumption is that different emotions are defined primarily in terms of physiological pattern of activation, facial expression, positive or negative valence, or level of arousal.

Interpersonal Model of Emotions: The Cases of China and Polynesian Cultures

According to *interpersonal model*, emotions are viewed in the *context of social relationships*, rather than in terms of internal states. From this perspective, different emotions are the transformations of the relationship between person and others. Accordingly, dimensions of emotions describe different aspects of the relations between self and other (De Rivera & Grinkis, 1986).

The *interpersonal model of emotions* generally prevails in East Asian cultures and views emotions as *interpersonally focused experience*, rather than intrapersonal experience. This *interpersonal model* is socio-centric and relationship-oriented. East Asian conceptions view *emotions* as *context-related experience*, and people verbally express their feelings of emotions not directly and openly, but rather in behavioral descriptions (Friedlmeier et al., 2015).

Individuals in these cultures favor the experience of a more balance between positive and negative emotional states, prefer to feel low versus high arousal positive states, they tend to suppress their expression of emotion, and suppression has beneficial outcomes.

The exploration of lay-people's theories of emotions (Uchida et al., 2009) has shown that Japanese understand and subjectively experience emotions as phenomena occurring in relationship between people.

In a similar way, the Chinese model of emotion focuses more on social relationships than on internal subjective experience. According to Chinese cultural values, an individual attains social meaning of their life primarily from social context, rather than from internal subjective states. People do not place high value on emotions in their social relationships and do not think that their emotions bring a sufficient rationale for their social actions. Emotions do not have the power to create, maintain, or dissolve social relationships. They are convinced that relationships exist independently of any emotion. The Chinese cultural values perceive "the continuity of the social order to exist independently of inner feelings" (Potter, 1988, p. 194).

Chinese cultural beliefs consider *interpersonal* processes associated with emotions as of primary importance. People are aware of their emotional experience and acknowledge that emotions exist. Emotions are viewed as a natural concomitant of life, but secondary in importance (Potter, 1988, p. 186).

Such an *interpersonal model of emotion* is also reflected in the words describing emotions. Different from the English emotion lexicon, which usually refers to internal feelings and states (Lutz, 1982), in some other cultures and corresponding languages emotion words explicitly denote the relations between a person and an event (or another person). The examples are the cultures of Polynesia, such as the Samoans' (Gerber, 1975), the Solomon Islands' (White, 1985), and that one of Pintupi Aborigines' (Myers, 1979). According to beliefs and vocabularies of people in those cultures, emotions refer to the relationships among people or between people and events. For example, the emotion words of native Malayo–Polynesian people inhabiting on Micronesian atoll in the Western Pacific represent the situations in which the emotion occurs. The 31 emotion words of Ifalukian language refer to the situations and social activity eliciting them.

Objectivized Model of Emotions: The Cases of India and China

Indian conception of emotions is an example of *objectified models*. According to the traditional Indian philosophical and aesthetic traditions, emotions tend to be objectivized, not internalized (Lynch, 1990). The linguistically specific term *rasa* explains the Indian cultural interpretation of emotion. The term *rasa* includes two meanings: artistic—referring to the act of production and aesthetic—referring to that of perception and enjoyment. The term designates the objective embodiment of the first process—artistic production, which causes the second process—the enjoyment of perception. The term *rasa* includes the subjectivity and objectivity (Thampi, 1965). The English language has no word with this multifaceted meaning. This linguistic artefact can partially explain the cultural differences between Anglo- and Indian cultural understanding of emotion.

A *rasa* also means the developed relishable state of mood, which is called *sthāyi-bhāva*. It is the global state of mind of an individual that is based on his or her emotional makeup.

The Indian philosophy makes a distinction between an *ordinary life-emotion* and an *emotional content of aesthetic experience*. The *life-emotion* is viewed as a disturbance, as an agitation in the consciousness. It stirs and moves out in action. The *poetic experience of emotions* does stir and agitate our mind, but not our behavior. In the poetic experience, the emotions are not simply undergone or suffered; they are observed and tasted.

In ordinary life, a person can control an emotion. He or she can destroy the emotion through concentration of attention on it. A detached contemplative attitude to emotional experience prevents the emotional disturbances of the heart (Thampi, 1965, p.77).

> "In poetic experience when we "distance" the emotions, i.e., when we apprehend them as having a non-ordinary relation to us, they do not disappear; on the contrary, they gain in clarity and become relishable. The liberative function of poetry, partly, is an outcome of this nature of poetic experience. Once we are able to formulate and precisely define the emo-

tions in a concrete and almost tangible way we gain a kind of mastery over them. We know their nature, potentialities, internal constituents and differentiations. This helps us understand and clarify human situations and experiences with enhanced efficiency. It helps us free ourselves from being a slave to emotions which are generally chaotic, blind, and powerful. This is one of the meanings of the statement that poetry makes our insight into life keener."

The Indian scholars believe that romantic poetry is not subjective, but rather objective. A poet objectifies feelings in terms of actions, images, and characters, detaching the experience from the subject—a personality. Once a person acquires such an attitude to emotion, he or she is capable to master the emotion. In contemporary India, the tradition of *rasa* is still being followed (Lynch, 1990; McDaniel, 1995).

The Indian school of acting in ancient Sanskrit drama and in modern Indian cinema illustrates this understanding of emotion, which is different from Western tradition. The Indian actors employ the *Rasa method of performance*, in which "empathetic emotions are conveyed by the performer and thus felt by the audience". This is contrastingly different from the Western *Stanislavski method of performance*, in which "the actor must become a living, breathing embodiment of a character rather than simply conveying emotion" (Saumi, 2016, p.52). While the Indian method of acting illustrates *objectification of emotion*, the Western method illustrates *internalization of emotion*.

Detachment and *self-reflexivity*, as the ways of *objectification of emotion*, are the cultural attitudes, which the Indian culture shares with the Chinese one. The Chinese notion of *savoring* is similar to the Indian concept of *rasa* (Sundararajan, 2010), and it is still being followed in contemporary China (Ye, 2007).

Self-reflexivity and *detachment* are some common grounds, which these two cultural attitudes to emotion have. *Self-reflexivity* engages two dimensions of consciousness: (1) first-order experience versus second-order awareness and (2) outward-directed attention versus self-directed (Lambie & Marcel, 2002). *Second-order awareness* is the awareness of the first-order experience that an individual can reflect and report. *Inwardly directed attention* is a self-reflexive consciousness, it constitutes awareness as "my" awareness. While tasting is the first-order experience of liking the flavors of food, savoring is the second-order awareness of knowing that one likes the flavors. The *savoring* allows to reflect tasting and, therefore, to manage this experience making the fine discriminations of it (Frijda & Sundararajan, 2007).

Such second-order awareness of emotional experience and inwardly directed attention to emotions are evident in the examples of other emotions as well. This explains how Chinese people can objectify and thus moderate the intensity of their emotions. These features make the Chinese culturally normative experience of emotion different from natural first-order and outward-directed emotion that is culturally normative for the Western internal subjective experience of the intense passionate emotions.

Interactive Model of Emotions: The Case of Polynesia

The *culture of Ifaluk* can represent Polynesian views on *emotions* as primarily inter-active processes. Emotions for people in those cultures are *interpersonal patterns of action* (e.g., sympathy, parting, and danger). They believe that emotions are insepa-rable from activity that triggers those emotions (Lutz, 1988).

Speakers in Polynesian culture distinguish emotions based on the situations in which the corresponding emotions arise. Five basic clusters of emotions are in accord with five typical situations: good fortune, danger, loss and connection with others, human error, and overly complex and misunderstood events and Ifalukian language (speaking in Polynesia) has 31 emotional words and no single word for *emotion* itself (Lutz, 1982, 1988).

5.1.4   Physiology Associated with Emotional Experience

Cross-Cultural Similarities in Physiology of Emotional Responses

Emotional experience consists of physiological processes and subjective psycho-logical feelings, which will be considered in this and the following section. Research demonstrated that autonomic nervous system activity is different among emotions and the physiological processes associated with emotions are substantially similar in different cultural contexts (Bond, 1993; Ekman, Levenson, & Friesen, 1983; Levenson, Ekman, Heider, & Friesen, 1992; Soto, Levenson, & Ebling, 2005; Tsai, Levenson, & Carstensen, 2000).

For instance, a study found that emotion-specific patterns in activity of auto-nomic nervous system of Minangkabau people (an indigenous ethnic group in Indonesia and West Sumatra) and Americans are similar (Levenson et al., 1992). Other researchers (Tsai et al., 2000; Tsai, Chentsova-Dutton, Freire-Bebeau, & Przymus, 2002) also did not find cultural differences in physiological responding during exposure of the emotionally inducing stimuli or reliving previous emotional episodes between Chinese Americans, Hmong Americans, and European Americans.

In other study (Soto et al., 2005), researchers found that physiological responses to emotion eliciting stimuli were similar in two cultural groups—Mexican Americans and Chinese Americans—no significant differences. Thus, autonomic physiology of emotional responding seems to be not affected by cultural influence. Nevertheless, Mexican Americans reported experiencing significantly more emotions than Chinese Americans. This means that despite absence of differences in physiological responses, participants from these cultures had different subjective experience.

In Western cultures, despite the data that women are more expressive of most emotions—that will be discussed in the following sections—men reveal equal or sometimes higher physiological arousal (e.g., greater blood pressure and cortisol responses). Men, being aroused internally, tend to keep their emotions inside, while women express their emotions freely (Buck, 1984; Chaplin, Hong, Bergquist, &

Sinha, 2008; Levenson, Carstensen, & Gottman, 1994; Stroud, Salovey, & Epel, 2002).

Other cross-cultural study of *physiological symptoms* (Scherer & Wallbott, 1994) of seven basic emotion categories (*joy, sadness, fear, anger, shame, guilt*, and *disgust*) with self-report questionnaires investigated experience of emotions. The data demonstrated that the reported patterns of emotional experiences substantially overlapped in 37 countries on all continents. However, the limitation of self-report data on physiological symptoms should be acknowledged.

Thus, despite some evidence of cross-cultural similarities in physiological patterns of emotional responses, many studies bring inconsistent results (see for review, Philippot & Rimé, 1997). The empirical findings are not sufficient to answer the questions about cross-cultural variations in physiology of emotion.

Culturally Modified Physiological Experience of Emotions

Emotional experience is affected by culture, and the patterns of cultural differences, as we will see in the following sections, exist. Even though physiological activity and subjective experience of basic emotions might be similar across culture, yet cultural norms, expression of complex emotions and attitudes are cross-culturally different.

There is some evidence that physiological experience of emotions can be modified by culture. For example, according to Chinese cultural tradition, extreme emotions are detrimental to social relationship and individual, therefore, moderation of emotional expressions and practice of emotional control are suggested (Klineberg, 1938; Potter, 1988; Russell & Yik, 1996; Wu & Tseng, 1985; Zheng & Berry, 1991). Therefore, people learn early in their social development that the strong emotional experience should be restrained and suppressed (Kleinman, 1986). Striving to achieve this suppression can result in "somatization" of emotions (Lynch, 1990)—manifesting emotions in bodily symptoms. For example, a person might complain about a stomachache when angry, rather than yell at a partner.

The whole human body and corresponding physiological processes are engaged in experience of emotions, yet indigenous cultures may attribute those to different parts. Emotions are the reflection of the processes that take place in a body. But where in the human body are physiological processes located? Head and heart are the vital organs, which are frequently associated with experience of emotion. More specifically, the *head* is the locus for rational thought, whereas the *heart* is the locus of emotions.

This *dualistic* view is typical understanding for many Western cultures. People *guided by their heart* are those guided by their emotions, rather than by their reasoning (Berendt & Tanita, 2011). This Western English-speaking belief represents a dichotomy of *mind* and *heart*, the *rational* and *emotional* parts of people's life.

Japanese and Thai languages and cultures represent a *monistic* view, which integrates the *rational* and *emotional* parts of people's life. Such integrative interpretation of emotions is present in the Japanese expressions of *hara* (belly/abdomen) and Thai expression of *jai* (heart).

Thai people use the word *jai* (heart) to reflect such aspects of mental life and behavior as conditions of the heart, thinking and making decisions, conduct and behavior, relationships and social life. Following the same *monistic* view, Japanese people, however, uses several key words *kokoro* (heart), *mune* (breast/chest), *hara* (belly) (Berendt & Tanita, 2011, p. 71).

Some languages and cultures embody emotions differently. Tahitians think that emotions arise from the intestines (Levy, 1973). For Malay indigenous people feeling and thoughts are located in the liver (Howell, 1981). According to some Turkish expressions, emotions are also located in the liver. However, idiomatic expressions of the Turkish words for *heart* (*yürek, kalp*) (Pérez, 2008). In some African cultures such as Nigeria, Akan people of Ghana and Cote d'Ivoire, the belly is the seat of emotional experience. It is worth noting that in those cultures, the body part *yam* (stomach) represents the entangled relationship between the stomach, the chest, the heart, the brain, and the womb (Agyekum, 2015).

5.1.5 Body Sensations Associated with Emotions

Similarities in the Cultural Patterns of Body Sensations Associated with Emotions

Generally, the patterns of bodily sensation describing each emotion are similar across studies using different methodological approaches (see for review Philippot & Rimé, 1997).

For example, the pattern of *joy* includes raised body temperature, accelerated heart rate, sensation of lump in the throat, and some changes in muscle symptoms. The patterns of *anger* include increased body temperature and heart rate, higher breathing rate, more intensive perspiration, and muscle tension. The pattern of *fear* has bodily sensations similar to *anger*, but different in some respects: (1) lower body temperature and (2) stomach symptoms. The pattern of *sadness* includes less bodily sensations, in particular in the areas of throat and stomach.

Are the patterns of bodily sensations physiologically or socially determined? Research on visceroception has demonstrated that people usually perceive their physiological changes as the diffuse and not well identifiable sensations of arousal. They often have difficulties in explaining and reporting of what they feel (Karandashev, 2019, p. 5; Philippot & Rimé, 1997, p.7). Findings suggest that people's bodily sensation of emotion is the constructive process unconsciously determined by the social schemata of the typical physiological changes associated with certain emotions (Rimé, Philippot, & Cisamolo, 1990).

Therefore, the understanding of the nature and origins of *social schemata* as *social constructions* (Averill, 1985) should help better explain the individual experience and cross-cultural variations in *bodily sensations*. The cross-cultural data collected in several studies (see for review Philippot & Rimé, 1997) have demonstrated that *social schemata* of bodily sensations for many emotions are quite *similar across cultures*.

The early studies of 1980s were not able to find cross-cultural variation in bodily sensations associated with experience of emotions. Cross-cultural similarities in body sensations related to emotions were predominant.

Cross-Cultural Differences in the Body Sensations Associated with Emotions

The later studies of 1990s employed the improved research methodology, in particular using more refined operationalization, extending the list of bodily sensations, increasing a number of cultures included in studies, and employing more powerful statistics (see for review Philippot & Rimé, 1997). Researchers used multivariate analysis of variance and found the distinctive patterns of bodily sensations associated with each emotion. Nevertheless, the data showed that culture significantly modifies these emotional profiles. Even though the cross-cultural similarities in these patterns were found to be prevalent, yet results suggest that these patterns vary across cultures statistically significant.

Researchers (see for review Philippot & Rimé, 1997) found that *social emotions* (joy, disgust, shame, and guilt) demonstrated more cultural variations compared to others (surprise, sadness, fear, and anger). Such *bodily sensations* as muscular sensations, respiratory and temperature changes had more cultural variations than others. Italian participants reported experience of less breathing and throat symptoms associated with anger and more muscular relaxation associated with sadness. These differences were especially large compared to Northern American participants. The Americans reported that in their experience of joy, fear, and anger, they felt the increased temperature more than participants from three other countries (Belgium, Bolivia, and Italy).

The processes engaged in generation of emotions may evolve differently depending on the type of emotions. *Biological emotions* have typical and discrete physiological patterns. Their sensations are fairly distinctive. Appraisal processes and self-reports of emotional experience are cross-culturally similar. *Cultural emotions* do not necessarily have unique typical and discrete physiological patterns. Their sensations can be mixed, complex, and overlapping. Appraisal processes and emotional experiences are more culturally dependent (Matsumoto & Hwang, 2012).

Verbal or visual self-reports of people about their emotional experience are probably the only way to know this aspect of their emotions. They can observe their behavior, but not the feelings. It is challenging for them to objectify and rationalize their physiological and subjective experiences (Karandashev, 2019, p. 5).

Cultural Abilities to Differentiate Body Sensations Across Emotions

The extensive studies of the relationships between body sensations and emotions have demonstrated (e.g., Scherer & Wallbott, 1994; Scherer, Wallbott, & Summerfield, 1986) that people across cultures have the similar ability to differentiate body sensations across emotions. A later study (Breugelmans et al., 2005) also advocated that body sensations associated with emotions such as *joy*, *anger*, *fear*, *sadness*, *disgust*, *surprise*, and *shame* are similar across cultures and suggested cross-cultural generalizability of body sensation profiles for these emotions, with some cultural deviations (e.g., for *anger* in the Rarámuri culture and *surprise* in the Javanese culture).

Later studies extended these findings employing new methodologies and including other cultures (Nummenmaa, Glerean, Hari, & Hietanen, 2014; Volynets, Glerean, Hietanen, Hari, & Nummenmaa, 2019). They demonstrated that people experience consistent topographically distinct and discrete, yet partially overlapping patterns of bodily sensations corresponding to each of the six basic emotions, seven nonbasic (complex) emotions, and a neutral state. Authors found that these patterns are culturally universal. Experimental studies replicated these patterns (body maps) using various stimuli: emotional words, stories, movies, and facial expressions.

> Most basic emotions were associated with sensations of elevated activity in the upper chest area, likely corresponding to changes in breathing and heart rate. Similarly, sensations in the head area were shared across all emotions, reflecting probably both physiological changes in the facial area (i.e., facial musculature activation, skin temperature, lacrimation) as well as the felt changes in the contents of mind triggered by the emotional events. Sensations in the upper limbs were most prominent in approach-oriented emotions, anger and happiness, whereas sensations of decreased limb activity were a defining feature of sadness. Sensations in the digestive system and around the throat region were mainly found in disgust. In contrast with all of the other emotions, happiness was associated with enhanced sensations all over the body. The nonbasic emotions showed a much smaller degree of bodily sensations and spatial independence, with the exception of a high degree of similarity across the emotional states of fear and sadness, and their respective prolonged, clinical variants of anxiety and depression. (Nummenmaa et al., 2014, p. 648)

In addition to the study administered with 701 participants in Finland, Sweden (West European cultures) and Taiwan (East Asian culture, Nummenmaa et al., 2014), researchers also supported cross-cultural similarity of these bodily sensation maps in an international sample of 3954 participants across 101 countries, with no gender differences (Volynets et al., 2019).

5.2   Cultural Appraisal of Emotion and Experience of Emotion

5.2.1   Appraisal as a Trigger of Emotion

Individually and Culturally Determined Appraisal

Experience of emotions is a complex of processes. As we saw in the previous sections, an appraisal is among those. Emotion is not a simple sensation; it evolves as a multifaceted emotional experience. Theory and research have demonstrated that an individual first appraises stimulus, event, or situation and then this appraisal triggers an emotion. The same situation being appraised differently causes different emotions (Ellsworth & Scherer, 2003; Frijda, 1993; Siemer, Mauss, & Gross, 2007).

The emotion being aroused activates physiology, feeling, thinking, and expressive behaviors. An assumption of general theory is that when people appraise situations in the same way, they experience the same emotions. Depending on a subjective appraisal of the consequences, which an event can bring to an individual, the event can produce a specific emotion. An evaluation of situation and circumstances from the point of how they are *pleasant-goal conducive* or *unpleasant-goal obstructive* produces the experience of either positive or negative emotions (Scherer, 1993; Smith & Lazarus, 1993).

An appraisal is individually subjective and culturally determined. A person with certain temperament and personality traits, or being in certain socioeconomic and life circumstances, or perceiving the meaning of a situation culturally specific, may be predisposed to evaluate situations as pleasant and goal conducive (or unpleasant and goal obstructive). Therefore, emotions are not universal and not experienced exactly the same way across individuals and societies.

Cultural appraisals determine an individual's experience of emotions and predispose people to view the life events and interpret actions of other persons in a certain way (Frijda, 1993; Lynch, 1990; Mesquita & Ellsworth, 2001). The differences in cultural understanding of an emotional situation, in the meaning of an event eliciting emotion cause the differences in the appraisal, construction of emotional experience and expression.

The *dimensions of appraisal*, which determine emotional experience, are largely similar across cultures. Researchers have identified multiple more or less complex dimensions of appraisal. Among those are (1) primitive dimensions such as *attentional activity*, *pleasantness*, *certainty*, *goal conduciveness*, and *coping ability*, (2) such more cognitively complex dimensions as *norm/self compatibility* and *legitimacy*, and (3) such complex dimensions as *responsibility*, *anticipated effort*, and *control* (Mauro, Sato, & Tucker, 1992).

Appraisal in the Light of the Cultural Value of Honor

Let us consider these differences with an example comparing the appraisals, experiences, and behaviors of Southern and Northern men in the United States of America in an experimental situation when they were offended (Cohen, Vandello, Puente, & Rantilla, 1999). Men in Southern cultural settings are different from men in Northern cultural settings in their attitude to the value of *honor*. Therefore, they are more sensitive to offense, especially when it is intentional, because it challenges their *honor* (Cohen, Nisbett, Bowdle, & Schwarz, 1996).

For the purpose of emotional self-regulation, the culture of Southerners has developed certain rules of politeness, which help people to be less receptive to small offenses and subtle hostilities. This way they implicitly avoid too frequent *experience of anger*. The culture of Northerners, however, prepares them well to notice such small hostilities and rudeness.

These cultural differences in appraisals were evident in the reactions of participants to experimental situation (Cohen et al., 1999) when an annoying confederate interfered with their task completion. In such situation, Southerners responded longer than Northerners with *emotion of anger*, as indicated in facial expression, verbal or physical confrontation. Nevertheless, once the Southern participants became angry owing to this annoying situation, they experienced and expressed their *anger* more intensely, being ready for verbal or physical confrontation. Thus, once Southerners took the offense seriously, they felt necessary to reciprocate and defend their *honor*. Despite these typical cultural tendencies in reactions to this experimental situation, there was variation in *individual experience of emotions*. Some Northerners and Southerners remained calm, while other became angry.

Thus, men from these two cultural models are predisposed to perceive the stimuli eliciting emotions in a certain way and appraise them accordingly. Those from interdependent cultural contexts (Southerners) perceive and appraise the social situation with attention to the relationship, while those from independent cultural context (Northerners) perceive and appraise the same social situation with focus on the individual. These differences trigger different types of emotional experience.

5.2.2 Appraisals of Social Situations Across Cultures

Cross-Culturally Common Appraisals

Appraisal of some situations and events are cross-culturally universal, while appraisal of others can vary across cultures depending on the culturally-specific meanings, which people attribute to these situations and events (Matsumoto & Hwang, 2012; Shweder, Haidt, Horton, & Joseph, 2008). For instance, death rituals may be perceived as grieving and mourning or as celebrations of life and consequently elicit different emotions (Hoy, 2013; Mead, 1943; Metcalf & Huntington, 1991).

The emotions, which events elicit, depend on appraisals, while the appraisals in turn may depend on culturally specific meaning of the events. Similar patterns of appraisal can evoke similar emotions, while different patterns cause cultural differences in emotions. Salience of certain appraisal dimensions and differences in their accessibility in different cultures explain the cultural differences in appraisal and consequently in experience of emotions (Mesquita & Ellsworth, 2001).

These appraisals in many ways are similar across cultures triggering the same emotions. Studies have demonstrated (Kuppens, Van Mechelen, Smits, & De Boeck, 2004; Scherer, Schorr, & Johnstone, 2001) that the underlying *patterns of appraisals*, which serve as the proximal elicitors of emotions, are overlapping. Emotions covary in different cultures depending on these appraisals. The results of the study (Kuppens, Ceulmans, Timmerman, Diener, & Kim-Prieto, 2006) suggest that

> the degree of overlap between two emotions' appraisal patterns may be similar across cultures as well: If two emotions are characterized by highly similar (respectively different)

appraisal patterns in one culture, it can be expected that they will be characterized by similar (respectively different) patterns in another culture as well. This does not imply, however, that the appraisal patterns themselves are similar across cultures. (p. 510)

The similarities in the patterns of appraisal eliciting emotions have been found in cross-cultural research. Comprehensive studies (see for review, Scherer, 1997a, 1997b) explored what types of situations elicit emotions of anger, disgust, fear, joy, sadness, shame, and guilt in 37 countries. The situations were classified into general groups (e.g., good news and bad news, temporary and permanent separation, success and failure). Results showed that all groups of events happen in people's lives in 37 cultures, and each event elicits certain emotions with the frequency relatively similar across countries. For instance, such events as "temporary meetings with friends," "relationships with friends," and "achievement situations" are the most frequent elicitors of happiness. Such events as "injustice" and "relationships" are the most frequent elicitors of anger. Such events as "death" and "relationships" are the most frequent elicitors of sadness. The cultural samples differ in the *frequencies* of how the events trigger an emotion and what the meanings of those events are.

Cross-Culturally Different Appraisals

Differences and specifics in appraisal and emotional experience can vary across culture due to mutual interaction of culture and emotion (e.g., Fontaine et al., 2002; Markus, Kitayama, & VandenBos, 1996; Mesquita & Frijda, 1992; Mesquita, Frijda, & Scherer, 1997; Shaver et al., 1992)—see more details below in this chapter.

The cultural differences have been revealed among Europeans, Americans, and Japanese (Scherer, Matsumoto, Wallbott, & Kudoh, 1988). In some cultural samples, the same events elicit certain emotions relatively more frequently than in others. And in some emotions there are culturally specific triggers. In particular,

- world news was a more frequent trigger of sadness for Europeans and Americans than for the Japanese
- problems in relationships, however, produced more sadness for the Japanese than for Americans or Europeans
- strangers and achievement-related situations elicited more fear for Americans, whereas novel situations, traffic, and relationships were more frequent elicitors of fear for the Japanese
- walking in the dark elicit less fear in Japan than in the United States
- situations involving strangers were more frequent elicitors of anger for the Japanese than for the Americans or Europeans
- situations involving relationships brought about more anger for Americans than for Japanese (cited in Matsumoto & Hwang, 2012, p. 100).

As I presented in earlier sections, the *cultural models of independent* and *interdependent self-construals* reflect on how people appraise a situation. The typical appraisal of a situation by a person in an *independent culture* involves the perception of *how the situation may impact individual goals*. Different from this, the typical appraisal of a situation by a person in an *interdependent culture* involves the perception of *how the situation may impact relational goals* (Mesquita & Leu, 2007, p.737).

5.2.3   Cultural Factors of Appraisal and Emotional Experience

Cultural Differences in Self-Construals and Experience of Emotions

Different *self-construals* of individuals in *independent* (more self-focused) and *interdependent* (more other-focused) *models of culture* can explain the differences in emotional reactions to a similar situation. The appraisal of *blaming other person* for *their offense* is the prevailing American path to experience *anger*, which consecutively triggers *assertive* and *aggressive* behavior. From another perspective, the typical Japanese appraisal of the similar situation is the *assumption that other person had a good reason* to behave in this way. Such appraisal of *sympathy with the offender* triggers the *decreased emotional experience* and probably in *doing nothing*. Thus, these two appraisals have caused difference in emotional experience and behavior (Mesquita & Leu, 2007).

As I commented in early sections, people in *independent model of culture* tend to be more self-focused, while in *interdependent model of culture*—more other-focused. According these differences, people from European American culture are more emotionally reactive when paying attention to individual aspects of the self, compared to Asian Americans. Different from this, people from Asian American cultures show similar or greater emotional reactivity than European Americans when paying attention to relational aspects of the self (Chentsova-Dutton & Tsai, 2010).

Sensitivity to Social Context and Experience of Emotions

People in *independent cultures* are *more self-focused*, while in *interdependent cultures* are *more relationship-focused*. Therefore, it is reasonable to expect that social context of situations can affect emotional experience of people in these two models of culture differently. A cross-cultural study (Oishi, Diener, Scollon, & Biswas-Diener, 2004) investigated emotional experience of students in Japan and India, American students in the Midwest (mostly European Americans) and Hispanic students in California. Participants completed a scale of positive and negative affective states five times a day indicating every time whether (1) they were alone, (2) with a friend, (3) with a classmate/coworker, (4) with a romantic partner, (5) with a stranger, or (6) with family. Results showed that in all cultural samples positive and negative affective states were largely consistent across situations. However, these emotional experiences varied from one social context to another. These variations were in a lesser degree in independent (European American) sample compared to two interdependent (Hispanic, Japanese) samples. The data of Indian participants were different from those obtained in the other interdependent cultural samples.

Results of the study (Oishi et al., 2004) have shown that in their emotional experience (particularly in positive affective states), the participants from interdependent cultural samples were more sensitive to different social contexts than participants from independent cultural sample. Those from the independent culture did not experience emotions differently in situations with or without others, yet those from the interdependent cultures experienced emotions differently depending on relationship circumstances. Thus, authors concluded that the social context influence emotional experience in interdependent cultures, but not in independent cultures.

In addition, authors (Oishi et al., 2004) analyzed a within-person variability of emotional experiences for each individual across six social situations. Overall, the larger variations were in positive than in negative affective states. Thus, the differences in social circumstances influenced variations in experience of positive emotions more than of negative ones. Moreover, researchers have revealed cross-cultural differences in the samples according to the relational orientation prevailing in interdependent cultures. In interdependent cultures, the particular social situations affected the individual level of positive and negative emotions more than in independent cultures.

The studies using a different methodology were in accord with these results (Masuda et al., 2008). Researchers investigated an observer's perspective on emotions rather than introspection of their own. Emotional experience was explored through the perception of emotional experience of people depicted on cartoons. Japanese and European American participants should rate the emotions of a central person who displayed happiness, sadness, or anger. This person was surrounded by four other persons with facial expressions displaying various emotions. Results showed that Japanese—consistent with an interdependent model of their culture—in their judgment of the emotional experience of central person took into account the emotions of all people depicted in the cartoon. However, European American participants—consistent with an independent model of their culture—rated the emotions of central person based solely on their expressions and did not pay attention to the emotions of the people around.

Other studies (Masuda et al., 2008; Tsang & Wu, 2005) used eye tracking when participants were completing the similar emotion judgment task. Researchers in both studies obtained similar results. The Japanese and Taiwanese participants were able to distribute their attention between the central person and other people in the cartoon, while Americans paid their attention mostly to the central person. Thus, results confirm that people from the *culture with independent models* perceive emotional experience from a *perspective of an individual*, whereas people from *the culture with interdependent models* perceive emotional experience from a *relational perspective*. For an individual from interdependent cultures, people in a situation are included in the emotion stimulus, if they belong to the same group, or related to the individual.

The Cultural Attitudes of Individual Agency and Personal Control and Experience of Emotions

For people in *interdependent cultures, relational meanings of* a *situation* are the leading contributing factors of appraisals. Different from this, for people in *independent cultures, individual agency* and *control* are the leading contributor to appraisals.

Studies have discovered that *individual agency* is a central dimension of emotional experience for Americans and people in several Western European countries (Frijda, Kuipers, & Ter Schure, 1989; Matsumoto, Kudoh, Scherer, & Wallbott, 1988; Scherer, 1984; Smith & Ellsworth, 1985). Thus, culturally specific appraisals of situations with accent on *agency* and *personal control* are more typical of individuals living in independent cultures (Ellsworth & Scherer, 2003; Frijda et al., 1989; Weiner, 1986). People in these cultural contexts (e.g., European American) tend to attribute the central events and outcomes in their life to their *personal agency*—independent and personal accomplishments (Markus & Kitayama, 1991).

However, the dimension of *individual agency* is much less important factor in appraisal of situations eliciting emotions for people in East Asian countries such as Japan, the People's Republic of China, and Hong Kong (Matsumoto et al., 1988; Mauro et al., 1992; Scherer, 1997a, b).

These culturally specific attitudes to agency and controllability substantially affect pleasantness and well-being of people in independent cultures. For example, such *emotion of agency* as *pride* is a strong predictor of the feeling of well-being among Americans. Different from this, in interdependent cultures, such as Japanese, *the feelings of relatedness* predict well-being of individuals better than emotions of agency (Kitayama, Markus, & Kurokawa, 2000, 2006; Mesquita & Karasawa, 2002).

People in individualistic independent cultures (e.g., West-Europeans and European Americans) perceive the world as *controllable* (Mesquita & Ellsworth, 2001; Morling, Kitayama, & Miyamoto, 2002; Weisz, Rothbaum, & Blackburn, 1984), whereas people in collectivistic interdependent cultures (e.g., Indians, Japanese, and Tahitians) do not have such an attitude (Miller, Bersoff, & Harwood, 1990; Savani, Morris, Naidu, Kumar, & Berlia, 2011). This *controllability–uncontrollability* dimension of cultural attitudes reflects on experience emotions. Let us consider examples of emotions associated with failure and success in achievement of goal.

Once the achievement of a goal is blocked, but this situation is interpreted as controllable, then it can be changed. The appraisal of Americans that things are within an individual's control causes their experience of frustration and anger (Frijda et al., 1989; Kuppens, Van Mechelen, Smits, & De Boeck, 2003; Stein, Trabasso, & Liwag, 1993). Thus, interpretation of events and situations through such cultural values cause differences in the intensity and frequency of anger and frustration, which are observed between European Americans and Indians (and Tahitians), and similarities between Indians and Tahitians.

The world, which is understood by people as *uncontrollable* and *unpredictable*, is less frustrating than the world, where individuals can reach anything possible. Studies (Levy, 1978; Roseman, Dhawan, Rettek, Naidu, & Thapa, 1995) are in support of this explanation. The Tahitian's common sense that individuals have limited control over nature and behavior of others determines the lack of anger in Tahitian culture (Levy, 1978, p. 226), which is different from American culture. Americans experience higher intensities of anger than Indians when they recall autobiographical events. In addition, the anger intensity is mediated by an appraisal of the events (Roseman et al., 1995).

These differences in the cultural attitudes toward *agency* also reflect on the corresponding emotions, motivations, and behaviors of *environmental control* prevalent in the cultures. European American and Western European cultures encourage the values of *influence* on physical and social environment and, therefore, they appreciate *high activation states*, which help individuals mobilize their energy on *influence*. The East Asian cultures encourage the values of *adjustment* to physical and social environment and, therefore, they appreciate *low activation states*, which help individuals pay attention to the important stimuli in physical and social environment (Tsai, Knutson, & Fung, 2006).

Cultural Tendencies in Attribution of Success and Failure and Experience of Emotions

European American individualistic culture encourages people to experience and express *pride* because this emotion demonstrates *high self-esteem* and *feeling of own accomplishment* (Mascolo, Fischer, & Li, 2003). *Chinese collectivistic culture*, however, discourages people to feel and express *pride* since personal accomplishments should be attributed to one's interpersonal relationships which gave support, rather than exclusively to the self. Instead, the Chinese culture encourages experiencing *shame*. This emotion promotes social cohesion and harmony.

In European American individualistic culture, for example, people often use *self-enhancing* and *self-protective attributions*. Different from this, in East Asian collectivistic cultures, people use these types of attribution substantially less frequently. For people in those cultures *self-criticism attribution* is more common than *self-enhancement* (see for review Imada & Ellsworth, 2011). Overall, people in individualist cultures of North America (such as European Americans and European Canadians) have strong motivation to enhance and maintain the positive self and positive emotions. Their culturally specific *self-serving appraisals* of events help to achieve such self-satisfaction. On the other side, people in collectivist cultures of East Asia (such as Japan and China) do not typically employ such *self-serving appraisals*. Instead they use modest, humble, and self-critical interpretations.

For instance, European Americans better remember occasions that increased their self-esteem, while Japanese better remember occasions that decreased their self-esteem (Kitayama, Markus, Matsumoto, & Norasakkunkit, 1997). European Americans tend to attribute success, yet do not attribute failure to their self, thus exhibiting pervasive *self-serving protective attribution*. However, Japanese tend to attribute not only success, but also failures to themselves (Heine & Lehman, 1997; Kitayama, Takagi, & Matsumoto, 1995; Markus & Kitayama, 1991). A Japanese individual usually evaluates himself or herself not better than Japanese people on an average. This tendency is exhibited even in the traits that are important in Japanese culture (e.g., cooperation and loyalty). Based on these two culturally different causal attributions (appraisals) of success and failure, people in individualist and collectivist cultures experience different emotions.

> If people attribute success to themselves, they experience emotions such as pride, satisfaction, superiority, and confidence (positive self-agency emotions), but if people believe that their success was due to other people, they experience quite different emotions such as gratitude, obligation, appreciation, and friendliness toward the people who helped them (positive other-agency emotions). If the success is seen as caused by impersonal circumstances, people feel lucky and happily surprised (positive situation-agency emotions). (Imada & Ellsworth, 2011, p. 330)

European Americans with their cultural tendency to be *self-enhancing* attribute success to themselves and therefore, tend to experience strong *positive self-agency emotions* (e.g., pride). *East Asians* with their cultural tendency to be *self-effacing* attribute success to external factors and therefore, tend to experience *positive other-agency* and *situation-agency emotions* (e.g., feeling lucky and grateful).

In support of this interpretation, in a cross-cultural experimental study of Americans and Japanese (Imada & Ellsworth, 2011) researchers asked participants to recall their personal experience and then imagine situations of success or failure and describe their agency appraisals and emotions. Results showed that different cultural attributions entail different emotions.

> In success situations, Americans reported stronger self-agency emotions (e.g., proud) than did Japanese, whereas Japanese reported a stronger situation-agency emotion (lucky). (Imada & Ellsworth, 2011, p. 329)

Thus, different self-enhancing motivation allowed explaining these cultural differences in attribution and experience of emotions. When the researchers induced the same type of attribution in Japanese and Americans, there were no significant cultural differences in emotions that they experience.

Cultural Dimensions of Society and Experience of Emotions

Gudykunst and Ting-Toomey (1988, p. 391) ran several analyses that allowed to conclude that Hofstede's theory can explain some of the cross-cultural variations in attitudes toward emotions and corresponding appraisals. The authors computed Spearman's rank order correlation between the seven cultures' rank order and the four dimensions of cultural variability, and then computed the percentage of respondents selected on the basis of the two most frequently cited emotions for each of the questions.

Few statistically significant correlations were found, many of those seems consistent with Hofstede's (1980/Hofstede, 1984) expectations. Uncertainty avoidance, as well as power distance showed negative correlation with dreading fear the most. The cultures with high power distance accept coercive power, yet it is not acceptable in the cultures with low power distance.

Researchers (Gudykunst & Ting-Toomey, 1988) also found that people in high masculinity cultures have the higher chance of experiencing distress the most, which can be nationally associated with their emphasis on decisiveness, achievement, and excelling. Feminine cultures, on another side, put more value on intuition, service, and not trying to do better than others, which is opposite to the values of masculine achievement culture.

Data indicated (Gudykunst & Ting-Toomey, 1988) that people in individualistic cultures tend to experience anger more. They also prefer variety of interests and pleasure over order and duty, while collectivistic cultures are opposite in this regard—they emphasize order and duty over variety and pleasure. These results are understandable because highly individualistic cultures expect individuals to be emotionally independent, while highly collectivistic cultures expect them to be emotionally dependent.

Gudykunst and Ting-Toomey (1988) also completed another interesting analysis of how cultural dimensions are associated with appraisal of emotions. They used the data from other study (Wallbott & Scherer, 1986b) and computed Spearman's rank order correlation of the percentage of respondents reporting the three most frequent antecedents of emotions with Hofstede's (1983) scores for the eight cultures (Great Britain, France, Belgium, West Germany, Italy, Spain, Switzerland, and Israel).

The authors found several significant relationships between Hofstede's (1983) dimensions of culture and the antecedents to specific emotions, which are consistent with Hofstede's theory. In particular, injustice and inequality are accepted as natural in the cultures of high power distance, while they are perceived as unacceptable in the cultures of lower power distance. Therefore, injustice as an antecedent to anger is more likely in the cultures of low power distance.

As for the novel situations being an antecedent to fear, they are more likely in the cultures of low uncertainty avoidance since in those societies they do not have formal rules for interaction. On another side, the cultures of high uncertainty avoidance have formal rules for interaction in novel situations, and then they do not fuel fear.

In addition, people in the cultures of high-power distance believe that there is an order of inequality in this world and everyone has his or her rightful place (Hofstede, 1980, p. 122). Therefore, novel situations should not threaten an individual and be an antecedent to fear because he or she is "protected" by the social order.

One more finding in that analysis (Gudykunst & Ting-Toomey, 1988) was that in the cultures of high masculinity, which value achievement and performance, novel situations are more likely to be an antecedent to fear because they can challenge individuals' capability to achieve these goals.

5.3   Norms and Experiences of Emotions Across Cultures

5.3.1   *Cultural Norms of Emotional Experience*

Types of Cultural Norms of Emotional Experience

There is a variety of cultural norms concerning regulation of emotional life. Cultures may prescribe their norms and suggest certain beliefs about how and when it is appropriate for people to feel some emotions (e.g, Hochschild, 1979; Mesquita & Frijda, 1992; Shweder, 1993; Soto et al., 2005). Such cultural norms of emotional experience represent *feeling rules* (Hochschild, 1979; Hochschild, 2003) and *cultural appropriateness of experiencing certain emotions* (Eid & Diener, 2001; Kuppens et al., 2006). These are common social conventions of what people should feel, should not feel, and would like to feel in certain social contexts. According to such rules, people are not supposed to experience, or at least, never express some feelings, while others are permissible, but only in particular contexts and according to culturally acceptable *expression rules.*

The cultural norms are the *focal, normative,* and *ideal representations of emotions* in the cultures (Mesquita & Leu, 2007). *Focal emotions* are those which are *admired* and *despised* in a culture (Mesquita & Ellsworth, 2001). They motivate behavior in a culturally desirable way. People seek out the *admired emotions* and avoid the *despised emotions.* Consequently, *admired emotions* occur frequently, while *despised emotions* occur rarely (Mesquita & Frijda, 1992; Mesquita & Leu, 2007). For instance, *happiness* is an example of admired focal emotion in *American culture.* Emotions of elevated happiness and excitement are the desired goals which individuals seek and cherish (D'Andrade, 1984). People feel better when they encounter positive events. They create and seek many occasions, such as awards, celebrations, and compliments, which bring them the state of happiness. They are more expressive communicating their happiness to others (see for review Mesquita & Leu, 2007).

The notion of cultural norms as desired emotions was proposed in the concept of *ideal affect* (how people want to feel). "Ideal affect is based on personal preferences, norms regarding emotional experience and feeling rules are based on consensual preferences. In other words, whereas people may agree about what is appropriate to feel or what they should feel, they may differ in the degree to which they endorse those states for themselves" (Tsai, 2007, p. 243). For example, Americans value the *positive affect of high arousal* (e.g., excitement) more than do Chinese (from Hong Kong). On the other side, Chinese value *positive affect of low arousal* (e.g., such as being calm) more than Americans do (Tsai, 2007; Tsai, Knutson, & Fung, 2006).

Cultural Value of Specific Emotions

Researchers have also found cross-cultural similarities in the value of experience for many emotions (e.g., Eid & Diener, 2001; Sommers, 1984b). These are those emotions, which are desirable in all cultures (e.g., joy, happiness, love) and those, which are dangerous and destructive in all cultures (e.g., rage, hate, anger, fear, worry). Generally, cross-cultural similarities exist in the value of experience for the emotions that are elicited from external and uncontrollable causes (e.g., anger, worry, joy) (Eid & Diener, 2001).

Cross-cultural differences are typically revealed in the value of emotions, which are elicited by internal and controllable causes, as in case of *self-conscious emotions* (e.g., pride, guilt) (Eid & Diener, 2001). In the same vein, *pride* can bear different cultural meanings and therefore, may differ in its specific value. For example, the Chinese, compared to Americans, consider *pride* of the achievements that are beneficial to others as more acceptable than *pride* of achievements that demonstrate personal accomplishments (Stipek, 1998). Here are some other specific accents in the cultural value of specific emotions. For people in the cultures of *West Indies* *pride* is an important emotion, for *Greeks*—the feeling of respect, for Americans— the experience of enthusiasm (Sommers, 1984b).

The results of the study cited here (Eid & Diener, 2001) showed that for people in independent cultures (the United States and Australia), *pride* was generally desirable and *guilt* mostly undesirable. The pattern desirability in two interdependent cultures (China and Taiwan) was somewhat similar, yet somewhat different. The pattern of norms for positive emotions in China considers *pride* and *contentment* as somewhat negative. The pattern of norms for positive emotions in Taiwan evaluates *contentment* as positive, but *pride* as neutral or negative. Many Chinese, and a smaller portion of Taiwanese viewed *guilt* as a positive or neutral emotion, while as I mentioned here, it is definitely evaluated as undesirable in independent cultures.

Similarly, the opposite norms of desirability of *pride* and *guilt* were found in the cultural contexts of African societies. A large study (Kim-Prieto & Eid, 2004) that was administered in Nigeria, Ghana, Tanzania, Zimbabwe, and South Africa, revealed that people in *more collectivistic African countries* view *pride* as *less desirable*, while guilt as *more desirable*, compared to those *African countries*, which are less collectivistic.

In a large study, cited here (Eid & Diener, 2001), it was found that across many cultural samples the high desirability of *anger* is associated with the low desirability of *guilt*. People in the cultural groups, who view anger as desirable, always view guilt as undesirable, and vice versa in cultural groups, which view anger as undesirable, guilt is viewed as desirable.

Norms of Emotions in Independent and Interdependent Models of Culture

Cultural differences between *individualistic* and *collectivistic cultures* and corresponding *independent* and the *interdependent self-construals* of people, which I reviewed in detail in the earlier section of this book, can predict variations in the cultural norms of experiencing emotions. Lee, Aaker, and Gardner (2000) found that people with these two *self-construals* prefer different regulatory focus: *approach* versus *avoidance*. Those with *independent self-construals* tend to focus more on how to *approach* their own wishes and aspirations. They pay more attentions on positive, rather than negative information about themselves. Those with *interdependent self-construals* tend to focus more on how to avoid and prevent their violation of social norms. They pay more attention on negative, rather than positive information about themselves.

A comprehensive study (Eid & Diener, 2001) compared the norms for experiencing emotions within and between countries among 1846 participants in collectivistic countries (China and Taiwan) and in individualistic countries (the United States and Australia). Researchers admitted that the *self-construals* and *regulatory focuses* might be associated with *cultural norms of emotional experience*, in particular, reflecting on differences in the experience of *self-conscious* or *self-reflective* emotions across cultures. As expected, the most differences between collectivistic and individualistic cultures were found in the norms for experience of *self-conscious and self-reflective emotions* (e.g., guilt and pride). Authors found that the *self-conscious emotions* elicited from a *success achieved by an individual's own efforts* (e.g., pride) have high value for people with *independent self-construals* and *promotion focus* (in *individualistic societies*). On the other side, the *self-conscious emotions* elicited from *violation of social norms* or from *failing to satisfy social obligations* (e.g., guilt) have high value for people with *interdependent self-construals* and *prevention focus* (in *collectivistic societies*) (Eid & Diener, 2001).

It should be noted that overall *collectivistic societies* revealed *greater diversity of emotional norms* than *individualistic ones*. The data showed (Eid & Diener, 2001) that such cultural norms in individualistic countries did not have much variation—particularly with regard to pleasant emotions—while in collectivistic countries researchers found substantial intranational variability.

Looseness-Tightness of Cultural Norms of Emotions

The concept of *tightness* (versus *looseness*) defines "the strength of social norms and the degree how a society sanction within societies" (Gelfand, Nishii, & Raver, 2006, p. 1225). The cultural dimension of *tightness–looseness* is a factor that can explain how societal culture is favorable or unfavorable to the experience of specific emotions and how strict the society regulates this aspect of people's behavior. Societies differ in the way how *tight* or *loose* they are in establishing and observing cultural norms of emotional experience (Gelfand et al., 2006; Pelto, 1968; Triandis, 1989; Triandis & Suh, 2002).

Tight cultures are quite homogeneous and authoritarian in their attitudes to norms. They impose the rigid norms and strict sanctions for deviation from those. Therefore, individuals in these societies experience a high pressure to follow these norms (Eid & Diener, 2001). *Loose cultures* are more heterogeneous and variable in their norms. They establish flexible norms and tolerate deviations from those. Therefore, individuals in such societies are relatively free to follow these norms.

For instance, the United States of America and Australia are fairly tight cultures regarding the norms for positive emotions. Individuals in these societies may experience the psychological pressure to feel joy, happy, pride, and love. These cultures seem to prescribe desirability of happiness. They even have their constitutional right to the pursuit of happiness. These are implicit cultural norms. Deviations from those norms impact personal life since unhappiness is considered as a failure. It is worth noting that even though these two societies are *loose* in their norms for *social behavior*, yet they are *tight* in the *domain of emotions* (Eid & Diener, 2001).

China and Taiwan are two *collectivistic*, but *relatively loose* cultures (Triandis, 1989). They seem loose in the domain of cultural norms for experience of positive emotions. Norms and attitudes toward emotions vary. Some people believe that positive emotions are undesirable; therefore, being unhappy is acceptable. Many people in these two societies view the feeling of *pride* as undesirable, yet many others consider emotion of *pride* as acceptable (Eid & Diener, 2001). Besides, individuals in the societies may have in mind the different meanings regarding the concept: *pride* as an achievement, which demonstrates a personal success, or as an achievement which benefits others (Stipek, 1998). Thus, the norms for experience of *positive emotions* are not very *tight* and do not imply that each individual has to follow them. Concerning the norms of *negative emotions*, all four societies (the United States, Australia, China, and Taiwan) are relatively heterogeneous and have loose norms for experience of *unpleasant emotions*, yet China is the most heterogeneous.

Cultural Norms and Experience of Emotions

The cultural patterns of emotional experience and frequency of individual emotions are substantially determined by the cultural norms that include the *focal, normative*, and *ideal representations of emotions* in the cultures. Intercultural analysis (Kuppens et al., 2006) has revealed that the average level of *experience of interpersonal emotions* (gratitude, shame, guilt, jealousy) differ across countries and highly correlates with cultural *norms of interpersonal emotions*. According to these data, people in different countries differ in frequency of their recall experiencing *interpersonal emotions*. People in *collectivistic cultures* experience *interpersonal emotions* more frequently compared to *individualistic cultures*. The finding may indicate that *interpersonal experiences* and *behaviors*, rather than *internal experiences*, are the sources of *emotions* in the societies with collectivistic values.

Authors (Kuppens et al., 2006) also suggest that the *cultural appropriateness* of specific emotions in a culture may influence how respondents recall the frequency of their experience of those emotions. *Cultural norms* may cause a person's expectation to experience (or not experience) those emotions, and in turn, determine the *appraisal process* eliciting emotion. Besides, these norms of emotional experience may implicitly encourage people to encounter certain situations, which prompt them to experience *culturally appropriate emotions* and to avoid other situations, which evoke *culturally inappropriate emotions*.

The data in support that emotional experiences are affected—to some extent—by cultural norms of emotions also came from another study (Eid & Diener, 2001) administered in United States of America and Australia (individualistic cultures) and China and Taiwan (collectivistic cultures). Researchers found the correlations of low and medium size between cultural norms of positive emotions in those countries and the frequency and intensity of emotional experience. The correlations were lower and less strong between cultural norms of negative emotions and emotional experience.

Cultural norms in Japan endorse socially engaging emotions, such as friendly feelings and guilt, whereas cultural norms in the United States of America encourage socially disengaging emotions, such as pride and anger. Results of the study (Kitayama, Mesquita, & Karasawa, 2006) showed that across various social situations, Japanese experienced engaging emotions more frequently and with higher intensity, compared with disengaging emotions. Opposite from this tendency, Americans experienced disengaging emotions more frequently and with higher intensity, compared with engaging emotions.

Studies showed (Kitayama et al., 2000; Kitayama, Mesquita, & Karasawa, 2006) that the *cultural norms* of the societies with the values of *interpersonal engagement of the self* (versus *disengagement*) and *interdependence* (versus *independent*) have impact on personal experience of positive emotions. According to their *cultural norms of interpersonal engagement of the self* and *interdependence*, the Japanese more frequently experience such positive emotions, as calm and elated, in association with their experience of such socially engaged positive emotions, as friendly feelings. Different from this, Americans, according to their *cultural norms of interpersonal disengagement of the self* and *independence*, more frequently experience these positive emotions in association with their experience of socially disengaged positive emotions, such as pride.

5.3.2   Experience of Basic Emotions, Their Dimensionality, Quality, and Frequency Across Cultures

Experience of Basic Emotions and Their Dimensionality

The data about emotional experience across cultures have been obtained in online self-report measurement of emotions, experience sampling, and retrospective reports. Research findings have demonstrated that emotional experiences have both cross-cultural similarities and differences. Many studies found many similarities in basic dimensions, basic emotions, and structure of emotional experience (e.g., Fontaine et al., 2002; Mesquita et al., 1997; Mesquita & Frijda, 1992; Osgood, May, & Mirron, 1975; Shaver et al., 1992)—see more details below in this chapter.

The data from many cultural samples have shown that the structure of emotional experience is substantially similar (see for review Kuppens et al., 2006). Similarities were identified first of all in some basic components and processes. Such dimensions of emotional experience as pleasantness–unpleasantness (positive affect vs. negative affect), arousal–sleepiness, or intensity, and potency appeared to be universal (Kuppens et al., 2006; Osgood et al., 1975; Russell & Feldman Barrett, 1999). The studies of these emotional dimensions in cross-cultural perspectives will be reviewed in the following sections.

Studies have found several aspects of similarity in self-reported subjective experience of basic emotions between Chinese Americans and European Americans (Lee & Levenson, 1992; Tsai, Levenson, & McCoy, 2006), between Japanese and European Americans (Lazarus, Tomita, Opton Jr., & Kodoma, 1966), between European Americans and Hmong Americans (Tsai et al., 2002).

In a wider international comparison, researchers administered surveys in several European countries (Scherer et al., 1986) and 27 countries on five continents (Wallbott & Scherer, 1986a, 1988). Across cultures, respondents reported rather universal experiences of such emotions as *joy, sadness, fear*, and *anger*. Intensity and duration of the emotional experience, self-perceived physiological symptoms, nonverbal and verbal reactions, and self-perceived capability to control emotions were quite similar.

A later study (Scherer & Wallbott, 1994), based on a large cross-cultural sample of 37 countries, investigated subjective experience and physiological symptoms associated with seven basic emotions—*joy, sadness, fear, anger, shame, guilt*, and *disgust*. Authors found the distinctive differences in the patterns of the experiences and symptoms associated with these emotions. The patterns of subjective emotional experience were stable across cultures with a substantial cross-cultural overlap. *Valence, intensity*, and *social engagement* are the *dimensions* of emotional experience that are cross-culturally similar in *basic emotions*.

Quality and Frequency of Emotional Experience

Many studies have revealed the differences in the mean level and frequency of experiencing certain emotions across cultures (Basabe et al., 2002; Kuppens et al., 2006; Matsumoto et al., 1988; Scherer et al., 1988; Scherer & Wallbott, 1994; Scollon, Diener, Oishi, & Biswas-Diener, 2004; Scollon, Diener, Oishi, & Biswas-Diener, 2005).

There are several factors that can affect the quality and intensity of emotional experience. Among those are individual differences in temperament and personality of people within a society (or between countries), cultural differences in beliefs and norms, as well as social and economic situations and events, which people encounter in their life and which bring positive and negative emotions. The study of *emotional experience* (Kuppens et al., 2006) based on recalled frequencies showed that such experience is predicted by *universal person-level factors* to a greater extent, while by *intercultural nation-level factors* to a smaller extent.

Authors (Basabe et al., 2002) reviewed six studies administered with a large sample of cultures in each of those (26, 27, 26, 33, 42, and 29 countries) and investigated self-ratings of two variables of emotional experience: (1) balance of pleasantness–unpleasantness and (2) intensity of emotions, comparing the national mean scores. Authors found that the average balance and relative frequency of positive and negative emotions differ across countries, and these differences are predicted by cultural and societal dimensions (individualism collectivism, masculinity–femininity, etc.).

Cultural Styles of Emotional Experience

Cultural models of emotions can be understood as the culturally *representative emotional styles*, which include the *typical* and the *most salient* ways to experience emotions. A *characteristic* and *distinctive pattern of emotional experience* describes the *emotional style*.

As I noted earlier, anthropologist Middleton (1989) proposed the concept of *emotional style* to define indigenous classification of emotions, their normative organization and ordering, relations with each other and with other cultural phenomena of a society. The concept of *emotional style* also includes the forms, intensities, and contexts of expression of emotions. Middleton, however, did not go further—beyond conceptual definition of emotional style, and did not explore *cultural emotional styles* empirically in cross-cultural perspective.

Various criteria can be set for *construction of emotional style*: the quality, valence, intensity, and frequency of emotions, as well as their expression. The simple examples of *emotional style* might be *passionate* and *dispassionate*, *positive* and *negative*, *expressive* and *suppressive*. Complexity of these styles depends on the number of parameters that are included in the construction of the model of emotional style.

5.4 Cultural Models of Basic and Complex Emotions

5.4.1 Cultural Models of Anger

Anger as Cross-Culturally Universal, Yet Culturally Different Emotion

Generally and universally in human societies, *anger* is an emotion, which arises when an individual is frustrated, harmed, or threatened. Yet, not the frustration itself makes a person angry, but rather the belief that the frustration, harm, or threat is unjustified. "The expression of anger is meant to redress this situation, to bring respect." (Myers, 1988, p. 594).

This meaning of anger seems universal. However, when people in different societies tell that they are "angry," they may talk about different feelings. Cultures may have their specific *social meanings of anger* and therefore have different cultural attitudes toward experience and expression of this emotion.

Anger in the Utku Eskimos Culture

Anthropological studies revealed, for example, that among *Utku Eskimos*—a tribe of Inuit in Northern Canada—norms of behavior disapprove the *expression of anger* (Briggs, 1970). According to their cultural beliefs, people with angry thoughts and behaviors are dangerous and frightening because they likely lose their self-control.

A *major moral principle* of the Utku Eskimo is *control of emotions*. The rules of *emotional self-control* and *expression*, however, differ when they are applied to children of early age (up to six years) and older children and adults. Parents allowed young children to shout, scream, weep uncontrollably, and throw tantrums. However, older children and adults are supposed to be under control of mind and reason (Briggs, 1970, pp. 111–112).

Expressions of anger are absent or rare among the Utku adults. Once a person shows up their anger, the other Eskimos disapprove this expression. These situations are so shameful and feared that the person is eager to avoid those. Due to such social sanctioning, people in the *Utku culture* have a little opportunity to elicit emotions of *anger* and have an amazing ability to control their anger.

The Utku people overall tend to be less expressive in other emotions as well. They believe that even *positive* emotions should not be expressed intensely. *Expression of personal happiness* is valued when it is timid. *Affection* and *protectiveness* toward others can interfere with the *value of personal independence*. Their expressions of *love* and *sadness* are scarcely perceptible. Husbands and wives, parents and their older children rarely show the loving gestures such as holding hands, embraces, and kisses. When loved ones separate and reunite, a gentle handshake is the only emotional expression. Tears are considered inappropriate.

Anger in the Kaluli Culture

The cultural spirit and beliefs of Kaluli (the culture in Papua New Guinea, the southwestern Pacific) is different from Utku Eskimos. People are encouraged to show their anger. Their cultural ideology emphasizes assertive energy, exuberant vigor, productive vitality, and personal dynamism. These attitudes are considered primarily as Kaluli male style; however, Kaluli females can also be assertive, yet in lesser degree. Due to this *value of assertion, anger* is important for men because it is the extreme expression of assertiveness. A *tendency to get angry* shows their character. Anger is an emotion both admired and feared among *Kaluli people* (Schieffelin, 1983).

> A man whose expectations have been frustrated or who has suffered wrong or injury at the hands of others does not usually suppress his annoyance. Rather he is likely to orchestrate his anger into a splendid frightening rage, projecting himself with threats and recriminations against his (often equally angry) opponent in a volatile exercise of social brinksmanship that occasionally leads to violence. (Schieffelin, 1983, p.183).

One can see that a *Kaluli* man's *expression of anger* conveys a message of his suffering and frustration. Implicitly, it is a form of appeal for others' support. The *expression of anger*, besides being intimidating to others, is in accord with their *assertive cultural spirit*.

Anger in the Samoan Culture

Similar in some way, but different in terms of meaning is the cultural interpretation of anger in Samoan culture. Gerber (1975) in the study of Samoan emotions describes *anger* as an emotion, which is morally justified in some relationship contexts. It is appropriate for Samoan men since it is an integral part of their identity as a dominant male in Samoan society. Wife and children may not like the *display of anger* by husband, yet they recognize that such expression is culturally appropriate. Anger being properly expressed is a part of Samoan male emotional style. Moreover, wife and children may feel alienated and unloved if man does not express anger occasionally (Gerber, 1975).

Anger in the Pintupi Culture

Another example is *the meaning* and *expression of anger* in *Pintupi*—the culture of Australian aborigines that I briefly discussed in earlier section. In *Pintupi* social life, the emotions of *anger* and *compassion* are dialectically related to each other. Cultural beliefs emphasize the values of *shared identity with others* and *compassion*. Yet, despite this emphasis, *anger* is not bad emotion in itself. Anger is considered acceptable and appropriate, while fight and violence is not a problem in a moderate extent (Myers, 1988).

It is important to note that violence among *Pintupi* does not pursue domination or control of others. A person's *anger* is understood as a reaction to a *rejection of relatedness*. People tend to accept *anger* and fighting as an expression of assertiveness and autonomy.

The question of special cultural interpretation is how sympathy, compassion (as relatedness) and anger, violence (as differentiation) are integrated in Pintupi culture (Myers, 1988). It looks like people evaluate any individual action in terms of the *shared identity*. Therefore, the emotions of being *compassionate* and *angry* both represent two aspects of the same Pintupi cultural value—*autonomy*. They are not primitive and isolated emotions, but rather emotions internally related to each other.

> Compassion, an expression of relatedness or identity with others, reflects Pintupi judge-ments that autonomy (the capacity and respect for self-direction such that no one is pre-pared to be told by others what to do) depends on sustaining relationships with others.

> Conversely, anger—understood by Pintupi as a negation of compassion (one who is angry typically has no compassion for the object of one's anger)—derives from perceived rejec-tion of relatedness, asserting autonomy in the face of loss. (Myers, 1988, p.596)

Thus, the cultural beliefs of Pintupi culture acknowledge two pathways of *auton-omy*: (1) sustaining *relatedness* (kinship) and (2) *differentiation* (conflict). This duality is resolved in a sense of *belonging together* or *shared identity*.

Generally, Pintupi people become angry when "they are not given food by some-one they consider to be related, when a spouse (or lover) is 'stolen' by another or runs away, when they are refused a request, and more generally when they are not supported in their wishes for help" (Myers, 1988, p.597). They perceive these actions as the *rejection* of the other to respect their *shared identity* and *relationship*. They also understand the lack of reciprocation in actions as the rejection of their *relatedness*. All these culturally specific interpretations make people *angry* (Myers, 1988).

5.4.2   Cultural Models of Self-Conscious Emotions

Compassionate Models of Emotions

Psycholinguistic analysis of the words expressing *sympathy*, *compassion*, and *empathy* in English and Moroccan Arabic revealed their meanings related the cul-tural models of interaction in Anglo and Moroccan cultures (Elasri, 2018). The cul-tural differences between English notions and their Moroccan Arabic equivalents correspond to the degree of closeness between a person experiencing emotion and other individual.

In English, the word *compassion* is used in the contexts of any relations with other individual—close and distant. Thus, in Anglo culture, the model of interper-sonal interaction does not distinguish between *close others* and *others who a person does not know*. The Moroccan Arabic uses two different equivalents of the word *compassion* that refer to the feelings toward close other and distant other. Thus, the Moroccan model of social interaction distinguishes a person's compassionate feel-ings toward an individual who the person knows well and an individual the person does not know. Subsequently, in the Moroccan model, *compassion* in relation with "close" people tend to be described as warm, open, and with an overt expression of compassion, while in relations with "distant" people as a more reserved (Elasri, 2018).

Other example of *compassionate model* of emotions can be illustrated by describ-ing emotional life of *Pintupi*—the cultural group of aborigines of Western Desert in

Australia (Myers, 1986). Experience and expression of *compassion* is the natural aspects of their daily life. It is evident in acts of sharing of manual work, nurturance, and concern for the welfare of others. Everyone strives to avoid the appearance of egotism and self-assertiveness. According to Myers (1986, p. 18), "The most salient aspect of living in Pintupi communities is its affective basis, the reliance on emotional criteria rather than on rules as the framework of action." Prescribed emotional tone carefully mediates interpersonal relations of kinship. Inappropriate emotional displays and improper acts prompt the feelings of embarrassment or shame. Emotion of shame, which is involved in the *model of compassion*, coordinates the needs of relatedness and personal autonomy. A *cultural ideal* of Pintupi is expressed in *compassion for others*. Subsequently, the moral *principle of compassion* encourages specific nurturing behavior toward others. Children in *Pintupi culture* acquire in early years when and how to be compassionate and interpret the behavior of others.

Cultural Models of Shame and Guilt

One more example is the cultural models of *shame* and *guilt*. Generally, a person experiences shame and guilt when he or she did something "bad" or "wrong" in the eyes of others or in their own eyes. *Shame* is usually experienced when the person is negatively evaluated by *others* (real or imagined), and *guilt* is generally experienced when the person is negatively evaluated by *oneself* (e.g., Smith, Webster, Parrott, & Eyre, 2002). Thus, *shame* is experienced as the fear of exposing one's defective self to others, while *guilt* is experienced as the fear of not living up to one's own standards (Benedict, 1946; Kitayama, Markus, & Matsumoto, 1995).

The early cultural models of shame and guilt in anthropology highlighted cultural differences in the *experience of shame* and *guilt* between American and Japanese cultures (Benedict, 1946) describing US culture as a "guilt culture," whereas Japanese culture as a "shame culture". Since that time, empirical studies have demonstrated substantial cultural variations in the elicitors, values, and behavioral consequences of shame and guilt (see for review, Wong & Tsai, 2007). Recent studies were able to identify that these differences are associated with *independent concept of the self* (typical for the United States), and *interdependent concept of the self* (typical for Japan, Korea, and China). Wong and Tsai (2007) concluded that the cultural model of shame and guilt associated with *independent concept of the self* (present in the United States as individualistic country) clearly differentiates between these two emotions. On the other hand, the cultural model of shame and guilt associated with *interdependent concept of the self* (present in Far East cultures, listed earlier as collectivistic countries) do not distinguish these two emotions. People in those cultures perceive those emotions more similar to each other. As Wong and Tsai (2007) summarized, "shame and guilt may be less differentiated in collectivistic contexts because in these contexts people do not view themselves as separate from their relationships with others, their contexts, or their actions."

(p. 231). Thus, the cultural *models of shame* and *guilt* present an example of the models based on cultural ability to differentiate between two emotions.

Experience and *expression of shame* depend on a culturally specific appraisal of situation. *In independent Western cultures*, a person feels *shame* when an appraisal of situation is discrepant with their *preferred personal identity* socially presented (Mesquita & Leu, 2007). The emotion of *shame* is elicited by the appraisal that a situation, which happened, is incompatible with person's identity causing the feeling of discrepancy with person's typical or desired characteristics (Tracy & Robins, 2004). Therefore, in *independent cultural contexts*, experience and expression of shame imply a personal unchangeable failure and the desire to disappear from others' view that hurts *personal identity*. The expression of shame pursues the goal to withdraw from the situation of a potential social rejection, as well as to avoid an internal dissonance between *positive personal identity* and the *situation that contradicts* this identity. Shame in *Western cultures* focuses on internal flaws (Crystal, Parrott, Okazaki, & Watanabe, 2001).

In *interdependent East Asian cultures*, an individual experiences *shame* when an appraisal of situation is discrepant with *relationship goals* (Mesquita & Leu, 2007). The emotion of *shame* is elicited by the appraisal that a situation is in contradiction with importance to fulfill responsibilities to others (parents, family, and community). This situation can also bring dishonor on the people to which the individual belongs. Shame in this cultural context is focused generally on negative social and relationship outcomes (Crystal et al., 2001). Experience and expression of shame in *East Asian cultures* intend to remedy the damage done to others and aim to restore relationships. (Frijda et al., 1989; Mesquita & Karasawa, 2004). Therefore, shame should be socially declared and publicly expressed in apologies with a statement of intention to alter shameful behavior and identity (Mascolo et al., 2003). Such a public acknowledgment of shame is supposed to motivate self-improvement and reassure that a person belongs to the social group.

Norms for experiencing guilt also differs in the cultural contexts of African societies. A cross-cultural study (Kim-Prieto & Eid, 2004) conducted in Nigeria, Ghana, Tanzania, Zimbabwe, and South Africa showed that *guilt* is viewed as *more desirable*, whereas *pride* as *less desirable* in *more collectivistic African societies*, when compared with less collectivistic African countries. Thus, once again one can see the opposite attitudes to *guilt* and *pride* in the culturally different models of emotions.

The *cultures of guilt* and *shame* have received extensive attention in cultural studies of recent decades. Scholars have explored their culturally specific psychological mechanisms, cultural appraisals that trigger them, their experience and expression (e.g., Bierbrauer, 1992; Casimir & Schnegg, 2002; Fontaine et al., 2006; Ha, 1995; Tangney & Fischer, eds.; Wallbott & Scherer, 1995; Wong & Tsai, 2007). The multiple publications on the topic go far beyond the scope and capacity of this book.

5.4.3   Cultural Models of Happiness

Universal and Culturally Specific in Cultural Models of Happiness

Studies (see for review Diener, Oishi, & Ryan, 2013) have provided strong evidence that national social environments and conditions and individual circumstances have impact on happiness and well-being. A multilevel review of multiple studies has shown that some social and personal parameters, such as income, the meeting of psychosocial needs, extraversion, are strongly associated with subjective well-being and life satisfaction across many cultures. Availability of social support correlates with experience of positive feelings. The countries that both wealthy and meet psychosocial needs are the most happy, while the countries that are poor and do not meet psychosocial needs are the least happy. Overall, the components of subjective well-being, their relationships, and societal factors affecting those have universal and culturally specific aspects.

As for the global cultural regions, the *models of happiness* have been usually compared between Western (*European American*) *cultural model of independent-self* and Eastern (*East Asian*) *cultural model of interdependent-self.* Euro-Americans associate happiness with individually centered subjective well-being, personal accomplishments, and pursuit for positive feelings. East Asians associate happiness with socially oriented subjective well-being, fulfilment of social role obligations, and dialectical balance of positive and negative hedonic feelings (e.g., Diener et al., 2002; Lu & Gilmour, 2004; Kitayama et al., 2000; Suh, Diener, Oishi, & Triandis, 1998; Uchida, Kitayama, Mesquita, Reyes, & Morling, 2008; Uchida & Kitayama, 2009).

These and other aspects of these global cultural models of happiness are described in the following sections.

American Model of Happiness

American model considers *happiness* primarily as a *personal happiness* stemming from *personal achievement.* Happiness is largely and predominantly *positive hedonic experience.* Among factors reflecting American *individualistic culture,* which are highly related to *happiness,* are personal accomplishment (Emmons, 1986), achievement of independent goals (Oishi & Diener, 2001), personal control (Kitayama, Karasawa, Curhan, Ryff, & Markus, 2010), and individual self-esteem (Campbell, 1981; Diener & Diener, 1995). On the other hand, in American culture relational harmony and social support have a weak effect on happiness (Uchida et al., 2008). The recent study (Uchida & Kitayama, 2009) analyzed the descriptions of happiness spontaneously produced by American and Japanese participants with multidimensional scaling and found that *American model of happiness* has two salient characteristics: it is *personal* and *positive.* This is consistent with *European American cultural model of self* as *independent.*

The idea of happiness for Americans is deemed as ultimate personal accomplishment and self-esteem. Several studies (Kwan, Bond, & Singelis, 1997; Uchida, Norasakkunkit, & Kitayama, 2004) explored the role of self-esteem, relationship harmony, and emotional support as the contributing factors of life satisfaction and found that in the North American sample, self-esteem was the only predictor of life satisfaction.

Many Americans strive to achieve personal happiness more than do Asians. According to some studies (e.g., Diener et al., 2002; Diener, Diener, & Diener, 1995; Kitayama et al., 2000; Oishi, 2002), Americans report experience of positive emotions more frequently than do Japanese. The subjective well-being of people in individualist cultures is much higher than in collectivist cultures.

From a methodological point of view, however, Oishi (2002) suggested that these cross-cultural differences may not reflect the difference in actual emotional experience. These differences might be partially due to a motivated tendency of Americans to pay more attention, remember and report positive emotional experience.

East Asian Models of Happiness

Japanese model, as an example of East Asian cultural models, views *happiness* as stemming primarily from *realization of social harmony* and believes in a holistic conception of happiness, admitting the natural co-existence of both positive and negative affective states. Japanese model of happiness is more social than personal and it is conceived as ambivalent experience. Among factors reflecting Japanese *collectivistic culture*, which are highly related to *happiness*, are positive social engagement (Kitayama et al., 2000; Kitayama, Mesquita, & Karasawa, 2006), fulfilling relational obligations and adaptation to social norms (Suh et al., 1998), achievement of interpersonal goals (Oishi & Diener, 2001) and relational harmony (Kang, Shaver, Sue, Min, & Jing, 2003; Kwan et al., 1997), receiving emotional support (Uchida et al., 2008). On the other hand, in Japanese culture self-esteem has less correlation with happiness (Diener & Diener, 1995).

Other than personal happiness, East Asians are motivated to pursue interpersonal and communal well-being and happiness, (Morling et al., 2002; Uchida et al., 2004). Happiness of individuals in East Asian cultures depends on their positive social relationship with others more than on their personal achievements and pleasures. Personal happiness can even disturb social relationship. Lack of modesty and excessive expression of a personal success may cause jealousy and envy by others. Therefore, individuals prefer to pursue relationship harmony and *social well-being*, rather than *personal happiness*. Happiness is deemed as an *intersubjective state*, rather than *introsubjective state*, with accent on *compassion, sympathy*, and *support*. A state of *happiness* is contingent on awareness of social harmony (Kitayama & Markus, 2000).

The same recent study cited here (Uchida & Kitayama, 2009), which compared the descriptions of happiness by Japanese and American participants, found that

Japanese model of happiness has two salient characteristics: it is *social* and *ambivalent*. The people's *conception of happiness* is highly *relational* with focus on the ultimate significance of social relationship. This is consistent with *Japanese cultural model of self* as *interdependent*.

Researchers (Kwan et al., 1997; Uchida et al., 2004) investigated the relative contribution of self-esteem, emotional support, and relationship harmony to *life satisfaction*. They discovered (Kwan et al., 1997) that among participants in Hong Kong (Asian culture), *relationship harmony* and *self-esteem* were equally important predictors of life satisfaction. The studies also found (Uchida et al., 2004) that among participants in Japan and the Philippines (two Asian cultures) perceived *emotional support* from close others and *self-esteem* were equal contributors to experience of happiness.

The emotional ambivalence of happiness might be linked to the idea of *yin* and *yang* in ancient Confucian philosophy: everything exists in duality as a unity of inseparable, opposing, and complementing aspects of life. Happiness for East Asians is not absolute state of being; it is rather dynamic, relative, and contextual experience. For instance, when American and Chinese participants were asked to represent the dynamics and change of happiness in the life (Ji, Nisbett, & Su, 2001), Americans more likely chose linear graphs, while Chinese more likely chose a non-linear graphs. The latter represented temporary and fluctuating nature of happiness.

Confucianism, as well as Buddhism and Taoism are Eastern Asian cultural ideologies that highlight a *holistic world view* assuming that everything is related with everything. In particular, positive affective states are connected and might be intertwined with negative ones. Unlike European-American cultural view, in which positive and negative affective states appear to be contradictory, East Asian cultures recognize them as complementary.

5.4.4   Cultural Model of Honor

Honor as a Cultural Phenomenon

Honor is the feeling of one's worth and respected self-concept in one's own view and in the perception of others. Honor is centered on the maintenance of a good personal reputation as well as collective reputation (e.g., family reputation). The *personal honor* is the feeling, which depends on one's own internal sense of honor (i.e., a concern for honor), which motivate one to act in honorable ways in order to avoid dishonor. However, only social recognition of a person really validates the person's claims for honor. *Collective honor* is the feeling that is shared by a group of people. *Collective honor* refers to different reference groups: close friends, political party, and family (Pitt-Rivers, 1968; Rodriguez Mosquera, 2013; Rodriguez Mosquera, Manstead, & Fischer, 2002; Stewart, 1994).

In the cultures of honor, many emotional events are appraised in reference to honor depending on their social consequences. An individual's feelings of strength and power over others trigger their emotions associated with honor are important because they determine their social rights (Abu-Lughod, 1986; Cohen, 1996; Cohen & Nisbett, 1994, 1997; Cohen et al., 1996; Davis, 1977/2016; Peristiany, 1965). In honor-based cultures, the social status and relationships of the individuals are the priorities in emotional appraisals. People perceive social position as natural and substantially depending on the status (Abu-Lughod, 1986/Abu-Lughod, 2000), yet negotiation can be sometimes possible (Cohen et al., 1996).

The Cultures of Honor Across Societies

In early research, importance of *honor* as cultural phenomenon was usually attrib- uted to the frontier regions, rather than in institutionalized societies (Nisbett & Cohen, 1996; Sommers, 2009; Stewart, 1994) and collectivist cultures, rather than individualist cultures (Abu-Lughod, 2000; Jakubowska, 1989; Peristiany, 1965).

Various *honor* concerns are also present in such diverse countries as Macedonia, New Zealand, Spain, Brazil, United Kingdom, the United States, Israel, and Japan, regardless of being individualist or collectivist society. According to the study of Guerra, Giner-Sorolla, and Vasiljevic (2013), in each of these cultures, people acknowledged *integrity, family honor, feminine honor,* and *masculine honor* as dis- tinct aspects of *honor*.

According to this categorization, southern Europe (i.e., Turkey, Pakistan) and southern US states are considered as *honor* cultures. The role of honor is high in the norms, beliefs, and social practices in rural and urban areas of Mediterranean cul- tures (e.g, Spain, see for review Mosquera, Manstead, & Fischer, 2002). South-east Asian countries (e.g., South Korea) are viewed as *face* cultures. Northern European countries (e.g., Germany) and northern American states are described as dignity cultures (Anjum, Kessler, & Aziz, 2019).

As Rodriguez Mosquera et al. (2002) claimed, although nowadays honor is less valued in north European countries (e.g., Netherlands.), yet it has been and still present in certain degree. Such Dutch expressions as "He is too proud to accept this offer," "he felt honored that he was invited" reflect the existence of a notion of honor.

Cross-regional research in the United States explored the nature of masculine *honor* in these cultures among White, non-Hispanic Northern, and Southern males. The question of interest was how they use anger and aggression in response to insults (Cohen et al., 1996; Cohen & Nisbett, 1994, 1997; Leung & Cohen, 2011; Vandello, Cohen, & Ransom, 2008).

Results demonstrated that people in *honor cultures* are prepared to protect their reputation for toughness with violence. The Southern men endorse violence in response to insults or threats. They express a stronger belief that insults damaged their reputation of toughness (Cohen et al., 1996). Therefore, individuals from the culture that accentuates the *value of honor* likely experience physiological, emo- tional, and behavioral signs of *rage* even to a minor insult.

A Culture of Honor in the United States

As I mentioned in earlier sections, some implicit cultural norms of the culture of Southern states in the United States differs from the norms of the culture in Northern states in the attitude and *value of honor* (Cohen et al., 1996).

Even though, people in Southern states are less receptive to subtle hostilities and small offenses, yet they are especially sensitive and over-reactive to big offenses. They unconsciously prefer not to notice the minor offensive words, gestures, and actions of others to avoid frequent *experience of anger*. However, when the offenses and insults are intentional and public, these actions seriously threat the feeling of *honor.* The insults are perceived as honor violations. Once the offense is serious, Southerners feel necessary to defend their *honor.*

When a situation is really annoying, Southerners become really angry expressing their *anger* and *aggressive responses* intensely, with possible verbal and physical confrontation. After they have expressed their anger, Southerners tend to be less resentful (compared to Northerners) since the strength is being shown and score is evened (Cohen et al., 1999).

These cultural tendencies have historical origins and still widely present (Cohen et al., 1999). Nevertheless, variation in individual and typological personality differences leads to *individual experience of emotions* associated with honor among Southerners.

Different Meanings of Honor

The concept of honor may bear different meanings across cultures and languages. Let us consider the examples of Spanish and Dutch cultures. Results of a study (Rodriguez Mosquera et al., 2002) showed that the values of social and family interdependence (e.g., humility, respect for parents, and elderly) are more important in Spanish culture than in Dutch one. Different from this, values of achievement and self-direction (e.g., ambition, capability, independence) are more important in Dutch culture compared to Spanish one.

In further cross-cultural research (Rodriguez Mosquera and colleagues), the concept of *honor* was expanded into four types: (1) *family honor*, the value of protection of the honor of one's family; (2) *integrity honor*, the value of reputation of an individual for honesty and fair dealings; (3) *masculine honor*, the value of "manly" reputation for endorsing assertive maleness (e.g., supporting a family, having sexual experiences); (4) *feminine honor*, the value of the obligation of a woman in light of her traditional gender role (e.g., maintaining chastity and sexual modesty (Rodriguez Mosquera, Tan, & Saleem, 2014).

Other theorists proposed *honor*, *face*, and *dignity* as three cultural categories (Leung & Cohen, 2011), depending on relative importance of the norms of honesty, trustworthiness, reciprocity, and punishment in a culture. In *honor* cultures, these norms are mainly external, internalized and lead to a loss of *honor* in the face of an insult. In *face* cultures, they are predominantly external and include hierarchy-based evaluations. Trustworthy people are highly concerned about saving their face. In *dignity* cultures, evaluation of the self is internal and everyone is treated as an equal.

People in the *honor cultures* favor the experience and expression of *anger* and *shame* for the purpose of defense. For instance, the emotions of *anger* and *shame* are afforded in Turkey because they are beneficial for the Turkish *culturally norma- tive understanding of honor*. In Japan, the emotion of *shame* is afforded, but *anger* is not, because these experiences and expressions of emotions are beneficial for the Japanese cultural norms of *keeping face* (Boiger, Gungor, Karasawa, & Mesquita, 2014).

5.5   Cultural Models Based on the Valence of Emotional Experience

5.5.1   The Value of Positive Versus Negative Affective States

The Concept of Emotional Valence in Cross-Cultural Research

From the early research, the dimension of *valence* distinguishing between positive and negative emotions consistently appears in cross-cultural studies (e.g., Diener & Emmons, 1985; Russell, 1980; Russell et al., 1989; Russell & Carroll, 1999; Van Hemert, Poortinga, & van de Vijver, 2007).

A large and comprehensive cross-cultural study (Kuppens et al., 2006) of emo- tional experiences of 9300 respondents from 48 nations has demonstrated that the groups of positive and negative emotions appear to be cross-culturally similar. Other study (Scollon et al., 2005) also brought the similar findings.

Another fact supporting the importance of distinction between positive and nega- tive groups of emotions in cross-cultural research comes from a study by Van Hemert et al. (2007). Sociopolitical and psychological variables aggregated across countries show the opposite patterns (with opposite sign) of correlations with self- reported experience of positive and negative emotions. Thus, the contrast between positive and negative emotions is relevant to cross-cultural research and reflects the opposite meanings of the two groups of emotions (Diener & Emmons, 1985; Van Hemert et al., 2007).

Positive and negative dimensions of emotional experience have been also reli- ably identified in many studies of affect and mood (Watson et al., 1988; Watson & Tellegen, 1985). In cross-cultural aspect, the distinction between positive affect and negative affect were confirmed by the studies conducted with cultural samples in China (Huang, Yang, & Li, 2003), Spain (Joiner Jr., Sandin, Chorot, Lostao, & Marquina, 1997), Mexico (Rodriguez & Church, 2003), and Italy (Terraciano, McCrae, & Costa Jr., 2003).

Cultural Norms and Experience of Positive and Negative Emotions

Cultural norms substantially influence how people experience emotions in different societies and in different relationship context. How individuals believe they want to experience emotion determines how they experience it. Cultural differences in social norms of appropriateness to feel certain emotions and people's actual emotional experience are interrelated (Eid & Diener, 2001). *Cultural norms of emotional experience* can regulate people's emotions. For instance, concerning the positive emotions:

> people who value positive emotions might be more alert to positive events, might seek situations that provoke positive emotions, might appraise positive events in a more positive way, might stay in positive situations longer, and might try to maintain their positive feelings or even enhance them. However, people who think that positive feelings are inappropriate are likely to avoid situations that cause positive feelings, might not be able to appraise positive situations in a positive way, might withdraw from positive situations much earlier, and might even try to dampen positive feelings (Eid & Diener, 2001, p. 870)

Studies (Eid & Diener, 2001; Kuppens et al., 2006) have shown that national differences in average level of *positive affect* are related to the *cultural appropriateness of experiencing positive emotions*. The same regulatory mechanism may be at work, when the *cultural appropriateness of experiencing negative emotions* can determine the experience of *negative affect*:

> people who think that negative emotions (e.g., anger) are appropriate might seek anger-provoking situations when they assume that these situations would be helpful (e.g., for clarifying conflicts, for asserting their goals). These people might be more prone to appraise situations with respect to the situation's potential for hindering their goal, they might not withdraw from anger situations, and they might try to maintain their anger as long as they think this would be necessary for asserting their goals. However, people who believe that the experience of anger is inappropriate might avoid anger-provoking situations. They might not focus on components of a situation that hinder a personal goal when appraising a situation, and they might try to withdraw from an anger situation early and try to suppress or dampen their anger reaction. (Eid & Diener, 2001, p. 870)

The differences in cultural values about ideal emotional experience do not always match the emotions that people actually experience. Real experience of emotions - how people actually feel (*actual affect*) may differ from cultural norms of desired emotions - how people want to feel (*ideal affect*). According to the studies (Tsai, 2007; Tsai, Knutson, & Fung, 2006), these differences might be because of cultural differences in *ideal affect* between cultures and also due to individual differences between persons. Personality traits and temperament of individuals greatly determine how they experience emotions (Tsai, Knutson, & Fung, 2006), and there might be a substantial variability of these individual differences within a culture, which are challenging at an average country/culture level.

The Value of Emotional Experience in Independent and Interdependent Models of Culture

Differences in emotional experience between *Western* and *East Asian cultures*, which are related to *independent* versus *interdependent models of self* are also in the value that they placed on experiencing positive (vs. negative) affective states, and on high versus low arousal positive states (Tsai & Clobert, 2019). According to the distinction between independent and interdependent models of self, Western people tend to maximize positive and minimizing negative emotion more than East Asian people.

Generally, positive emotions make people feel that they are better than others, that they are special. Frequently these emotions elicit envy from others and make people less sensitive to others' needs. On the other hand, negative emotions make people feel bad about themselves. These emotions often do not elicit envy from others and can make people more sensitive to other people's pain.

Stemming from independent model of self, Westerners want to differentiate their self from others in positive ways: stand out, be unique, and demonstrate how special they are. Easterners, with their interdependent model of self, want to fit in with others, adjust to others, conform to the group, and demonstrate how similar they are to others.

Although many people wish to feel positively more than negatively, yet the magnitude of this difference varies by culture. People in all cultures want to experience positive affective states more than negative one, yet due to cultural difference, this tendency is less pronounced in East Asian cultures—they value a balance of positive to negative emotions.

5.5.2   Experience of Positive and Negative Emotions Across Cultures

European American Model of Experience of Positive and Negative Emotions

European Americans perceive positive and negative emotional experience as bipolar opposites (Bagozzi, Wong, & Yi, 1999). They tend to maximize the positive and minimize negative emotional states, prefer to feel high versus low arousal positive states, and they openly express emotions that result in beneficial outcomes. Experience of positive emotions is relatively more prevalent among North Americans than among Asians. In particular, European Americans experience positive (pleasant) emotions more intensely and frequently, while they experience negative (unpleasant) emotions less intensely and less frequently (Mesquita & Karasawa, 2002; Oishi, 2002; Scollon et al., 2004; Tsai & Levenson, 1997).

European Americans also remember and describe their past emotional experience in a situation more positively, compared to Asian Americans, than they actually felt at the time of that task (Oishi, 2002). However, other studies did not replicate this positive memory bias of European Americans (Scollon et al., 2004).

East Asian Model of Experience of Positive and Negative Emotions

For East Asians, positive and negative emotions often co-occur in their subjective experience. They experience these emotions in a simultaneous way (Bagozzi et al., 1999). Although a mixture of emotions may occasionally happen in the life of European Americans, yet studies found that such emotional ambivalence prevail among people in East Asian societies more than in Western ones (Bagozzi et al., 1999; Schimmack, Oishi, & Diener, 2002; Scollon et al., 2005).

East Asians (e.g., Chinese, Koreans, Japanese, Indians, and Asian Americans) appreciate and experience more than Westerners (e.g., European Americans, Hispanics in the United States) a balance of positive to negative affective states (Scollon et al., 2005; Sims et al., 2015). This can explain why East Asians tend to dampen their experiences of positive emotions compared with Westerners.

For example, when Japanese individuals recall positive events in their lives, they savor their happiness less and dampen their happiness more during those positive events (Miyamoto & Ma, 2011). When Chinese individuals are in dating relationships, they tend to experience emotional balance. In a study, during conversations about their relationship, Chinese Americans prefer to moderate and control their emotions, experiencing fewer periods and less variability in positive emotions, compared to European Americans (Tsai & Levenson, 1997).

As I discussed in earlier sections, people in an East Asian culture can naturally accept co-occurrence of positive and negative emotions, "mixed" emotions. For people in a Western culture, it is more challenging; therefore, they tend to avoid such experience. European Americans, for instance, feel less mixed emotions, compared to Chinese American and Hong Kong Chinese (Sims et al., 2015).

Further studies explored the details of such experience. In particular, researchers found that in many cultures people rarely feel pleasant and unpleasant emotions at the same time (Scollon et al., 2005) and dialectical mixture of positive and negative emotions usually occurs in positive situations (Leu et al., 2010). East Asian bicultural individuals living in Western countries can switch their mode of emotional experience. When they identify themselves with an Asian culture or communicate in an Asian language, they are more likely to experience a dialectical mixture of emotions. However, when they identify themselves with a Western culture or communicate in a non-Asian language, they tend to experience such dialectical emotions less (Perunovic, Heller, & Rafaeli, 2007).

East Asians are more comfortable than Westerners with mixed emotional experiences (Aaker, Drolet, & Griffin, 2008; Hong & Lee, 2010; Kim, Seo, Yu, & Neuendorf, 2014; Williams & Aaker, 2002), recognize the events of their life—even the positive ones—as more mixed with emotions than European Americans (Leu et al., 2010; Miyamoto, Uchida, & Ellsworth, 2010), and describe happiness as a more mixed emotion (Uchida & Kitayama, 2009).

Regulatory Styles for Positive and Negative Emotional Experience in Western and Eastern Cultures

Mesquita and Leu (2007) interpret these Eastern–Western differences in emotional experience by culturally specific regulatory styles in *independent* (Western) and *interdependent* (Eastern) cultures. When something bad has happened, individuals in both East Asian and Western cultures attempt to find the positive aspect of the event, thus feeling a positive emotion as well. On the other end, when something good has happened, only individuals in East Asian cultures make an effort to find the negative aspect of the event. This characterizes two cultural approaches to emotional regulation: European American style—with an emphasis on maximizing positive feelings and minimizing negative feelings, and East Asian style—with an emphasis on moderation of positive and negative emotions.

Findings at the country level (Grossmann, Huynh, & Ellsworth, 2016) supported a major role of *independent model of self* (prevalent in individualistic cultures) versus *interdependent model of self* (prevalent in collectivistic cultures) in shaping these cultural differences.

Interdependent Cultures and Their Models of Experience of Positive and Negative Emotions: Mexican Versus Japanese Comparison

Mexican interdependent culture seems very different from Japanese in terms of emotional experience. People in East Asian culture (e.g., Japanese) tend to moderate their positive emotions to fulfill their social roles and fit in relationships with others. People in Mexican culture do not use such emotion moderation. Positive emotions and emotional expressivity are encouraged and valued (Klein, 2001). Mexican cultural norms explicitly consider personal happiness and happy events as compatible with role fulfillment, interdependence in relationships, and social adjustment, while negative events are downplayed.

People in *Mexican interdependent collectivistic culture* tend to experience emotions substantially different than in *Japanese interdependent collectivistic culture* (Mesquita & Leu, 2007). *Philosophical dialectic tradition* of East Asian cultures, rather than East Asian *collectivism* contributes to the pattern of relation between pleasant emotions and unpleasant emotions when positive and negative emotions do not correlate to each other (Schimmack et al., 2002). Different from *Asian interdependent cultures* (such as Japanese and Indian), people in some *non-Asian interdependent cultures* (such as Mexican) experience high positive affective states, even higher than in *European American culture*. Three groups of measures (global self-reports, an experience-sampling for 1 week, and participants' recall of their emotions from the experience-sampling week) brought convergent evidence.

The measures showed cultural differences (Scollon et al., 2004). Hispanic students in California experienced considerably higher positive emotions than European American university students. Positive emotions of Asian students in the United States, as well as in Japan and India were lower. Besides, Hispanics, as well as European Americans experienced lower negative emotions compared to both Asian samples. Thus, one can see that Hispanics and Asians, both belonging to interdependent cultures, are substantially different in their experience of emotions.

Development of Cultural Values of Emotional Experience in Childhood

Some studies found that preferences in experience of positive and negative affective states develop quite early in childhood. According to parents' ratings of the temperamental trait "positive affectivity," infants in Western societies, such as the United States, Italy, Spain, and Finland, experience positive emotions with high-intensity pleasure, reactivity, and smiling/laughter. These studies also revealed that infants in Asian cultures, such as Japan, China, Russia, Poland, tend to experience more "negative affectivity," distress, and fear (Gaias et al., 2012; Gartstein et al., 2006; Gartstein, Slobodskaya, & Kinsht, 2003; Gartstein, Slobodskaya, Zylicz, Gosztyla, & Nakagawa, 2010; Slobodskaya, Gartstein, Nakagawa, & Putnam, 2013).

Among Western countries, the comparison of American infants with Spanish and Italian ones found some subtle differences. Nevertheless, the affective traits of Spanish and Italian children were overall more similar to American than to Chinese children. The older Spanish and Italian children revealed the higher tendency to smile and laugh. The American children, however, were more stable in "positive affectivity" (Gartstein et al., 2006; Montirosso, Cozzi, Putnam, Gartstein, & Borgatti, 2011). Cultural differences in parental practices can influence these differences in children's affectivity. European American parenting encourages early assertiveness and individuality in infants, whereas Italian parent–child interactions and close physical contact foster affiliation and connectedness (Bornstein et al., 2012; Bornstein, Tamis-LeMonda, Hahn, & Haynes, 2008).

Polish and Russian infants had affectivity profiles close to each other. This similarity might be due to their shared Slavic cultural background. Comparison of data in Russian, Polish, and American samples revealed higher "negative affectivity" and lower "positive affectivity" of Russian children compared to Americans, yet similarity between Polish and American children on both "positive affectivity" and "negative affectivity" traits (Gartstein et al., 2003; Gartstein et al., 2010; Gartstein, Knyazev, & Slobodskaya, 2005).

These societal differences in emotional expressivity might be interpreted as a result of cultural differences in parenting practices. Many studies, which were cited here, are in support of this.

An alternative temperamental explanation is also possible. These differences in emotional expressivity and reactivity appear quite early in childhood. Results of some studies suggested that Asian infants tend to experience lower arousal compared to Caucasian infants (Caudill & Weinstein, 1969; Freedman & Freedman,

1969; Kagan, Kearsley, & Zelazo, 1978; Lewis, 1989; Lewis, Ramsay, & Kawakami, 1993). In particular, Freedman and Freedman (1969) discovered that newborn Asian-Americans are less labile and less willing to take away a cloth placed on their face; they are calmer and easier to console when distressed compared with European-Americans. Caudill and Weinstein (1969) found that Japanese infants tend to be less easily aroused compared to European-American infants in the United States. Several researchers (Lewis, 1989; Lewis et al., 1993) revealed that during baby examinations Japanese infants are less reactive compared to European-American infants. They also less often display intense distress to an inoculation. Data showed (Kagan et al., 1978) that Chinese-American infants are less active, less vocal, and display fewer smiles in response to visual and auditory events compared to European-American infants. In the later study (Kagan et al., 1994) of 4-month-old infants from the United States (Boston), Ireland (Dublin), and China (Beijing) researchers demonstrated cross-cultural differences in level of reactivity to visual, auditory, and olfactory stimuli. The observations showed that Chinese infants are significantly less active, irritable, and vocal than American and Irish infants. The American infants revealed the highest level of reactivity.

Since these temperamental differences are observed in very young children, some authors suggested that genetic factors might also play their role in contributing to these cross-cultural differences (Kagan et al., 1994).

5.5.3 The Effect of Negative and Positive Emotional Experience on Physical and Mental Health

Effect of Negative Emotions on Health and Well-Being

It is worth noting that empirical findings showed that the cultural importance of positive versus negative experience determines how actual experiences of negative and positive emotions affect physical and mental health. Many studies have demonstrated that negative emotions are accompanied by multiple negative physiological and psychological outcomes (e.g., increased pain and fatigue, increased cardiovascular disease, increased risk of cancer, decreased life satisfaction, and faster mortality (see for detailed review, Tsai & Clobert, 2019). In the survey of more than 150,000 individuals from 142 countries about their emotions and health, researchers (Pressman, Gallagher, & Lopez, 2013) discovered that in industrialized, as well as in developing nations, people experiencing more negative affect have the worse health. These detrimental effects of negative affective states on negative physiological and psychological outcomes, however, vary across cultures in the magnitude (Consedine, Magai, Cohen, & Gillespie, 2002; Curhan et al., 2014; Diener & Suh, 2000; (Kuppens, Realo, & Diener, 2008; Miyamoto et al., 2013; Miyamoto & Ryff, 2011). Such cultural differences arose even when objective markers of physical health were used (see for review, Tsai & Clobert, 2019).

Effect of Positive Emotions on Health and Well-Being

As for the effect of positive emotions on health and life satisfaction, the findings were optimistic. The study of relations between emotions and life satisfaction in 46 countries, which was mentioned earlier (Kuppens et al., 2008), found that positive emotions had stronger predictive power for life satisfaction, compared to negative emotions, across countries.

Another study (Leu, Wang, & Koo, 2011) revealed that experience of positive emotions was less associated with depression symptoms among European Americans, as well as among Asian Americans born in the United States. However, the degree of this association of positive emotions with less depressive symptoms was bigger among European Americans than Asian-Americans. Nevertheless, different from this trend, experience of positive emotions was not associated with depressive symptoms among Asian immigrants to the United States.

5.6 Cultural Models Based on Intensity of Emotional Experience

5.6.1 Emotional Arousal Across Cultures

The Cultural Values of Low and High Emotional Arousal

Cultures differ in their *attitudes* to the experience of *low* and *high arousal*, in *emotions of low* and *high intensity*. The norms of Eastern (collectivist) cultures encourage experiencing the low arousal emotions more than the high arousal emotions. These culturally normative attitudes are related to the desirable psychological qualities in such cultures – conforming and adjusting to other people. The low arousal emotions work better to achieve this goal, compared to the high arousal emotions.

The norms of Western (individualist) cultures, on the other hand, suggest experiencing the high arousal emotions more than the low arousal emotions. The culturally normative attitudes of these cultures encourage people to influence others. The high arousal emotions are well suitable and effective to achieve these goals (Lim, 2016).

Culturally Different Experience of Low and High Emotional Arousal

These differences in the culturally encouraging norms of emotional arousal levels also appear in the actual arousal levels of emotional experience: people in Eastern cultures tend to experience prevalently the low arousal emotions in their everyday life, whereas the emotional experience of people in Western cultures engages more frequently the high arousal emotions (Lim, 2016).

The results of research demonstrated that people in different cultures vary in the level of emotional arousal of actual and ideal emotions (Lim, 2016). Several cross-cultural studies (see for review, Lim, 2016) showed that men and women in Eastern cultures experience the low arousal emotions more frequently than the high arousal emotions. Different from this, people in Western cultures experience the high arousal emotions more frequently than the low arousal emotions (Lim, 2016).

5.6.2 Models of Passionate and Dispassionate Life

The Importance of Emotions in People's Life

Cultural values of a society may consider emotions as the vital forces, or as the disruptive episodes in people's lives (Wierzbicka, 1999). Consequently, people perceive strong emotions either as a welcome or troublesome experience of living.

Cultural attitudes may favor passionate or dispassionate way of life. Solomon (1995) believes that Lord Byron was a cultural proponent of a *passionate ideal*, typical of Western mentality, while a Buddhist bodhisattva was an advocate of *dispassionate ideal* of living, typical of Eastern mentality. The Western ideals of passionate life encourage experience and expression of passion in various situations. Love and hatred can be and shall be strong. The Eastern ideals of dispassionate life consider experience and expression of passion undesirable. This cultural attitude still admits the life full of emotions of modest intensity.

As for the real experience of emotions, the studies (Roseman et al., 1995) showed that Indians generally report lower intensity of emotions than Americans do. Cultural differences in appraisal mediate these differences in emotional intensity.

Passionate Ideals

Western cultures suggest that a person has a right to experience and express emotion naturally, while Eastern cultures inspire to moderate emotion (Pennebaker & Graybeal, 2001). These differences are still gender specific. Within American and Chinese cultures, gender norms allow women to experience and express intense emotions naturally and openly, yet the norms suggest that men should moderate their emotions, using *disengagement* emotion-regulation strategies (Davis et al., 2012).

Dispassionate Ideals

Asians are less expressive and less assertive. They prefer to suppress expression of negative messages and confrontations (see for detailed review Lim, 2003, p. 64. Courtesy for them is more important than truthfulness (Gudykunst & Kim, 1984, p. 142).

Therefore, when they expect that a straight and factual answer might be embarrassing or unpleasant, they would rather give a pleasant and agreeable answer to a question (Hall & Whyte, 1960). In the Japanese, as well as in the Thai cultures, people tend to make efforts not to cause trouble for others and not to hurt their feelings (Lebra, 1976; Smurkupt & Barna, 1976; Suzuki, 1986).

According to cultural tradition, being emotional in Asian reflects a lack of self-control. Therefore, Asians tend to suppress expression of their emotions. They prefer to say *good*, rather than *fantastic* and *not very good*, rather than *terrible*. Even when they express strong personal affection, they prefer a style of indirectness and hesitancy. The direct verbal expressions of love and respect may give them impression of being suspicious and not genuine. An excessive compliment or verbal praise can make a partner feel embarrassed (Gudykunst & Kim, 1984, p. 142).

Value of Moderation and Control in Emotional Experience: The Case of China

Chinese culture illustrates the Eastern cultural beliefs that extreme emotions are disruptive and dangerous to social harmony and relationship; they also may trigger illness of an individual (Klineberg, 1938; Potter, 1988; Russell & Yik, 1996; Wu & Tseng, 1985; Zheng & Berry, 1991). According to ethnographic research, Chinese values consider emotions as less relevance and lower significance for social relationship and people's life, compared with American values (Potter, 1988). Cultural attitudes consider emotional experience as irrelevant, sometime dangerous for social relationship. Therefore, Chinese cultural norms place greater emphasis on emotional control and moderation than the mainstream European-American culture (Potter, 1988; Russell & Yik, 1996; Song, 1985; Wu & Tseng, 1985).

Chinese and Chinese Americans tend to experience *inhibition* and *restrain* in their experience and expression of emotions. According to the recent cross-cultural studies (e.g., Eid & Diener, 2001), Chinese participants reveal the lowest frequency and intensity of both positive and negative emotions, compared to Taiwanese, Australians, and European Americans. This effect is present even in the experience of emotions, which are viewed in Chinese culture as desirable (e.g., guilt). Probably, the cultural values of moderation and suppression of emotions, which are generally highly valued in China, have impact on real emotional experience. Cross-cultural differences in the experience of emotions across countries might be due to social norms, genetics, physiology of emotional responses, personality, or life circumstances in societies.

It should be noted, however, that the Chinese cultural group can vary substantially between China and America, as well as in the extent of acculturation among individuals within the United States (e.g., Chinese and Chinese Americans). They may endorse and adopt more or less the customs and practices of their culture of origins (Triandis, & Kashima, Y,, Shimada, E.,, & Villareal, M., 1986). Therefore, for example, "the Chinese Americans who are more acculturated to mainstream European American culture demonstrate less emotional moderation and control than Chinese Americans who are less acculturated to mainstream European

American culture" (Tsai & Levenson, 1997, p. 604). Experimental results, however, only partially support these cultural differences (Tsai & Levenson, 1997).

Diversity of Cultural Attitudes Toward Experience of Emotions in European Cultures

The Western cultural attitudes to the experience of emotions also vary. For example, Anglo academic psychology frequently conveys culture-specific attitudes to a state of emotion (quoted in Fehr & Russell, 1984) as a departure from a normal state of composure. From this view, the experience of very intense emotions is a state, which seriously impairs the ability to control behavior. Such implicit assumptions are in accord with the cultural values of an influential stream within Anglo-American culture. Even though similar attitudes may be present in other cultures as well, yet Wierzbicka (1999) argues that they are reflected in the English language. Therefore, I believe they can be a part of Anglo-American cultural model of emotions implicitly discouraging from intense emotional experience.

Different from this model, such assumptions and attitudes to emotion are less evident in mainstream German, Italian, or Russian culture. For instance, in the view of traditional Russian culture, the emotions of "joy," "delight," "sadness," "sorrow," and so on are deemed as people's natural states, while absence of "emotions" would be a deadening state of a person's heart and soul. In addition to this observation, Wierzbicka (1999) noted that Russian lexicon frequently conceptualizes emotions as active, rather than passive experience. Emotions are "inner activities in which one engages rather than states which one passively undergoes, and so they are often designated by verbs rather than adjectives" (p.18), e.g., *to rejoice*, rather than *to be joyful*, *to rage*, rather than *to be angry*. The notion of "composure" as a person's "normal state" is NOT the Russian cultural ideal. Therefore, I believe that the embracing of intense emotional experience is a part of Russian cultural model of emotions.

Of course, societies are heterogeneous and changing over time. People may vary in their attitudes to emotion—some may be more emotional than others. Nevertheless, in certain historical periods language reflects the prevailing *emotionology* of cultures (Wierzbicka, 1999). Lexicon and conceptual metaphors partially constitute cultural reality (Kövecses, 2005, p.189).

5.6.3   Passionate Western and Dispassionate Eastern Cultural Models of Emotions

Emotional Intensity in the Framework of Independent and Interdependent Models of the Self

As it was mentioned in the earlier sections, people commonly want to experience more positive over negative emotions, yet due to their cultural background they may prefer different types of positive emotions and the level of emotional arousal, which they ideally wish to feel. The *models of self*, for individuals with *independent* and *interdependent models of the self*, explain these dissimilarities (Tsai & Clobert, 2019).

Individuals with independent model of the self (like Americans) are culturally encouraged to influence others. Such actions require the increased physiological arousal. Consequently, people in these cultures favor high arousal positive states with energy, excitement, and enthusiasm as ideal.

On the other hand, individuals with interdependent model of self (e.g., Chinese or Japanese) are culturally encouraged to adjust to others. In order to adjust, they should learn what others want and change their own actions accordingly. This needs the decreased action accompanied by decreased physiological arousal. Consequently, the individuals in these cultures generally favor the experience of emotions of low frequency, intensity, and duration. According to cultural beliefs of moderation in emotions, they strive to experience even positive emotional states with peacefulness, calm, and serenity (Bond, 1993; Tamir et al., 2016; Tsai, Knutson, & Fung, 2006; Tsai, Miao, Seppala, Fung, & Yeung, 2007).

A series of studies have supported these interpretations (Tsai, Levenson, & McCoy, 2006; Tsai, Louie, & Uchida, 2007). European Americans want to feel enthusiasm, excitement, and other high arousal positive emotions as more ideal states than Hong Kong Chinese, whereas Hong Kong Chinese want to feel peacefulness, calm, and other low arousal positive emotions as more ideal states than European Americans. Chinese Americans with equal orientation to both European and Chinese cultures, value high-arousal positive states as much as their European American counterparts and value low-arousal positive states as much as their Hong Kong Chinese counterparts (Tsai, Levenson, & McCoy, 2006; Tsai, Louie, & Uchida, 2007). Again, studies confirm that these differences are due to cultural differences in the goals to influence or adjust. In survey and experimental studies across various cultures, people wanting to influence others tend to like high arousal positive states, and people wanting to adjust to others, tend to like low arousal positive states. Cultural differences in an *ideal affect* correspond with actual affective states, which individuals experience and what they actually feel (Tsai, Miao, & Seppala, 2007).

The differences in preferences of positive states of high or low arousal entail how people perceive others, what people feel good about, and how they regard illness and well-being. For example, European Americans depict more exciting and fewer calm activities compared to Hong Kong Chinese, when they think about their ideal vacations, and they are more likely to choose excited music than Asian Americans (Tsai, 2007; Tsai, Louie, & Uchida, 2007). In consumer behavior, European Americans tend to choose the excited (vs. calm) products more than Beijing Chinese, Hong Kong Chinese, and Chinese Americans (Tsai, Chim, & Sims, 2015).

Culturally Ideal Affect and Well-Being

As for implications of a *culturally ideal affect* for health and well-being, a study (Tsai, Knutson, & Fung, 2006) found that among Hong Kong Chinese, Chinese Americans, and European Americans, the greater discrepancies between how people ideally wish to feel and how they really feel are related to more depressive symptoms. However, these relations vary across cultures. Among European Americans, discrepancies in ideal and actual high arousal positive states predicted depressive symptoms, but discrepancies in ideal and actual low arousal positive states did not. Among Hong Kong Chinese, only discrepancies in ideal and actual low arousal positive states predict depression. Among Chinese Americans, equally oriented to both cultures, both types of discrepancies are associated with depression.

In the same vein, another study (Young, Sims, Charles, & Tsai, 2013) revealed that among European Americans, low arousal negative emotions like feeling sluggish, dull, as the opposite of high arousal positive emotions, are related to physical health problems, while among Chinese Americans, high arousal negative states like feeling afraid, nervous, and others, as the opposite of low arousal positive states are related to increased physical health problems.

The empirical data also show that the absence of high arousal positive emotions is frequently associated with depression. These relations are stronger among European Americans than among Hong Kong Chinese. However, the absence of low arousal positive emotions is linked with depression more among Hong Kong Chinese than among European Americans (Tsai & Clobert, 2019).

As all these results demonstrate, European American culture (with value of independent model of self) favors high arousal positive emotional states more and low arousal positive emotional states less than East Asian cultures (with value of interdependent model of self). The findings support the theory that *culturally ideal affect* can predict and explain what people feel good about, as well as their conceptions of well-being, depression, and their health outcomes.

5.6.4 Cultural Differences in Intensity of Emotional Experience

Individualism Versus Collectivism and Intensity of Emotions

Individualism and *collectivism* as cultural dimensions are associated with intensity of experience of emotions. As I commented in the earlier sections, people in *individualistic cultures* tend to focus their attention on *internal individual emotional experiences*, while people in *collectivistic cultures* focus attention on *external interactional aspects of their emotions*, thinking of how their actions affect others. These cultural differences can reflect on intensity of emotional experience. Studies suggest that individuals feel their emotions more intensely in *individualistic* rather than in *collectivistic cultures* (Basabe et al., 2000; Markus & Kitayama, 1991; Matsumoto, 1991; Scherer et al., 1988).

The results of some studies (e.g., Arrindell et al., 1997; Diener et al., 1995) showed that *individualism* as a cultural dimension was associated with high intensity of ego-focused emotions. Data from other studies (Basabe et al., 2000; Diener, Diener & Diener, 1995) also supported the findings that public acceptance, social desirability, and experience of high intensity of negative and positive emotions are a social norm in individualistic cultures.

Societal Power Distance and Intensity of Emotions

.   Data (Basabe et al., 2000) showed that people in the cultures of *high-power distance* experience the moderated emotions of lower intensity and lower variability. Results of several studies (see for review Basabe et al., 2000) have demonstrated that cultural norms of the cultures *high* in *power distance* appreciate the value of respect and submission, while depreciate the value of individual emotional experience. Multivariate analysis of data (Basabe et al., 2000) revealed that *high power distance* was one of the strongest predictors of *low emotion intensity*. In these cultures, both positive emotions (satisfaction, joy, and pride) and negative emotions (sadness, fear, and anger) are less socially desirable and less intense. In the societies high in inequalities, social norms of experiencing of lower intensity emotions are suitable and functional. High intensity of anger and other negative emotions in these cultures implies the lack of interpersonal respect and submission. Therefore, social norms socialize people in such a way that they minimize the occurrence of situations eliciting negative emotions and their antecedents. Or, they may not pay too much attention on their internal feelings, associated with such situations.

Cultural femininity was unrelated to intensity of emotional experience (Basabe et al., 2000).

Socio-Economic Parameters of Society and Intensity of Emotions

Socio-economic development also plays an important role in affecting the intensity of subjective experience of emotions (e.g., Arrindell et al., 1997; Basabe et al., 2000; Diener et al., 1995; Wallbott and Scherer (1988)). In particular, Wallbott and Scherer (1988) revealed that people in the countries with low income tend to experience emotions of higher intensity. Authors suggest that people in poor countries perceive social life as less controllable, and their emotional reactions to the difficult life events are more intense and longer-lasting.

Desirability of Emotions and Intensity of Their Experience

Desirability and *appropriateness* of certain *emotions* in societies can also determine the intensity of emotional experience. Socialization plays an important role in this case. If people know that certain emotions are desirable in a culture, they feel themselves free to experience these emotions intensely. Conversely, if they are aware that particular emotions are inappropriate or undesirable, they can learn to regulate the intensity of their experience downward. The *norms of desirability* and *actual emotional experiences* in terms of frequency and intensity correlate to each other higher for positive emotions than for negative emotions (Eid & Diener, 2001).

References

Aaker, J., Drolet, A., & Griffin, D. (2008). Recalling mixed emotions. *Journal of Consumer Research, 35*, 268–278.

Abu-Lughod, L. (2000). *Veiled sentiments: Honor and poetry in a Bedouin society*. Berkeley, CA: University of California Press. (Original work published 1986).

Agyekum, K. (2015). Akan metaphoric expressions based on yam 'stomach'. *Cognitive Linguistic Studies, 2*(1), 94–115.

Anjum, G., Kessler, T., & Aziz, M. (2019). Cross-cultural exploration of honor: Perception of honor in Germany, Pakistan, and South Korea. *Psychological Studies*, 1–14.

Arrindell, W. A., Hatzichristou, C., Wensink, J., Rosenberg, E., van Twillert, B., Stedema, J., & Meijer, D. (1997). Dimensions of national culture as predictors of cross-national differences in subjective well-being. *Personality and Individual Differences, 23*, 37–53.

Averill, J. R. (1985). The social construction of emotion: With special reference to love. In K. J. Gergen & K. E. Davis (Eds.), *The social construction of the person*. New York, NY: Springer.

Averill, J. R. (1990). Inner feelings, works of the flesh, the beast within, diseases of the mind, driving force, and putting on a show: Six metaphors of emotion and their theoretical extensions. In D. E. Leary (Ed.), *Metaphors in the history of psychology* (pp. 104–132). New York, NY: Cambridge University Press.

Bagozzi, R. P., Wong, N., & Yi, Y. (1999). The role of culture and gender and the relationship between positive and negative affect. *Cognition and Emotion, 3*, 641–672.

Basabe, N., Paez, D., Valencia, J., Gonzalez, J. L., Rimé, B., & Diener, E. (2002). Cultural dimensions, socioeconomic development, climate, and hedonic level. *Cognition & Emotion, 16*, 103–125.

Basabe, N., Paez, D., Valencia, J., Rimé, B., Pennebaker, J., Diener, E., & González, J. L. (2000). Sociocultural factors predicting subjective experience of emotion: A collective level analysis. *Psicothema, 12*(Suppl 1), 55–69.

Benedict, R. (1946). *The chrysanthemum and the sword: Patterns of Japanese culture*. Boston, MA: Houghton Mifflin.

Berendt, E. A., & Tanita, K. (2011). The 'heart' of things: A conceptual metaphoric analysis of heart and related body parts in Thai, Japanese and English. *Intercultural Communication Studies, 20*(1), 65–78.

Bierbrauer, G. (1992). Reactions to violation of normative standards: A cross-cultural analysis of shame and guilt. *International Journal of Psychology, 27*(2), 181–193.

Bilimoria, P., & Wenta, A. (Eds.). (2015). *Emotions in Indian thought-systems*. New Delhi, India: Routledge.

Bockover, M. I. (1995). The concept of emotion revisited: A critical synthesis of Western and Confucian thought. In J. Marks & R. T. Ames (Eds.), *Emotions in Asian thought* (pp. 161–180). Albany, NY: State University of New York Press.

Boiger, M., Gungor, D., Karasawa, M., & Mesquita, B. (2014). Defending honour, keeping face: Interpersonal affordances of anger and shame in Turkey and Japan. *Cognition and Emotion, 28*(7), 1255–1269.

Bond, M. H. (1993). Emotions and their expression in Chinese culture. *Journal of Nonverbal Behavior, 17*(4), 245–262.

Bornstein, M. H., Putnick, D. L., Suwalsky, J. T. D., Venuti, P., de Falco, S., Zingman de Galperin, C., … Heslington Tichovolsky, M. (2012). Emotional relationships in mothers and infants: Culture-common and community-specific characteristics of dyads from rural and metropolitan settings in Argentina, Italy, and the United States. *Journal of Cross-Cultural Psychology, 43*, 171–198. https://doi.org/10.1177/0022022110388563

Bornstein, M. H., Tamis-LeMonda, C. S., Hahn, C., & Haynes, O. M. (2008). Maternal responsiveness to young children at three ages: Longitudinal analysis of a multidimensional, modular, and specific parenting construct. *Developmental Psychology, 44*, 867–874. https://doi.org/10.1037/0012-1649.44.3.867

Breugelmans, S. M., Ambadar, Z., Vaca, J. B., Poortinga, Y. H., Setiadi, B., Widiyanto, P., & Philippot, P. (2005). Body sensations associated with emotions in Rarámuri Indians, rural Javanese, and three student samples. *Emotion, 5*(2), 166–175.

Briggs, J. L. (1970). *Never in anger: Portrait of an Eskimo family*. Cambridge, MA: Harvard University Press.

Buck, R. (1984). *The communication of emotion*. New York, NY: Guilford Press.

Campbell, A. (1981). *The sense of well-being in America*. New York, NY: McGraw-Hill.

Casasanto, D. (2009). Embodiment of abstract concepts: Good and bad in right-and left-handers. *Journal of Experimental Psychology: General, 138*(3), 351–367.

Casimir, M. J., & Schnegg, M. (2002). Shame across cultures: The evolution, ontogeny and function of a "moral emotion". In H. Keller, Y. H. Poortinga, & A. Schölmerich (Eds.), *Between culture and biology: Perspectives on ontogenetic development* (pp. 270–302). Cambridge, UK: Cambridge University Press.

Caudill, W., & Weinstein, H. (1969). Maternal care and infant behavior in Japan and America. *Psychiatry, 32*, 12–43.

Chaplin, T. M., Hong, K., Bergquist, K., & Sinha, R. (2008). Gender differences in response to emotional stress: An assessment across subjective, behavioral, and physiological domains and relations to alcohol craving. *Alcoholism: Clinical and Experimental Research, 32*(7), 1242–1250.

Chentsova-Dutton, Y. E., & Tsai, J. L. (2010). Self-focused attention and emotional reactivity: The role of culture. *Journal of Personality and Social Psychology, 98*, 507–519.

Cohen, D. (1996). Law, social policy, and violence: The impact of regional cultures. *Journal of Personality and Social Psychology, 70*(5), 961–978.

Cohen, D., & Nisbett, R. E. (1994). Self-protection and the culture of honor: Explaining southern homicide. *Personality and Social Psychology Bulletin, 20*, 551–567. https://doi.org/10.1177/0146167294205012

Cohen, D., & Nisbett, R. E. (1997). Field experiments examining the culture of honor: The role of institutions in perpetuating norms about violence. *Personality and Social Psychology Bulletin, 23*, 1188–1199. https://doi.org/10.1177/01461672972311006

Cohen, D., Nisbett, R. E., Bowdle, B. F., & Schwarz, N. (1996). Insult, aggression, and the southern culture of honor: An experimental ethnography. *Journal of Personality and Social Psychology, 70*, 945–960. https://doi.org/10.1037/0022-3514.70.5.945

Cohen, D., Vandello, J., Puente, S., & Rantilla, A. (1999). "When you call me that, smile!": How norms for politeness, interaction styles, and aggression work together in Southern culture. *Social Psychology Quarterly, 62*(3), 257–275.

Consedine, N. S., Magai, C., Cohen, C. I., & Gillespie, M. (2002). Ethnic variation in the impact of negative emotion and emotion inhibition on the health of older adults. *Journals of Gerontology, Series B: Psychological Sciences, 57*, 396–408.

Crystal, D. S., Parrott, W. G., Okazaki, Y., & Watanabe, H. (2001). Examining relations between shame and personality among university students in the United States and Japan: A developmental perspective. *International Journal of Behavioral Development, 25*(2), 113–123.

Curhan, K. B., Sims, T., Markus, H. R., Kitayama, S., Karasawa, M., Kawakami, N., … Ryff, C. R. (2014). Just how bad negative affect is for your health depends on culture. *Psychological Science, 25*, 2277–2280.

D'Andrade, R. G. (1984). Cultural meaning systems. In R. A. Shweder & R. A. LeVine (Eds.), *Culture theory: Essays on mind, self, and emotion* (pp. 88–119). Cambridge, UK: Cambridge University Press.

Danzinger, K. (1997). *Naming the mind: How psychology found its language*. London, UK: Sage.

Davidson, R. J. (1992). Anterior cerebral asymmetry and the nature of emotion. *Brain and Cognition, 20*(1), 125–151.

Davis, J. (1977/2016). *People of the Mediterranean: An essay in comparative social anthropology*. London, UK: Routledge.

Davis, E., Greenberger, E., Charles, S., Chen, C., Zhao, L., & Dong, Q. (2012). Emotion experience and regulation in China and the United States: How do culture and gender shape emotion responding? *International Journal of Psychology, 47*(3), 230–239.

De Rivera, J., & Grinkis, C. (1986). Emotions as social relationships. *Motivation and Emotion,* *10*(4), 351–369.

Diener, E., & Diener, M. (1995). Cross-cultural correlates of life satisfaction and self-esteem. *Journal of Personality and Social Psychology, 68*, 653–663.

Diener, E., Diener, M., & Diener, C. (1995). Factors predicting the subjective Well-being of nations. *Journal of Personality and Social Psychology, 69*, 851–864.

Diener, E., Lucas, R. E., & Oishi, S. (2002). Subjective well-being: The science of happiness and life satisfaction. In C. R. Snyder & S. J. Lopez (Eds.), *The handbook of positive psychology* (pp. 63–73). Oxford, England: Oxford University Press.

Diener, E., & Emmons, R. A. (1985). The independence of positive and negative affect. *Journal of Personality and Social Psychology, 47*, 1105–1117.

Diener, E., Oishi, S., & Ryan, K. L. (2013). Universals and cultural differences in the causes and structure of happiness: A multilevel review. In C. Keyes (Ed.), *Mental well-being* (pp. 153–176). Dordrecht, The Netherlands: Springer.

Diener, E., & Suh, E. M. (Eds.). (2000). *Culture and subjective well-being.* Cambridge, MA: The MIT Press.

Eid, M., & Diener, E. (2001). Norms for experiencing emotions in different cultures: Inter- and intra-national differences. *Journal of Personality and Social Psychology, 81*(5), 869–885.

Ekman, P., Levenson, R. W., & Friesen, W. V. (1983). Autonomic nervous system activity distinguishes among emotions. *Science, 221*(4616), 1208–1210.

Elasri, K. (2018). A linguistic and cultural analysis of sympathy, compassion, empathy and pity in English and Moroccan Arabic. *International Journal of Linguistics and Literature, 7*(4), 81–90.

Ellsworth, P. C., & Scherer, K. R. (2003). Appraisal processes in emotion. In R. J. Davidson, H. Goldsmith, & K. R. Scherer (Eds.), *Handbook of the affective sciences* (pp. 572–595). New York, NY/Oxford, UK: Oxford University Press.

Emmons, R. A. (1986). Personal strivings: An approach to personality and subjective well-being. *Journal of Personality and Social Psychology, 51*, 1058–1068.

Fehr, B., & Russell, J. A. (1984). The concept of emotion viewed from a prototype perspective. *Journal of Experimental Psychology: General, 113*(3), 464–486.

Fontaine, J. R. J., Luyten, P., de Boeck, P., Corveleyn, J., Fernandez, M., Herrera, D., et al. (2006). Untying the Gordian knot of guilt and shame: The structure of guilt and shame reactions based on situation and person variation in Belgium, Hungary, and Peru. *Journal of Cross-Cultural Psychology, 37*, 273–292.

Fontaine, J. R. J., Poortinga, Y. H., Setiadi, B., & Markam, S. S. (2002). Cognitive structure of emotion terms in Indonesia and The Netherlands. *Cognition & Emotion, 16*, 61–86. https://doi. org/10.1080/02699933014000130

Fontaine, J. R. J., Scherer, K. R., Roesch, E. B., & Ellsworth, P. (2007). The world of emotion is not two-dimensional. *Psychological Science, 18*(12), 1050–1057. https://doi. org/10.1111/j.1467-9280.2007.02024.x

Fontaine, J. R. J., Scherer, K. R., & Soriano, C. (Eds.). (2013). *Components of emotional meaning: A sourcebook.* Oxford, UK: Oxford University Press.

Freedman, D. G., & Freedman, N. C. (1969). Behavioural differences between Chinese–American and European–American newborns. *Nature, 224*(5225), 1227–1227.

Friedlmeier, W., Corapci, F., & Benga, O. (2015). Early emotional development in cultural perspective. In L. Jensen (Ed.), *Oxford handbook of human development and culture: An interdisciplinary perspective* (pp. 127–148). New York, NY: Oxford University Press. https://doi. org/10.1093/oxfordhb/9780199948550.013.9

Frijda, N. H. (1993). The place of appraisal in emotion. *Cognition and Emotion, 7*, 357–387.

Frijda, N. H., Kuipers, P., & ter Schure, E. (1989). Relations among emotion, appraisal, and emotional action readiness. *Journal of Personality and Social Psychology, 57*(2), 212–228. https:// doi.org/10.1037/0022-3514.57.2.212

Frijda, N. H., & Sundararajan, L. (2007). Emotion refinement: A theory inspired by Chinese poetics. *Perspectives on Psychological Science, 2*, 227–241.

Gadea, M., Espert, R., Salvador, A., & Martí-Bonmatí, L. (2011). The sad, the angry, and the asymmetrical brain: Dichotic listening studies of negative affect and depression. *Brain and Cognition, 76*(2), 294–299.

Gaias, L. M., Raikkonen, K., Komsi, N., Gartstein, M. A., Fisher, P. A., & Putnam, S. P. (2012). Cross-cultural temperamental differences in infants, children, and adults in the United States of America and Finland. *Scandinavian Journal of Psychology, 53*, 119–128. https://doi.org/10.1111/j.1467-9450.2012.00937.x

Gartstein, M. A., Gonzalez, C., Carranza, J. A., Ahadi, S. A., Ye, R., Rothbart, M. K., & Yang, S. W. (2006). Studying the development of infant temperament through parent report: Commonalities and differences for the People's Republic of China, the United States of America, and Spain. *Child Psychiatry and Human Development, 37*, 145–161.

Gartstein, M. A., Knyazev, G. G., & Slobodskaya, H. R. (2005). Cross-cultural differences in the structure of infant temperament: United States of America (US) and Russia. *Infant Behavior and Development, 28*, 54–61. https://doi.org/10.1016/j.infbeh.2004.09.003

Gartstein, M. A., Slobodskaya, H. R., & Kinsht, I. A. (2003). Cross-cultural differences in temperament in the first year of life: United States of America (US) and Russia. *International Journal of Behavioral Development, 27*, 316–328. https://doi.org/10.1080/01650250244000344

Gartstein, M. A., Slobodskaya, H. R., Zylicz, P. O., Gosztyla, D., & Nakagawa, N. (2010). A cross-cultural evaluation of temperament development: Japan, United States of America, Poland and Russia. *International Journal of Psychology and Psychological Therapy, 10*, 55–75. https://doi.org/10.1177/016502541142218

Gelfand, M. J., Nishii, L. H., & Raver, J. L. (2006). On the nature and importance of cultural tightness-looseness. *Journal of Applied Psychology, 91*(6), 1225–1244. https://doi.org/10.1037/0021-9010.91.6.1225

Gerber, E. R. (1975). *The cultural patterning of emotions in Samoa*. San Diego, CA: University of California.

Gillioz, C., Fontaine, J. R. J., Soriano, C., & Scherer, K. R. (2016). Mapping emotion terms into affective space: Further evidence for a four-dimensional structure. *Swiss Journal of Psychology, 75*(3), 141–148. https://doi.org/10.1024/1421-0185/a000180

Glenberg, A. M., Sato, M., Cattaneo, L., Riggio, L., Palumbo, D., & Buccino, G. (2008). Processing abstract language modulates motor system activity. *The Quarterly Journal of Experimental Psychology, 61*(6), 905–919.

Grossmann, I., Huynh, A. C., & Ellsworth, P. C. (2016). Emotional complexity: Clarifying definitions and cultural correlates. *Journal of Personality and Social Psychology, 111*(6), 895–916. https://doi.org/10.1037/pspp0000084

Gudykunst, W. B., & Kim, Y. Y. (1984). *Communicating with strangers: An approach to intercultural communication*. Reading, MA: Addison-Wesley.

Gudykunst, W. B., & Ting-Toomey, S. (1988). Culture and affective communication. *American Behavioral Scientist, 31*(3), 384–400.

Guerra, V. M., Giner-Sorolla, R., & Vasiljevic, M. (2013). The importance of honor concerns across eight countries. *Group Processes and Intergroup Relations, 16*, 298–318. https://doi.org/10.1177/1368430212463451

Ha, F. I. (1995). Shame in Asian and Western cultures. *American Behavioral Scientist, 38*, 1114–1131.

Hall, E. T., & Whyte, W. E. (1960). Intercultural communication. Human Organization, 19, 5–12.

Heine, S. J., & Lehman, D. R. (1997). The cultural construction of self-enhancement: An examination of group-serving biases. *Journal of Personality and Social Psychology, 72*, 1268–1283.

Hochschild, A. (1979). Emotion work, feeling rules, and social structure. *American Journal of Sociology, 85*(3), 551–575.

Hochschild, A. (2003). *The commercialization of intimate life: Notes from home and work*. Berkeley, CA: University of California Press.

Hofstede, G. (1983). Dimensions of national cultures in fifty countries and three regions. In J. B. Deregowski, S. Dziurawiec, & R. C. Annis (Eds.), *Expisications in cross-cultural psychology* (pp. 335–355). Lisse, NL: Swets & Zeitlinger.

Hofstede, G. (1984). *Culture's consequences: International differences in work-related values.* Newbury Park, CA: SAGE. Originally published in 1980.

Hong, J., & Lee, A. Y. (2010). Feeling mixed but not torn: The moderating role of construal level in mixed emotions appeals. *Journal of Consumer Research, 37,* 456–472.

Howell, S. (1981). Rules not words. In P. Heelas & A. Lock (Eds.), *Indigenous psychologies: The anthropology of the self* (pp. 133–143). San Diego, CA: Academic.

Hoy, W. (2013). *Do funerals matter? The purposes and practices of death rituals in global perspective.* New York, NY: Routledge. https://doi.org/10.4324/9780203072745

Huang, L., Yang, T., & Li, Z. (2003). Applicability of the positive and negative affect scale in Chinese. *Chinese Mental Health Journal, 17,* 54–56.

Imada, T., & Ellsworth, P. C. (2011). Proud Americans and lucky Japanese: Cultural differences in appraisal and corresponding emotion. *Emotion, 11*(2), 329–345.

Jakubowska, L. (1989). A matter of honor. *The world and I, 4,* 670–677.

Ji, L. J., Nisbett, R. E., & Su, Y. (2001). Culture, change, and prediction. *Psychological Science, 12*(6), 450–456.

Joiner, T. E., Jr., Sandin, B., Chorot, P., Lostao, L., & Marquina, G. (1997). Development and factor analytic validation of the SPANAS among women in Spain: (More) cross-cultural convergence in the structure of mood. *Journal of Personality Assessment, 68,* 600–615.

Kagan, J., Arcus, D., Snidman, N., Feng, W. Y., Hendler, J., & Greene, S. (1994). Reactivity in infants: A cross-national comparison. *Developmental Psychology, 30*(3), 342–345. https://doi.org/10.1037/0012-1649.30.3.342

Kagan, J., Kearsley, R. B., & Zelazo, P. R. (1978). *Infancy: Its place in human development.* Cambridge, MA: Harvard University Press.

Kang, S., Shaver, P. R., Sue, S., Min, K., & Jing, H. (2003). Culture-specific patterns in the prediction of life satisfaction: Roles of emotion, relationship quality, and self-esteem. *Personality and Social Psychology Bulletin, 29,* 1596–1608.

Karandashev, V. (2019). *Cross-cultural perspectives on the experience and expression of love.* New York, NY: Springer.

Kim, J., Seo, M., Yu, H., & Neuendorf, K. (2014). Cultural differences in preference for entertainment messages that induce mixed responses of joy and sorrow. *Human Communication Research, 40,* 530–552.

Kim-Prieto, C., & Eid, M. (2004). Norms for experiencing emotions. *Journal of Happiness Studies, 5*(3), 241–268.

Kitayama, S., Karasawa, M., Curhan, K. B., Ryff, C. D., & Markus, H. R. (2010). Independence and interdependence predict health and wellbeing: Divergent patterns in the United States and Japan. *Frontiers in Psychology, 1,* 163.

Kitayama, S., & Markus, H. R. (2000). The pursuit of happiness and the realization of sympathy: Cultural patterns of self, social relations, and well-being. In E. Diener & E. M. Suh (Eds.), *Culture and subjective well-being* (pp. 113–161). Cambridge, MA: MIT Press.

Kitayama, S., Markus, H. R., & Kurokawa, M. (2000). Culture, emotion, and well-being: Good feelings in Japan and the United States. *Cognition and Emotion, 14,* 93–124.

Kitayama, S., Markus, H. R., & Matsumoto, H. (1995). Culture, self, and emotion: A cultural perspective on "self-conscious" emotions. In J. P. Tangney & K. W. Fischer (Eds.), *Self-conscious emotions: The psychology of shame, guilt, embarrassment, and pride* (pp. 439–464). New York, NY: Guilford Press.

Kitayama, S., Markus, H. R., Matsumoto, H., & Norasakkunkit, V. (1997). Individual and collective process in the construction of the self: Self-enhancement in the United States and self-criticism in Japan. *Journal of Personality and Social Psychology, 72,* 1245–1267.

Kitayama, S., Mesquita, B., & Karasawa, M. (2006). Cultural affordances and emotional experience: Socially engaging and disengaging emotions in Japan and the United States. *Journal of Personality and Social Psychology, 91*(5), 890–903.

Kitayama, S., Takagi, H., & Matsumoto, H. (1995). Causal attribution of success and failure: Cultural psychology of the Japanese self. *Japanese Psychological Review, 38,* 247–280.

Klein, A. M. (2001). Tender machos: Masculine contrasts in the Mexican baseball league. In A. Yiannakis & M. J. Melnick (Eds.), *Contemporary issues in the sociology of sport* (pp. 291–303). Champaign, IL: Human Kinetics.

Kleinman, A. (1986). *Social origins of distress and disease: Depression, neuraesthenia, and pain in modern China*. New Haven, CT: Yale University Press.

Klineberg, O. (1938). Emotional expression in Chinese literature. *The Journal of Abnormal and Social Psychology, 33*(4), 517–520.

Kovecses, Z. (2000). *Metaphor and emotion: Language, culture, and body in human feeling*. Cambridge, UK: Cambridge University Press.

Kövecses, Z. (2005). *Metaphor in culture: Universality and variation*. Cambridge, UK: Cambridge University Press.

Kuppens, P., Ceulmans, E., Timmerman, M. E., Diener, E., & Kim-Prieto, C. (2006). Universal intracultural and intercultural dimensions of the recalled frequency of emotional experience. *Journal of Cross-Cultural Psychology, 37*(5), 491–515.

Kuppens, P., Realo, A., & Diener, E. (2008). The role of positive and negative emotions in life satisfaction judgment across nations. *Journal of Personality and Social Psychology, 95*, 66–75.

Kuppens, P., Van Mechelen, I., Smits, D. J. M., & De Boeck, P. (2003). The appraisal basis of anger: Specificity, necessity and sufficiency of components. *Emotion, 3*(3), 254–269.

Kuppens, P., Van Mechelen, I., Smits, D. J. M., & De Boeck, P. (2004). Associations between emotions: Correspondence across different data types and componential basis. *European Journal of Personality, 18*, 159–176.

Kwan, V. S. Y., Bond, M. H., & Singelis, T. M. (1997). Pancultural explanations for life satisfaction: Adding relationship harmony to self-esteem. *Journal of Personality and Social Psychology, 73*(5), 1038–1051. https://doi.org/10.1037/0022-3514.73.5.1038

Lambie, J., & Marcel, A. (2002). Consciousness and emotion experience: A theoretical framework. *Psychological Review, 109*, 219–259.

Larsen, R. J., & Diener, E. (1992). Promises and problems with the circumplex model of emotion. In M. S. Clark (Ed.), *Review of personality and social psychology: Emotion* (pp. 25–59). Newbury Park, CA: Sage.

Lazarus, R. S., Tomita, M., Opton, E., Jr., & Kodoma, M. (1966). A cross-cultural study of stress-reaction patterns in Japan. *Journal of Personality and Social Psychology, 4*, 622–633.

Lebra, T. S. (1976). *Japanese patterns of behavior*. Honolulu, HI: University Press of Hawaii.

Lee, A. Y., Aaker, J. L., & Gardner, W. L. (2000). The pleasures and pains of distinct self-construals: The role of interdependence in regulatory focus. *Journal of Personality and Social Psychology, 78*, 1122–1134.

Lee, K. J., & Levenson, R. W. (1992, October). *Ethnic similarities in emotional reactivity to an unanticipated startle*. Poster session presented at the meeting for the Society for Psychophysiological Research, San Diego, CA.

Leu, J., Mesquita, B., Ellsworth, P. C., Zhang, Z., Yuan, H., Bucktel, E., … Masuda, T. (2010). Situational differences in dialectical emotions: Boundary conditions in a cultural comparison of North Americans and East Asians. *Cognition and Emotion, 24*(3), 419–435.

Leu, J., Wang, J., & Koo, K. (2011). Are positive emotions just as "positive" across cultures? *Emotion, 11*, 994–999.

Leung, A. K. Y., & Cohen, D. (2011). Within- and between-culture variation: Individual differences and the cultural logics of honor, face, and dignity cultures. *Journal of Personality and Social Psychology, 100*, 507–526. https://doi.org/10.1037/a0022151

Levenson, R. W., Carstensen, L. L., & Gottman, J. M. (1994). Influence of age and gender on affect, physiology, and their interrelations: A study of long-term marriages. *Journal of Personality and Social Psychology, 67*(1), 56–68.

Levenson, R. W., Ekman, P., Heider, K., & Friesen, W. V. (1992). Emotion and autonomic nervous system activity in Minangkanau of West Sumatra. *Journal of Personality and Social Psychology, 62*, 972–988.

Levy, R. I. (1973). *Tahitians*. Chicago, IL: University of Chicago Press.

Levy, R. I. (1978). Tahitian gentleness and redundant controls. In A. Montagu (Ed.), *Learning non-aggression: The experience of non-literate societies* (pp. 222–235). New York, NY: Oxford University Press.

Lewis, M. (1989). Culture and biology: The role of temperament. In P. R. Zelazo & R. G. Barr (Eds.), *Challenges to developmental paradigms:Implications for theory assessment and treatment* (pp. 203–223). Hillsdale, NJ: Erlbaum.

Lewis, M., Ramsay, D. S., & Kawakami, K. (1993). Differences between Japanese infants and Caucasian American infants in behavioral and cortisol response to inoculation. *Child Development, 64*(6), 1722–1731.

Lim, N. (2016). Cultural differences in emotion: Differences in emotional arousal level between the East and the West. *Integrative Medicine Research, 5*(2), 105–109.

Lim, T.-S. (2003). Language and verbal communication across cultures. In W. B. Gudykunst (Ed.), *Handbook of international and intercultural communication* (pp. 53–71). Thousand Oaks, CA: Sage.

Lu, L., & Gilmour, R. (2004). Culture and conceptions of happiness: Individual oriented and social oriented SWB. *Journal of Happiness Studies, 5*, 269–291.

Lutz, C. (1982). The domain of emotion words on Ifaluk. *American Ethnologist, 9*(1), 113–128.

Lutz, C. (1988). *Unnatural emotions: Everyday sentiments on a Micronesian atoll and their challenge to Western theory*. Chicago, IL: University of Chicago Press.

Lynch, O. M. (1990). *Divine passions*. Berkeley, CA: University of California Press.

Markus, H., Kitayama, S., & VandenBos, G. R. (1996). The mutual interactions of culture and emotion. *Psychiatric Services, 47*(3), 225–226. https://doi.org/10.1176/ps.47.3.225

Markus, H. R., & Kitayama, S. (1991). Culture and the self: Implications for cognition, emotion, and motivation. *Psychological Review, 98*, 224–253.

Marmolejo-Ramos, F., Elosúa, M. R., Yamada, Y., Hamm, N. F., & Noguchi, K. (2013). Appraisal of space words and allocation of emotion words in bodily space. *PLoS One, 8*(12).

Mascolo, M. J., Fischer, K. W., & Li, J. (2003). Dynamic development of component systems of emotions: Pride, shame, and guilt in China and United States. In R. J. Davidson, K. Scherer, & H. H. Goldsmith (Eds.), *Handbook of affective science* (pp. 375–408). Oxford, UK: Oxford University Press.

Masuda, T., Ellsworth, P. C., Mesquita, B., Leu, J., Tanida, S., & Van de Veerdonk, E. (2008). Placing the face in context: Cultural differences in the perception of facial emotion. *Journal of Personality and Social Psychology, 94*(3), 365–381. https://doi.org/10.1037/0022-3514.94.3.365

Matsumoto, D. (1991). Cultural influences on facial expressions of emotion. *Southern Communication Journal, 56*, 128–137.

Matsumoto, D., & Hwang, H. S. (2012). Culture and emotion: The integration of biological and cultural contributions. *Journal of Cross-Cultural Psychology, 43*(1), 91–118.

Matsumoto, D., Kudoh, T., Scherer, K. R., & Wallbott, H. (1988). Antecedents of and reactions to emotions in the United States and Japan. *Journal of Cross- Cultural Psychology, 19*(3), 267–286.

Mauro, R., Sato, K., & Tucker, J. (1992). The role of appraisal in human emotions: A cross-cultural study. *Journal of Personality and Social Psychology, 62*(2), 301–317.

McDaniel, J. (1995). Emotion in Bengali religious thought: Substance and metaphor. In J. Marks & R. T. Ames (Eds.), *Emotions in Asian thought* (pp. 39–63). Albany, NY: SUNY Press.

Mead, M. (1943). *Coming of age in Samoa: A study of adolescence and sex in primitive societies*. New York, NY: Penguin Books.

Mesquita, B., & Ellsworth, P. C. (2001). The role of culture in appraisal. In K. R. Scherer & A. Schorr (Eds.), *Appraisal processes in emotion: Theory, methods, Research* (p. 233248). New York, NY: Oxford University Press.

Mesquita, B., & Frijda, N. H. (1992). Cultural variations in emotions: A review. *Psychological Bulletin, 112*(2), 179–204. https://doi.org/10.1037/0033-2909.112.2.179

Mesquita, B., Frijda, N. H., & Scherer, K. R. (1997). Culture and emotion. In P. Dasen & T. S. Saraswathi (Eds.), *Handbook of cross-cultural psychology. Basic processes and human development* (Vol. 2, pp. 255–297). Boston, MA: Allyn & Bacon.

Mesquita, B., & Karasawa, M. (2002). Different emotional lives. *Cognition & Emotion, 16*(1), 127–141.

Mesquita, B., & Karasawa, M. (2004). Self-conscious emotions as dynamic cultural processes. *Psychological Inquiry, 15,* 161–166.

Mesquita, B., & Leu, J. (2007). The cultural psychology of emotion. In S. Kitayama & D. Cohen (Eds.), *Handbook of cultural psychology* (pp. 734–759). New York, NY: Guilford Press.

Metcalf, P., & Huntington, R. (1991). *Celebrations of death: The anthropology of mortuary ritual* (2nd ed.). Cambridge, UK: Cambridge University Press.

Middleton, D. R. (1989). Emotional style: The cultural ordering of emotions. *Ethos, 17*(2), 187–201.

Miller, J. G., Bersoff, D. M., & Harwood, R. L. (1990). Perceptions of social responsibilities in India and in the United States: Moral imperatives or personal decisions? *Journal of Personality and Social Psychology, 58,* 33–47.

Miyamoto, Y., & Ma, X. (2011). Dampening or savoring positive emotions: A dialectical cultural script guides emotion regulation. *Emotion, 11,* 1346–1357.

Miyamoto, Y., Morozink Boylon, J., Coe, C. L., Curhan, K. B., Levine, C. S., Markus, H. R., … Ryff, C. D. (2013). Negative emotions predict elevated interleukin-6 in the United States but not in Japan. *Brain, Behavior, and Immunity, 34,* 79–85.

Miyamoto, Y., & Ryff, C. D. (2011). Cultural differences in the dialectical and non-dialectical emotional styles and their implications for health. *Cognition and Emotion, 25,* 22–39.

Miyamoto, Y., Uchida, Y., & Ellsworth, P. C. (2010). Culture and mixed emotions: Cooccurrence of positive and negative emotions in Japan and the United States. *Emotion, 10,* 404–415.

Montirosso, R., Cozzi, P., Putnam, S. P., Gartstein, M. A., & Borgatti, R. (2011). Studying cross-cultural differences in temperament in the first year of life: United States and Italy. *International Journal of Behavioral Development, 35,* 27–37. https://doi.org/10.1177/0165025410368944

Morling, B., Kitayama, S., & Miyamoto, Y. (2002). Cultural practices emphasize influence in the United States and adjustment in Japan. *Personality and Social Psychology Bulletin, 28*(3), 311–323.

Myers, F. R. (1979). Emotions and the self: A theory of personhood and political order among Pintupi aborigines. *Ethos, 7*(4), 343–370.

Myers, F. R. (1988). The logic and meaning of anger among Pintupi aborigines. *Man, 23,* 589–610.

Niedenthal, P. M., Barsalou, L. W., Winkielman, P., Krauth-Gruber, S., & Ric, F. (2005). Embodiment in attitudes, social perception, and emotion. *Personality and Social Psychology Review, 9*(3), 184–211.

Nisbett, R. E., & Cohen, D. (1996). *Culture of honor: The psychology of violence in the south.* Boulder, CO: Westview Press.

Nummenmaa, L., Glerean, E., Hari, R., & Hietanen, J. K. (2014). Bodily maps of emotions. *Proceedings of the National Academy of Sciences, 111*(2), 646–651.

Oishi, S. (2002). The experiencing and remembering of well-being: A cross-cultural analysis. *Personality and Social Psychology Bulletin, 28,* 1398–1406.

Oishi, S., & Diener, E. (2001). Goals, culture, and subjective well-being. *Personality and Social Psychology Bulletin, 27,* 1674–1682.

Oishi, S., Diener, E., Scollon, C. N., & Biswas-Diener, R. (2004). Cross-situational consistency of affective experiences across cultures. *Journal of Personality and Social Psychology, 86,* 460–472.

Osgood, C. E., May, W. H., & Mirron, M. S. (1975). *Cross-cultural universals of affective meanings.* Urbana, IL: University of Illinois Press.

Pelto, P. J. (1968, April). The difference between "tight" and "loose" societies. *Transactions, 5,* 37–40.

Pennebaker, J. W., & Graybeal, A. (2001). Patterns of natural language use: Disclosure, personality, and social integration. *Current Directions in Psychological Science, 10*(3), 90–93.

Pérez, R. G. (2008). A cross-cultural analysis of heart metaphors. *Revista Alicantina de Estudios Ingleses, 2,* 25–56.

Peristiany, J. G. (Ed.). (1965). *Honour and shame: The values of Mediterranean society*. London, UK: Weidenfeld and Nicolson.

Perunovic, W. Q. E., Heller, D., & Rafaeli, E. (2007). Within-person changes in the structure of emotion: The role of cultural identification and language. *Psychological Science, 18*(7), 607–613.

Philippot, P., & Rimé, B. (1997). The perception of bodily sensations during emotion: A cross-cultural perspective. *Polish Psychological Bulletin, 28*, 175–188.

Pitt-Rivers, J. (1968). Honor. In D. Sills (Ed.), *International encyclopedia of the social sciences* (pp. 503–511). New York, NY: Macmillan.

Potter, S. H. (1988). The cultural construction of emotion in rural Chinese social life. *Ethos, 16*(2), 181–208.

Pressman, S. D., Gallagher, M. W., & Lopez, S. J. (2013). Is the emotion-health connection a "first-world problem"? *Psychological Science, 24*, 544–549.

Rimé, B., Philippot, P., & Cisamolo, D. (1990). Social schemata of peripheral changes in emotion. *Journal of Personality and Social Psychology, 59*, 38–49.

Rodriguez, C., & Church, A. T. (2003). The structure and personality correlates of affect in Mexico: Evidence of cross-cultural comparability using the Spanish language. *Journal of Cross Cultural Psychology, 34*, 211–230.

Rodriguez Mosquera, P. M. (2013). In the name of honor. On virtue, reputation, and violence. *Group Processes and Intergroup Relations, 16*, 271–388. https://doi.org/10.1177/1368430212472590

Rodriguez Mosquera, P. M., Manstead, A. S., & Fischer, A. H. (2002). Honor in the Mediterranean and northern Europe. *Journal of Cross-Cultural Psychology, 33*(1), 16–36.

Rodriguez Mosquera, P. M., Tan, L. X., & Saleem, F. (2014). Shared burdens, personal costs on the emotional and social consequences of family honor. *Journal of Cross-Cultural Psychology, 45*(3), 400–416. https://doi.org/10.1177/0022022113511299

Roseman, I. J., Dhawan, N., Rettek, S. L., Naidu, R. K., & Thapa, K. (1995). Cultural differences and cross-cultural similarities in appraisals and emotional responses. *Journal of Cross-Cultural Psychology, 26*, 23–48.

Rubin, D. C., & Talarico, J. M. (2009). A comparison of dimensional models of emotion: Evidence from emotions, prototypical events, autobiographical memories, and words. *Memory, 17*(8), 802–808.

Russell, J. A. (1980). A circumplex model of affect. *Journal of Personality and Social Psychology, 39*(6), 1161–1178. https://doi.org/10.1037/h0077714

Russell, J. A., & Carroll, J. M. (1999). On the bipolarity of positive and negative affect. *Psychological Bulletin, 125*, 3–30.

Russell, J. A., & Feldman Barrett, L. (1999). Core affect, prototypical emotional episodes, and other things called emotion: Dissecting the elephant. *Journal of Personality and Social Psychology, 76*, 805–819.

Russell, J. A., Lewicka, M., & Niit, T. (1989). A cross-cultural study of a circumplex model of affect. *Journal of Personality and Social Psychology, 57*, 848–856.

Russell, J. A., & Yik, M. S. M. (1996). Emotion among the Chinese. In M. H. Bond (Ed.), *The handbook of Chinese psychology* (pp. 166–188). Hong Kong, China: Oxford University Press.

Saumi, M. M. (2016). Indian cinema and pop culture. *Epitome: International journal of multidisciplinary research, 2*(5), 49–57. Retrieved from http://www.epitomejournals.com/VolumeArticles/FullTextPDF/124_Research_Paper.pdf

Savani, K., Morris, M. W., Naidu, N. V. R., Kumar, S., & Berlia, N. V. (2011). Cultural conditioning: Understanding interpersonal accommodation in India and the United States in terms of the modal characteristics of interpersonal influence situations. *Journal of Personality and Social Psychology, 100*(1), 84–102.

Scherer, K. R. (1984). Emotion as a multicomponent process: A model and some cross-cultural data. In P. Shaver (Ed.), *Review of personality and social psychology* (Vol. 5, pp. 37–63). Beverly Hills, CA: Sage.

Scherer, K. R. (1993). Studying the emotion-antecedent appraisal process: An expert system approach. *Cognition and Emotion, 7*, 325–355.

Scherer, K. R. (1997a). Profiles of emotion-antecedent appraisal: Testing theoretical predictions across cultures. *Cognition and Emotion, 11*(2), 113–150.

Scherer, K. R. (1997b). The role of culture in emotion-antecedent appraisal. *Journal of Personality and Social Psychology, 73*(4), 902–922.

Scherer, K. R., Matsumoto, D., Wallbott, H. G., & Kudoh, T. (1988). Emotional experience in cultural context: A comparison between Europe, Japan, and the United States. In K. R. Scherer (Ed.), *Facets of emotion: Recent research* (pp. 5–30). Hillsdale, NJ: Lawrence Erlbaum.

Scherer, K. R., Schorr, A., & Johnstone, T. (2001). Appraisal processes in emotion. In *Theory, methods, research*. New York, NY: Oxford University Press.

Scherer, K. R., & Wallbott, H. G. (1994). Evidence for universality and cultural variation of differential emotion response patterning. *Journal of Personality and Social Psychology, 66*(2), 310–328.

Scherer, K. R., Wallbott, H. G., & Summerfield, A. B. (Eds.). (1986). *European monographs in social psychology. Experiencing emotion: A cross-cultural study*. New York, NY/Paris, France: Cambridge University Press/Editions de la Maison des Sciences de l'Homme.

Schieffelin, E. L. (1983). Anger and shame in the tropical forest: On affect as a cultural system in Papua New Guinea. *Ethos, 11*(3), 181–191.

Schimmack, U., Oishi, S., & Diener, E. (2002). Cultural influences on the relation between pleasant emotions and unpleasant emotions: Asian dialectic philosophies or individualism-collectivism? *Cognition and Emotion, 76*(6), 705–719.

Schnall, S. (2014). Are there basic metaphors? In M. Landau, M. D. Robinson, & B. P. Meier (Eds.), *The power of metaphor: Examining its influence on social life* (pp. 225–247). Washington, DC: American Psychological Association. https://doi.org/10.1037/14278-010

Scollon, C. N., Diener, E., Oishi, S., & Biswas-Diener, R. (2004). Emotions across cultures and methods. *Journal of Cross-Cultural Psychology, 35*(3), 304–326.

Scollon, C. N., Diener, E., Oishi, S., & Biswas-Diener, R. (2005). An experience sampling and cross-cultural investigation of the relation between pleasant and unpleasant affect. *Cognition and Emotion, 19*(1), 27–52.

Shaver, P., Schwartz, J., Kirson, D., & O'Connor, C. (1987). Emotion knowledge: Further exploration of a prototype approach. *Journal of Personality and Social Psychology, 52*, 1061–1086. https://doi.org/10.1037/0022-3514.52.6.1061

Shaver, P. R., Wu, S., & Schwartz, J. C. (1992). Cross-cultural similarities and differences in emotion and its representation. In M. S. Clark (Ed.), *Review of personality and social psychology* (Vol. 13, pp. 175–212). Thousand Oaks, CA: Sage.

Shweder, R. A. (1993). The cultural psychology of emotions. In M. Lewis & J. Hovland (Eds.), *Handbook of emotions* (pp. 417–437). New York, NY: Guilford Press.

Shweder, R. A., Haidt, J., Horton, R., & Joseph, C. (2008). The cultural psychology of the emotions: Ancient and renewed. In M. Lewis, J. M. Haviland-Jones, & L. Feldman Barrett (Eds.), *Handbook of emotions* (pp. 409–427). New York, NY: Guilford Press.

Siemer, M., Mauss, I., & Gross, J. J. (2007). Same situation–different emotions: How appraisals shape our emotions. *Emotion, 7*(3), 592–600. https://doi.org/10.1037/1528-3542.7.3.592

Sims, T., Tsai, J. L., Jiang, D., Wang, I., Fung, H. H., & Zhang, X. (2015). Wanting to maximize the positive and minimize the negative: Implications for mixed affective experience in American and Chinese contexts. *Journal of Personality and Social Psychology, 109*, 292–315.

Slobodskaya, H. R., Gartstein, M. A., Nakagawa, A., & Putnam, S. P. (2013). Early temperament in Japan, the United States, and Russia. Do cross-cultural differences decrease with age? *Journal of Cross-Cultural Psychology, 44*, 438–460. https://doi.org/10.1177/0022022112453316

Smith, C. A., & Ellsworth, P. C. (1985). Patterns of cognitive appraisal in emotion. *Journal of Personality and Social Psychology, 48*, 813–838.

Smith, C. A., & Lazarus, R. S. (1993). Appraisal components, core relational themes, and the emotions. *Cognition and Emotion, 7*, 233–269.

Smith, R. H., Webster, J. M., Parrott, W. G., & Eyre, I. L. L. (2002). The role of public exposure in moral and nonmoral shame and guilt. *Journal of Personality and Social Psychology, 83*, 138–159.

Smurkupt, S., & Barna, L. (1976). Impact of nonverbal communication in an intercultural setting: Thailand. In F. Casmir (Ed.), *International and intercultural communication annual* (Vol. 3). Falls Church, VA: Speech Communication Association.

Solomon, R. C. (1995). The cross-cultural comparison of emotion. In J. Marks & R. T. Ames (Eds.), *Emotions in Asian thought* (pp. 253–294). Albany, NY: State University of New York Press.

Sommers, S. (1984b). Adults evaluating their emotions: A cross-cultural perspective. In C. Z. Malatesta & C. Izard (Eds.), *Emotions in adult development* (pp. 319–338). Beverly Hills, CA: Sage.

Sommers, T. (2009). The two faces of revenge: Moral responsibility and the culture of honor. *Biology and Philosophy, 24*, 35–50. https://doi.org/10.1007/s10539-008-9112-3

Song, W. (1985). A preliminary study of the character traits of the Chinese. In W. S. Tseng & D. Y. H. Wu (Eds.), *Chinese culture and mental health* (pp. 47–55). Orlando, FL: Academic Press.

Soto, J. A., Levenson, R. W., & Ebling, R. (2005). Cultures of moderation and expression: Emotional experience, behavior, and physiology in Chinese Americans and Mexican Americans. *Emotion, 5*(2), 154–165.

Stein, N. L., Trabasso, T., & Liwag, M. (1993). The representation and organization of emotional experience: Unfolding the emotion episode. In M. Lewis & J. M. Haviland (Eds.), *Handbook of emotions* (pp. 279–300). New York, NY: Guilford Press.

Stewart, F. H. (1994). *Honor*. Chicago, IL: Chicago University Press.

Stipek, D. (1998). Differences between Americans and Chinese in the circumstances evoking pride, shame, and guilt. *Journal of Cross- Cultural Psychology, 29*, 616–629.

Stroud, L. R., Salovey, P., & Epel, E. S. (2002). Sex differences in stress responses: social rejection versus achievement stress. *Biological Psychiatry, 52*(4), 318–327.

Suh, E., Diener, E., Oishi, S., & Triandis, H. C. (1998). The shifting basis of life satisfaction judgements across cultures: Emotions versus norms. *Journal of Personality and Social Psychology, 74*, 482–493.

Sundararajan, L. (2010). Two flavors of aesthetic tasting: Rasa and savoring a cross-cultural study with implications for psychology of emotion. *Review of General Psychology, 14*(1), 22–30.

Suzuki, T. (1986). Language behavior in Japan: The conceptualization of personal relations. In T. S. Lebra & W. R Lebra (Eds.), *Japanese culture and behavior* (Rev. ed., pp. 142–157). Honolulu, HI: University Press of Hawaii.

Tamir, M., Schwartz, S. H., Cieciuch, J., Riediger, M., Torres, C., Scollon, C., … Vishkin, A. (2016). Desired emotions across cultures: A value-based account. *Journal of Personality and Social Psychology, 111*, 67–82.

Terraciano, A., McCrae, R. R., & Costa, P. T., Jr. (2003). Factorial and construct validity of the Italian Positive and Negative Affect Schedule (PANAS). *European Journal of Psychological Assessment, 19*, 131–141.

Thampi, G. M. (1965). "Rasa" as aesthetic experience. *Journal of Aesthetics and Art Criticism, 24*(1), 75–80.

Thayer, R. E. (1989). *The biopsychology of mood and arousal*. New York, NY: Oxford University Press.

Tracy, J. L., & Robins, R. W. (2004). Putting the self into self-conscious emotions: A theoretical model. *Psychological Inquiry, 15*(2), 103–125.

Triandis, H., & Kashima, Y,, Shimada, E., & Villareal, M. (1986). Acculturation indices as a means of confirming cultural differences. *International Journal of Psychology, 21*(1), 43–70.

Triandis, H. C. (1989). The self and social behavior in differing cultural contexts. *Psychological Review, 96*, 506–520.

Triandis, H. C., & Suh, E. M. (2002). Cultural influences on personality. *Annual Review of Psychology, 53*, 133–160.

Tsai, J. L. (2007). Ideal affect: Cultural causes and behavioral consequences. *Perspectives on Psychological Science, 2*(3), 242–259.

Tsai, J. L., Chentsova-Dutton, Y., Freire-Bebeau, L., & Przymus, D. E. (2002). Emotional expression and physiology in European Americans and Hmong Americans. *Emotion, 2*(4), 380–397.

Tsai, J. L., Chim, L., & Sims, T. L. (2015). Understanding affect and consumer behavior across cultures: The role of ideal affect. In A. Y. Lee & S. Ng (Eds.), *Handbook of culture and consumer behavior* (pp. 68–98). New York, NY: Oxford University Press.

Tsai, J. L., & Clobert, M. (2019). Cultural influences on emotion: Empirical patterns and emerging trends. In S. Kitayama & D. Cohen (Eds.), *Handbook of cultural psychology* (2nd ed., pp. 292–318). New York, NY: Guilford Press.

Tsai, J. L., Knutson, B., & Fung, H. H. (2006). Cultural variation in affect valuation. *Journal of Personality and Social Psychology, 90*(2), 288–307.

Tsai, J. L., & Levenson, R. W. (1997). Cultural influences on emotional responding: Chinese American and European American dating couples during interpersonal conflict. *Journal of Cross-Cultural Psychology, 28*(5), 600–625.

Tsai, J. L., Levenson, R. W., & Carstensen, L. L. (2000). Autonomic, subjective, and expressive responses to emotional films in older and younger Chinese Americans and European Americans. *Psychology and Aging, 15*(4), 684–693.

Tsai, J. L., Levenson, R. W., & McCoy, K. (2006). Cultural and temperamental variation in emotional response. *Emotion, 6*(3), 484–497.

Tsai, J.L., Louie, J.Y., Chen, E.E, & Uchida, Y (2007). Learning what feelings to desire: Socialization of ideal affect through children's storybooks. Personality and Social Psychology Bulletin, 3, 17–30.

Tsai, J. L., Miao, F., & Seppala, E. (2007). Good feelings in Christianity and Buddhism: Religious differences in ideal affect. *Personality and Social Psychology Bulletin, 33*, 409–421.

Tsai, J. L., Miao, F. F., Seppala, E., Fung, H. H., & Yeung, D. Y. (2007). Influence and adjustment goals: Sources of cultural differences in ideal affect. *Journal of Personality and Social Psychology, 92*, 1102–1117.

Tsang, S., & Wu, C. (2005). *What constitutes my subjective well-being: Is the subjective well-being of interdependent-self individuals rooted in others' subjective well-being?* Paper presented at the sixth biennial conference of the Asian Association of Social Psychology, Wellington, New Zealand.

Uchida, Y., & Kitayama, S. (2009). Happiness and unhappiness in east and west: Themes and variations. *Emotion, 9*, 441–456.

Uchida, Y., Kitayama, S., Mesquita, B., Reyes, J. A. S., & Morling, B. (2008). Is perceived emotional support beneficial? Well-being and health in independent and interdependent cultures. *Personality and Social Psychology Bulletin, 34*, 741–754.

Uchida, Y., Norasakkunkit, V., & Kitayama, S. (2004). Cultural constructions of happiness: Theory and empirical evidence. *Journal of Happiness Studies, 5*(3), 223–239.

Uchida, Y., Townsend, S. S. M., Markus, H. R., & Bergsieker, H. B. (2009). Emotions as within or between people? Cultural variation in lay theories of emotion expression and inference. *Personality and Social Psychology Bulletin, 35*, 1427–1439.

Van Hemert, D. A., Poortinga, Y. H., & van de Vijver, F. J. (2007). Emotion and culture: A meta-analysis. *Cognition and Emotion, 21*(5), 913–943.

Vandello, J. A., Cohen, D., & Ransom, S. (2008). U.S. Southern and Northern differences in perceptions of norms about aggression: Mechanisms for the perpetuation of a culture of honor. *Journal of Cross Cultural Psychology, 39*, 162–177. https://doi.org/10.1177/0022022107313862

Volynets, S., Glerean, E., Hietanen, J. K., Hari, R., & Nummenmaa, L. (2019). Bodily maps of emotions are culturally universal. *Emotion*. Advance online publication. https://doi.org/10.1037/emo0000624

Wallbott, H. G., & Scherer, K. R. (1986a). How universal and specific is emotional experience? Evidence from 27 countries on five continents. *Information (International Social Science Council), 25*(4), 763–795.

Wallbott, H. G., & Scherer, K. R. (1986b). The antecedents of emotional experiences. In K. Scherer, H. Wallbott, & A. Summerfield (Eds.), *Experiencing emotion: A cross-cultural study* (pp. 69–83). Cambridge, UK: Cambridge University Press.

Wallbott, H. G., & Scherer, K. R. (1988). How universal and specific is emotional experience?: Evidence from 27 countries on five continents. In K. R. Scherer (Ed.), *Facets of emotion: Recent research* (pp. 31–56). Hillsdale, NJ: Lawrence Erlbaum Associates.

Wallbott, H. G., & Scherer, K. R. (1995). *Cultural determinants in experiencing shame and guilt.* New York, NY: Guilford Press.

Watson, D., Clark, L. A., & Tellegen, A. (1988). Development and validation of brief measures of positive and negative affect: The PANAS scales. *Journal of Personality ad Social Psychology, 54,* 1063–1070.

Watson, D., & Tellegen, A. (1985). Toward a consensual structure of mood. *Psychological Bulletin, 98*(2), 219–235. https://doi.org/10.1037/0033-2909.98.2.219

Weiner, B. (1986). *An attributional theory of motivation and emotion.* New York: Springer-Verlag.

Weisz, J. R., Rothbaum, F. M., & Blackburn, T. C. (1984). Standing out and standing in: The psychology of control in America and Japan. *American Psychologist, 39*(9), 955–969.

White, G. M. (1985). Premises and purposes in a Solomon Islands ethnopsychology. In G. M. White & J. Kirkpatrick (Eds.), *Person, self, and experience: Exploring Pacific ethnopsychologies* (pp. 328–366). Berkeley, CA: University of California Press.

Wierzbicka, A. (1999). *Emotions across languages and cultures: Diversity and universals.* Cambridge, UK: Cambridge University Press.

Wierzbicka, A. (2004b). Preface: Bilingual lives, bilingual experience. *Journal of Multilingual and Multicultural Development, 25*(2–3), 94–104.

Williams, P., & Aaker, J. L. (2002). Can mixed emotions peacefully coexist? *Journal of Consumer Research, 28*(4), 636–649.

Wilson, N. L., & Gibbs, R. W., Jr. (2007). Real and imagined body movement primes metaphor comprehension. *Cognitive Science, 31*(4), 721–731.

Wong, Y., & Tsai, J. (2007). Cultural models of shame and guilt. In J. L. Tracy, R. W. Robins, & J. P. Tangney (Eds.), *The self-conscious emotions: Theory and research* (pp. 209–223). New York, NY: Guilford Press.

Wu, D. Y., & Tseng, W. S. (1985). Introduction: The characteristics of Chinese culture. In *Chinese culture and mental health* (pp. 3–13). New York, NY: Academic.

Ye, Z. (2007). Taste as a gateway to Chinese cognition. In A. Schalley & D. Khlentzos (Eds.), *Mental States (Language and cognitive structure)* (Vol. 2, pp. 109–132). Amsterdam, The Netherlands: John Benjamins.

Young, H. R., Sims, T., Charles, A., & Tsai, J. L. (2013) *Western Affective Representations of Illness Collide with Asian Americans' Affective Indicators of Illness.* Poster Presentation. Society for Personality and Social Psychology, New Orleans, LA. January 19, 2013.

Zheng, X., & Berry, J. W. (1991). Psychological adaptation of Chinese sojourners in Canada. *International Journal of Psychology, 26*(4), 451–470.

Chapter 6
Cultural Models Based on Expression of Emotions

6.1 Expression of Emotions and Culture

6.1.1 The Diverse Channels to Express Emotions

Nonverbal and Verbal Expression of Emotions Across Cultures

Emotions are expressed externally via verbal and nonverbal communication, inter-action, and behavior. People use facial expressions, gestures, body language and posture, vocal, tactile, and kinesthetic sensory systems to convey their feelings and emotions. All expressive modalities are involved in emotion communication. However, visual and auditory channels have received more research attention and coverage than others. Facial and vocal expressions were of a particular interest to scholars.

Some postures, gestures, facial expressions, and other nonverbal signals appear as cross-culturally similar in their forms and meanings. For instance, the eyebrow flash, and a 1/6th second raise of the brows, demonstrate nonverbal greetings in such different cultures as the Papuans, Samoans, Balinese, Bushmen, Europeans, and Native South Americans. The facial displays of flirting and embarrassment were also similar in those societies (see for review Keating, 1994).

Nevertheless, *same gestures* can mean *different things* for people in different cultures, while *different gestures* can have *different meanings* in different cultures. Gestures and their meanings are cultural conventions. For instance,

> shaking your head "no" to convey disagreement in the West would convey agreement in India. Just as awkwardly, the three-fingers up, thumb and index finger circled, "OK" sign in the West signals "money" in Japan, and invites a sexual encounter in much of South America (see for review Keating, 1994, p. 178)

Culture plays an important role in verbal and nonverbal expression of emotions. It affects facial expression, gaze, speech quality, tone of voice, interpersonal space, gestures, body-part movements, and whole-body movements (Cosnier, Dols, &

Fernandez, 1986; Matsumoto, 2006a; Wallbott, Ricci-Bitti, & Banninger-Huber, 1986). Several cross-cultural studies of 1980-90s reported the results for verbal and nonverbal reactions and expressions of emotions (Cosnier et al., 1986; Keating, 1994; Wallbott et al., 1986), exploring emotional response patterns. In particular, research revealed that Americans are more verbally and nonverbally emotionally expressive than Japanese are (Matsumoto, Kudoh, Scherer, & Wallbott, 1988).

The ways how people express their emotions might be qualitatively different due to different cultural meanings of certain forms of emotional expression. For instance, if Americans and many West Europeans smile to express joy, the Chinese and Japanese people may smile when they experience distress in the presence of a high-status person. They often attempt to hide anger and embarrassment by smiling (Ekman, 1972).

Cross-Cultural Patterns of Nonverbal Expressivity in Emotions

On a broader cross-cultural perspective, a large-scale study (Wallbott et al., 1986) involving eight European countries identified the typical patterns of nonverbal emotional expressive behaviors for the four emotions studied: joy, fear, sadness, and anger. It was found that for joy the distinctive expressive characteristics were "laughing and smiling," "expansive movements," and "movements towards another person." For anger, "changes in speech quality" and "changes in movement quality" were quite typical. These differences in reaction patterns of nonverbal behaviors of the emotions, however, were similar across cultural samples. Only the quantity of nonverbal reactions and the degree of control were different in those countries. Nonetheless, other researchers (Cosnier et al., 1986) in the same data set discovered significant cultural differences for the types of verbal expressions: the "nothing" response, exclamation (e.g., word, humming, and vocal emblems) and discussion (e.g., sentence, complete expression, and discussion) for the four emotions.

A cross-cultural study (Scherer & Wallbott, 1994) of seven basic emotion (*joy, sadness, fear, anger, shame, guilt,* and *disgust*) with self-report questionnaires of *expressive behavior* administered in 37 countries also found similar findings for several cultural differences in emotion regulation, symbolic representation, and expression. Approach behavior, nonverbal behavior, paralinguistic behavior, and verbal behavior were among those. Authors found the distinctive reaction patterns which were consistent and strong across the seven emotions; however, no cultural differences were found. Cultural specificity was only in the absolute level, but not in the patterns of the emotion responses.

6.1.2   The Role of Culture in Expression of Emotion

Cultural Dimension of Individualism and Expression of Emotions

What are the relations between expression of emotions and the dimensions of culture? Based on the data obtained in the earlier studies (Scherer & Wallbott, 1994; Wallbott et al., 1986), Gudykunst and Ting-Toomey (1988) computed rank order correlations between the dimensions of culture and the percentage of respondents in a culture who reported the specific type of reactions.

Verbal and nonverbal reactions (e.g., body reactions) positively correlate with individualism. Taking the United States and Japan as examples, individualistic cultures prefer the verbal aspects of communication, including direct emotional expressions, while collectivistic cultures do not fully trust the verbal dimension and pay attention to indirect messages (Gudykunst & Ting-Toomey, 1988; Okabe, 1983). Despite these latter differences, research showed that people in individualistic cultures use nonverbal expression more often than people in collectivistic cultures (see for reviews, see La France & Mayo, 1978; Ramsey, 1979).

A meta-analysis of many studies conducted across 26 countries (Van Hemert, Poortinga, & van de Vijver, 2007) brought an additional support to these findings: people in the societies, which are higher on *individualism dimension*, tend to be more emotionally expressive.

However, the influence of individualism-collectivism on the expression of emotion (more at the cultural and less at the individual level) is generally moderate, especially taking into account multifaceted and multidimensional nature of this broad dimension that includes the cluster of several cultural characteristics (Stephan, Stephan, Saito, & Barnett, 1998).

Cultural Dimension of Uncertainly Avoidance and Expression of Emotions

The picture of cross-cultural differences in nonverbal and verbal expression of emotion becomes more complex when researchers take into account the combinations of two cultural dimensions in their analyses. The following studies show such interaction between the influence of *individualism* and *uncertainty avoidance*.

According to the early studies, people in the cultures of *high uncertainty avoidance* express their emotions more than those in the cultures of *low uncertainty avoidance*. For example, in initial interactions with strangers, Japanese—the culture of high uncertainty avoidance—generally display nonverbal affiliative expressions more, compared to Americans—the culture of low uncertainty avoidance (Gudykunst & Kim, 1984; Hofstede, 1984). However, in the case of *collectivistic culture with the high uncertainty avoidance* (such as Japan), people limit their display to *positive emotions* (e.g., gratitude) because the display of *negative emotions* (e.g., anger) would decrease the harmony in the group. This cultural tendency was demonstrated in several studies (Argyle, Henderson, Bond, Iizuka, & Contarello, 1986; Matsumoto, 1990) using the samples from Japan, the United States, Hong Kong, Italy, and England. For example, the Italians and English—both from the *cultures with lower uncertainty avoidance and individualistic* scores—endorse the display of anger and distress across relationships, while the Japanese—the *culture of lower uncertainty avoidance and collectivistic* scores—did not endorse the display of anger and distress (Argyle et al., 1986). According to meta-analysis across 26 countries (Van Hemert et al., 2007), people in the *societies with high uncertainty avoidance* tend to show *more negative emotions*.

Modernization of Societies and Expression of Emotions

In light of these findings, it is important to take into account several cultural dimensions, which characterize a society, to better understand their associations with patterns of emotional expression. In this regard, an important concept of *modernization* was proposed by Inglehart and colleagues (Inglehart, 1997; Inglehart & Baker, 2000; Inglehart & Welzel, 2005); see the earlier chapter of this book for details, which distinguishes between traditional societies (characterized by *survival values*) and modernized societies (characterized by *self-expression values*). The cultural norms of societies *high in modernization dimension* encourage individuals to openly express emotions.

Cultural Dimension of Tightness-Looseness and Expression of Emotions

The cultural dimension of *tightness-looseness*, discussed in earlier sections, also affects the norms of how desirable or permissible in a society the expressions of particular emotions are (Gelfand, Nishii, & Raver, 2006; Pelto, 1968; Triandis & Suh, 2002). The societies with *tight culture* have the rigid norms for emotional expression and sanction more severely the deviation from those norms. Therefore, people tend to be reserved and reticent. They restrain themselves, as well as other members of cultural community, from overly expressive emotional behavior.

The *loose cultures* are more flexible and have fewer cultural restrictions on emotional behaviors and less strict social norms of emotional expressions permitting more deviation from the norms. The range of possible self-expressions is wider than in tight cultures. Therefore, people tend to be more emotionally expressive.

Cultural Dimension of Power Distance and Expression of Emotions

Results of several studies (Basabe et al., 2000) showed that people in the societies of *high-power distance* experience many negative emotions, yet they are less emotionally expressive. This might be because public expression of negative emotions is non-normative in these cultures.

In a culture of *high-power distance*, such as Chinese, which is characterized by *inequality of power*, the carefully monitored self-expression of emotions is very important. The disruptive displays of specific emotions and inappropriate emotional expressions are social controlled by shame techniques during socialization (see for review, Bond, 1993; Bond, Wan, Leung, & Giacalone, 1985).

The role of *high-power distance* characteristics of society in *expression of emotions* is especially important for differences in *higher- and low-status interactions*. People tend to modify their emotional expressions depending on the status of power relationships between self and others. Individuals in a society learn through emotional socialization what the appropriate emotional behavior and expressions are toward others depending on status differences.

Generally, in *high-power-distance cultures,* the emotions that *preserve status differences* are encouraged (Matsumoto, 1991). Expressing positive emotions to people of higher status and negative emotions to those of lower status is a cultural norm (Collins, 1984). Individuals prefer to *suppress emotions* toward *superiors* because their expression can threaten status differences, which are highly valued.

In *low power-distance* cultures, on the other hand, emotions that *minimize power status differences* are encouraged (Matsumoto, 1991). People tend to express positive emotions to people of lower status and negative emotions to those of higher status. In this type of egalitarian culture, individuals believe they can express negative emotions to those who are higher in status. They feel free from the fear of sanctions and necessity to suppress emotions, which threaten status differences, because the status differences in society or community are minimal.

In the *high-power-distance* societies, the differences in the style of emotional expressions toward persons of high-status and persons of low-status are larger. Conversely, in the *low power-distance* societies, such differences are smaller.

Ecological, Economical, Sociopolitical Factors and Expression of Emotions

In addition to culture, *ecological, economical, and sociopolitical* parameters may play their role in the expression of emotions. As for the temperature parameter, researchers (Pennebaker, Rimé, & Blankenship, 1996) found a small, but statistically significant positive correlation between latitude of the region where people live and their self-reported emotional expressions. It was a relatively small predictor across 26 countries (Pennebaker et al., 1996). However, the meta-analysis of other studies conducted on the topic did not find support for this temperature factor (Van Hemert et al., 2007).

As for *economic parameters*, the same comprehensive meta-analysis (Van Hemert et al., 2007) found no significant correlations. Thus, the economic wealth does not play the role in emotional expressivity. However, several *political parameters* correlate with expressivity. In the countries *with more human rights and democracy,* people tend to be generally *more emotionally expressive.* People *in more stable societies* are *higher in expression of positive emotions.* As for Hofstede's values, people in societies with higher *individualism* and *short-term orientation* tend to be more expressive in their emotions.

Psychological Factors and Expression of Emotions

Psychological variables of people being aggregated across countries can also explain the expression of emotions typical for a culture. Among those are evidently *extraversion*, subjective *well-being, optimism*, predominance of experience of *positive affect*—the variables, which positively correlate with general emotional expressivity, the tendency to express positive emotion, but negatively with the tendency to express negative emotions (Van Hemert et al., 2007).

As I commented in earlier sections, experiences of positive and negative emotions are the variables independent from each other (not necessarily opposite). The differences in self-reported experience of these two groups of emotions are frequently revealed in cross-cultural research (e.g., Diener & Emmons, 1985; Russell, 1980; Russell & Carroll, 1999; Van Hemert et al., 2007). Independence of these groups of emotions was also supported in the study of recognition of nonverbal emotional vocalizations of basic emotions across two cultures (two English and two Himba groups, Sauter, Eisner, Ekman, & Scott, 2010). Results showed that vocalizations of negative emotions are recognized across cultures, whereas vocalizations of most positive emotions are recognized with cultures. This finding supports the importance of differentiation between positive and negative emotions not only in experience but also in expression of emotions. Authors (Sauter et al., 2010) believe that this difference reflects an affiliative function of positive emotions. Expressive nonverbal vocal signals of several positive emotions are recognized within each culture, but not across cultural groups. Thus, these emotional signals are shared by members of cultural in-group. This result of their study can be interpreted as evidence that expressions of positive emotion serve affiliative social functions.

Expression of Emotions Toward Members of In-Groups and Out-Groups Across Cultures

The *cultural norms of emotion expression* also depend on the *target person* with who an individual communicates. People in different cultures tend to distinguish within their social network those individuals who belong to their in-group ("us") and out-group ("them"). For example, they may express more intense and frequent negative emotions toward out-group members and less toward in-group members. This difference reflects strong distinction between in-group (as us) and out-group (as them), as well as the concern for harmony of relationship with in-group.

Societies differ in their culturally specific conceptions of these two types of groups (Triandis, 1994). In particular, people in collectivistic cultures—due to their high conformity necessary to preserve unity and harmony within groups—tend to differentiate strongly between people who are the members of their in-group and who are not. People in individualistic societies do not distinguish, at least noticeably, between individuals who belong to their in-group and out-group. They generally feel less attachment to any group. Here is one example to illustrate these cultural differences. In the study of emotion expression (Safdar et al., 2009), the Japanese participants (from a collectivistic culture) were able to differentiate between close, medium, and distal groups better than Americans and Canadians (individualistic culture).

How does this ability to distinguish between in-group and out-group in cultures reflect on the display rules for emotion expression? Do cultures differ in this respect? American and Japanese students were asked to rate whether the expression of certain emotions is appropriate toward such target persons as family members, friends, and acquaintances (Matsumoto, 1990). According to the results of that study,

Americans, compared to Japanese, view the expression of sadness toward family members and friends as more appropriate. On the other side, Japanese, compared to Americans, consider the expression of anger toward persons outside of their extended family and close friends as more appropriate.

The similar results, partially in accord with the earlier study (Matsumoto, 1990), were obtained in the later research (Safdar et al., 2009). Authors revealed that Japanese participants, compared to Americans and Canadians, tend to differentiate better the display rules for expression of powerful emotions (anger, contempt, disgust) between close, medium, and distal groups.

6.1.3 Early Enculturation of Emotional Responses

**Enculturation of Emotional Expressions Through Interaction
with Caregivers**

Emotion patterns are acquired early in infancy. Initially, they evolve naturally and, therefore, they are largely similar across cultures. Infants' expression of emotions signals to their caregivers about their needs and affective states. Infants have limited ability to regulate expression of their emotions.

Over time, infants learn the normative character of emotions and regulation skills through interactions with caregivers. Children acquire the ways how to express and modulate emotions. Such emotional socialization involves modeling of emotions and their expression by caregivers, as well as displaying specific reactions to emotion-eliciting situations (Thompson & Meyer, 2007).

In an observational study, Japanese and American mothers reacted with the same slightly exaggerated expressions in response to the positive emotions displayed by infants. The mothers of both cultures almost never showed negative affect to their infants (Kanaya, Bradshaw, Nakamura, & Miyake, 1988; Kanaya, Nakamura, & Miyake, 1989).

The learning of culturally specific spontaneous emotional expressions begins also during infancy and early childhood. For instance, when researchers (Camras et al., 1998) observed 11-month Japanese, Chinese, and European Americans, they revealed that the Chinese were less expressive than the European American and Japanese infants. Caregivers' models of responses to emotionally charged situations of interaction with a child vary in different cultures (e.g., in the United States, Turkey, and Romania, Corapci et al., 2018). The expressive behavior that mothers display enculturates the regulation of infants' and toddlers' expressions of emotion, perhaps due to imitation (Camras et al., 1998; Friedlmeier, Corapci, Susa-Erdogan, Benga, & Kurman, 2019; Kanaya et al., 1988; Kanaya et al., 1989).

Another cross-cultural study (Friedlmeier et al., 2019 investigated mothers' behavioral patterns in a situation of delay of gratification and observed their effect on toddlers' emotional reactions. Authors found cultural similarities in these variables in the samples of Israeli-Jewish and European-Americans, representing mostly individualistic cultures, but different from the samples of Turkish and Romanians, representing collectivistic cultures.

Gender Differentiation of the Patterns of Emotional Expression in Early Childhood

Many cultures also encourage early gender differentiation of the patterns of emotion expressivity in childhood (Brody, 1999; Maccoby, 1988). Studies on child emotion expressivity have been conducted mostly in Canada, the United States, and some Western European countries with White middle and upper middle-class youth (Chaplin, 2015).

Children acquire expressive behaviors consistent with their gender roles via social learning (Chaplin, 2015). In particular, they may express or not express their emotions in certain situations according to the models exhibited by their parents. For instance, mothers may display patterns of "feminine" emotion expression when they express cheeriness even when they do not really feel it. Observing this behavior, girls may follow this feminine pattern of emotion expression in an appropriate context.

Another way how parents can develop the gender-specific expressive behavior of their children is to show greater attention to children's emotions, which are consistent with their gender-role. A study of parent–child interactions conducted with preschoolers (the age of 4 and 6 years from American White middle-class) found that girls tend to express more submissive emotions, compared to boys. Authors (Chaplin, Cole, & Zahn-Waxler, 2005) observed that fathers (surprisingly not mothers) were more responsive to situational *expressions* of *sadness, anxiety,* and other submissive by girls than boys, yet they were more responsive to situational expression of anger and other disharmonious emotions by boys than girls. This parental behavior at preschool age implicitly socializes girls to openly express *sadness* but limit their expression of *anger.*

6.2   Expressive and Nonexpressive Cultural Models

6.2.1   Cultural Display Rules for Expression of Emotions

The Concept of Cultural Display Rules

Cultures differ in beliefs about how and when emotions should be expressed (e.g. Ekman, 1972; Hochschild, 1979; Mesquita & Frijda, 1992; Shweder, 1993; Soto, Levenson, & Ebling, 2005). The societal norms of expression of emotions are called *cultural display rules* (Ekman & Friesen, 1969, 1971; Matsumoto, Yoo, Hirayama, & Petrova, 2005). People of different cultures learn the ways how to decode cultural rules. These rules are learnt early in childhood and youth and prescribe the nature and types of emotion which are acceptable to reveal in specific contexts. They impose when some feelings have to be expressed, others can never be expressed, while others only according to *expression rules* and in some contexts.

Researchers found typical expressive modes, such as amplification, deamplification, qualification, masking, in several cultural contexts (Matsumoto et al., 2005; Matsumoto, Yoo, & Fontaine, 2009; Matsumoto, Yoo, & Nakagawa, 2008). The authors describe those expressive modes as follows:

1. Express the feeling as is with no inhibitions.
2. Express the feeling, but with less intensity than one's true feelings.
3. Express the feeling, but with more intensity than one's true feelings.
4. Try to remain neutral; express nothing.
5. Express the feeling, but together with a smile to qualify one's feelings.
6. Smile only, with no trace of anything else, in order to hide one's true feelings.
   (Matsumoto et al., 2005, p. 40)

Display rules provide individuals a guidance of the normative behaviors which are appropriate to social roles (e.g., wife, husband, mother, father, daughter, son). A person should regulate their experience of emotions and expressive behaviors to act according to a social role. The display rules regulating emotional expressions are commensurate with culturally defined social roles and thus assist group survival and its social coordination.

Cross-Cultural Comparison in the Display Rules of Emotional Expressivity

Studies revealed differences in cultural display rules among four ethnic groups in the United States (Matsumoto, 1993). Researchers found cultural differences among American, Japanese, and Russian participants (Matsumoto et al., 2005). Complex patterns of cultural similarities and differences were revealed in expression of different emotions. Americans expressed fear and disgust more than Russians, while happiness more than did both Russians and Japanese. Both Americans and Russians expressed contempt and anger more than Japanese.

The Japanese participants tend to deamplify more than the Americans and the Russians. On the other hand, while Americans tend to amplify more than Russians on sadness and disgust, Japanese are inclined to amplify surprise and fear more than Russians.

A large cross-cultural study (Fernandez, Carrera, Sanchez, Paez, & Candia, 2000) included samples from 21 cultures to explore the display rules for joy, sadness, and anger in both the verbal and nonverbal domains. Results showed that participants from North American and European cultures reported higher level of emotional verbal and nonverbal expression, compared to Latin American and Asian cultures, in *sadness* and *anger*. Participants from Asian cultures reported the lowest level of emotional expression equally for *all emotions*, including *joy*. Different from Asian, but similar to Euro-American participants, Latin Americans reported higher levels of emotional expression in *joy*.

Researchers (Fernandez et al., 2000) used a broad set of cultural samples and multivariate analysis, which showed that previous studies overestimated the important of *individualism* for high *emotional expressivity*. Other cultural, social, and economic parameters may play their role.

Their results indicated that people in Latin American countries showed the lower expression of negative emotions than North Americans and Europeans, but similar to Asians. However, they revealed the higher expression of positive emotions (e.g., joy, sympathy). Latin Americans belonging to relatively collectivistic cultures highlight the importance of sociability. Therefore, they reluctantly express their negative emotions and willing to express rather positive emotions.

Another study (Safdar et al., 2009) compared emotional display rules among Japanese, US American (including White, Asians, Latinos, African American), and Canadian university students. Results showed that the display rules of Japanese culture endorse less expression of powerful emotion (e.g., contempt, anger, and disgust), compared to the two North American societies. The Japanese display rules also discourage expressing positive emotions (e.g., surprise, happiness), compared to Canadian society. The participants in Japanese and two North American samples did not differ in the display rules for expression of powerless emotions (Safdar et al., 2009). These findings generally suggest that the cultures of the United States and Canada are *expressive*, while the Japanese one is *nonexpressive*.

Interpersonal Relationships and Display Rules Across Cultures

Expressiveness versus *nonexpressiveness in display rules* also *depends* on how the affective modes of emotion affect *interpersonal relationships*. Across many cultural contexts, people tend to express positive emotions much as they feel, and they tend to control their expression of negative emotions (Matsumoto et al., 2008). Expression of positive emotions generally attracts people to each other, while expression of negative emotions repulses them from each other. The results of studies showed that such negative emotion as *contempt*, *anger*, and *disgust* are potentially disruptive to social relationships in any culture and, therefore, must be controlled. Because of this destructive effect on interpersonal relationship, the cultural norms of many societies encourage to minimize the expression of these emotions toward in-group members and individuals of higher status (Gottman & Levenson, 2000; Matsumoto & Hwang, 2012; Rozin, Lowery, Imada, & Haidt, 1999).

The *display rules* are found to be different in relationships with people from in-group and out-group. They tend to be more expressive toward the members of in-groups than to the members of out-groups (Matsumoto et al., 2008). People within in-group relationship share their past and present experiences, expectations for the future. They feel like they belong to these groups, with a sense of familiarity and trust. Therefore, they experience less anxiety, less ambiguity and uncertainty that allow them to be more expressive. The results of the study (Matsumoto, Yoo, Fontaine, et al., 2008) demonstrated that this in-group versus out-group difference in expressivity is cross-culturally similar. Participants across all 32 countries think that the expression of emotions toward members of in-groups is more appropriate than toward members of out-groups. In addition, authors conclude that these cultures have different display rules for family (close friends) and strangers. People tend to express their positive emotions when they are with family and close friends, but prefer to suppress negative emotions when they are with strangers. Some empirical data show that the *display rules coincide* with *actual expressions of emotions* which people display (e.g., Matsumoto & Hwang, 2012; Matsumoto & Kupperbusch, 2001; Wagner & Smith, 1991).

Among specific emotions, *fear, disgust,* and *contempt* are rated as the least suitable emotions with both the members of in-group and out-group. The expressions of these emotions are disturbing for social relationships, as studies showed (Gottman & Levenson, 2000; Matsumoto, Yoo, Fontaine, et al., 2008; Rozin et al., 1999).

Display rules, however, *may not correspond* to *real emotion expression.* Although the Japanese participants in Matsumoto's study (Matsumoto, 1990) stated that they would be more likely than Americans to express negative emotions to out-groups, the Japanese subjects in Friesen's study of 1972 (as quoted in Matsumoto, 1990) of spontaneous emotional expressions smiled to mask their negative feelings in the presence of other. Thus, the values and real behavior do not always coincide.

Dimensions of Culture and Display Rules

The early research revealed the effect of *individualism* and *collectivism*, as well as *power distance* on display rules among Japanese and Americans (Matsumoto, 1990). In comparison of Japanese (as a collectivistic culture with high power distance) and Americans (as an individualistic culture with low power distance), Matsumoto found that the Americans considered sadness and disgust in in-group as more appropriate to express than did Japanese; it is because the American culture is tolerant of negative emotions in in-group and do not see such expression as threatening factor to cohesion or harmony. The Americans also consider happiness in *public* as more appropriate than the Japanese did; it is because American culture does not sanction, but rather encourage positive emotions to out-group. Thus, cultural differences in individualism-collectivism explain these results very well.

The Japanese believed that anger is appropriate to express in out-group and with lower-status others. In Japanese culture the value of *power distance* (power, status, and hierarchical relationships) is very high. Therefore, the Japanese culture allows the expression of negative emotions toward lower-status others to maintain power distances within vertical relationships, to foster greater differentiation between in-groups and out-groups, and facilitate in-group harmony. According to collectivistic values, greater distinctions toward out-groups increase the greater degree of harmony in the in-groups. The American culture, on the other side, emphasizes equality and therefore, discourage displays of negative emotions to lower-status others as these emphasize differences (Matsumoto, 1990).

Later studies of 1990s-2000s have demonstrated association of *individualism* and *collectivism,* as a cultural dimension, with *expressivity norms* using more cultural samples (e.g., Matsumoto, Takeuchi, Andayani, Kouznetsova, & Krupp, 1998; Matsumoto, Yoo, Fontaine, et al., 2008; Safdar et al., 2009).

The results of questionnaire study (Matsumoto et al., 1998) of cultural differences in display rules across seven emotions in four countries (the United States, Russia, Japan, and South Korea) were also in support of this role of *individualism-collectivism* in the cultural groups measured in that study at the individual level as *idiocentrism* (an individualistic personality trait))and *allocentrism* (a collectivistic personality trait). In another study (Matsumoto & Kupperbusch, 2001) researchers found that *idiocentric* participants did not mask their negative feelings to a higher status experimenter, whereas *allocentric* participants did. *Allocentric participants* masked not only negative, but also positive emotions. Thus, the display rules of collectivistic culture encourage the suppression of all emotions.

The survey study across 32 countries (Matsumoto, Yoo, Fontaine, et al., 2008) showed that the higher cultural *individualism* in a country is accompanied by the norms of higher expressivity, especially for positive emotions. On the other end, the countries, which are high in cultural *collectivism,* have the *display rule* norms encouraging less overall expressivity. Authors attempted to interpret this finding by the fact that the higher *individualism* is correlated with higher country-level extraversion, as a personality trait characterizing expressiveness. However, I believe this association of individualism with higher expressivity can be better explained via distinction between *traditional* and *modern societies* (Inglehart, 1997; Inglehart & Baker, 2000; Inglehart & Welzel, 2005), which I described in details in previous sections. *Traditional societies* encourage *survival values,* while *modern societies* encourage *self-expression values. Traditional societies* tend to be predominantly *collectivistic,* whereas *modern societies* tend to be predominantly *individualistic.*

Another cross-cultural study of *display rules* (Safdar et al., 2009), cited in an earlier section, found differences in the norms of expression of emotions in the Japanese, the US American, and Canadian samples (Safdar et al., 2009). These differences generally reflect the common cultural norms of collectivistic and individualistic societies (Eid & Diener, 2001).

The tendencies of people to suppress their emotions are associated with several cultural values (Matsumoto, Yoo, & Nakagawa, 2008). In societies, which concern about the maintenance of *social order,* with corresponding high value in *embeddedness*, *hierarchy*, *long-term orientation,* and low value in individual *affective autonomy* and *egalitarianism,* people tend to suppress their emotions. The social norms of these cultures encourage suppression of emotional expression because such regulation is important to adapt to relationships in a given social context.

In the study that was cited in earlier sections (Fernandez et al., 2000) authors were able to identify several cultural parameters of societies, which were associated with verbal and nonverbal expression of emotions. These are *high individualism, cultural femininity,* and *low power distance.* In these cultures, people do not mask their genuine emotions. They believe that the expression of emotions will not break their social relationships.

People in the cultures of *high collectivism, cultural masculinity, high power distance*, and *low uncertainty avoidance* tend to be less expressive in their emotions both verbally and nonverbally. The data from that study did not find the straight association between *uncertainty avoidance* and *emotional expressivity*.

The other parameters probably mediate their relations. For example, the *high uncertainty avoidance* of *Latin American* countries is different compared to *high uncertainty avoidance* of *southern European* countries. The expression of emotion in Latin American societies is lower; their cultural norms suggest emotional regulation suppressing emotions (Fernandez et al., 2000).

Cultural Comparison in the Expression of Positive and Negative Emotions

In many individualistic countries (in particular, in the United States), experience of positive emotions (especially *happiness*) is a high priority. Social norms put an extensive pressure on people to feel *joyful* and *happy* and to express these feelings. Therefore, people look for joyful and happy situations in their life. *Unhappiness* is perceived as a personal failure and its expression as deviation (Eid & Diener, 2001).

In many *collectivistic countries* (e.g., China) experience and *expression of positive emotions* are perceived as *undesirable*. For instance, Chinese participants of cross-cultural study reported the lower intensity and frequency of positive emotions (e.g., *joy* and *happiness*) compared to America and Australia (Eid & Diener, 2001). According to other study (Safdar et al., 2009), however, the Japanese attitudes toward expression of positive emotion are less definite. Thus, collectivistic culture (in this case Japan) does not differ from individualistic cultures (American and Canada) in this attitude.

People in *collectivistic cultures* tend to *avoid open expression of emotions*. This cultural disposition in display rules is particularly important for *negative powerful emotions*. The open expressions of *contempt, disgust*, and *anger* are culturally inappropriate in *the collectivistic societies*, such as Japanese (Miyake & Yamazaki, 1995), because such expressions *threaten authority* and *disrupt interpersonal harmony*.

Another study (Matsumoto et al., 1998), however, revealed that the Japanese keep under control more than do Americans. They tend to limit not only the display of powerful negative emotions, but also such a positive emotion as happiness.

The positivity tendency in expressive behavior was demonstrated in the study where dating couples talked about conflicts in their relationships (Tsai, Levenson, & McCoy, 2006). Even though the data did not show any differences in autonomic reactivity and emotional experience in two cultural samples, yet results revealed that European American dating partners displayed in their conversations more positive and less negative emotional expressions compared to Chinese American partners.

In *individualistic cultures*, such as the US American and Canadian societies, people view the *expression of negative powerful emotions*, such as contempt, disgust, and anger, as *functional*. When they are expressed in a proper way, such expressions promote self-assertion and protect freedom and individual rights (Eid & Diener, 2001). Many people in those cultures believe that the expression of anger may help to clarify a situation (Eid & Diener, 2001). Therefore, they are more tolerant to expressions of these emotions (Safdar et al., 2009). In earlier study, participants in an American sample exhibited less control over contempt, anger, and disgust than participants from collectivistic countries (Matsumoto et al., 1998).

The *attitudes toward expression of powerless emotions,* such as sadness and fear, are *less definite in collectivistic cultures* because they do not obviously threaten intragroup unity and interpersonal harmony. They withdraw an individual from a group, but not disrupt relationship. Therefore, collectivistic cultures do not differ from individualistic in this regard (Safdar et al., 2009). In earlier study, however, participants from an American sample—*individualistic culture   exhibited more control* over displays of sadness and fear than participants from collectivistic countries (Matsumoto et al., 1998).

Another more comprehensive study of display rules (Matsumoto et al., 2009) involved 32 countries to survey display rules for emotions of anger, contempt, disgust, fear, happiness, sadness and surprise in public and private settings during interaction with several target figures: father, mother, brother, sister, close friend, acquaintance, when alone, and so on.

However, even within Western, presumably individualistic cultures, a diversity of expression can occur. For example, *in the expression of sympathy Americans tend to avoid negative emotions* more than Germans do since they feel not comfortable expressing the sympathy with only negative feelings (Koopmann-Holm & Tsai, 2014). Another example is the difference between Americans and Canadians in the display rules for expression of contempt. *Americans think that people should express contempt* more than the Canadians do (Safdar et al., 2009). Authors explain this difference referring to the representation of personality in these two societies (Terracciano & McMcrae, 2007). Canadians believe that the typical personality trait of a Canadian is agreeableness, while Americans think that the typical personality trait of an American is assertiveness. Since it is more valuable for Canadians to appear agreeable, compared to Americans, then they believe that they should constrain the expression of contempt (Safdar et al., 2009).

6.2.2   Cultural Model of Emotional Expression and Cultural Model of Emotional Control

Effect of Cultural Dimensions on the Values of Expression Versus Suppression of Emotions

Some cultural traditions encourage *freedom of emotional expression,* while others suggest *exercising emotional control.* Comparison of expressive style between Westerners (e.g., Americans) and Easterners (e.g., Chinese and Japanese) can illustrate this distinction. For example, *Americans* tend to be more *extroverted in their emotions,* whereas members of many *Asian cultures* believe in the *importance of moderating and controlling their emotions* (see for review, Tsai & Levenson, 1997).

However, the following sections demonstrate that this East-West distinction does not fully explain the diversity of emotional expressivity styles in many cultures.

Individualism (versus *collectivism*), *power distance, cultural masculinity*, and some other cultural variables at the country level of analysis frequently showed their relations with emotional expressivity. For example, it was found that people in the United States—*individualistic culture*—are *more expressive* in their *negative emotions* compared to people in Costa Rica and Japan—collectivistic cultures (Stephan et al., 1998; Stephan, White, & Cabezas, 1996).

The people in *collectivistic* societies and *high-power distance* are generally *less emotionally expressive*. However, the *expression of good feelings* (e.g., sympathy) to others is more typical for the countries *high in collectivism* and *power distance*, where respect and harmony are especially valued. The public expression of distress, anger, and even excessive joy may be understood by others as the lack of respect. Thus, the cultures with *high power distance* endorse the emotional expressions which legitimize differences in social status (Fernandez et al., 2000).

Independent and Interdependent Models of Self and Expression of Emotions

Differences in emotions between Western and East Asian cultures, which come from their *independent* vs. *interdependent models of self*, are in the importance, which they place on emotional *expression* or *suppression* (Markus & Kitayama, 1991; Tsai & Clobert, 2019). As it was described in previous sections, people with *independent model of self* recognize them-selves as separate from others. They believe in priorities of personal needs, desires, beliefs, and preferences. Conversely, people with *interdependent models of self* recognize them-selves as related to others. They believe in priorities of others' needs, duties, and affiliations with others.

Due to the self-conceptions in these two types of culture, people have different attitudes toward expression of emotions. *Norms of Western cultures* encourage not only *independent models of self*, but also a *free expression of emotion* since such an open expression highlights the self of a person as separate and unique. In addition, emotional expression is viewed as important to psychological health. Since *Western cultures* place *high value on emotional expression*, then *emotional control and suppression are harder* for European Americans, and it might be harmful because it is contrary to their cultural ideal (e.g., Butler, Lee, & Gross, 2007; Mauss & Butler, 2010, see for more detailed review, Tsai & Clobert, 2019).

In contrast with this, *Eastern cultures* encourage *interdependent models of self*, and *discourage open expression of emotions*. Cultural norms suggest that an open expression of emotions can make others feel bad and, thus, may be damaging for interpersonal harmony (Soto et al., 2005). *Easterners*, compared with Westerners, tend to *control emotions*. They are *less expressive in their emotions* (Heine, 2010; Henrich, Heine, & Norenzayan, 2010; Kitayama & Cohen, 2007; Markus & Kitayama, 1991). People in Eastern cultures usually do not impose their emotions on others because this can be detrimental for maintaining harmonious relationships.

In such cultural contexts, people, instead of expressing their emotions, tend to suppress them (Ford & Mauss, 2015; Matsumoto, 1990; Su, Wei, & Tsai, 2014; Wei, Su, Carrera, Lin, & Yi, 2013). Since *Eastern cultures* place *high value on suppression*, rather than *emotional expression*, then emotional control and suppression are in accordance with their cultural ideal, and it is beneficial for Asians (Butler et al., 2007; Le & Impett, 2013; Mauss & Butler, 2010, see also for more detailed review, Tsai & Clobert, 2019). Due to their cultural norms, which they are learned, East Asians down-regulate and suppress their emotions easier, and this requires fewer resources than it does for European Americans (Murata, Moser, & Kitayama, 2013).

The cultural tradition to employ *passive withdrawal* as a defensive tactics is common for several Asian cultures. The avoiding communication of their views, decreasing involvement and further interaction with others are the hidden psychological ways to deal with negative emotions. The most favored reactions are of the *passive* type, rarely *active* (Barnlund, 1975, p.448).

Results of research showed that in a variety of social situations and relationships Asian people consider emotional expressions as less "appropriate" than do European Americans (Matsumoto, 1993). These cultural norms affect the ability of emotional self-regulation. According to research (Soto, Perez, Kim, Lee, & Minnick, 2011), Asian and European Americans reveal the same level of emotion displayed when asked to suppress emotional reactions in emotionally evoked situation. However, the European Americans are more capable than Asian Americans to display their emotion when they need to amplify their emotional reactions. These conclusions were supported by psychophysiological, behavioral, and self-report measures. As I commented elsewhere, these differences are in accord with the cultural benefits of suppression for Asian Americans and the utility of expression for European Americans.

Socialization of Emotion Regulation in Childhood

Cultural norms of emotion expression and regulation are acquired by children quite early. They learn how to adjust their expression of emotions according to the culturally accepted display rules about when, where, and how to express emotions (Saarni, 1999).

For development of *emotion regulation* abilities, it is important to distinguish between emotion experience and emotion expression. As a result, display rules evolve. A cross-cultural study (Joshi & MacLean, 1994) compared English and Indian preschoolers of the age 4–5 years and found that Indian girls were able to differentiate experience of emotions and their expressions better than Indian boys, as well as better than English girls and boys. They explained that the expression of emotion is based on social norms, which expect their respect to elders, submission to authority, and social obligations. *Concealment* of negative emotions is an example of those *cultural display rules.*

Another study (Raval, Martini, & Raval, 2007) explored further the *display rules* of Indian children. Authors found that the urban Indian Gujarati children of age 5–9 years view *sadness* and *anger* as less appropriate for overt expression than *pain.* Girls expressed *sadness* more often than *anger.* When the girls expressed their sadness and anger, they did this indirectly—in a subtle way. Thus, Indian girls and boys tend to control their emotions. However, gender differences were also present. Girls attempted to control their *anger* more frequently than boys.

Other study compared emotion regulation between Nepalese and American children. Authors found that *Brahman Nepalese* children of early school age (first through fifth grade) are more aware of the need to conceal anger than *Tamang Nepalese* or *American* children (Cole, Bruschi, & Tamang, 2002; Cole & Tamang, 1998);

Similarly, comparison of preschool children of age 4–5 years in Japan and the United States (Zahn-Waxler, Friedman, Cole, Mizuta, & Hiruma, 1996) showed that Japanese children attempted to regulate their emotions (e.g., in response to conflict) more frequently and expressed less anger and aggression than American children.

Other example presents a comparison of emotional expressions displayed by Chinese-American and European-American children of age 4 and 7 years (Garrett-Peters & Fox, 2007). Researchers investigated the emotion display rules in a disappointing situation—upon receipt of an undesirable gift. European American children of 7 years old were able to mask their disappointment and express positive emotion better than those of 4 years old. This looks as an evolving socialization of emotional regulation through these years. However, the expression of positive emotion by Chinese-American children of 7 years old was still the same low, as their 4 years old counterparts. The latter fact seems surprising due to the emphasis that Chinese culture places on emotional restraint. Interpreting this unexpected finding, authors assume that Chinese cultural norms might endorse emotional restraint of sadness and anger, but not disappointment.

Acculturation seems also play its role: the Chinese-American children who were more adapted to American culture displayed the emotion expression similar to European American children (i.e., they masked the disappointment and showed positive expression). As for gender differences, girls displayed less negative expressions than boys in both cultural groups (Garrett-Peters & Fox, 2007).

Development of *emotional regulation* of *positive emotions* in childhood is also culturally specific. Children in Eastern and Western societies differ in how they express *positive emotions.* Eastern children learn their *cultural norm of modesty* and therefore, prefer to *conceal the expression of positive emotions.* In particular, researchers (Lee, Aaker, & Gardner, 2000) found that Chinese and Taiwanese children of 11 years old thought that it is good and acceptable to keep unnoticed, even concealed, their own good deeds and achievements compared to younger children of 7 years of age. Similarly, Japanese preschool children expressed less pride (rather embarrassment) when they achieved a success, compared to European-American and African-American children (Lewis, Takai-Kawakami, Kawakami, & Sullivan, 2010).

Thus, children acquire the cultural norms for expression of emotions quite early. The studies have revealed so far cross-cultural differences in their display rules consistent with traditional opposition of Western, individualistic and Eastern, collectivistic cultures. In individualistic societies, parents encourage and children accept the norms of open expression of emotions as self-expression of their individuality. In collectivistic societies, parents endorse and children acquire quite early their cultural norms of social harmony and modesty and the corresponding display rules of concealment of positive and negative emotions.

These differences are consistent with *emotional competence models* of emotional development (Friedlmeier, Corapci, & Cole, 2011). According to *individualistic emotional competence* model, which is based on *independent self-construal* (prevalent in Western cultures), emotions reflect individual needs and, therefore, should be openly communicated and respected. Different from that, *relational emotional competence* model, which is based on *interdependent self-construal* (prevalent in Eastern cultures), emotions have lesser importance in life than in-group interests. Therefore, respect to others and proper demeanors have priority over open emotion expression. These cultures endorse the open expression only for socially engaging emotions (such as shame and guilt) which promote the regulation of social relationships and maintenance of social harmony. Multiple studies have shown how children acquire these culturally specific *emotional competences* and how emotion socialization fosters cultural differences in emotion expression (see for review, Friedlmeier, Corapci, & Benga, 2015).

Chinese Style of Emotion Expression

Chinese moral idea of *moderation in emotions* has originated from ancient Confucian teachings. Therefore, children are socialized to control their impulses (Ho, 1994). Social harmony, being associated with self-control of emotions, is of higher priority than individual self-expression (Klineberg, 1938; Wu & Tseng, 1985). Studies suggest (see for review, Bond, 1993) that Chinese tend to carefully regulate their expression of emotion. This cultural norm is driven by the concern that excessive expressivity would disrupt status hierarchy and group harmony.

In Chinese culture, the *feelings in close relationship* are *assumed*, but are *not communicated*. Chinese tend to avoid discussing and expressing the nature of their emotions in family relationships. "The son does not know the mother's heart; the mother does not know the son's heart"—a Chinese proverb among villagers says (Potter, 1988, p. 201). The same way, a father does not openly express his affection to a son. A cultural tradition of appropriate behavior recommends to exhibit the due distance between parents and children. Chinese believe that social and physical distance, rather than display of affection, is a better way to maintain a proper relationship. They think that an open expression of emotion can weaken the strength of the relationship between parent and their children, in which the patterns of obedience and respect supposed to be fundamental.

To the Chinese, the *speaking about emotion* to affirm relationships is alien and is *not relevant for their close relationships* (Potter, 1988). The *capacity to do something good*, rather than the capacity to feel and express, is viewed as the most important.

Even though generally, Chinese exhibit emotional displays sparsely, yet Potter (1988) observed that Chinese villagers do not hide their emotions and do not avoid their expression. They *can be expressive* in their daily life, but *do not consider talking about their emotions as important*.

Japanese Style of Emotion Expression

Japanese expressive style contains many *respectful, humble* forms, and a variety of strategies for marking *politeness*. The context of conversation is important in order to elicit the meaning beyond the words. Japanese rarely use personal names (Nishimura, Nevgi, & Tella, 2008).

The study of early 1970s (Barnlund, 1975), conducted among Japanese students, discovered highly consistent profiles of their expressive culture, both from Japanese and American view. The Japanese perceived themselves and were viewed by Americans as "formal," "reserved," "evasive," and "cautious." The Japanese also added such terms as "silent," "serious," and "dependent." Thus, *Japanese favor formal encounters*. They are cautious and *reserved in expressing themselves*, preferring to be silent and evasive rather than frank and open. Their highly contained self is controlled and cautiously expressed. Their larger private self is hidden and unknown. These attributes are consistent with early publications of scholars (e.g., Benedict, 1946, Doi, 1962, Nakamura, 1964, Nakane, 1970, see for detailed review and references Barnlund, 1975).

Japanese prefer to *limit their personal disclosure*: both verbally and nonverbally. Their average level of self-disclosure is 0.75 (compared to Americans—1.12, Barnlund, 1975). However, for trusted people (male and female friends, mother and father) Japanese self-disclosure scores are higher—1.00 (compared to Americans—1.44). Thus, the Japanese maintain greater interpersonal distance than Americans, even with closest associate and intimates. About half of their interpersonal communication with intimates involves a moderately full exposure of the inner self. Mainly, the Japanese tend to talk—even with their parents and closest friends—only in the general terms.

As for the ideal husband-wife communication, 54% of the husbands and 71% of the wives agreed that "discussing matters freely and openly" is important, 43% of the husbands and only 23% of the wives agreed with the statement that "in an ideal marriage the husband and wife understand each other without speaking" (Morsbach, 1988b, p. 210).

Physical contact is a sensitive indicator of interpersonal distance. People in Japan acquire different rules concerning physical contact than in the United States. Japanese—similar Americans—had their closest contact with opposite sex friend, then with mothers, then with same sex friends, and lastly with fathers. However, there were some cultural differences (Barnlund, 1975). Japanese consider opposite sex friends as somewhat more eligible as mothers or same sex friends.

Touch in a close relationship is used in Japan the same way as in the United States. Receiving and initiating physical contact are reciprocal: lower or higher frequency of being touched is related to a lower or higher frequency of touching. Nevertheless, in both cultures men have slightly more "touching" contact with the opposite sex, whereas females experience a relatively higher incidence of "being touched." (Barnlund, 1975).

In case of messages that intrude their private life, themselves, or their view of the world, Japanese prefer such defensive tactics as "passive withdrawal." Although they may use various forms and content in their reaction, nevertheless, the hidden psychological theme is to avoid communication of their views, and decrease involvement and further interaction with others.

They often select to "say I did not want to discuss it," "hint verbally I preferred not to answer," and "remain silent." They rarely report "tell him to mind his own business," "use humor or sarcasm to put him in his place," or "defend myself by explanation and argument." The most favored replies are of the "passive" type, rarely "active." (Barnlund, 1975, p. 448).

Indian Style of Emotion Expression

Expressive style in Indian culture is characterized by *interpersonal distance*. People talk to elderly persons in respectful forms. Younger brothers and sisters never call their elder sibling by their first name; only as *tai* (eldest sister), *mai* (second eldest sister), and *bhau* (eldest brother). (Nishimura et al., 2008, p. 792). Indian English is formal, poetic, and polite with expressions of humility and respect terminology.

For Indian people, verbal and nonverbal expressive behavior does not have the purpose to exchange facts and knowledge, or share emotions; communication is rather the way to maintain harmony and forge relationships (Lewis, 1996, 2003; Pakiam, 2007). Indians tend to use long sentences and ambiguous expressions with multiple meanings. That can lead to misunderstandings between communicators from high-context Indian and Western low-contact cultures (Zaidman, 2001).

Indians are *family-oriented, loyal to their group*; they obey to a hierarchical system, obligations, and duties of being a member of the family. They are *collectivist in their local group*, but *individualistic in relations with outsiders* (Lewis, 1996, 2003).

Kaluli Style of Emotion Expression

The *Kaluli* are the nonliterate indigenous people living in the tropical forest in Papua New Guinea. It is an *egalitarian society*—there are no positions of fixed authority or status. Individuals undertake their own initiatives and encourage cooperation of others. The force of character and energetic assertiveness are in the cultural spirit of *Kaluli* men.

The strong personal energy determines the emotional style, which Schieffelin (1983) characterized as *expressively passionate*. When *Kaluli people* experience a strong emotion, such as embarrassment, fear, rage, grief, and compassion, they do not hide their feelings, but rather openly expressed it. Expressing their emotions, they tend to influence others. They frighten them, as in case of anger, or elicit their compassion and support, as in case of grief. *Distress and grief are openly expressed* to prompt sympathy and support of others. Thus, as Schieffelin (1983) highlights, this display of emotions function rather "as declarations of mind, motivation, and/or intention than as mere cathartic expressions of feeling" (p. 183).

In this regard, for the *Kaluli* people, an *expression of anger* implies that the angry person suffers some kind of loss, an unfulfilled desire, or frustrated hope. A display of anger is not only frightening, but it frequently means a vigorous plea for support. Yelling about a distress for all to hear, the person intends to arouse their sympathetic attention. Expression of anger for the Kaluli is a rhetorical and legitimate force of their assertive cultural spirit.

6.2.3 Diversity of Expressiveness Within Western Cultures

The Norms of Emotional Expression in Homogeneous and Heterogeneous Societies

It is reasonable to expect that *emotional expression* depends on how *homogeneous* or *heterogeneous* the societies are in their historical cultural perspectives: whether contemporary population of a country has descended from migration from few or numerous countries over a period of 500 years (Rychlowska et al., 2015). People in historically homogeneous societies have a common language, norms, and cultural practices, while people in historically heterogeneous societies are diverse in this regard.

The theory proposes that *people* in historically *heterogeneous societies* should be able to *amplify their emotional expressions* in order to convey their feelings accurately. When researchers re-analyzed the data on display rules from 32 countries (Matsumoto, Yoo, Fontaine, et al., 2008), they discovered that people in historically more heterogeneous countries have stronger beliefs that emotions should be expressed openly, rather than suppressed. They also agreed that smiling serve social bonding, rather than status signaling functions (Rychlowska et al., 2015).

Some cultures have strong norms about regulating emotions to fulfill institutional roles and standards—*institutional orientation*—while other cultures value expressing unregulated emotions—*impulsive orientation* (Gordon, 1989). Both orientations can be used by people of any culture, depending on the context. France represents a culture with impulsive orientation, whereas the United States represents the culture with the institutional orientation toward emotional behavior.

Grandey, Fisk, and Steiner (2005) suggest the United States as an example of a culture with a strong institutional orientation toward emotion. For Americans, there is a strong norm to act positively and hide negative feelings to make good impressions (Schneider, 1981). Americans in their style of verbal communication often use the headline style: they usually announce what they are going to talk about at the beginning. Americans tend to smile in greeting and during formal introductions (Hall & Hall, 1990, p. 142) and are more concerned with inhibiting anger than European and Asian students (Sommers, 1984a, b).

American Expressive Style

Americans prefer to be direct in their messages and sometimes miss such nonverbal cues as slight changes in body posture, breathing, and subtle shifts in voice. Americans like to brag, boast, and exaggerate their emotions. They admire a good sense of humor, jokes, and tend to use humor to reduce tensions in social situations. Americans prefer to maintain their social conversations light, not engaging in serious philosophical discussions, viewing philosophy as an abstract and theoretical field (Hall & Hall, 1990).

Americans also differ from Germans in their expression of sympathy as a response to someone's suffering. Americans tend to avoid negative emotion more than Germans do. Wanting to avoid negative emotion, Americans feel less comfortable with expressions of sympathy mentioning only negative feelings. Comparing American and German sympathy cards (Tsai, Koopmann-Holm, Miyazaki, & Ochs, 2013), researchers found that American sympathy cards are more positive and optimistic than German cards (e.g., "May you find comfort"), whereas German sympathy cards are more negative (e.g., "I hope these words show how much I share your pain").

Americans also differ from Japanese in their expression of emotion. The study of early 1970s (Barnlund, 1975) discovered highly consistent profiles of their expressive culture, viewed both from American and Japanese perspectives. Americans saw themselves and were perceived by Japanese as "informal," "talkative," "frank," "self-assertive," and "spontaneous." Japanese perceived Americans as "humorous," while Americans perceived themselves rather "impulsive." Thus, the Americans favor informal encounters, they are self-expressive, self-assertive, talkative, and spontaneous. They are frank and open sharing their experience. Regarding verbal and nonverbal disclosure, overall, Americans showed a higher level of self-revelation. The average level of disclosure among Americans exceeds verbal disclosure of Japanese—even in their intimate relationships. Americans lovers need to hear frequently that their partners love them.

As for physical contact as an indicator of interpersonal distance, in all categories of relationships, physical contact of Americans was twice frequent compared to Japanese. Americans perceive opposite sex friends as most attractive. Most Americans mentioned that they had physical contact with an opposite sex friend in all areas of the body. Americans seems to be more physically accessible and more physically expressive in all close relationships.

Anger seems to be common in American culture. Tavns suggested (1982) that "the individualism of American life. .. creates anger and encourages its release; for when everything is possible, limitations are irksome" (p. 65). Thus, the widespread expressions of anger stems from the extent of American sense of their rights. The Americans' notion of *individualism* and their extensive rights constituted their *cultural meaning of anger*.

In case when others intrude personal space of Americans, private life, or challenge their view of the world, they employ "active aggression" strategy. They prefer to increase their involvement, further elaborate their beliefs, and aggressively reply to those who challenge their beliefs. They respond with threatening communication and use active forms such as "answer the remark directly, even though uncomfortable," "defend myself by explanation and argument," and "use humor and sarcasm to put him in his place." They rare select to "ask others what they think," "laugh," and "change the subject" (Barnlund, 1975, p.449). There are no significant gender differences in both American and Japanese cultures; cultural differences override sexual ones.

It is commonplace that *European American culture encourages* people to *express their emotions openly*; there is a belief that such nonrestrained emotional self-expression promotes relationship satisfaction and health. It is worthwhile to note that cultural groups in the United States are quite heterogeneous; therefore, it is not quite correct and adequate to compare emotional expressiveness of Asians with Americans or Europeans (so called Westerners).

Among *European Americans*, *expression of emotions* also *depends on their immigration descent*. Normative cultural differences in expression of emotions remain consistent with their country of origins. For instance, European Americans of Scandinavian descent tend to be less expressive, while European Americans of Irish descent are more inclined to be more expressive (Tsai & Chentsova-Dutton, 2003). And these differences are especially large in the expression of love and happiness.

French Expressive Style

France, on another side, is an example of a *culture with impulsive orientation toward emotion*. The French have a very emotional way to do things: they can be very joyous and engaging. Yet, sometimes the French temper lashes out (Hallowell, Bowen, & Knoop, 2002, p. 14) that indicate an impulsive orientation compared with Americans. The French do not concern about "phony chumminess" or false informalities (Hall & Hall, 1990, p. 117). "Service with a smile" is present in the United States not only in business and service sphere, but in other areas of life as well, while the French do not care about this.

Hall and Hall (1990, p. 102) characterize the French communication style as *eloquent, indirect, and frank*. That is in some contrast not only with American, but also with neighboring German culture, where a direct approach to communication is a norm.

French people relish small talks and conversations. Every engagement begins with general conversation. They are usually informed about current events and willingly discuss those. Being high-context communicators, in their dialogues the French prefer to leave a room for imagination not spelling out some details. In verbal communication, they admire sophistication, mystery, and nuances of expression.

The *French high-context communication style* has some similarity, yet differences with Japanese high-context culture. The French frequently talk about something without explicit expression, assuming that a listener understands the hidden message intuitively. In this regard, their communication style is similar to the Japanese culture. Yet, their style is different because they enjoy spirited discussion with logical rhetoric.

As for emotional life and actions, the early Mediterranean cultures influenced the modern *French culture* and people's behavior substantially *more similar to the cultures of southern Europe* than to the *cultures of other northern European countries*. The French are traditionalists; they respect status, formalities, and have a good sense of humor.

The French seemingly contradictory behavior might be due to internal conflicts between emotion, logic, and pragmatism. French people *experience emotions intensely and openly*, sometimes demonstratively, express their affection, love, displeasure, and anger. They tend to actively defend their opinion in discussion and mentally engage in highly detailed problems of great complexity, not giving up until it is solved.

The French are impatient, have a tendency to internal conflicts between emotions and pragmatism or logic. Patience is not on the top French values, may be because of their temperament. People act in fast tempo: move rapidly and think quickly, expecting a simple yes or no, not lengthy discussion, seeking to make a decision (Hall & Hall, 1990).

The Catholic faith teaches them forgiveness. Parents teach them self-discipline, obedience, and good manners. In adult life, they expect obedience from subordinates. The French are conservative traditionalists and resistant to change, even though throughout recent decades, they are becoming more open to new experiences.

The *French* are very *individualistic people*, not always responsive to other people's needs. They are also not responsive to public pressure or to pressures from others. Unlike Germans, *they are nonconformists*. The French are meticulous about social norms being strongly perfectionist in style, behavior, dress, and manners. They are polite and expect precision in language using the proper approach in social interactions. The stance and posture of a person during interaction convey correctness and formality. They do not favor informal and casual style of Americans (Hall & Hall, 1990).

German Expressive Style

German expressive style is usually characterized as direct, straightforward, and detailed *in its verbal expression. Germans*, as the people of *low-context culture*, tend to provide much more information and explanations than people from high-context cultures actually need. They like examples, facts, and figures logically and orderly outlining those to preserve credibility. The summary of all major points at the end of communication is very important, even if they have already been explained earlier (Hall & Hall, 1990, pp. 49–50).

Some grammatical and lexical features of German language reflect on their culture of verbal communication. The verb frequently comes at the end of a German sentence; thus, it takes a while for a listener to fully understand what a German speaker is going to say until the end of the speech. The German language is more literal than English and the meanings of words are usually precise. While many English words can be used in various senses, each German word has an exact meaning (Hall & Hall, 1990).

Germans are *conformists*. They are serious, frank, realistic, and prefer a conservative approach to both manners and dress. Germans are persistent, stubborn, and might be arrogant. Drastically different from Americans, they are serious and dislike social chit-chat and small talks. They are not open to casual acquaintances or strangers, and do not "make conversation" at social gatherings. Well-mannered Germans do not raise their voices (Hall & Hall, 1990, pp. 52–53).

Having serious and sometimes unapproachable appearance, Germans have a deep need to be understood and respected. They value respect more than admiration; nevertheless, they have a need to be liked. Even though Germans do not show many emotions, their feelings are intense. Their experience of mood is frequently melancholic and pessimistic.

Germans tend to develop deep friendship relations, in which they discuss their private feelings and problems. In private conversation with close friends they like to discuss the philosophical meaning of life. Germans view most American friendships as superficial.

Irish Expressive Style

According to ethnographic observations, Irish cultural values and norms of emotional expression appreciate humor and laughter as a means to convey one's feelings. Expressions of suffering are also acceptable (Greeley, 1979; McGoldrick, 1996). The influence of the origins of their ancestors is still noticeable among immigrants of Irish descent who likely have never have been in contact with original Irish culture in Ireland. The modern European Americans of Irish descent highly value emotional expression. In experimental situation of reliving emotions, they are very expressive. These expressive features are especially pronounced in the expression of love and happiness (Tsai & Chentsova-Dutton, 2003).

Scandinavian Expressive Style

Many *people in Scandinavian countries* (Denmark, Sweden, Norway, Finland, and Iceland) are typically *reserved*. Their cultural legacy is centered on twin implicit ethics: "Don't think you're so special" and "Keep to yourself" (Erickson, 2005, p. 642).

For Scandinavians, the socialist idea that society is more important than the individual is very important in their life. Egalitarianism, tolerance, nonviolence, and moderation are essential values for them. They keep strict bounds between the private and the public. Other ethnic groups would label this trait as being shy. Scandinavians have desire for autonomy and penchant for solitude. While many Americans believe that shy people are less intelligent, less competent, and less socially desirable, thus considering shyness as negative trait, yet for Scandinavians, shyness is positive: they see shy people as sensitive, reflective, and nonpushy (Daun, 1995; Erickson, 2005).

Even though others may interpret such behavior as introversion, withdrawal, rejection, and anxiety, yet Scandinavians themselves attribute it to being less verbal, vocal, and intrusive. Scandinavians tend to avoid meddling questions, deep and elaborate discussions with people outside of their close relationships. They may seem passive in conversation.

Their social norms endorse *emotional control* and *moderation in expression of emotions* (Midelfort & Midelfort, 1982; Pennebaker et al., 1996; Rodnick, 1955). Individuals in those cultures appear as more *inhibited emotionally* than in other European cultures. In Norway, for example, people prefer to reduce the expression of certain negative emotions (e.g., "excessive" anger) because "expressing them would interfere with neighborly relationships" (Midelfort & Midelfort, 1982; Rodnick, 1955, p. 14). Norwegians also tend to minimize the experience of pleasure and other positive emotions (Erickson & Simon, 1996).

It is interesting that Scandinavian languages do not contain a rich vocabulary of aggressive words. This can reflect the avoidance of conflict, holding back aggressiveness and preferring practical solutions instead. In case of a loss and unresolved grief, however, the lack of expressiveness can have negative consequences: they can be susceptible to developing physical or psychological symptoms (Erickson, 2005).

Finland represents the typical example of Scandinavian expressive style. Communication of Finns is silent and quite monologic, with slow-moving turns of speech, relatively long pauses. Finish speakers do not like of being interrupted with verbal exclamations, applause, or other superficial external feedback. They listen to a speaker without external evidence that they pay attention; yet actually, this is their way of listening most attentively (Nishimura et al., 2008; Tella, 2005, cited in Nishimura et al., 2008, p.788).

Americans of Scandinavian descent who likely have never have been in contact with their original culture in Europe continue to follow the cultural values of emotional control, as their ancestors. In experimental situation of reliving emotions, they were less expressive, keeping more emotional control compared to Americans of Irish descent. They were quite reserved even in the expression of happiness and love (Tsai & Chentsova-Dutton, 2003).

6.2.4 Gender Differences in Emotional Expressions Across Cultures

Cultural Stereotypes of Gender Differences in Emotional Expressivity

Oscar Wilde once noted that "A man's face is his autobiography; a woman's face is her work of fiction" (quoted in La France & Mayo, 1979, p. 96). That implies that a man's face is truly reflective of his inner state, whereas a woman's face is fabrication.

A woman's face may be less reflective of her own inner state than of the inner states of those with whom she is interacting. This may occur because the gender role expectations in many societies call for women to be reactive and responsive. In contrast, across many cultures, men are expected to be proactive, independent, self-confident, and decisive. They are less tuned to the socio-emotional aspects of human relationships and more concerned with getting the job done (La France & Mayo, 1979, p.96).

The *cultural belief that women are more emotional than men* is well known, and the research on gender stereotypes demonstrated its presence (Birnbaum, Nosanchuk, & Croll, 1980; Fabes & Martin, 1991; Fischer, 1993). "Being emotional" is not characteristic of the *male cultural model*. Females are perceived and really are more emotional than men across several cultural contexts (Fernandez et al., 2000; Simon & Nath, 2004; Timmers, Fischer, & Manstead, 2003).

Feminine and Masculine Expressive Rules for Emotions

However, some researchers doubted that empirical support for such gender differences in emotional expression and experience is sufficient (e.g., Brody & Hall, 1993; Fischer, 1993; La France & Banaji, 1992; Shields, 1991). The studies (Brody, 1999; Fischer & Manstead, 2000) conducted within Western cultures demonstrated gender differences in emotional expressivity (Brody, 1999; Fischer & Manstead, 2000).

Certain emotional *display rules* are *prevalent among women and men across cultures* (Brody & Hall, 2008). In European American and many Western European countries, cultures expect that women display more intense positive emotions (e.g., joy, happiness, hope, interest) and internalize negative emotions (e.g., sadness, fear, anxiety, shame, and guilt) (Brody & Hall, 2008). These feminine display rules to express positive and internalize negative emotions reflect women's cultural gender roles which expect that they would be oriented on interpersonal relations, nurturing, and accommodating (Zahn-Waxler, Cole, & Barrett, 1991). Expressed positive and internalized negative emotions promote closeness with others and facilitate relationships. Shared happiness promotes bonding. Expressed sadness elicits sympathy from others and brings individuals together in shared mourning (Barrett & Campos, 1987; Izard & Ackerman, 2000).

Different from these feminine display rules, European American and many Western European cultures expect that men express such "tender" negative emotions as sadness and anxiety as internalized, less intensely and less frequently. On the other hand, since contempt and anger as negative emotions promote overcoming obstacles by pushing outward, cultural norms allow men to express these emotions openly and intensely, rather than internalizing them. Such display rules permitting men to externalize and express certain emotions are consistent with their gender roles to be independent, assertive, and aggressive (Brody, 1999, 2000; Brody & Hall, 2008).

It is important to note that these *gender role differences in expression of emotions* manifest *variably in different social and cultural contexts* and in interpersonal interaction within specific situations (Brody, 1999; Chaplin, 2015). The social-constructionist theory proposed that an individual displays fewer gender differences in emotion expression when they are alone or when they are in presence of a person who they know well and trust. In these cases, they feel more comfortable and therefore allow themselves to express any emotions, not taking into consideration their gender roles. However, an individual exhibits more gender differences when they are in presence of an unfamiliar person or a peer (Chaplin & Aldao, 2013; La France, Hecht, & Paluck, 2003; Zeman & Garber, 1996). They tend to behave in a "socially acceptable" way with such a person adhering to gender roles.

Cultural backgrounds and ethnicities can affect gender roles for expression of emotions, even though the data demonstrating this is still limited (Chaplin, 2015). A recent cross-cultural study (Safdar et al., 2009) showed that gender differences in display rules—how people should express their emotions—are similar across three cultural groups: Canadians, US Americans, and Japanese. The gender differences in the display rules were larger or smaller across cultures, depending on emotion and contact partner.

Men tend to express *powerful emotions* (e.g., anger) more than women, and *women* tend to express *powerless emotions* (e.g., sadness, fear) and happiness more than men. As for specific target figures, both men and women believe they should use the same display rules to express *powerful emotions* toward people in *close relationship* (in-group members) and *powerless emotions* toward people in *distal relationship* (out-group members). Thus, the display rules of men and women are differentiated depending on the specific relationship context (Safdar et al., 2009).

Contrary to their expectations, authors (Safdar et al., 2009) did not reveal larger gender differences in Japan, compared to the United States and Canada. However, they discovered that the largest gender differences in display rules for expression of emotions were among Canadians and the smallest differences were among Japanese. The authors explain the smaller differences between men and women in Japan by their general cultural norms of politeness discouraging emotional display. These norms of moderation in expression of emotion make a gender effect less influential.

Despite equal frequency of emotional experience of women in the United States (Simon & Nath, 2004), they express their emotions more readily than men. In cultural perspective, *expression* of emotion is more affected by socialization than the *experience* of emotion (e.g., Brody, 1993; Kring & Gordon, 1998).

From cultural norms, *men learn to conceal their feelings*, whereas *women learn to more freely express their emotions*. Taking cultural context into account, these expressive gender differences are even more contrasting. For example, in cultural norms of European American and some other Western cultures women should smile often, regardless of their mood and emotions at the time. On the other hand, it is more culturally proper for Muslim men in some West African cultures to display only muted emotional reactions. The same way, young men in traditional Masai society in East Africa should expose "stony-faced and long, unbroken stares" (Keating, 1994, p.178).

Gender Differences in Expression of Specific Emotions

The studies found that experience and expressivity of emotions can be inconsistent with each other, and men and women differ in this regard: men have more intense emotional experiences, while women have higher emotional expressivity. These *gender differences* also depend *on the type of emotion* (Deng, Chang, Yang, Huo, & Zhou, 2016). In some contexts, men are more expressive than women in anger, aggression, and pride (Archer, 2004; Brebner, 2003; Brody & Hall, 1993; Kring & Gordon, 1998; La France & Mayo, 1979; La France et al., 2003, see for detailed review Chaplin, 2015).

As for specific emotions, studies showed that women express *fear* verbally and nonverbally more often, with more intensity, and more frequent facial expressions than do men, more crying and freezing when they are afraid (Allen & Haccoun, 1976; Brody & Hall, 1993; Fischer, 1993; Kring & Gordon, 1998; Wallbott et al., 1986). Studies also found that women express *sadness* with more intensity and frequency, more often and to a greater extent than do men. When they cry, it is more intensive, frequent, with nonverbal expressions and changes in voice quality (Allen & Haccoun, 1976; Balswick & Avertt, 1977; Brody & Hall, 1993; Dosser, Balswick, & Halverson Jr., 1983; Fischer, 1993; Kring & Gordon, 1998; Lombardo, Cretser, Lombardo, & Mathis, 1983; Oliver & Toner, 1990; Wallbott et al., 1986).

As for *anxiety* and *depression*, although women express more anxiety and depression than do men, there is not strong evidence that they actually experience these emotions more intense and more frequently. Research does not always show consistent gender differences: some studies found that women experience more intense and more frequent fear or anxiety than do men (e.g., Allen & Haccoun, 1976; Berenbaum, Fujita, & Pfennig, 1995; Dillon, Wolf, & Katz, 1985; Scherer, Wallbott, & Summerfield, 1986), however others do not reveal significant gender differences (e.g., Gotlib & Meyer, 1986; Kring & Gordon, 1998; Small, Gessner, & Ferguson, 1984; Sprecher & Sedikides, 1993; Stapley & Haviland, 1989, see detailed review of these studies Madden, Barrett, & Pietromonaco, 2000). The same can be said about *sadness* and *depression*. Some studies found that women experience these emotions more intense and more frequent than do men (e.g., Allen & Haccoun, 1976; Eisenberg et al., 1994; Grossman & Wood, 1993; Scherer et al., 1986; Sprecher & Sedikides, 1993), other studies, however, did not reveal differences (e.g., Ganong & Coleman, 1984; Gotlib & Meyer, 1986; Kring & Gordon, 1998; Small et al., 1984; Watson & Clark, 1992, see detailed review of these studies Madden et al., 2000). A recent meta-analytic review of studies on gender differences revealed that many of those are somewhere in the middle (Petersen & Hyde, 2010).

Negative Emotionality of Women

The differences, yet relatively small, evidently exist in the domain of *negative emotions,* (Brody & Hall, 2008; Chaplin & Aldao, 2013; Else-Quest, Higgins, Allison, & Morton, 2012; Fischer, Rodriguez Mosquera, Van Vianen, & Manstead, 2004; McLean & Anderson, 2009). *Across cultures,* women are universally higher than men in *social anxiety* (Caballo et al., 2014) and *test anxiety* (Bodas & Ollendick, 2005).

The *cross-cultural studies,* which investigated the actual daily life expression of emotions with observer reports and clinical evaluations, also revealed *negative emotionality of women* (Diener, Sandvik, & Larsen, 1985; Fujita, Diener, & Sandvik, 1991; Seidlitz & Diener, 1998), yet not always (Barrett, Robin, Pietromonaco, & Eyssell, 1998). In addition, in their coping with negative emotions, women tend to use negative emotion-related strategies, such as cognitive rumination and seeking emotional support (Tamres, Janicki, & Helgeson, 2002). It appears there are also differences in relationship situations that provoke negative emotionality. Men express more negative emotions when their partners demand more intimacy, while women express more negative emotionality when their partners reject them (Brody, Muderrisoglu, & Nakash-Eisikovits, 2002).

Several theories were proposed to explain these gender differences. Some of them focus on socio-economic factors, such as the role of stereotypes, stigmatization of women, social roles, the role of power, while others focus—on such cognitive processes as appraisal, differences in memory for emotional experience, and reliance on implicit beliefs (see for detailed review, Madden et al., 2000). Among the most prominent recent theories are the *expectation states theory* (Correll & Ridgeway, 2006), which explains the relation between gender-emotion beliefs and social roles, and the theory of *doing emotion as doing gender* (Shields, 2002; Shields & Dicicco, 2011), which explains connections between emotional expressions, beliefs about emotion, and gendered sense of self.

Feminine Emotional Expressivity in Social Interaction

According to the earlier studies (see for review, La France & Mayo, 1979), women demonstrated higher nonverbal sensitivity than men, however, the later studies demonstrated inconsistency in this regard. Therefore, a recent study on gender differences in emotion recognition (Fischer, Kret, & Broekens, 2018) attempted to test the emotional sensitivity hypothesis on a large sample and overall, found no gender differences.

Women have difficulty in conversation when they could not see the other person. Women smile more than men. The bubbles of personal space surrounding women are smaller than are those surrounding men. Women are more affiliative and friendlier toward others than men are. Women are capable to be responsive and being submissive in their dealings with men. As for touch in emotional expression, research confirms gender differences and reflects the stereotype that women are passive while men are active in relationships. Cultural stereotypes characterize women as more talkative. However, research demonstrated the opposite: in most intergender encounters, men talk and women listen (see review of the studies, La France & Mayo, 1979).

Another gender difference is in the style of nonverbal behavior expressing emotion (La France & Mayo, 1979). This gender difference is in line with typical cultural norms that expect for women to be *reactive*, while for men to be *proactive*. The women's reactivity is displayed in being more sensitive to others' expressivity and tendency to complement their partner's behavior. On another side, men's proactivity is displayed in more frequent talking, interrupting, and overall being nonverbally dominant, especially with women.

Cultural Factor of Gender Differences in Expression of Emotions

However, gender differences in emotional expressivity depend on cultural parameters of societies. Generally, in the study of 37 countries (Fischer & Manstead, 2000) *women experience more intense emotions and display more overt emotional expressions than men*. Yet, the *gender differences* in the intensity of experiences and the *degree of expression of joy, shame, disgust, and guilt* are *bigger* in *independent* than in *interdependent cultures*.

Generally, in American and Europe women tend to be more expressive than men facially and vocally. Studies in the United States and some Western European countries have reported small significant gender differences in expressions of emotion: women show more emotional expression than men, especially for positive emotions (e.g. joy and happiness), yet internalizing negative emotions (e.g., sadness and anxiety). Data obtained with observation of women's written and verbal behavior found that women express more negative emotions than men do (e.g., Burke, Weir, & Harrison, 1976; Levenson, Carstensen, & Gottman, 1994).

Other study (Fernandez et al., 2000) explored the importance of *masculinity-femininity* as a cultural dimension in predicting high emotional verbal and nonverbal expressivity of emotions. Results revealed that gender differences in emotional expressivity among Asian participants were lower than among North American participants. The North Americans revealed the higher gender differences in *joy, sadness,* and the lower differences in verbal expression of *anger*. According to the authors' interpretation, the *higher masculinity* of the *North American society* can explain these results. The American culture tends to emphasize gender differences and still legitimizes such assertive emotions as anger (Hofstede, 1998).

Societal and Socioeconomic Factors of Gender Differences in Emotional Expressions

Gender differences for emotion expressions vary in societies, depending on socio-economic conditions, ethnicity, and cultures. Ethnic groups may have different gender specific display rules for expression of emotions. For instance, in a US sample (Matsumoto, 1993), Caucasian adults viewed the displays of fear as more appropriate, compared to Hispanic adults, and sadness as more appropriate, compared to African Americans and Asian Americans. As Chaplin (2015) commented this data, "Caucasian parents in the US may be more likely to encourage sadness expressions among girls, whereas African American parents may be more likely to discourage sadness expressions, possibly for both boys and girls." (p. 19).

Meta-analysis (La France et al., 2003) showed that ethnicity moderates gender differences in expression of positive emotions. In particular, among Caucasians there are larger sex differences in smiling—females smile more than males—in comparison with other ethnic groups, such as Asians and African Americans groups. This suggests that ethnicity and culture can play their roles in emotion expressions.

A comprehensive study (37 countries of the world, Fischer et al., 2004) on gender differences in 6 emotions discovered that gender-specific patterns of emotional experience and expressions, found in studies in Western samples, are cross-culturally universal. Women tend to experience more powerless emotions (e.g., sadness, fear), while men tend to experience more powerful emotions (e.g., anger). It was also found that these gender differences are not related to the status of women and their roles in their respective countries (operationalized by the Gender Empowerment Measure, GEM).

Another cross-cultural study (Schmitt, 2015) suggested that it is unlikely that gender differences in emotions are caused by gender role socialization in cultures. Surprisingly and unexpectedly, author found the smallest gender differences in more patriarchal countries, while the largest sex differences—in Scandinavian egalitarian countries.

Other findings are also in support of this interpretation. Across cultures gender differences in neuroticism—the trait mostly about negative emotionality—and depression are apparent and *larger* in countries with higher sociopolitical gender equity, not smaller as would be expected if gender differences come only from gender roles, gendered socialization, and patriarchy (Hopcroft & McLaughlin, 2012; Hyde, Mezulis, & Abramson, 2008; Schmitt, 2015; Van de Velde, Bracke, & Levecque, 2010). And these differences are *wider in high gender equity societies* than in low gender equity societies.

Thus, gender differences in emotion expressions depend on cultural background and ethnicity. Gender roles and stereotypes of other cultures can affect their experience and expression of emotion. However, the studies of gender differences in experience and expression of emotions in other cultures are not readily available. Thus, we cannot generalize the findings reviewed above, and further research is needed.

6.3 Facial Expressiveness of Emotion

6.3.1 Methods to Study Facial Expression of Emotions Across Cultures

Methodology of Facial Recognition

Throughout recent several decades, researchers have extensively explored *facial expression* and *recognition of emotions* in cross-cultural perspective. In particular, the studies investigating the expression of basic emotions have frequently employed *methodology of facial expression recognition* (e.g., Ekman, 1992; Ekman et al., 1987; Elfenbein & Ambady, 2002; Izard, 1994; Jack, Blais, Scheepers, Schyns, & Caldara, 2009; Jack, Garrod, Yu, Caldara, & Schyns, 2012; Jack, Sun, Delis, Garrod, & Schyns, 2016; Matsumoto, 1992; Mesquita & Frijda, 1992). In this research design, participants look on slides (or photos) with faces and select an appropriate emotion term for portrayed emotion from a list of alternatives. In cross-cultural studies, the percentage of responses and participants which selected the intended emotion term from different cultures is compared. The high percentage demonstrates cross-cultural universality of facial recognition of basic emotions (Matsumoto, 1992).

Eye Tracking Technologies and Neuroimaging of Facial Expression

The new *eye tracking technologies, neuroimaging,* and statistical analysis techniques allowed investigators to monitor attention that observers pay to various aspects of expressive (or nonexpressive) face. The main cultural differences, which researchers identified, were in observation and decoding strategies, the parts of the face, which people focus on in their emotion recognition, in perception of individuals from cultural in-group and out-group (e.g., Blais, Jack, Scheepers, Fiset, & Caldara, 2008; Jack et al., 2016; Yuki, Maddux, & Masuda, 2007).

This line of research usually follows categorical approach and assumes that emotions have distinctive patterns of facial movements. That might be true for basic emotions (e.g., joy, anger). However, more complex emotions (e.g., regret, grief) and social emotions in particular (e.g., shame and guilt) have been outside the scope of such comparative research since they do not reveal distinctive patterns of facial expressions.

Facial Recognition of Morphed Photographs of Emotional Expression

The use of *morphed photographs of facial expressions* of emotions is another interesting and productive way to study basic emotions from categorical approach (Calder, Young, Perrett, Etcoff, & Rowland, 1996; Wang et al., 2006). Gradually altering facial features in such morphed photographs of facial expressions, and forced-choice labeling technique allow researchers to investigate categorical perception of the facial expressions anchoring basic emotions. A drastic change in observer's judgments at the category boundaries for basic emotions can serve as an indication of the distinct patterns of recognition for each of basic emotions. The judgment of expressions within categories as more similar, compared to judgment of expressions across categories, is also an indication of categorical perception. Empirical data have discovered existence of discrete peaks for correct identification of each basic emotion and confusions in identification of midpoint of adjacent emotional regions, thus supporting categorical perception, rather than dimensional perception of emotional expression (Calder et al., 1996; Etcoff & Magee, 1992; Wang et al., 2006).

6.3.2   Cross-Cultural Similarities in Facial Expression of Emotions

Cross-Cultural Universality in Facial Expression of Emotions

Early studies revealed the empirical evidence of cross-cultural universality in facial expression of several emotions (e.g., anger, disgust, fear, happiness, sadness, and surprise). They employed various methodologies (e.g., Ekman, 1972; Izard, 1971; Mesquita, Frijda, & Scherer, 1997). The series of studies of Ekman and his colleagues was an early landmark (Ekman, 1972; Ekman et al., 1987; Ekman & Friesen, 1971; Ekman, Sorenson, & Friesen, 1969). Researchers investigated the similarity in facial expressions of emotions in different cultures and the cross-cultural capability for recognition of facial expressions as an indication of universality of a number of *basic* emotions (e.g., Ekman et al., 1987; Ekman & Friesen, 1971).

The evidence was consistent from those experiments and conclusively demonstrated universal facial expressions of emotion with data from Western and Eastern countries, on literate and preliterate cultures. The participants in those samples spoke six different language groups: Dani, English, Fore, Japanese, Portuguese, and Spanish. The results showed that people do not learn facial expressions from the mass media and contacts with literate Westerners. For instance, people in preliterate cultures of New Guinea and Borneo recognized correctly six basic emotions (happiness, sadness, disgust, surprise, anger, and fear, Ekman et al., 1969). Reporting cross-cultural universality of facial expressions, Ekman (1972), however, did not report any cultural differences.

Following this Ekman's original study, Canadian, German, French, and Japanese researchers found evidence for the universality of facial expressions of emotion in their cultural samples. Thus, it appears that the universality of facial expressions of emotion is not a debated issue anymore (see for review Matsumoto, 2000; Matsumoto, 2006a).

Methodological Concerns on Facial Recognition of Emotions in Cross-Cultural Research

Plenty of studies provided evidence that facial expressions of emotion are cross-culturally universal, and by late 1980s this conclusion seemed no longer questioned in psychology (Matsumoto, 1990, p. 195). However, some researchers (e.g., Russell, 1994) reviewed in details the internal, convergent, and ecological validity of those cross-cultural results. The findings looked less convincing than before. Even though participants were able to associate facial expressions with emotion labels, but this association varied with culture and it was loose and not sufficiently consistent with various alternative accounts (Russell, 1994, p.102).

6.3.3   Cross-Cultural Differences in Facial Expression of Emotions

Cultural Diversity in Facial Expression of Emotions

Cross-cultural studies have explored two separate and distinct psychological phenomena concerning facial expression of emotions: *emotion expression* and *emotion recognition.* In this section, I review the studies on *emotion expression,* while in the next one—*emotion recognition.*

Even though emotions are expressed in the same way across cultures, yet specific cultural display norms differ and affect the people's own expressions as well as their judgment of others' expression according to social context.

Many studies reported the findings on cross-cultural comparisons which questioned universality of facial expression of emotions. Their data have demonstrated the impact of culture on facial expression of emotions (e.g., Jack et al., 2009; Jack et al., 2012). Authors provided the results that show that among Western participants, the six basic emotions are displayed with different sets of facial movements, while Eastern participants do not display such diverse facial expressions. As for emotional intensity, Easterners display it via dynamic eye activity. (Jack et al., 2012, p. 7241).

As for particular emotions, Edelmann et al. (1987) presented self-reports of participants in their *displays of embarrassment*, when they recalled an actual (or typical) event, in the countries of Italy, Spain, Greece, West Germany, and the United Kingdom. Across all samples, nonverbal response included the combination of smiling, grinning or laughing and avoiding eye contact. The Greek participants more smiled/grinned but less averted gaze. They experienced much more intense embarrassment of longer duration compared to their counterparts in other four nations. And they made more effort to control their embarrassment. The British participants, maybe being "lighter" in their nature, experienced embarrassment of less intensity and shorter duration, compared to the other samples, and displayed extensive laughter and smiling/grinning in response to embarrassing situation (Edelmann et al., 1986; Edelmann et al., 1987).

Another example is the expression of happiness. In the interdependent collectivistic cultures that emphasize *harmony in relationships* the expression of *high-activation happiness* is quite rare (Lutz, 1987; Tsai, Chentsova-Dutton, Freire-Bebeau, & Przymus, 2002). Cultural norms consider the extensively expressive happiness as potentially disruptive for relationships since it may contrast with the sad or moderate emotions of others, thus making other people emotionally dissonant and uncomfortable (Lutz, 1987; Mesquita & Leu, 2007).

Many other researchers examined cultural differences in facial emotional expression (e.g., Argyle et al., 1986; Gudykunst & Kim, 1984; Gudykunst & Ting-Toomey, 1988; see for detailed review Matsumoto, Franklin, Choi, Rogers, & Tatani, 2003; Matsumoto, 2006a). Some of those are reviewed in the earlier sections—about display rules.

Cultural Differences in Smile as Expression of Emotions

In *European American culture*, people think that *smile is a natural expression of positive emotions*, especially among women. They are especially known as extensively smiley. Smiling is a sign of happiness, certainty, and confidence. Smiling is a sign of positive attitudes, respect, and friendliness.

Americans believe that it is good to smile, and that *smile makes the world smiles*. The feeling happy seems naturally expressed in smile. On the other hand, the simple smiling of a person can make them feel happy. Smiling appears reciprocal: a person tends to smile back at someone who smiles, and this response is frequently involuntary (Beamish, Foster, Edwards, & Olbers, 2019).

Despite common association of smile with happiness, studies have demonstrated that people can express in smile other emotions (Gorvett, 2017; Martin, Rychlowska, Wood, & Niedenthal, 2017), such as embarrassment, distress, and confusion.

Generally, *smile can express* three different types of functionally different emotional experiences: *enjoyment, affiliation*, and *dominance* (Niedenthal, Mermillod, Maringer, & Hess, 2010). People express enjoyment smiles spontaneously during their experiences of pleasure. Affiliative smile expresses the affiliative emotions associated with positive intentions to create and maintain social relations. Dominance smiles express emotions associated with feeling of pride, awareness of social status, and ability to control. The study (Rychlowska et al., 2015) has demonstrated that people in different cultures are able to distinguish these three types of smile.

On the other side, perception, and interpretation of smile can be different depending on cultural norms. This perspective sheds light on the cultural way of emotional expression and smile. For people in Western cultures, the mouth region is most important for interpretation of facial expressions and smile, while the eye region is most important in Easterner cultures (Mai et al., 2011).

The judgment of smiling may be culturally different, and smile may have not only positive, but also negative associations. Even though in many cultures, smiling people are judged as attractive, friendly, happy, approachable, and communal, yet in some cultures they can be perceived as less intelligent and less trustworthy (Krys et al., 2016). *Cultural opinion in some countries*, like Norway, Russia, and Poland for example, are *frown on smiling*. Being smiley for them is associated with being insane, foolish, or tricky (Bedford, Fallon, & McAdam, 2008; EURES, 2010; Krys et al., 2016).

People in East Asian cultures are also well-known as *not smiley*. Compared to European Americans, Japanese tend to control and mask their expression of smile to fit to cultural traditions (Matsumoto et al., 1998).

Cultural and Societal Factors of Smile

Several cultural and societal factors can contribute to the different perception and interpretation of smiley expression of emotions. Among those are *heterogeneous* versus *homogeneous cultural backgrounds, corruption of a society, independent* versus *interdependent self-construal.*

The *heterogeneity* is the cultural dimension characterizing the societies, in which a population of present-day descended from migration from many countries of origins over a long period of time. *Homogeneity,* on the other side, characterizes the societies in which a present-day population descended from migration from few countries of origins (Rychlowska et al., 2015). Authors discovered that people in *heterogeneous societies* tend to endorse *affiliative smiles*, while people in *homogeneous societies* endorse *dominance smiles*.

For example, *North America* has always been a *heterogeneous culture*. Many immigrants have been settled in the United States speaking different languages. Therefore, in the world of strangers who need to communicate others, nonverbal expressions and smile were the faster means to express a good will and a wish of peace (Khazan, 2017).

The cultural dimension of *uncertainty avoidance* also affects the perceptions of smile. In particular, people living in the countries with *low uncertainty avoidance* tend to judge a smiling person as less intelligent. Besides, the research shows that the societal level of *corruption* undermines the positive meaning of smile and weakens its trustworthiness (Krys et al., 2016).

People in *independent cultures* tend to express high-activation happiness with more expansive behavior and smile. In an experimental situation (Tsai et al., 2002), European American participants and Hmong American participants were asked to relive their high-intensity emotions (such as happiness) recalling very emotional episodes of their past.

Even though physiological activity and subjective feelings associated with the relived emotions did not differ in these cultural groups, yet the recorded facial behavior of participants showed that European Americans (Western independent culture) expressed significantly more social smiles compared to Hmong Americans (East Asian interdependent culture). However, more acculturated Hmong Americans, which adopted American culture, displayed a higher frequency of social smiles during happiness. As interpretation of these findings, authors say that social smiles of European Americans and highly acculturated Hmong Americans may express the nonverbal messages to other people. Since they experience happiness, the socially desirable emotion in independent culture (the United States), then they are successful.

Due to socialization and strong stereotypical expectations, women are more communal and therefore tend to smile more (La France et al., 2003). When researchers (La France et al., 2003) analyzed the sex differences in smiling based on the multiple cross-cultural studies, they revealed that women generally smile more than men. However, these differences varied by nationality, ethnicity, and age.

Development of Culturally Specific Expression of Emotion in Childhood

The questions remain (1) in which period of individual development these cultural differences emerge and (2) whether they are due to biological ethnic origins or due to cultural influence. The studies of early childhood are useful in this regard.

For instance, developmental psychologists (Camras, Oster, Campos, Miyake, & Bradshaw, 1992) discovered that the expressions of negative emotions in an arm restraint procedure are similar among American and Japanese infants (of 5 months), yet American children reacted more quickly.

Overall, Chinese children, and in a lesser extent Japanese children, tend to show less negative and positive emotions and have a longer latency of emotional response, compared to American children (Camras et al., 1998). The differences in emotional expressivity between European American and Chinese infants (of 11 months) are more robust than between European American and Japanese infants. Chinese and Japanese infants also differ significantly. Thus, Chinese infants demonstrated less overall expressivity, compared to Japanese and American infants of that age. Chinese infants had a longer latency in their facial display of distress after a situation of anger/frustration (gentle arm restraint), and after a procedure inducing fear (growling toy gorilla head). Cross-cultural differences were revealed for some specific midface facial, brow, cheek actions (e.g., brows lowered).

Smile is among the most obvious facial expression of pleasure in humans. Infants typically begin to display it when they are around 2 to 3 months old. The frequency of smile increases in the following months reaching its peak at around 4 months. This age is similar and probably universal across many cultural samples (e.g., Israel,

Japan, the United States, and Uganda). However, the increasing cultural divergence emerges in subsequent months of infancy (Super & Harkness, 2010).

Culturally specific differences in emotional expressivity are also found in subsequent years of childhood. For example, researchers (Camras, Bakeman, Chen, Norris, & Cain, 2006) studied girls of four cultural groups: Mainland Chinese, Chinese-American adopted by US families, Chinese-American (nonadopted), and the European Americans. The results showed that the European girls were generally more expressive and, in particular, they displayed more disgust-related expressions than Mainland Chinese girls. They also exhibited more smiles than the other groups. The American Chinese girls, who were adopted by American families, revealed more disgust expressions compared to Mainland Chinese girls. They probably already learned the expressive norms pf their adoptive culture.

6.3.4   Cross-Cultural Similarities and Differences in Perception of Facial Expression of Emotions

Perception of Emotions Across Cultures

This section reviews cross-cultural studies of *perception of emotional expression.* While *emotion expression* research design investigates how people display certain emotions (upon instruction or naturally), *emotion recognition* design investigates how people—observers—perceive and recognize emotions. Still, the latter design gives a useful window for researchers into *emotion expression.* The studies on both research designs bring the results quite consistent with each other (Yuki et al., 2007).

A number of studies in 1970-1990s have documented cross-cultural similarities in the judgments of expressions for several emotions, their rating of intensity, how people associate the perceived expression of intensity with subjective experience of other. At the same time, many studies found substantial differences in emotion recognition, ethnic differences in intensity ratings, attributions of intensity, inferences about experiences underlying facial expression of emotion, and how cultural dimensions contribute to emotional judgment across countries (see for detailed review Matsumoto, 1992; Matsumoto et al., 2003).

Studies on emotions recognition also demonstrate cross-cultural differences. East Asian participants consistently show lower recognition of some negative facial expressions, compared to Western Caucasian participants (Elfenbein & Ambady, 2002; Matsumoto, 1992; Mesquita & Frijda, 1992; Russell, 1994). Recently, researchers found that during recognition task, Eastern participants employ a decoding strategy which does not allow them to adequately differentiate facial expressions of "disgust and "fear." They typically fixate on the eye region, whereas Western participants allocate their fixations evenly across the face. These *differences in decoding strategies* create confusion among Eastern people in emotion recognition (Jack et al., 2009).

The results of other cross-cultural studies are in accord with those, which are presented above. In one study (Blais et al., 2008), researchers explored how Western Caucasian (presumably Glasgow, Scotland) and East Asian (Chinese and Japanese international students in Glasgow) participants learned, recognized, and categorized facial expression of emotions. Authors have discovered Western-Eastern differences in observation strategies recording the participants' eye movements when those attempted to obtain information from faces. Western Caucasians exhibited scattered patterns of fixations on faces with focus on triangle (two eyes and mouth). Different from this, East Asians fixated more on the central region of the face (eyes and nose). Thus, people from these two cultures tend to process information from human face paying attention to different aspects of face information.

Recognition of Emotions Displayed by Cultural In-Group Versus Out-Group Members

It is worth to note that observers from various cultural samples are more accurate at recognizing the faces and facial expression of emotions from individuals of their own cultural in-group, compared to individuals of out-group (Blais et al., 2008; Elfenbein & Ambady, 2002, 2003; Meissner & Brigham, 2001). People tend to rely on specific nonverbal communication skills of their own culture when they interpret other's facial expression of emotions. Some researchers called such skills as facial "accents" or "dialects" (Elfenbein & Ambady, 2002, 2003; Marsh, Elfenbein, & Ambady, 2003).

Observers recognize emotions of people from their cultural in-group easier because they know better the typical facial cues predominant in that culture. The ability to adequately judge facial emotional expressions of individuals from other cultural group may change over time once observers are more exposed to and gain better knowledge of other culture and their culturally specific nonverbal expressive norms. When observers become more familiar with that culture, they become more accurate in judging emotions of people from that culture (Elfenbein & Ambady, 2002, 2003; Elfenbein, Mandal, Ambady, Harizuka, & Kumar, 2004; Marsh et al., 2003; Shimoda, Argyle, & Ricci Bitti, 1978).

Yuki et al. (2007) in their study found that according to cultural norms of emotion expression, people tend to use their culturally specific facial cues to recognize emotions. For example, Japanese relied predominantly on the eyes, while Americans on the mouth, when they interpreted the happiness and sadness emotions displayed in illustrated faces and computer-edited facial expressions of real people (Yuki et al., 2007). Authors' interpretation stems from the fact that when individuals express their emotions it is harder for them to control the muscles around the eyes than the muscles around the mouth (Ekman, 1992; Ekman & Friesen, 1975; Ekman, Friesen, & O'Sullivan, 1988). Therefore, in Japanese culture, where emotional restrain is a norm, the eyes of other people are more informative of their true emotional states. On the other side, in American society, where open expression of emotions is the cultural norm, the dynamic and expressive mouth is more informative for recognition of emotional states.

Recognition of Qualities and Intensity of Facial Expressions

Many researchers also revealed the cultural differences in how people judge and attribute the qualities of facial expressions and intensity. In particular, studies found that Asian and Asian American participants (Hong Kong, Japan, Sumatra countries, and the United States) tend to attribute less emotional intensity to facial expressions of Caucasians depicted on photographs compared to non-Asian participants (Ekman et al., 1987; Matsumoto, 1993), however, in other study Japanese rated Australians as more expressive.

Asian Americans assessed the lower intensity of facial expressions on photographs depicted European Americans, Australians, and Japanese (Ekman et al., 1987; Matsumoto, 1993; Pittam, Gallois, Iwawaki, & Kroonenberg, 1995). These results suggest that Japanese, as well as people from other Asian cultures, may conceptualize emotions as less intense than Western cultures.

As for intensity attributions, a study of ten countries (Ekman et al., 1987) revealed cross-national differences in how people attribute intensity to others' facial expressions. For majority of emotions, Americans judged the expressions more intensely than the Japanese. The differences might be due cultural decoding rules (Matsumoto & Ekman, 1989). The later studies also replicated these findings (e.g., Biehl et al., 1997; Matsumoto, 1990). In the United States among four ethnic groups (Matsumoto, 1993) differences were revealed in affect intensity, emotion judgments, display rule attitudes, and self-reported emotional expression.

Cultural differences found also in the inferences, which people make regarding a presumed subjective experience underlying facial expressions of emotion (Matsumoto, Kasri, & Kooken, 1999). The cultural differences depend on the strength of the expression being judged. While Americans judged external display of emotions much higher than internal experience when perceived strong expressions, Japanese did not reveal any differences in this regard. On weak expressions, however, the Japanese judged internal experience higher than external display, whereas no difference found among Americans. These differences in judgment the authors explain from the assumed display decoding rules, which differ in two cultures.

Cultural dimensions of *individualism-collectivism*, *power distance*, *uncertainty avoidance*, and *masculinity-femininity* (Hofstede, 1984, 1983) contribute to cross-national *differences in emotion recognition* rates. Matsumoto (1989) in the sample of 15 cultures found correlations between recognition of selected emotions with these four cultural dimensions. A later meta-analysis (Schimmack, 1996) also found how emotion perception differ contingent of cultural dimensions.

6.4   Models of Direct and Indirect Expression of Emotions

6.4.1   Diversity of Cultures in Terms of Direct and Indirect Emotion Expression

Directness and Indirectness in Expression of Emotion as Cultural Styles

Generally, it is common for many languages—even in Western societies—that people mean more than they actually say. Since interpretation depends on the knowledge of context they attempt to elaborate meanings (Grice, 1975).

In the West, such grammatical features as the longer grammatical structures, the subjunctive and conditional moods convey indirectness. *Indirectness* is a useful linguistic way in expression of emotions, feelings, and experiences in some relationship situations.

In the East, people use another approach to express *indirectness*: obscuring the meaning and avoiding verbalization. Japanese, for example, prefer not to say what they want, and tend to avoid specification and precision (Mizutani & Mizutani, 1987). In the same vein in Javanese culture, societal norms favor high degrees of indirectness and concealment of one's thoughts and feelings in some socially challenging situations. Accordingly, people are unwilling to face issues in their naked truth, they prefer not to say what is on their mind and what they really thinks (rather beating about the bush), they never show their real feelings directly (Geertz, 1976; Wierzbicka, 1991).

Cultural Differences in Direct and Indirect Ways to Express Emotions

Western versus Eastern comparison might be not quite adequate reflection of the cultural models of expressiveness. Western countries are quite diverse in this regard. The findings suggest that British English and North American English, rather than European languages, tend to emphasize the rights for expression and the emotional autonomy of individuals (Wierzbicka, 1991). Otherwise, directness of expression varies in Western societies.

For instance, English cultural norms (of Western Europe and the United States) being compared with Polish norms (Central Europe) favor indirectness (Wierzbicka (1991), whereas compared with African American norms and Australian Aboriginal norms, they rather encourage directness in seeking information from the addressee (Abrahams, 1976; Eades, 1982; Sansom, 1980).

Compared with the English-speaking societies (American and British), Greek cultural norms expect a much higher level of indirectness in social interaction (Tannen, 1981), whereas the Israeli cultural norms encourage to be generally more direct. People in Israel are not much concerned with social distance, and they orient their interaction style toward solidarity politeness (Blum-Kulka, Danet, & Gherson, 1985).

People in Slavic cultures, Italian culture, Jewish culture, and African American culture are very expressive. Whether the feelings are good or bad, these cultures value uninhibited emotional expression (Wierzbicka, 1991). German, Polish, Russian, Serbo-Croatian, and Spanish speakers are also more direct than English speakers in their expression of thoughts and emotions (Wierzbicka, 1991).

Asian societies, being high-context cultures, may also substantially contrast in their expressiveness. For instance, Arabic cultures in Middle East are different from East Asian cultures and tend to be overly expressive (Gudykunst & Kim, 1984; Suleiman, 1973). The Arabic language has many grammatical structures for exaggeration and assertion: "some common-ending words are designed to emphasize the meaning, the doubling of the sounds of some consonants creates stronger effects, and the repetition of pronouns and words increases assertiveness" (Lim, 2003, p. 64). Arabic metaphors, analogies, long arrays of adjectives, as rhetorical and stylistic devices, bring even stronger exaggerations (Suleiman, 1973). People in Arabic cultures, being over-expressive and over-assertive, have the communication tendency to emphasize image over meaning, form over function, and affect over accuracy (Zahanrna, 1995). What is interesting, Asian preferences, as a high-context culture, are in directly opposite way.

6.4.2   Eastern Ways to Express Emotions Indirectly

Honorific System

Since Asians do not have an abundance of grammatical forms to express emotions *indirectly,* then being in a situation where they need to verbalize their meanings, they employ the well-developed honorific system. Such *honorifics*—carrying certain degrees of respect for other—are intended to compensate for the likely face threat. In other situations, for instance, when Asians speak to a friend, when they argue, when they speak in English, the use of honorifics is inadequate. Then, they can be very direct.

Indirect and Ambiguous Verbalization

Low *expressiveness and low assertiveness,* typical for *East Asians,* bring high ambiguity to their messages. Some East Asian languages have grammatical constructions that cultivate ambiguity. For example, in the *Japanese* and the *Korean* languages, the subject of a sentence is frequently omitted, the numerals are not specific, incomplete sentences are abundant, the verbs come at the end of sentence, and thus the meaning of a sentence can be determined only until the whole sentence has been spoken.

The Japanese attitudes toward verbalization create genuine ambiguity. They can talk for hours, yet not expressing clearly their opinion (Morsbach, 1976), they may say *hai* (yes) several times and do not necessarily imply agreement. Both a speaker and a listener understand this *hai* as "I understand what you are saying."

High-Context Communication

Due to these cultural traditions of expressing their emotions and thoughts *indirectly*, people in the East—emphasizing *high-context communication*—have developed special strategies to decode the message accurately. In Japanese, as Yoshikawa (1978) mentioned, what a person intended to verbally express and what he/she actually expresses are two different things. To understand the intended meaning, it is important to know the contextual information, as well as to have good intuition acquired through a history of contacts with the speaker. In the same vein, Koreans develop *noon-chi* (literally translated as "eye-measure") to figure out the intention, desire, mood, and attitude of the speaker from the ambiguous message. It is a vital ability of their competence in communication (Lim & Choi, 1996). Some persons have more experience and use *noon-chi* better than others. Once an individual does not have the good ability to use *noon-chi*, this can threaten the speaker's face since he/she would be forced to say explicitly something (Lim & Choi, 1996).

Eye Contact

Across cultures, the *eye contact* is recognized as important for daily communication. It is reflected in "eye" metaphors across cultures. For example, in North America people say "Eyes are the windows to the soul," while in Japan people say "Eyes are as eloquent as the tongue." However, eye contact may be used more or less frequently, directly or indirectly, with direct and averted gaze.

Overall, people tend to perceive a person maintaining *eye contact* as more likable, intelligent, trustworthy, and dominant than a person displaying less eye contact. Excessive eye contact of communicator, however, can make a person feel uncomfortable (Kleinke, 1986). The value and norms of *gaze* in communication, however, differ across cultures.

Generally, people in Western cultures view *eye contact* during social interaction as more important than people in East Asian cultures (Akechi et al., 2013). In particular, respondents from Italy and the United Kingdom rated eye contact during a conversation as more important than respondents from Japan and Hong Kong (Argyle et al., 1986). People in North America display more eye contact than do Japanese. Generally, indirectness in East Asian cultures is the social norm that discourages excessive and direct eye contact and encourages avoiding gaze (Argyle & Cook, 1976). In addition, it should be noted that in Japanese culture avoidance of eye contact is a sign of respect and humble submission (Argyle et al., 1986).

A recent study (Akechi et al., 2013) investigated evaluative ratings of eye contact with a person who displays an emotionally neutral expression. As independent variable (stimuli), authors use two types of gaze—direct and averted. They did a comparison of people's physiological responses and ratings of facial expression from Western European (Finnish) and East Asian (Japanese) cultures.

Results revealed cross-cultural similarities and differences. As for similarities, in both cultures, observers reacted with greater deceleration of heart rate, shorter gazing times, and higher ratings of subjective arousal to a face displaying a *direct gaze* as compared to an *averted gaze*. Cultural differences were found in evaluative responses (pleasantness, approachability, dominance, and basic emotions displayed at face) of observers to different kinds of eye contact—*direct* versus *averted gaze*. These dissimilarities might be due to cultural norms and specific display rules.

Compared to the Finish sample, Japanese participants perceived a face with display of direct eye contact as unpleasant, unapproachable, dominant, angrier, and sadder. Japanese individuals tend to over interpret the frequent and long direct eye contact of faces as signaling anger and making an unapproachable impression. Thus, *direct* and *averted gazes* have culturally specific influence on perception of facial affect (Akechi et al., 2013, p. 9).

6.4.3   Silence, Handshaking, Bowing as Indirect Ways to Express Emotions

Silence as Nondirect Expressive Behavior

Many people in Western cultures are unwilling to tolerate *silence* in communication around them. Some individuals in the West, of course, appreciate importance of silence in communication. It seems, however, a natural aspect of Japanese behavior (Morsbach, 1988b).

The Japanese are often regarded as "silent." They tend to hide the real feelings. When a person is in public settings, he or she tends to conceal their real emotions behind blank and still faces or smiles. For instance, silence is the "typical" and traditional way for females to hide their emotions of surprise by covering the mouth with the palm of the hand. The nearly motionless Japanese face reveals little of their inner feelings. Japanese seems slow in conversation; it takes slightly longer for them to answer questions, even if they understand perfectly. They are comfortable with silence and do not dread stillness as much as do Americans.

Japanese culture has the pervasive influence of *Zen Buddhism*, where silence, not words, is regarded very highly. Silent communication is idealized in Japan, but it can be a myth (Morsbach, 1988b). In modern Japan, *Zen Buddhism* is rare, and silence is the ideal, rather than real. In practice, things are different.

Americans, on the other hand, are much more expressive—nonverbally and verbally. Japanese, with their cultural norms of stillness and silence, frequently perceive Americans as "verbose," associating this with a "shallow character" (Morsbach, 1988b, p. 206). Americans move forehead and eyebrows constantly when they speak and these motions express the inner feelings behind the words. Americans tend to display their joy and anxiety quite openly.

Handshaking as Nonverbal Expressive Behavior

In many modern countries, the *handshaking* greeting is a common expression of emotion in communication. It is widespread in Europe and Africa, although there are regional differences. In Britain, people shake hands only on meeting again after a long time, while the French shake everyone's hand on meeting at a party and again when taking their leave. Shaking hands comes "naturally" to many Westerners. It is a "democratic" sign of equality. Japanese culture is an exception in this regard—people there rarely handshake. Koreans followed Japanese practice until the end of World War II, but now it is an accepted custom of shaking hands (Morsbach, 1988a).

Bowing as Nonverbal Expressive Behavior

In some cultures, there are various peculiar nonverbal expressions of emotions in communication. In many non-Western countries, people use *bowing* in their expressive behavior. In the Western societies, bowing was of great importance throughout the Middle Ages, yet the practice has disappeared since then. Nowadays, bowing is considered as uniquely Japanese. It is not a natural motion, it has to be learned: bowing can be of different depth, of different position (in standing or sitting), and different in various social situation (Morsbach, 1988a). Currently, Westerners interpret bowing as something negative, while for Japanese, it is an important way of interpersonal communication expressing status and emotions in their culture, which is socially complex and hierarchical. It is present not only in formal situations but also in other type of relationships.

References

Abrahams, R. D. (1976). *Talking black*. Rowley, MA: Newbury House.

Akechi, H., Senju, A., Uibo, H., Kikuchi, Y., Hasegawa, T., & Hietanen, J. K. (2013). Attention to eye contact in the West and East: Autonomic responses and evaluative ratings. *PLoS One, 8*(3), e59312.

Allen, J. G., & Haccoun, D. M. (1976). Sex differences in emotionality: A multidimensional approach. *Human Relations, 29*, 711–722.

Archer, J. (2004). Sex differences in aggression in real-world settings: A meta-analytic review. *Review of General Psychology, 8*(4), 291–322.

Argyle, M., & Cook, M. (1976). *Gaze and mutual gaze*. Cambridge, UK: Cambridge University Press.

Argyle, M., Henderson, M., Bond, M., Iizuka, Y., & Contarello, A. (1986). Cross-cultural variations in relationship rules. *International Journal of Psychology, 21*(1–4), 287–315.

Balswick, J., & Avertt, C. P. (1977). Differences in expressiveness: Gender interpersonal orientation, and perceived parental expressiveness as contributing factors. *Journal of Marriage and the Family, 39*, 121–127.

Barnlund, D. C. (1975). Communicative styles in two cultures: Japan and the United States. In A. Kendon, R. M. Harris, & M. R. Key (Eds.), *Organization of behavior in face-to-face interaction* (pp. 427–456). The Hague, The Netherlands: Mouton.

Barrett, K. C., & Campos, J. J. (1987). Perspectives on emotional development: II. A functionalist approach to emotions. In J. D. Osofsky (Ed.), *Handbook of infant development* (2nd ed., pp. 555–578). New York, NY: Wiley.

Barrett, L. F., Robin, L., Pietromonaco, P. R., & Eyssell, K. M. (1998). Are women the "more emotional" sex? Evidence from emotional experiences in social context. *Cognition & Emotion, 12*, 555–578.

Basabe, N., Paez, D., Valencia, J., Rimé, B., Pennebaker, J., Diener, E., & González, J. L. (2000). Sociocultural factors predicting subjective experience of emotion: A collective level analysis. *Psicothema, 12*(Suppl 1), 55–69.

Beamish, A. J., Foster, J. J., Edwards, H., & Olbers, T. (2019). What's in a smile? A review of the benefits of the clinician's smile. *Postgraduate Medical Journal, 95*(1120), 91–95.

Bedford, N., Fallon, S., & McAdam, M. (2008). *Lonely planet—Destination Poland*. Oakland, CA: LPP.

Benedict, R. (1946). *The chrysanthemum and the sword: Patterns of Japanese culture*. Boston, MA: Houghton Mifflin.

Berenbaum, H., Fujita, F., & Pfennig, J. (1995). Consistency, specificity, and correlates of negative emotions. *Journal of Personality and Social Psychology, 68*, 342–352.

Biehl, M., Matsumoto, D., Ekman, P., Hearn, V., Heider, K., Kudoh, T., & Ton, V. (1997). Matsumoto and Ekman's Japanese and Caucasian Facial Expressions of Emotion (JACFEE): Reliability data and cross-national differences. *Journal of Nonverbal Behavior, 21*, 3–22.

Birnbaum, D. W., Nosanchuk, T. A., & Croll, W. L. (1980). Children's stereotypes about sex differences in emotionality. *Sex Roles, 6*, 435–443.

Blais, C., Jack, R. E., Scheepers, C., Fiset, D., & Caldara, R. (2008). Culture shapes how we look at faces. *PLoS One, 3*(8), e3022.

Blum-Kulka, S., Danet, B., & Gherson, R. (1985). The language of requesting in Israeli society. In J. P. Forgas (Ed.), *Language and social situations* (pp. 113–139). New York, NY: Springer.

Bodas, J., & Ollendick, T. H. (2005). Test anxiety: A cross-cultural perspective. *Clinical Child and Family Psychology Review, 8*(1), 65–88.

Bond, M. H. (1993). Emotions and their expression in Chinese culture. *Journal of Nonverbal Behavior, 17*(4), 245–262.

Bond, M. H., Wan, K. C., Leung, K., & Giacalone, R. (1985). How are responses to verbal insult related to cultural collectivism and power distance? *Journal of Cross-Cultural Psychology, 16*, 111–127.

Brebner, J. (2003). Gender and emotions. *Personality and Individual Differences, 34*(3), 387–394.

Brody, L. R. (1993). On understanding gender differences in the expression of emotion: Gender roles, socialization, and language. In S. L. Ablon, D. Brown, E. Khantzian, & J. Mack (Eds.), *Human feelings: Explorations in affective development and meaning* (pp. 89–121). Hillsdale, NJ: Analytic Press.

Brody, L. R. (1999). *Gender, emotion, and the family*. Cambridge, MA: Harvard University Press.

Brody, L. R. (2000). The socialization of gender differences in emotional expression: Display rules, infant temperament, and differentiation. In A. H. Fischer (Ed.), *Gender and emotion: Social psychological perspectives* (pp. 24–47). New York, NY: Cambridge University Press.

Brody, L. R., & Hall, J. A. (1993). Gender and emotion. In M. Lewis & J. M. Haviland (Eds.), *Handbook of emotions* (pp. 447–460). New York, NY: Guilford Press.

Brody, L. R., & Hall, J. A. (2008). Gender and emotion in context. In M. Lewis, J. M. Haviland-Jones, & L. F. Barrett (Eds.), *Handbook of emotions* (pp. 395–408). New York, NY: Guilford Press.

Brody, L. R., Muderrisoglu, S., & Nakash-Eisikovits, O. (2002). Emotions, defenses, and gender. In R. F. Bornstein & J. M. Masling (Eds.), *The psychodynamics of gender and gender role* (pp. 203–249). Washington, DC: American Psychological Association.

Burke, R. J., Weir, T., & Harrison, D. (1976). Disclosure of problems and tensions experienced by marital partners. *Psychological Reports, 38*, 531–542.

Butler, E. A., Lee, T. L., & Gross, J. J. (2007). Emotion regulation and culture: Are the social consequences of emotion suppression culture-specific? *Emotion, 7*(1), 30–48.

Caballo, V. E., Salazar, I. C., Irurtia, M. J., Arias, B., Hofmann, S. G., & Research Team, C. I. S. O.-A. (2014). Differences in social anxiety between men and women across 18 countries. *Personality and Individual Differences, 64*, 35–40.

Calder, A. J., Young, A. W., Perrett, D. I., Etcoff, N. L., & Rowland, D. (1996). Categorical perception of morphed facial expressions. *Visual Cognition, 3*, 81–117.

Camras, L. A., Bakeman, R., Chen, Y., Norris, K., & Cain, T. R. (2006). Culture, ethnicity, and children's facial expressions: A study of European American, mainland Chinese, Chinese American, and adopted Chinese girls. *Emotion, 6*, 103–114. https://doi.org/10.1037/1528-3542.6.1.103

Camras, L. A., Oster, H., Campos, J., Campos, R., Ujie, T., Miyake, K., … Meng, Z. (1998). Production of emotional facial expressions in European American, Japanese, and Chinese infants. *Developmental Psychology, 34*(4), 616–628.

Camras, L. A., Oster, H., Campos, J. J., Miyake, K., & Bradshaw, D. (1992). Japanese and American infants' responses to arm restraint. *Developmental Psychology, 28*, 578–583. https://doi.org/10.1037/0012-1649.28.4.578

Chaplin, T. M. (2015). Gender and emotion expression: A developmental contextual perspective. *Emotion Review, 7*(1), 14–21. https://doi.org/10.1177/1754073914544408

Chaplin, T. M., & Aldao, A. (2013). Gender differences in emotion expression in children: A meta-analytic review. *Psychological Bulletin, 139*, 735–765.

Chaplin, T. M., Cole, P. M., & Zahn-Waxler, C. (2005). Parental socialization of emotion expression: Gender differences and relations to child adjustment. *Emotion, 5*(1), 80–88.

Cole, P. M., Bruschi, C. J., & Tamang, B. L. (2002). Cultural differences in children's emotional reactions to difficult situations. *Child Development, 73*, 983–996. https://doi.org/10.1111/1467-8624.00451

Cole, P. M., & Tamang, B. L. (1998). Nepali children's ideas about emotional displays in hypothetical challenges. *Developmental Psychology, 34*, 640–646. https://doi.org/10.1037/0012-1649.34.4.640

Collins, R. (1984). The role of emotion in social structure. In K. Scherer & P. Ekman (Eds.), *Approaches to emotion* (pp. 385–396). New York, NY: Erlbaum.

Corapci, F., Friedlmeier, W., Benga, O., Strauss, C., Pitica, I., & Susa, G. (2018). Cultural socialization of toddlers in emotionally charged situations. *Social Development, 27*(2), 262–278.

Correll, S. J., & Ridgeway, C. L. (2006). Expectation states theory. In J. Delamater (Ed.), *Handbook of social psychology* (pp. 29–51). Boston, MA: Springer.

Cosnier, J., Dols, J. M. F., & Fernandez, A. J. (1986). The verbalization of emotional experiences. In K. R. Scherer, H. G. Wallbott, & A. B. Summerfield (Eds.), *Experiencing emotion: A cross-cultural study* (pp. 117–128). Cambridge, UK: Cambridge University Press.

Daun, A. (1995). *Swedish mentality*. University Park, PA: Penn State University Press.

Deng, Y., Chang, L., Yang, M., Huo, M., & Zhou, R. (2016). Gender differences in emotional response: Inconsistency between experience and expressivity. *PLoS One, 11*(6), e0158666.

Diener, E., & Emmons, R. A. (1985). The independence of positive and negative affect. *Journal of Personality and Social Psychology, 47*, 1105–1117.

Diener, E., Sandvik, E., & Larsen, R. J. (1985). Age and sex effects for emotional intensity. *Developmental Psychology, 21*, 542–546.

Dillon, K. M., Wolf, E., & Katz, H. (1985). Sex roles, gender, and fear. *The Journal of Psychology, 119*, 355–359.

Doi, L. T. (1962). Amae: A key concept for understanding Japanese personality structure. In R. J. Smith & R. K. Beardsley (Eds.), *Japanese culture: Its development and characteristics* (pp. 307–313). Chicago: Aldine.

Dosser, D. A., Balswick, J. O., & Halverson, C. F., Jr. (1983). Situational context of emotional expressiveness. *Journal of Counseling Psychology, 30*, 51–66.

Eades, D. (1982). You gotta know how to talk: Information seeking in south-east Queensland aboriginal society. *Australian Journal of Linguistics, 2*, 61–82.

Edelmann, R. J., Asendorpf, J., Conrtarello, A., Georgas, J., Villanueva, C., & Zammuner, V. (1987). Self-reported verbal and non-verbal strategies for coping with embarrassment in five European cultures. *Social Science Information, 26*, 869–883.

Edelmann, R. J., Asendorpf, J., Contarello, A., Zammuner, V., Georgas, J., & Villanueva, C. (1986). *Self-reported expression of embarrassment in five European cultures.* Paper presented at the 8th international congress of Cross-cultural psychology, Istanbul, Turkey.

Eid, M., & Diener, E. (2001). Norms for experiencing emotions in different cultures: Inter- and intra-national differences. *Journal of Personality and Social Psychology, 81*(5), 869–885.

Eisenberg, N., Fabes, R. A., Murphy, B., Karbon, M., Maszk, P., Smith, M., … Suh, K. (1994). The relations of emotionality and regulation to dispositional and situational empathy-related responding. *Journal of Personality and Social Psychology, 66*, 776–797.

Ekman, P. (1972). Universals and cultural differences in facial expressions of emotion. In J. Cole (Ed.), *Nebraska Symposium Motivation, 1971* (Vol. 19, pp. 207–282). Lincoln, NE: University of Nebraska Press.

Ekman, P. (1992). Are there basic emotions? *Psychological Review, 99*, 550–553.

Ekman, P., & Friesen, W. (1969). The repertoire of nonverbal behavior: Categories, origins, usage, and coding. *Semiotica, 1*, 49–98.

Ekman, P., & Friesen, W. V. (1971). Constants across cultures in the face and emotion. *Journal of Personality and Social Psychology, 17*, 124–129.

Ekman, P., & Friesen, W. V. (1975). *Unmasking the face: A guide to recognizing emotions from facial clues.* Englewood Cliffs, NJ: Prentice Hall.

Ekman, P., Friesen, W. V., & O'Sullivan, M. (1988). Smiles when lying. *Journal of Personality and Social Psychology, 54*, 414–420.

Ekman, P., Friesen, W. V., O'Sullivan, M., Chan, A., Diacoyanni-Tarlatzis, I., Heider, K., … Tzavaras, A. (1987). Universals and cultural differences in the judgments of facial expressions of emotion. *Journal of Personality and Social Psychology, 53*(4), 712–717. https://doi.org/10.1037/0022-3514.53.4.712

Ekman, P., Sorenson, E. R., & Friesen, W. V. (1969). Pancultural elements in facial displays of emotion. *Science, 164*, 86–88.

Elfenbein, H. A., & Ambady, N. (2002). On the universality and cultural specificity of emotion recognition: A meta-analysis. *Psychological Bulletin, 128*(2), 203–235. https://doi.org/10.1037/0033-2909.128.2.203

Elfenbein, H. A., & Ambady, N. (2003). When familiarity breeds accuracy: Cultural exposure and facial emotion recognition. *Journal of Personality and Social Psychology, 85*, 276–290.

Elfenbein, H. A., Mandal, M. K., Ambady, N., Harizuka, S., & Kumar, S. (2004). Hemifacial differences in the in-group advantage in emotion recognition. *Cognition and Emotion, 18*, 613–629.

Else-Quest, N. M., Higgins, A., Allison, C., & Morton, L. C. (2012). Gender differences in self-conscious emotional experience: A meta-analysis. *Psychological Bulletin, 138*, 947–982.

Erickson, B. M. (2005). Scandinavian families: Plain and simple. In M. G. McGoldrick, J. Nydia, & N. Garcia-Preto (Eds.), *Ethnicity and family therapy* (3rd ed., pp. 641–654). New York, NY: Guilford Press.

Erickson, B. M., & Simon, J. S. (1996). Scandinavian families: Plain and simple. In M. McGoldrick, J. Giordano, & J. K. Pearce (Eds.), *Ethnicity and family therapy* (p. 595–608). Guilford Press.

Etcoff, N. L., & Magee, J. J. (1992). Categorical perception of facial expression. *Cognition, 44*, 227–240.

EURES. (2010). *Living and working in Norway.* http://www.eures.dk/JobSeeker/Landeinfo-og-jobdatabaser/Norden/Living_and_working_in_Norway_%28engelsk%29.aspx

Fabes, R. A., & Martin, C. L. (1991). Gender and age stereotypes of emotionality. *Personality and Social Psychology Bulletin, 17*, 532–540.

Fernandez, I., Carrera, P., Sanchez, F., Paez, D., & Candia, L. (2000). Differences between cultures in emotional verbal and non-verbal reactions. *Psicothema, 12*(Suppl 1), 83–92.

Fischer, A. H. (1993). Sex differences in emotionality: Fact or stereotype? *Feminism & Psychology, 3*, 303–318.

Fischer, A. H., Kret, M. E., & Broekens, J. (2018). Gender differences in emotion perception and self-reported emotional intelligence: A test of the emotion sensitivity hypothesis. *PLoS One, 13*(1), e0190712.

Fischer, A. H., & Manstead, A. S. R. (2000). The relation between gender and emotion in different cultures. In A. H. Fischer (Ed.), *Gender and emotion: Social psychological perspectives* (pp. 71–98). New York, NY: Cambridge University Press.

Fischer, A. H., Rodriguez Mosquera, P. M., Van Vianen, A. E., & Manstead, A. S. (2004). Gender and culture differences in emotion. *Emotion, 4*, 87–94.

Ford, B. Q., & Mauss, I. B. (2015). Culture and emotion regulation. *Current Opinion in Psychology, 3*, 1–5.

Friedlmeier, W., Corapci, F., & Benga, O. (2015). Early emotional development in cultural perspective. In L. Jensen (Ed.), *Oxford handbook of human development and culture: An interdisciplinary perspective* (pp. 127–148). New York, NY: Oxford University Press. https://doi.org/10.1093/oxfordhb/9780199948550.013.9

Friedlmeier, W., Corapci, F., & Cole, P. (2011). Emotion socialization in cross-cultural perspective. *Social and Personality Psychology Compass, 5*, 410–427. https://doi.org/10.1111/j.1751-9004.2011.00362.x

Friedlmeier, W., Corapci, F., Susa-Erdogan, G., Benga, O., & Kurman, J. (2019). Cultural variations of maternal emotion regulation of toddler's emotions in a delay of gratification context. *Culture and Brain, 7*, 1–27. https://doi.org/10.1007/s40167-018-0076-0

Fujita, F., Diener, E., & Sandvik, E. (1991). Gender differences in negative affect and well-being: The case for emotional intensity. *Journal of Personality and Social Psychology, 61*, 427–434.

Ganong, L. H., & Coleman, M. (1984). Sex, sex roles, and familial love. *Journal of Genetic Psychology, 148*, 45–52.

Garrett-Peters, P. T., & Fox, N. A. (2007). Cross-cultural differences in children's emotional reactions to a disappointing situation. *International Journal of Behavioral Development, 31*, 161–169. https://doi.org/10.1177/0165025407074627

Geertz, C. (1976). *The religion of Java*. Chicago, IL: Chicago University Press.

Gelfand, M. J., Nishii, L. H., & Raver, J. L. (2006). On the nature and importance of cultural tightness-looseness. *Journal of Applied Psychology, 91*(6), 1225–1244. https://doi.org/10.1037/0021-9010.91.6.1225

Gordon, S. L. (1989). Institutional and impulsive orientations in selective appropriating emotions to self. In D. D. Franks & D. McCarthy (Eds.), *The sociology of emotions: Original essays and research papers* (pp. 115–136). Greenwich, CT: JAI Press.

Gorvett, Z. (2017, April 10). There are 19 types of smile but only six are for happiness. *BBC Future*, Retrieved on May 24, 2020, http://www.bbc.com/future/story/20170407-why-all-smiles-are-not-the-same

Gotlib, I. H., & Meyer, J. P. (1986). Factor analysis of the multiple affect adjective check list: A separation of positive and negative affect. *Journal of Personality and Social Psychology, 50*, 1161–1165.

Gottman, J. M., & Levenson, R. W. (2000). The timing of divorce: Predicting when a couple will divorce over a 14-year period. *Journal of Marriage & the Family, 62*, 737–745.

Grandey, A. A., Fisk, G. M., & Steiner, D. D. (2005). Must "service with a smile" be stressful? The moderating role of personal control for American and French employees. *Journal of Applied Psychology, 90*(5), 893.

Greeley, A. M. (1979). The American Irish: A report from great Ireland. *International Journal of Comparative Sociology, 20*, 67–81.

Grice, H. R. (1975). Logic and conversation. In P. Cole & J. L. Morgan (Eds.), *Syntax and semantics: Vol. 3. Speech acts* (pp. 41–58). New York, NY: Academic.

Grossman, M., & Wood, W. (1993). Sex differences in intensity of emotional experience: A social role interpretation. *Journal of Personality and Social Psychology, 65*, 1010–1022.

Gudykunst, W. B., & Kim, Y. Y. (1984). *Communicating with strangers: An approach to intercultural communication.* Reading, MA: Addison-Wesley.

Gudykunst, W. B., & Ting-Toomey, S. (1988). Culture and affective communication. *American Behavioral Scientist, 31*(3), 384–400.

Hall, E. T., & Hall, M. R. (1990). *Understanding cultural differences.* Yarmouth, ME: Intercultural Press.

Hallowell, R., Bowen, D. E., & Knoop, C. I. (2002). Four seasons goes to Paris. *Academy of Management Executive, 16*(4), 7–24.

Heine, S. I. (2010). Cultural psychology. In S. T. Fiske, D. T. Gilbert, & G. Lindzey (Eds.), *Handbook of social psychology* (Vol. 2, 5th ed., pp. 1423–1464). New York, NY: Wiley.

Henrich, J., Heine, S. J., & Norenzayan, A. (2010). The weirdest people in the world? *Behavioral and Brain Sciences, 33*, 61–83.

Ho, D. Y. F. (1994). Cognitive socialization in Confucian cultures. In P. M. Greenfield & R. R. Cocking (Eds.), *Cross-cultural mots of minority child development.* Hillsdale, NJ: Lawrence Erlbaum.

Hochschild, A. (1979). Emotion work, feeling rules, and social structure. *American Journal of Sociology, 85*(3), 551–575.

Hofstede, G. (1984). *Culture's consequences: International differences in work-related values.* Newbury Park, CA: SAGE. Originally published in 1980.

Hofstede, G. (1998). Attitudes, values and organizational culture: Disentangling the concepts. *Organization Studies, 19*(3), 477–493.

Hopcroft, R. L., & McLaughlin, J. (2012). Why is the sex gap in feelings of depression wider in high gender equity countries? The effect of children on the psychological well-being of men and women. *Social Science Research, 41*, 501–513.

Hyde, J. S., Mezulis, A. H., & Abramson, L. Y. (2008). The ABCs of depression: Integrating affective, biological, and cognitive models to explain the emergence of the gender difference in depression. *Psychological Review, 115*, 291–313.

Inglehart, R. (1997). *Modernization and postmodernization: Cultural, economic, and political change in 43 societies.* Princeton, NJ: Princeton University Press.

Inglehart, R., & Baker, W. E. (2000). Modernization, cultural change, and the persistence of traditional values. *American Sociological Review, 65*(1), 19–51. https://doi.org/10.2307/2657288

Inglehart, R., & Welzel, C. (2005). *Modernization, cultural change, and democracy: The human development sequence.* Cambridge, UK: Cambridge University Press.

Izard, C. E. (1971). *The face of emotion.* East Norwalk, CT: Appleton-Century-Crofts.

Izard, C. E. (1994). Innate and universal facial expressions: Evidence from developmental and cross-cultural research. *Psychological Bulletin, 115*(2), 288–299. https://doi.org/10.1037/0033-2909.115.2.288

Izard, C. E., & Ackerman, B. P. (2000). Motivational, organizational, and regulatory functions of discrete emotions. In M. Lewis & J. M. Haviland-Jones (Eds.), *Handbook of emotions* (2nd ed., pp. 253–264). New York, NY: Guilford Press.

Jack, R. E., Blais, C., Scheepers, C., Schyns, P. G., & Caldara, R. (2009). Cultural confusions show that facial expressions are not universal. *Current Biology, 19*(18), 1543–1548.

Jack, R. E., Garrod, O. G., Yu, H., Caldara, R., & Schyns, P. G. (2012). Facial expressions of emotion are not culturally universal. *Proceedings of the National Academy of Sciences, 109*(19), 7241–7244.

Jack, R. E., Sun, W., Delis, I., Garrod, O. G., & Schyns, P. G. (2016). Four not six: Revealing culturally common facial expressions of emotion. *Journal of Experimental Psychology: General, 145*(6), 708–730.

Joshi, M. S., & MacLean, M. (1994). Indian and English children's understanding of the distinction between real and apparent emotion. *Child Development, 65*, 1372–1384. https://doi.org/10.1111/j.1467-8624.1994.tb00822.x

Kanaya, Y., Bradshaw, L. B., Nakamura, C., & Miyake, K. (1988). Expressive behavior of Japanese mothers in response to their 5-month-old infants' negative and positive emotion expression. Annual Report 1986-1987, 10, 55–59, Research and Clinical Center for Child Development, Faculty of Education, Hokkaido University.

Kanaya, Y., Nakamura, C., & Miyake, K. (1989). Cross-cultural study of expressive behavior of mothers in response to their 5-month-old infants' different emotion expression. *Research and Clinical Center for Child Development, Annual Report, 11*, 25–31.

Keating, C. F. (1994). World without words: Messages from face and body. In W. J. Lonner & R. Malpass (Eds.), *Psychology and culture* (pp. 175–182). Boston, MA: Allyn & Bacon.

Khazan, O. (2017, May 3). Why Americans smile so much: How immigration and cultural values affect what people do with their faces. *The Atlantic*, Retrieved on May 24, 2020, https://www.theatlantic.com/science/archive/2017/05/why-americans-smile-so-much/524967/

Kitayama, S., & Cohen, D. (Eds.). (2007). *Handbook of cultural psychology*. New York, NY: Guilford Press.

Kleinke, C. L. (1986). Gaze and eye contact: A research review. *Psychological Bulletin, 100*(1), 78–100.

Klineberg, O. (1938). Emotional expression in Chinese literature. *The Journal of Abnormal and Social Psychology, 33*(4), 517–520.

Koopmann-Holm, B., & Tsai, J. L. (2014). Focusing on the negative: Cultural differences in expressions of sympathy. *Journal of Personality and Social Psychology, 107*, 1092–1115.

Kring, A. M., & Gordon, A. H. (1998). Sex differences in emotion: Expression, experience, and physiology. *Journal of Personality and Social Psychology, 74*(3), 686–703.

Krys, K., Vauclair, C. M., Capaldi, C. A., Lun, V. M. C., Bond, M. H., Domínguez-Espinosa, A., … Antalíková, R. (2016). Be careful where you smile: Culture shapes judgments of intelligence and honesty of smiling individuals. *Journal of Nonverbal Behavior, 40*(2), 101–116.

La France, M., & Banaji, M. (1992). Toward a reconsideration of the gender emotion relationship. In M. S. Clark (Ed.), *Review of personality and social psychology: Emotion and social behavior* (Vol. 14, pp. 178–202). Newbury Park, CA: Sage.

La France, M., Hecht, M. A., & Paluck, E. L. (2003). The contingent smile: A meta-analysis of sex differences in smiling. *Psychological Bulletin, 129*(2), 305–334.

La France, M., & Mayo, C. (1978). Cultural aspects of nonverbal communication. *International Journal of Intercultural Relations, 2*(1), 71–89.

La France, M., & Mayo, C. (1979). A review of nonverbal behaviors of women and men. *Western Journal of Communication (includes Communication Reports), 43*(2), 96–107.

Le, B. M., & Impett, E. A. (2013). When holding back helps: Suppressing negative emotions during sacrifice feels authentic and is beneficial for highly interdependent people. *Psychological Science, 24*, 1809–1815.

Lee, A. Y., Aaker, J. L., & Gardner, W. L. (2000). The pleasures and pains of distinct self-construals: The role of interdependence in regulatory focus. *Journal of Personality and Social Psychology, 78*, 1122–1134.

Levenson, R. W., Carstensen, L. L., & Gottman, J. M. (1994). Influence of age and gender on affect, physiology, and their interrelations: A study of long-term marriages. *Journal of Personality and Social Psychology, 67*(1), 56–68.

Lewis, M., Takai-Kawakami, K., Kawakami, K., & Sullivan, M. W. (2010). Cultural differences in emotional responses to success and failure. *International Journal of Behavioral Development, 34*, 53–61. https://doi.org/10.1177/0165025409348559

Lewis, R. D. (1996). *When cultures collide. Managing successfully across cultures*. London, UK: Nicholas Brealey Publishing.

Lewis, R. D. (2003). The cultural imperative: Global trends in the 21st century. Helsinki, Finland: Intercultural Press.

Lim, T., & Choi, S. (1996). Interpersonal relationships in Korea. In W. B. Gudykunst, S. Toomey, & T. Nishida (Eds.), *Communication in personal relationships across cultures* (pp. 122–136). Thousand Oaks, CA: Sage.

Lim, T.-S. (2003). Language and verbal communication across cultures. In W. B. Gudykunst (Ed.), *Handbook of international and intercultural communication* (pp. 53–71). Thousand Oaks, CA: Sage.

Lombardo, W. K., Cretser, G. A., Lombardo, B., & Mathis, S. L. (1983). 'Fer cryin' out loud – There is a sex difference. *Sex Roles, 9,* 987–996.

Lutz, C. (1987). Goals, events, and understanding in Ifaluk emotion theory. In N. Quinn & D. Holland (Eds.), *Cultural models in language and thought* (pp. 290–312). Cambridge, UK: Cambridge University Press.

Maccoby, E. E. (1988). Gender as a social category. *Developmental Psychology, 24,* 755–765.

Madden, T. E., Barrett, L. F., & Pietromonaco, P. R. (2000). Sex differences in anxiety and depression: Empirical evidence and methodological questions. In *Gender and emotion: Social psychological perspectives* (pp. 277–298). Paris, France: Cambridge University Press.

Mai, X., Ge, Y., Tao, L., Tang, H., Liu, C., & Luo, Y. J. (2011). Eyes are windows to the Chinese soul: Evidence from the detection of real and fake smiles. *PLoS One, 6*(5), e19903.

Markus, H. R., & Kitayama, S. (1991). Culture and the self: Implications for cognition, emotion, and motivation. *Psychological Review, 98,* 224–253.

Marsh, A. A., Elfenbein, H. A., & Ambady, N. (2003). Nonverbal "accents": Cultural differences in facial expressions of emotion. *Psychological Science, 14,* 373–376.

Martin, J., Rychlowska, M., Wood, A., & Niedenthal, P. (2017). Smiles as multipurpose social signals. *Trends in Cognitive Sciences, 21*(11), 864–877.

Matsumoto, D. (1990). Cultural similarities and differences in display rules. *Motivation and Emotion, 14*(3), 195–214.

Matsumoto, D. (1991). Cultural influences on facial expressions of emotion. *Southern Communication Journal, 56,* 128–137.

Matsumoto, D. (1992). American-Japanese cultural differences in the recognition of universal facial expressions. *Journal of Cross-Cultural Psychology, 23*(1), 72–84.

Matsumoto, D. (1993). Ethnic differences in affect intensity, emotion judgments, display rule attitudes, and self-reported emotional expression in an American sample. *Motivation and Emotion, 17*(2), 107–123.

Matsumoto, D. (2006a). Culture and nonverbal behavior. In V. Manusov & M. L. Patterson (Eds.), *The SAGE handbook of nonverbal communication* (pp. 219–235). Newbury Park, CA: Sage.

Matsumoto, D., & Ekman, P. (1989). American-Japanese differences in intensity ratings of facial expressions of emotion. *Motivation and Emotion, 13,* 143–157.

Matsumoto, D., Franklin, B., Choi, J., Rogers, D., & Tatani, H. (2003). Cultural influences on the expression and perception of emotions. In W. B. Gudykunst (Ed.), *Handbook of international and intercultural communication* (pp. 91–110). Thousand Oaks, CA: Sage.

Matsumoto, D., & Hwang, H. S. (2012). Culture and emotion: The integration of biological and cultural contributions. *Journal of Cross-Cultural Psychology, 43*(1), 91–118.

Matsumoto, D., Kasri, R., & Kooken, K. (1999). American-Japanese cultural differences in judgments of expression intensity and subjective experience. *Cognition and Emotion, 13,* 201–218.

Matsumoto, D., Kudoh, T., Scherer, K. R., & Wallbott, H. (1988). Antecedents of and reactions to emotions in the United States and Japan. *Journal of Cross- Cultural Psychology, 19*(3), 267–286.

Matsumoto, D., & Kupperbusch, C. (2001). Idiocentric and allocentric differences in emotional expression, experience, and the coherence between expression and experience. *Asian Journal of Social Psychology, 4*(2), 113–131.

Matsumoto, D., Takeuchi, S., Andayani, S., Kouznetsova, N., & Krupp, D. (1998). The contribution of individualism vs. collectivism to cross-national differences in display rules. *Asian Journal of Social Psychology, 1*(2), 147–165.

Matsumoto, D., Yoo, S. H., & Fontaine, J. (2009). Hypocrisy or maturity? Culture and context differentiation. *European Journal of Personality, 23*(3), 251–264.

Matsumoto, D., Yoo, S.-H., Fontaine, J., Anguas-Wong, A. M., Arriola, M., Ataca, B., et al. (2008). Mapping expressive differences around the world: The relationship between emotional display rules and individualism vs. collectivism. *Journal of Cross-Cultural Psychology, 39,* 55–74.

Matsumoto, D., Yoo, S. H., Hirayama, S., & Petrova, G. (2005). Development and validation of a measure of display rule knowledge: The display rule assessment inventory. *Emotion, 5*(1), 23–40.

Matsumoto, D., Yoo, S. H., & Nakagawa, S. (2008). Culture, emotion regulation, and adjustment. *Journal of Personality and Social Psychology, 94*(6), 925–937.

Mauss, I., & Butler, E. A. (2010). Cultural context moderates the relationship between emotion control values and cardiovascular challenge versus threat responses. *Biological Psychology, 84*, 521–530.

McGoldrick, M. (1996). Irish families in America. *Aisling Magazine*, Retrieved from http://www.aislingmagazine.com/aislingmagazine/articles/TAM19/Irish%20families.html

McLean, C. P., & Anderson, E. R. (2009). Brave men and timid women? A review of the gender differences in fear and anxiety. *Clinical Psychology Review, 29*, 496–505.

Meissner, C. A., & Brigham, J. C. (2001). Thirty years of investigating the own-race bias in memory for faces: A meta-analytic review. *Psychology, Public Policy, and Law, 7*(1), 3–35. https://doi.org/10.1037/1076-8971.7.1.3

Mesquita, B., & Frijda, N. H. (1992). Cultural variations in emotions: A review. *Psychological Bulletin, 112*(2), 179–204. https://doi.org/10.1037/0033-2909.112.2.179

Mesquita, B., Frijda, N. H., & Scherer, K. R. (1997). Culture and emotion. In P. Dasen & T. S. Saraswathi (Eds.), *Handbook of cross-cultural psychology. Basic processes and human development* (Vol. 2, pp. 255–297). Boston, MA: Allyn & Bacon.

Mesquita, B., & Leu, J. (2007). The cultural psychology of emotion. In S. Kitayama & D. Cohen (Eds.), *Handbook of cultural psychology* (pp. 734–759). New York, NY: Guilford Press.

Midelfort, C. F., & Midelfort, H. C. (1982). Norwegian families. In J. Giordano (Ed.), *Ethnicity and family therapy* (pp. 438–456). New York, NY: Guilford Press.

Miyake, K., & Yamazaki, K. (1995). Self-conscious emotions: The psychology of shame, guilt, embarrassment, and pride. In J. P. Tangney & K. W. Fischer (Eds.), *Self-conscious emotions: The psychology of shame, guilt, embarrassment, and pride* (pp. 488–504). New York, NY: Guilford Press.

Mizutani, O., & Mizutani, N. (1987). *How to be polite in Japanese*. Tokyo, Japan: The Japan Times.

Morsbach, H. (1976). Aspects of nonverbal communication in Japan. In L. Samovar & R. Porter (Eds.), *Intercultural communication: A reader* (2nd ed.). Belmont, CA: Wadsworth.

Morsbach, H. (1988a). Nonverbal communication and hierarchical relationships: The case of bowing in Japan. In F. Poyatos (Ed.), *Cross-cultural perspectives in nonverbal communication* (pp. 189–199). Lewinston, NY: Hogrefe.

Morsbach, H. (1988b). The importance of silence and stillness in Japanese nonverbal communication: A cross-cultural approach. In F. Poyatos (Ed.), *Cross-cultural perspectives in nonverbal communication* (pp. 201–215). Lewinston, NY: Hogrefe.

Murata, A., Moser, J. S., & Kitayama, S. (2013). Culture shapes electrocortical responses during emotion suppression. *Social Cognitive and Affective Neuroscience, 8*, 595–601.

Nakamura, H. (1964). Consciousness of the Individual and the Universal Among the Japanese. *Philosophy East and West, 14*(3/4), 333–351.

Nakane, C. (1970). *Japanese society*. University of California Press.

Niedenthal, P., Mermillod, M., Maringer, M., & Hess, U. (2010). The simulation of smiles (SIMS) model: Embodied simulation and the meaning of facial expression. *Behavioral and Brain Sciences, 33*, 417–433.

Nishimura, S., Nevgi, A., & Tella, S. (2008). Communication style and cultural features in high/low context communication cultures: A case study of Finland, Japan and India. *Teoksessa A. Kallioniemi (toim.), Uudistuva ja kehittyvä ainedidaktiikka.* Ainedidaktinen symposiumi, 8(2008), 783–796.

Okabe, R. (1983). Cultural assumptions of East and West: Japan and the United States. In W. Gudykunst (Ed.), *Intercultural communication theory: Current perspective* (pp. 21–44). Beverly Hills, CA: Sage.

Oliver, S. J., & Toner, B. B. (1990). The influence of gender role typing on the expression of depressive symptoms. *Sex Roles, 22,* 775–791.

Pakiam, A. (2007, December 17, updated 2011, April). "Face-saving" in cross-cultural communication. *The Hindu Business Line.* Retrieved from http://www.thehindubusinessline.com/manager/2007/12/17/stories/2007121750321100.htm

Pelto, P. J. (1968, April). The difference between "tight" and "loose" societies. *Transactions, 5,* 37–40.

Pennebaker, J. W., Rimé, B., & Blankenship, V. E. (1996). Stereotypes of emotional expressiveness of Northerners and Southerners: A cross-cultural test of Montesquieu's hypotheses. *Journal of Personality and Social Psychology, 70*(2), 372–380.

Petersen, J. L., & Hyde, J. S. (2010). A meta-analytic review of research on gender differences in sexuality, 1993–2007. *Psychological Bulletin, 136,* 21–38.

Pittam, J., Gallois, C., Iwawaki, S., & Kroonenberg, P. (1995). Australian and Japanese concepts of expressive behavior. *Journal of Cross-Cultural Psychology, 26*(5), 451–473.

Potter, S. H. (1988). The cultural construction of emotion in rural Chinese social life. *Ethos, 16*(2), 181–208.

Ramsey, S. J. (1979). Nonverbal behavior: An intercultural perspective. In M. K. Asante, E. Newmark, & C. A. Blake (Eds.), *Handbook of intercultural communication* (pp. 71–89). Beverly Hills, CA: Sage.

Raval, V. V., Martini, T. S., & Raval, P. H. (2007). 'Would others think it is okay to express my feelings?' Regulation of anger, sadness and physical pain in Gujarati children in India. *Social Development, 16,* 79–105. https://doi.org/10.1111/j.1467-9507.2007.00373.x

Rodnick, D. (1955). *The Norwegians: A study in national culture.* Washington, DC: Public Affairs Press.

Rozin, P., Lowery, L., Imada, S., & Haidt, J. (1999). The CAD triad hypothesis: A mapping between three moral emotions (contempt, anger, disgust) and three moral codes (community, autonomy, divinity). *Journal of Personality and Social Psychology, 75*(4), 574–585.

Russell, J. A. (1980). A circumplex model of affect. *Journal of Personality and Social Psychology, 39*(6), 1161–1178. https://doi.org/10.1037/h0077714

Russell, J. A. (1994). Is there universal recognition of emotion from facial expression? A review of the cross-cultural studies. *Psychological Bulletin, 115*(1), 102–141. https://doi.org/10.1037/0033-2909.115.1.102

Russell, J. A., & Carroll, J. M. (1999). On the bipolarity of positive and negative affect. *Psychological Bulletin, 125,* 3–30.

Rychlowska, M., Miyamoto, Y., Matsumoto, D., Hess, U., Gilboa-Schechtman, E., Kamble, S., … Niedenthal, P. M. (2015). Heterogeneity of long-history migration explains cultural differences in reports of emotional expressivity and the functions of smiles. *Proceedings of the National Academy of Sciences, 112,* 2429–2436.

Saarni, C. (1999). *The development of emotional competence.* New York, NY: Guilford Press.

Safdar, S., Friedlmeier, W., Matsumoto, D., Yoo, S. H., Kwantes, C. T., Kakai, H., & Shigemasu, E. (2009). Variations of emotional display rules within and across cultures: A comparison between Canada, USA, and Japan. *Canadian Journal of Behavioural Science/Revue canadienne des sciences du comportement, 41*(1), 1–10. https://doi.org/10.1037/a0014387

Sansom, B. (1980). *The camp at Wallaby cross: Aboriginal fringe dwellers in Darwin.* Canberra, Australia: Australian Institute of Aboriginal Studies.

Sauter, D. A., Eisner, F., Ekman, P., & Scott, S. K. (2010). Cross-cultural recognition of basic emotions through nonverbal emotional vocalizations. *Proceedings of the National Academy of Sciences, 107*(6), 2408–2412.

Scherer, K. R., & Wallbott, H. G. (1994). Evidence for universality and cultural variation of differential emotion response patterning. *Journal of Personality and Social Psychology, 66*(2), 310–328.

Scherer, K. R., Wallbott, H. G., & Summerfield, A. B. (Eds.). (1986). *European monographs in social psychology. Experiencing emotion: A cross-cultural study.* New York, NY/Paris, France: Cambridge University Press/Editions de la Maison des Sciences de l'Homme.

Schieffelin, E. L. (1983). Anger and shame in the tropical forest: On affect as a cultural system in Papua New Guinea. *Ethos, 11*(3), 181–191.

Schimmack, U. (1996). Cultural influences on the recognition of emotion by facial expressions: Individualistic or Caucasian cultures? *Journal of Cross-Cultural Psychology, 27,* 37–50.

Schmitt, D. P. (2015). The evolution of culturally-variable sex differences: Men and women are not always different, but when they are…it appears not to result from patriarchy or sex role socialization. In V. A. Weekes-Shackelford & T. K. Shackelford (Eds.), *The evolution of sexuality* (pp. 221–256). New York, NY: Springer.

Schneider, D. J. (1981). Tactical self-presentations: Toward a broader conception. In J. T. Tedeschi (Ed.), *Impression management theory and social psychological research* (pp. 23–40). New York, NY: Academic.

Seidlitz, L., & Diener, E. (1998). Sex differences in the recall of affective experiences. *Journal of Personality and Social Psychology, 74,* 262–276.

Shields, S. A. (1991). Gender in the psychology of emotion: A selective review. In K. T. Strongman (Ed.), *International review of studies on emotion* (pp. 227–247). New York, NY: Wiley.

Shields, S. A. (2002). *Speaking from the heart: Gender and the social meaning of emotion.* Cambridge, UK: Cambridge University Press.

Shields, S. A., & Dicicco, E. C. (2011). The social psychology of sex and gender: From gender differences to doing gender. *Psychology of Women Quarterly, 35*(3), 491–499.

Shimoda, K., Argyle, M., & Ricci Bitti, P. (1978). The intercultural recognition of emotional expressions by three national racial groups: English, Italian, and Japanese. *European Journal of Social Psychology, 8,* 169–179.

Shweder, R. A. (1993). The cultural psychology of emotions. In M. Lewis & J. Hovland (Eds.), *Handbook of emotions* (pp. 417–437). New York, NY: Guilford Press.

Simon, R. W., & Nath, L. E. (2004). Gender and emotion in the United States: Do men and women differ in self-reports of feelings and expressive behavior? *American Journal of Sociology, 109*(5), 1137–1176.

Small, A., Gessner, T., & Ferguson, T. (1984). Sex role and dysphoric mood. *Sex Roles, 11,* 627–638.

Soto, J. A., Levenson, R. W., & Ebling, R. (2005). Cultures of moderation and expression: Emotional experience, behavior, and physiology in Chinese Americans and Mexican Americans. *Emotion, 5*(2), 154–165.

Soto, J. A., Perez, C. R., Kim, Y. H., Lee, E. A., & Minnick, M. R. (2011). Is expressive suppression always associated with poorer psychological functioning? A cross-cultural comparison between European Americans and Hong Kong Chinese. *Emotion, 11*(6), 1450–1455.

Sprecher, S., & Sedikides, C. (1993). Gender differences in perceptions of emotionality: The case of close heterosexual relationships. *Sex Roles, 28,* 511–530.

Stapley, J. C., & Haviland, J. M. (1989). Beyond depression: Gender differences in normal adolescents' emotional experiences. *Sex Roles, 20,* 295–308.

Stephan, C. W., Stephan, W. G., Saito, I., & Barnett, S. M. (1998). Emotional expression in Japan and the United States: The nonmonolithic nature of individualism and collectivism. *Journal of Cross-Cultural Psychology, 29*(6), 728–748.

Stephan, W. G., White, C., & Cabezas, M. (1996). Emotional expression in Costa Rica and the United States. *Journal of Cross-Cultural Psychology, 27,* 147–160.

Su, J. C., Wei, M., & Tsai, H. T. (2014). Running away from unwanted feelings: Culture matters. *Cognition and Emotion, 28*(7), 1313–1327.

Suleiman, Y. (1973). The Arabs and the west: Communication gap. In M. Prosser (Ed.), *Intercomnunication among nations and peoples.* New York, NY: Harper & Row.

Super, C. M., & Harkness, S. (2010). Culture and infancy. In G. Bremner & T. D. Wachs (Eds.), *Blackwell handbook of infant development* (Vol. 1, 2nd ed.). Oxford, UK: Blackwell. https://doi.org/10.1002/9781444327564.ch21

Tamres, L. K., Janicki, D., & Helgeson, V. S. (2002). Sex differences in coping behavior: A meta-analytic review and an examination of relative coping. *Personality and Social Psychology Review, 6,* 2–30.

Tannen, D. (1981). New York Jewish conversational style. *International Journal of the Sociology of Language, 30,* 133–149.

Tella, S. (2005). Multi-, inter- and transdisciplinary affordances in foreign language education: From singularity to multiplicity. In J. Smeds, K. Sarmavuori, E. Laakkonen, & R. de Cillia (Eds.), *Multicultural communities, multilingual practice: Monikulttuuriset yhteisöt, monikielinen käytäntö* (pp. 67–88). Turku, Finland: Annales Universitatis Turkuensis B 285.

Terracciano, A., & McMcrae, R. R. (2007). Perceptions of Americans and the Iraq invasion: Implications for understanding national character stereotypes. *Journal of Cross-Cultural Psychology, 38,* 695–710.

Thompson, R. A., & Meyer, S. (2007). Socialization of emotion regulation in the family. In J. J. Gross (Ed.), *Handbook of emotional regulation* (pp. 249–268). New York, NY: Guilford Press.

Timmers, M., Fischer, A. H., & Manstead, A. S. R. (2003). Ability versus vulnerability: Beliefs about men's and women's emotional behavior. *Cognition and Emotion, 17,* 41–63.

Triandis, H. C. (1994). *Culture and social behaviour.* New York, NY: McGraw-Hill.

Triandis, H. C., & Suh, E. M. (2002). Cultural influences on personality. *Annual Review of Psychology, 53,* 133–160.

Tsai, J. L., & Chentsova-Dutton, U. (2003). Variation among European Americans in emotional facial expression. *Journal of Cross-Cultural Psychology, 34*(6), 650–657.

Tsai, J. L., Chentsova-Dutton, Y., Freire-Bebeau, L., & Przymus, D. E. (2002). Emotional expression and physiology in European Americans and Hmong Americans. *Emotion, 2*(4), 380–397.

Tsai, J. L., & Clobert, M. (2019). Cultural influences on emotion: Empirical patterns and emerging trends. In S. Kitayama & D. Cohen (Eds.), *Handbook of cultural psychology* (2nd ed., pp. 292–318). New York, NY: Guilford Press.

Tsai, J. L., Koopmann-Holm, B., Miyazaki, M., & Ochs, C. (2013). The religious shaping of feeling: Implications of affect valuation theory. In R. F. Paloutzian & C. L. Park (Eds.), *Handbook of the psychology of religion and spirituality* (2nd ed., pp. 274–291). New York, NY: Guilford Press.

Tsai, J. L., & Levenson, R. W. (1997). Cultural influences on emotional responding: Chinese American and European American dating couples during interpersonal conflict. *Journal of Cross-Cultural Psychology, 28*(5), 600–625.

Tsai, J. L., Levenson, R. W., & McCoy, K. (2006). Cultural and temperamental variation in emotional response. *Emotion, 6*(3), 484–497.

Van de Velde, S., Bracke, P., & Levecque, K. (2010). Gender differences in depression in 23 European countries. Cross-national variation in the gender gap in depression. *Social Science & Medicine, 71,* 305–313.

Van Hemert, D. A., Poortinga, Y. H., & van de Vijver, F. J. (2007). Emotion and culture: A meta-analysis. *Cognition and Emotion, 21*(5), 913–943.

Wagner, H. L., & Smith, J. (1991). Facial expression in the presence of friends and strangers. *Journal of Nonverbal Behavior, 15,* 201–214.

Wallbott, H. G., Ricci-Bitti, P., & Banninger-Huber, E. (1986). Non-verbal reactions to emotional experiences. In K. R. Scherer, H. G. Wallbott, & A. B. Summerfield (Eds.), *Experiencing emotion: A cross-cultural study* (pp. 98–116). Cambridge, UK: Cambridge University Press.

Wang, K., Hoosain, R., Lee, T. M., Meng, Y., Fu, J., & Yang, R. (2006). Perception of six basic emotional facial expressions by the Chinese. *Journal of Cross-Cultural Psychology, 37*(6), 623–629.

Watson, D., & Clark, L. A. (1992). On traits and temperament: General and specific factors of emotional experience and their relation to the five factor model. *Journal of Personality, 60,* 441–476.

Wei, M., Su, J. C., Carrera, S., Lin, S.-P., & Yi, F. (2013). Suppression and interpersonal harmony: A cross-cultural comparison between Chinese and European Americans. *Journal of Counseling Psychology, 60*, 625–633.

Wierzbicka, A. (1991). *Cross-cultural pragmatics: The semantics of human interaction.* Berlin, Germany: Mouton de Gruyter.

Wu, D. Y., & Tseng, W. S. (1985). Introduction: The characteristics of Chinese culture. In *Chinese culture and mental health* (pp. 3–13). New York, NY: Academic.

Yoshikawa, M. (1978). Some Japanese and American cultural characteristics. In M. Prosser (Ed.), *The cultural dialogue* (pp. 220–251). Boston, MA: Houghton Mifflin.

Yuki, M., Maddux, W. W., & Masuda, T. (2007). Are the windows to the soul the same in the East and West? Cultural differences in using the eyes and mouth as cues to recognize emotions in Japan and the United States. *Journal of Experimental Social Psychology, 43*(2), 303–311.

Zahn-Waxler, C., Cole, P. M., & Barrett, K. C. (1991). Guilt and empathy: Sex differences and implications for the development of depression. In J. Garber & K. A. Dodge (Eds.), *The development of emotion regulation and dysregulation* (pp. 243–272). New York, NY: Cambridge University Press.

Zahn-Waxler, C., Friedman, R. J., Cole, P. M., Mizuta, I., & Hiruma, N. (1996). Japanese and United States preschool children's responses to conflict and distress. *Child Development, 67*, 2462–2477. https://doi.org/10.1111/j.1467-8624.1996.tb01868.x

Zaidman, N. (2001). Cultural codes and language strategies in business communication: Interactions between Israeli and Indian businesspeople. *Management Communication Quarterly, 14*(3), 408–441.

Zeman, J., & Garber, J. (1996). Display rules for anger, sadness, and pain: It depends on who is watching. *Child Development, 67*(3), 957–973.

Conclusion

The book has presented the concept of culture in a broad perspective—in the variety of types of cultures and in the wide array of its cultural and social parameters. It has shown that in addition to global, national, and ethnic cultures, researchers shall more frequently include regional, socioeconomic, religious, and mixed cultural groups. Intersection and mixture of these types and dimensions of culture bring a better understanding of diversity across cultures. Such a broader perspective will enrich the scope and details of cross-cultural research of emotions.

For example, many studies presented in the book have recognized that individualism-collectivism is a more multifaceted construct than early research admitted. In particular, an individualistic society, such as the United States, is not homogeneously individualistic when the cultures of socioeconomic status and ethnic and religious cultures are taken into account. Individualism as a general cultural ideal of the American society is evident in the minds, social expectations, and behaviors of many. Individualism as the reality of social relationship is present in practice and behavior of some societal circles of modern American population, yet not in others. Generalization would be rather simplification of social life.

Collectivism, on the other side, is not omnipotent in collectivistic society and may be present in one type of relationship, but not in others. For example, individuals can be collectivistic in their interpersonal relations with members of their group, but individualistic in their relations with individual outside their group. Examples of Indian culture presented in the book illustrate this.

Studies of recent decades presented in the book have shown that *individualism* and *collectivism* are still viable dimensions for cultural explanation of many emotional phenomena, especially in light of *independent* and *interdependent self-construals* associated with them. Yet these dimensions are multifaceted and closely intertwined with other cultural and societal parameters. Therefore, their complex and typological understanding will benefit the research of cultural models of emotions.

© The Author(s), under exclusive license to Springer Nature Switzerland AG 2021   317
V. Karandashev, *Cultural Models of Emotions*,
https://doi.org/10.1007/978-3-030-58438-2

The temporal perspective of cultures is also important, yet sometime is neglected in cross-cultural research of emotions. Cultures are in flux and their cultural dimensions and values change and evolve over time. The examples of the United States, Japan, and China presented in the book show the dynamic nature of individualism and collectivism. The old assumption that the United States is individualistic while Japan is collectivistic culture may not fully reflect the modern changes that have happened in those societies. The updated measurement of these parameters, taking into account their modern multifaceted understanding, is important. Measurement of individual variables associated with individualism and collectivism is also important because not all individuals accept the cultural norms of their society.

The book has presented extensive research on how *individualism–collectivism, power distance, uncertainty avoidance, gender roles equality* versus *gender roles inequality (cultural femininity-masculinity)*, and *context differentiation* as cultural dimensions are associated with specific patterns of emotional experience and expression.

Chapters 1 and 2 have proposed to extend the scope of cultural dimensions to *immediacy, temporal patterns of cultures, survival and self-expression cultural values, relational mobility*, and *cultural values* in cross-cultural research of emotions. Any types of cultures, any cultural or social parameters, which are presented in Chaps. 1 and 2, or their combination, can be the candidates for manifold cultural research of emotions. Researchers can go beyond individualistic–collectivistic and Western–Eastern dichotomies in their constructions of *cultural models of emotions*. The possible types of such models are briefly outlined in Chap. 3 for future researchers, along with methodology that can be employed.

Multiple studies presented in the book have demonstrated that basic emotional processes, including physiology of emotional response, are quite similar across cultures. Nevertheless, cultural conceptions of emotions and emotional complexity differ substantially from culture to culture. Culturally specific meanings of emotions, social norms, appraisals of situations, subjective experience of emotional qualities and emotional arousal, as well as expression of emotions vary across cultures. The studies of all of these aspects of emotional life, which have been conducted throughout recent several decades, are extensively reviewed in Chaps. 4, 5, and 6.

The *concept of cultural model* has recently attracted attention of many scholars in anthropology, sociology, psychology, and communication studies. Cultural models are considered as the cognitive schemas organizing knowledge in systemic, relatively simple, or complex units that are shared by the members of a society. They have intellectual and pragmatic knowledge of how people *must, should*, or *actually* think, feel, and behave. Cultural models exist both on cultural and individual levels. They can represent an ideal model of how people in a culture understand it or the typical model of real patterns of behavior, thought, and feelings. A *cultural model* conveys to people a *framework* reflecting expectations of a society.

The typology of cultural models of emotions and methods to explore those were outlined in Chap. 3. Various categorical, dimensional, or structural models of emotions are possible. Their construction depends on methodological preferences of researchers. Chapter 3 briefly reviewed available options.

Based on multiple cross-cultural studies of emotions, which are reviewed in this book, several *cultural models of emotions* have been *constructed*. In terms of locus of emotions, many cultures tend to interpret those as intrapersonal while others as interpersonal processes. Divergent from those, two other models exist: objectivized and interactive models of emotions.

Cultural models of emotions also differ in terms of value, which cultures place on the experience of positive and negative emotions, and intensity of emotional experience. Most drastic differences are between models of passionate and dispassionate life. It is worthy to note that these polar differences are typically found between Western and Eastern cultures. However, such generalization is probably not quite adequate since in many studies the United States is usually considered as representative of Western cultures while Japan or China as representative of Eastern cultures. A few studies have demonstrated that many European cultures are quite different from American. The Eastern cultures are also quite diverse. Thus, further research should go beyond this Western–Eastern dichotomy and dig deeper in cultural diversity.

In terms of the ways how cultures expect people to express their emotions, analysis of multiple studies allowed to identify several cultural models of emotions. Expressive versus nonexpressive models are the most salient ones. Stereotypically, they split between Western as expressive and Eastern as nonexpressive. However, this division cannot be viewed as adequate—there are several North-European cultures which are geographically Western, yet cultural norms there are of being reserved. Another distinction is between the cultural models of direct expression, more prevalent in Western cultures, and nondirect expression of emotions, more prevalent in Eastern cultures. Studies also reveal that besides facial expression, there are various culturally specific ways to express emotions.

Overall, I believe that this book will inspire future researchers of emotions to explore the effect of many other cultural parameters of societies on experience and expression of emotions. Besides those already extensively investigated, such as *individualism–collectivism, power distance*, and others, it is worthwhile to explore how such cultural dimensions as *immediacy, temporal dimensions of societies, relational mobility*, and others affect the emotional life of people.

I also encourage researchers to go beyond the traditional dichotomy of Western (presumably individualistic) and Eastern (presumably collectivistic) cultures, exploring the cultural diversity of the world societies.

On a personal note, my intention in this book was to comprehensively present all varieties of cultural models of emotions. However, it turned out to be impossible because of an enormous number of studies that have been conducted and published on emotions in cultural and cross-cultural perspectives throughout recent several decades. Although the list of sources and references, which have been covered in the book, are very extensive, I was not able to present many others which are also worthwhile in the context of the topic. Time and book capacity constraints have not permitted me to accomplish that ambitious goal.

Another challenge was the overwhelming amount of knowledge and research findings collected in several disciplines dealing with emotions, from various theoretical perspectives and methodological approaches. They had their own conceptual frameworks and purposes, sometimes not related to each other. They focused on their research tasks. They went their ways. *My goal* was to compile all these findings in *structured, consistent,* and possibly *comprehensive representations* of *cultural models of emotions.* It was like herding cats—sometimes it worked, sometimes it did not.

It often worked, and I was able to describe several cultural models of emotions in Chaps. 4, 5, and 6. They are relatively well-structured and consistent. Nonetheless, these cultural models of emotions are too far from being comprehensive and complete.

Once I had finished the text, I realized that the book turned out to be *like a Lego constructor* for future scholars. Some houses and streets have been constructed. As for the rest of the town, Chaps. 1, 2, 4, 5, and 6 of the book have provided many building blocks, which can be used for future construction. The construction guide is also provided (Chap. 3). Now it is the time to continue this work.

Index

© The Author(s), under exclusive license to Springer Nature Switzerland AG 2021
V. Karandashev, *Cultural Models of Emotions*,
https://doi.org/10.1007/978-3-030-58438-2